Development
and Democratization
in the Third World

Development and Democratization in the Third World:
Myths, Hopes, and Realities

Edited by
Kenneth E. Bauzon
Yeshiva University
New York

CRANE RUSSAK
A member of the Taylor & Francis Group
Washington • Philadelphia • London

USA	Publishing Office:	Taylor & Francis 1101 Vermont Ave., NW, Suite 200 Washington, DC 20005-3521 Tel: (202) 289-2174 Fax: (202) 289-3665
	Distribution Center:	Taylor & Francis Inc. 1900 Frost Road Suite 101 Bristol, PA 19007-1598 Tel: (215) 785-5800 Fax: (215) 785-5515
UK		Taylor & Francis Ltd. 4 John St., London WC1N 2ET

DEVELOPMENT AND DEMOCRATIZATION IN THE THIRD WORLD: Myths, Hopes, and Realities

1 2 3 4 5 6 7 8 9 0   E B E B   9 8 7 6 5 4 3 2

This book was set in Times Roman by Hemisphere Publishing Corporation. The editors were Stephen Summerlight and Joyce Duncan; the production supervisor was Peggy M. Rote; and the typesetter was Anahid Alvandian. Cover design by Michelle Fleitz.
Printing and binding by Edwards Brothers, Inc.

A CIP catalog record for this book is available from the British Library.

∞ The paper in this publication meets the requirements of the ANSI Standard Z39.48-1984(Permanence of Paper)

Library of Congress Cataloging-in-Publication Data

Development and democratization in the Third World : myths, hopes, and
  realities / edited by Kenneth E. Bauzon.
    p.   cm.
  Includes bibliographical references and index.

    1. Developing countries—Economic conditions.   2. Economic
development.   3. Democracy—Developing countries.   I. Bauzon,
Kenneth España.
HC59.69.D45   1992
338.9'009172'4—dc20
                                                      92-6894
                                                      CIP

ISBN 0-8448-1722-8 (case)
ISBN 0-8448-1723-6 (paper)

For Rosaida

Contents

Part Three
Human Rights and the Ethical Basis of Development

Contents   *xiii*

Preface

Since Plato's time, thinkers have argued the meaning of democracy. Interpretations of the term abound, but regardless of what has been said and written about it, a discernible pattern in its evolution is undeniable. The classical Greek thinkers have normally thought of the term as befitting mob activity characterized by lack of order and discipline. According to Plato, the people, because of their vulgarity and ignorance, were not to be trusted and had to be ruled by a philosopher-king.

The appeal of democracy, nevertheless, has persisted. Despite the negative meaning attached to the term, its essence was not lost to ordinary citizens who may not have necessarily possessed the fine attributes of the philosopher-king. Thus, ordinary citizens—as subjects of authority—strove to have a share in the exercise of this authority and, in the process, lent meaning to their early experience with democracy. The Athenian experiment in direct democracy remains to this day an exemplary model that has since inspired both admirers and detractors.

Through the Middle Ages, courageous dissenters challenged the claim to universal ecclesiastical authority by the Roman Catholic Church. Martin Luther contributed in no small measure when he enunciated the principle of priesthood of all believers, bypassing the Church as an intermediator between God and the faithful, unleashing a powerful movement called the Reformation, and giving the Church a taste of religious democracy.

In the early modern period, the Scientific Revolution allowed various thinkers to explore various areas of human knowledge, giving rise—at least in the European context—to such disciplines as physics, astronomy, chemistry, and biology. With this development, democracy has earned another meaning associated with academic or intellectual freedom.

This freedom was to be extended to its political and economic meanings through the works of the social contract writers and the utilitarians of the eighteenth and nineteenth centuries. The writings of John Locke and Adam Smith, reflecting on the conditions in England where political evolution was much more placid than in continental Europe, elaborated on individualism as a cornerstone of liberal democracy. Members of the rising middle class, freed from the bondage of the land and more mobile with their money, would henceforth pursue their own political and economic destiny—and preserve their newly acquired status in society—without being encumbered by government.

In continental Europe, where struggles were much more vigorous and often bloody, the middle class and the aristocracy were forced, under threat of losing their heads, to yield to the demands of the lower classes. Jean Jacques Rousseau contributed his share in fueling the French Revolution, and Karl Marx challenged the liberal conception of rule of law by elaborating on the nature of conflict and revolution as normal components of the historical process. In so doing, Marx gave the working class the needed justification to seize political power and extend democracy to themselves.

People in the colonial areas, in the wake of capitalist expansion and consolidation in the non-Western world, were determined not to be left out. Resistance to colonial rule took various forms, but the theme of freedom was common to all. Frantz Fanon, in his provocative and highly influential *The Wretched of the Earth,* explained the insidiousness of colonialism by making its victims accept and even justify their lot. This was possible, Fanon argued, because colonialism transformed the consciousness of its subjects and no less than violence against the colonizers would be needed to reverse and undo what colonialism has done. Mahatma Gandhi, meanwhile, taught his followers the principle of militant non-violent civil disobedience in his campaign to oust the British from India. The principle of *satyagraha,* to which Gandhi adhered closely, instilled in the minds of his followers the virtues of tolerance and love while opposing unjust and oppressive governance.

With these movements, democratization, at least in its political sense, became highly appealing and, as a process, it was difficult to reverse. The peoples of the Third World struggled hard in the hope that their newly won freedom and self-government would not be lost. To them, their dignity and self-worth were intertwined with these.

Many of the developments in the post-World War II period, however, brought a new awareness among Third World countries that somehow something was lacking. The failure of development programs, vulnerability to external forces, and the rise of native dictatorships in many of these countries, brought home the realization that their political independence was an empty gesture. Indeed, it was realized too that having just political democracy, with the attendant guarantees of freedom to participate in a competitive political process, to enjoy due process of law, and work within a liberal political framework, was not in and of itself sufficient to give democracy its full meaning. This inadequacy has, unfortunately, contributed in large measure to the erosion of sovereignty in the Third World leading, among other things, to artificially induced debt and environmental crises—problems that were preventable.

To extend democracy to its fullest meaning, therefore, it is necessary to look beyond the political dimension. Much has been written about the social, economic, and ethical foundations of democracy. This volume lends its weight to these other works in emphasizing that without the requisite socioeconomic and ethical conditions—in addition, of course, to the political condition—democracy would be meaningless. The meaning of democracy has to be extended, therefore, so that it also means social justice.

In their particular ways, the essays in this volume contribute to the elaboration of the above theme. Although a few of them were written specifically for this volume, most of them were originally prepared for various fora (e.g., the Third World Lecture Series organized by this editor at Lynchburg College, Lynchburg, Virginia, in the spring semester of 1990; the annual meeting of the Association for the Advancement of Policy, Research and Development in the Third World held in Mexico City in November 1990; the International Conference on Human Rights in the Twenty-first Century: A Global Challenge, sponsored by the Faculty of Law of the University of Calgary, held in November 1990 in Banff, Alberta, Canada; and the Regional Dialogue on Governmental-Nongovernmental Relations: Prospects and Challenges for Improving the Policy Environment for People-Centered Development held in Chiengmai, Thailand in March 1991).

Authored by individuals with distinguished credentials, these pieces were solicited on the basis of their timeliness, relevance, and rigor in discussing the topics being addressed. Each of these contributions complements the others in much the same manner that the issues they discuss are all very much interrelated. This is not to say, however, that the issues discussed here are exhaustive; rather, they are among the most pressing issues that need to be addressed when considering development and democratization in the Third World. The volume, for instance, has not touched on gender issues, e.g., the role of women in development. Nothing here is intended to reduce the significance of issues such as these. We hope that this volume stimulates further discussion on these issues so that one may get a more comprehensive and integrated understanding of how these issues affect development and democratization in the Third World.

One of the characteristics of this volume is its multidisciplinary approach to the subject matter. A good number of disciplines are herein represented includ-

ing political science, economics, business, sociology, theology, mass communications, and history. If this is so, it is only because the subject matter—by its
nature global and controversial—also crosses disciplinary boundaries, and anyone who is serious in attempting to understand it must necessarily embark on a
journey into these and other related disciplines.

Having stated such, nothing here implies that every author in this volume
(including the editor) agrees with every specific point or argument that the other
authors make. Nor should it be inferred that the contributors agree with or
endorse every point or assumption that I as the editor have made. Suffice it to
say that on the broader scheme of things, all the contributions here complement
and, in some instances, support each other.

The completion of this work would not have been possible without the support and encouragement of certain individuals and organizations. At Lynchburg
College, the college administrators and the sponsoring organizations were generous in their support of the Third World Lecture Series mentioned earlier. The
lectures in that series became the core of this compendium. My special thanks
go to Dr. Kern Lunsford, Chairman of the Department of Languages at Lynchburg College, and to Ms. Vicki Lunsford, Instructor of English, also at Lynchburg College, for sharing their time and talent in the translation and the
editing, respectively, of the contribution by Dr. Enrique Dussel (which was
originally prepared in Spanish for the said lecture series). Appreciation also
goes to the sponsors and/or organizers of the other fora mentioned earlier for
giving consent, both explicitly and implicitly, in order that some of the papers
presented there could be included (although in somewhat revised form) in this
compendium.

To Dr. Ralph Salmi, a dear friend and colleague at the California State
University in San Bernardino, goes my sincere thanks not only for his valuable
advice but also for his encouragement, especially during the early stage when I
felt like abandoning the enterprise.

To Mr. David Crugnola, Reference Librarian of Yeshiva University, who
went beyond the call of duty to assist in the search for missing bibliographic
details and who exemplifies a truly dedicated professional librarian, my respect
and appreciation go to him.

To all the contributors to this volume, I would also like to express my
wholehearted appreciation for the forbearance and prompt and courteous cooperation they have shown while the project was in progress. I feel very fortunate,
indeed, to have had the privilege of working and corresponding with these
individuals who have made such distinguished contributions in their own respective fields of endeavor.

On the home front, the generous support and affection of my wife, Rosaida, have been invaluable. In a very real sense, without these, this project would not have been completed. Her understanding of the long hours that I had to spend in front of the computer monitor has been quite admirable. But I appreciate her even more for her own conviction that this project is truly a worthwhile one.

Kenneth E. Bauzon
Yeshiva University
New York City

Introduction

Democratization in the Third World—Myth or Reality?

Kenneth E. Bauzon

INTRODUCTION

The last three decades have witnessed the gradual transition of many regimes around the world from authoritarian, totalitarian, or military rule to more consensual and competitive political systems. In Western Europe, we have seen fascist regimes in Spain, Portugal, and Greece replaced by popularly accountable governments. In Latin America, the "bureaucratic-authoritarian" regimes in Brazil, Argentina, and Chile have given way to more representative types of government. In Asia, the dictatorships in the Philippines, South Korea, and Pakistan have either eased or been overthrown. In Africa, meanwhile, Nigeria's military-dominated Second Republic and Ghana's Third Republic have broken down and been replaced by popularly based civilian governments. This is not to mention the overthrow of a brutal dictator in Uganda as well as the gradual dismantling of the apparatus of apartheid in South Africa, which improved the prospects for the establishment of a broader-based, multiethnic, and nonracial government.

During the second half of the 1980s, dramatic changes in the former Soviet Union and Eastern Europe took place. The *glasnost* and *perestroika* reforms introduced by Mikhail Gorbachev, following his ascendancy to the position of General Secretary in 1985, have had profound consequences but at the same time have opened the floodgates of irreversible changes. Politically, the Communist Party of the Soviet Union moved to abandon its long-standing vanguard status. Pluralism on a scale never dreamed of by Stalin was introduced leading to the emergence of previously repressed autonomous associational groups. Economically, grassroots capitalism was allowed to complement joint ventures being encouraged between foreign capitalists and certain state-controlled indus-

1

tries. Efforts were also underway to facilitate conversion of the ruble into foreign currencies so as to expedite the country's integration into the world capitalist network. But even these piecemeal reforms were not sufficient. The various republics, irrepressible in their nationalism, took bold steps to achieve full independence culminating in the formation during the 1991–1992 period of the Commonwealth of Independent States thus effectively bringing about the demise of the Soviet Union.

In Eastern Europe, holdover Stalinist regimes have been overthrown in Romania and Czechoslovakia, while in Poland, a formerly banned labor organization—Solidarity—ascended to power. The two Germanies underwent a successful, albeit costly, reunification. In Bulgaria, the country's communist party changed its name to something less odious. The rest of the countries of the region—most notably Albania—have followed suit, embracing one reform or another. In the case of Albania, which enjoyed the reputation as a redoubt of communist rule and of having Europe's most despotic regime, one-party rule was belatedly terminated in 1991 and a parliament was freely elected a year later.

The apparent failure of the socialist system, accompanied by demands for reforms toward greater personal freedom, has led many observers to believe that democracy—much similar to that experienced in Western Europe and North America—is the wave of the future.

That greater personal freedom and more open political systems abound in the West are no accidents of history. They are definite outgrowths of a long process of evolution and institutionalization consciously pursued by historical forces under unique conditions that enabled the seed of individualism to grow and prosper. Whether this experience can be replicated in other parts of the world has been the subject of much debate and discussion.

DEMOCRATIZATION LITERATURE: SOME BASIC POSTULATES

In any case, a growing number of observers believe that the events taking place in the Third World as well as in the former Soviet Union and in Eastern Europe toward apparent democratization are evidence of the enduring quality and the pervasiveness of influence of liberal democratic values.[1]

This group of observers has compiled a formidable and voluminous set of writings. A cursory review of this literature reveals certain fundamental beliefs shared commonly by its authors about the nature of democracy and the direction it is taking. Democracy, for instance, is defined as

> a system of government that meets three essential conditions: meaningful and extensive *competition* among individuals and organized groups (especially political parties) for all effective positions of government power, at regular intervals and excluding the use of force; a highly inclusive level of *political participation* in the selection of leaders and policies, at least through regular and fair elections,

such that no major (adult) social group is excluded; and a level of *civil and political liberties*—freedom of expression, freedom of the press, freedom to form organizations—sufficient to ensure the integrity of political competition and participation.[2]

Democracy is distinguished from two other types of political system in the continuum. At one end is totalitarianism, which has been described as possessing certain characteristics including, but not limited to, the following: a highly centralized political and administrative structure; the lack of a regularized and institutionalized mechanism for the orderly transfer of power; the absence of public accountability on the part of the rulers; an elaborate ideology designed to instill loyalty and to legitimize and validate the regime; the regimentation of society to ensure conformity; the loss of autonomy of voluntary associations (e.g., labor unions, the church, etc.); and the establishment of a vanguard party that subordinates all other groups in society. A manifest consequence of all of these is the blurring of the distinction between the private and the public realms and the emergence of the state as the omnipotent and omniscient power.[3]

At the other end of the continuum is authoritarianism, which is acknowledged to contain some of the above-mentioned characteristics although on a lesser scale. Authoritarian regimes, thus, are generally said to have no pervasive ideology, to allow political pluralism but in a limited way, to have no overt or systematic thought control program, to tolerate autonomous groups so long as they do not pose a threat to the regime, and to maintain a semblance of difference between private and public affairs.[4]

In this conventional literature, the authors leave no doubt as to which of the three types of political systems they prefer. Liberal democracy is the clear choice because, as Larry Diamond puts it, "[a]fter all, democracy is the only form of government that commands widespread and deep legitimacy in the world today." He further explains that "[t]he great competing ideologies of the twentieth century have largely been discredited as a vital force in World War II, and the appeals of Marxism-Leninism have visibly declined with the harsh repressiveness, glaring economic failures, and loss of revolutionary idealism of the existing communist regimes."[5]

The presumption, thus, is that liberal democracy and its economic expression—capitalism—is the wave of the future. Despite legitimate questions pertaining to its internal logical consistency as well as its applicability in non-Western settings, proponents regard these as mere distractions that have no bearing on the overall historic thrust of liberal democracy as an ideological force with which to be reckoned. Convinced that no other ideological rivals exist to challenge liberal democracy's dominance (as Brzezinski believes), the authors in this set of literature have proceeded to analyze the various conditions in which it might be weak (as suggested by the title *Breakdown of Democratic Regimes*), in which it might be strengthened (as suggested by the title "Strategies for Democratization"), in which certain regimes might be persuaded and encouraged to be more democratic (as suggested by the titles "Facilitating and Obstructing Factors" and "Will More Countries Become Democratic?"), in which certain criteria of democratization may be formulated and generated (as attempted by *Freedom in the World* and *Process of Democratization*), and in which the gains toward democratization may be preserved and expanded (as suggested by the title "The Problems of Consolidation of Political Democracy").

Examining more closely some of the basic postulates of this literature, one can gather that the significant factors affecting the stability of democratic regimes, particularly in the Third World, include the following:[6]

1. A public perception of the legitimacy of the regime tied to the degree to which the consent of the people is sought as well as the effectiveness of the regime in delivering services.
2. The prevalence of norms and values, as embedded in the country's political culture, that serve as mediating mechanisms between the governors and the governed thus lessening the potential for conflict and violence and enhancing, instead, nonconflictual competition or even collaboration.
3. The adaptation of social and political structures to socioeconomic changes that may create pressures and instability as well as the implementation of these changes (e.g., land reform) in a manner that enhances democratization.
4. The degree to which autonomous associations—which may be based on religion, ethnicity, occupation, and geography, among others—are allowed to exert influence over the state, particularly in the exercise of power, the formulation and implementation of policy, and the recruitment of members into political positions.
5. The degree to which both political and administrative power is either centralized or devolved in response to cleavages generated by ethnic or regional rivalries.
6. The manner in which both the state and society interact such that an efficient and cooperative, rather than antagonistic, relationship is evolved, thus allowing the state to carry out development programs, distribute resources equitably, and maintain social order without resorting to coercion.
7. The manner in which external factors (e.g., diplomatic, economic, and military pressures) are mediated so that these would enhance, rather than obstruct, the prospects for democracy domestically.

Hinting about their supposedly thorough and objective approach, the authors suggest that these factors were identified only after a consideration of the historical experiences of countries in Asia, Africa, and Latin America, with the goal of discovering certain patterns from which generalizations may be based. Equipped with this information, it was hoped that one would be in a better position to formulate strategies with which democratization may be induced. For instance, Diamond, in a piece cited earlier, enumerates many of these strategies. He rationalizes such an endeavor by observing that "[t]here is nothing inevitable about the progress—or the stability—of democracy in the world." He then explains that "[t]he intrinsic openness and competitiveness of democracies imply a certain element of fragility, and outside the deeply institutionalized polities of the industrialized West, this fragility has been acute. As a result, those concerned about how countries can move 'beyond authoritarianism and totalitarianism' must also ponder the conditions that permit such movement to endure."[7]

Thus, a deliberate, calculated, and systematic program to induce democratization around the world is not only desirable, but also imperative considering the "acute" nature (referring to the "fragility") of democratic institutions outside Western Europe and North America. The first of the strategies concerns the domestic political actors. A "firm and forceful commitment" must be made by the leaders themselves because they are in control of the government and are presumed to be in a better position to fashion the manner, timing, and pace of the transition to democracy. This would involve a skillful building of a consensus with respected citizens and other political leaders and the encouragement of a broad-based "process of popular debate, consultation, and participation." In the event that rulers are reluctant or even unwilling to democratize, "popular pressure" is deemed essential, although the degree and nature varies from place to place. In any case, this must be tempered by the willingness of the opposition forces "to negotiate with the regime in some coherent way." This means that the opposition forces themselves must have an "effective organization," an "effective leadership," particularly with respect to the mobilization of members, one that is comprehensive enough to include diverse but not necessarily competing groups representing a wide range of backgrounds, motives, and interests.

The second strategy involves the role of international actors: for example, foreign governments or international lending agencies. Diamond argues that foreign intervention per se is not bad but that it must be oriented around "democratic objectives." As an example, Diamond cites economic assistance, which he credits for having helped struggling democracies survive, such as Costa Rica in the decades following 1946 and Colombia in the 1960s and 1970s. Other examples are political initiatives and diplomatic pressures that, if exerted under propitious conditions and in a judicious manner, could dissuade a dictatorship from indiscriminately repressing its citizens or fraudulently attempting to steal elections. Such measures could even hasten the departure of certain dictators to avoid or minimize bloodshed.

With the above examples serving as context, Diamond suggests specific measures that could be taken by international actors. First, international assistance could be refocused in a manner that fosters "pluralism and autonomy in organizational life and the flow of information." The assumption here is that any activity that enhances the ability of the people to organize autonomously from the government improves the prospects for democracy. Second, such actors could encourage efforts to develop and enhance legal institutions so as to strengthen the rule of law. This would involve, for example, support for human rights organizations in monitoring and exposing violations, aid to victims of abuse, and training programs for administrators of the law including judges, lawyers, court clerks, paralegal and human rights workers, and even prosecutors and the police in democratic principles and practices. Third, increased funding—as funneled through such organizations as the National Endowment for Democracy (NED) and the Agency for International Development (AID)—could be used to affirm U.S. claims "to have the promotion of democracy and human rights" as one of its major foreign policy goals. The presumption is that the building of the "organizational, informational, and legal infrastructures of democracy" is not possible unless adequate financial and human resources are committed. Last, economic measures such as sanctions and debt relief could be judiciously used to exert pressure on an authoritarian regime or to bolster newly emergent democracies. Economic sanctions, for instance, could serve as a "potent form of pressure and an effective component of a larger strategy for isolating and shaming a regime internationally." In another instance, a program of debt relief could be geared in such a way that it is made consistent with development needs and requirements. Debt servicing could be reduced so that the much needed funds could be rechanneled to areas where they are most needed. "Simply providing new loans," Diamond explains, "to roll over existing debts may stave off an international financial panic . . ., but it will not renew economic growth in the developing world."

CRITIQUE OF THE CONVENTIONAL LITERATURE

Social Darwinists of the late nineteenth century were, in large measure, content in their conviction that civilization had reached its zenith and that democracy was its manifestation. Societies outside of the Western world, social Darwinists believed in their usual deterministic manner, would seek to develop themselves by evolving, in stages as in an organism, in the image of the Western industrialized countries. To hasten these societies' evolution, the "White Man's Burden" had to be assumed in as altruistic a way as possible if the West's "Manifest Destiny" of bringing these peoples to the doorsteps of modern civilization was to be realized.

At the close of the twentieth century, much of the Social Darwinists' vision remains unfulfilled. On the contrary, a large portion of what is now referred to as the Third World has slipped further backward in the wake of or as a consequence of the unabashed colonialism of Western powers. Colonialism has left a legacy of economic despoliation, political violence, and cultural distortion. In many cases, the departure of colonial administrators left the business of administration in the hands of native elites who, in turn, ruled over their countrymen.

Colonialism per se was undemocratic, whatever form it took. Its political and administrative apparatus was meant for ruling, not as a vehicle of representation. And it was established for the purpose of pursuing colonial policies, not for advancing the interests of the colonized. Contrary to stated aims, colonial administrators did not prepare the colonial peoples for any meaningful independence and self-government. Instead, elaborate arrangements were made, wittingly or unwittingly, to prepare for the coming phase of neocolonialism. This assured that, even under conditions of formal independence, the former colonies would remain subservient to or dependent on their specific "Mother countries" and on industrialized countries in general. Much has been written about unequal treaties that were negotiated on the eve of independence and designed to favor the soon-to-be former colonial powers. But even after independence, one would learn of the disastrous effects and consequences of the "aid, trade, and investments" that Third World countries too naively believed were in their best national interests. Thus, even without deliberate attempts to subvert the former colonies, the political, economic, and cultural patterns that were already shaped during the period of colonialism—for example, the introduction of secular concepts of bureaucracy, single-crop economies, and colonial consciousness—would ensure that the newly emergent countries would remain tied to the "apron strings" of their respective mother countries for a long time to come.

In short, the lack of democracy in vast portions of the Third World is as much a legacy of the colonial past as it is a consequence of the contemporary inequitable structure of relationships between the developing countries of the Third World and the industrialized countries of Western Europe, North America, and Japan. Through a series of policies and practices (applied either bilaterally or multilaterally), the industrialized countries have sought to maintain their hegemony over the rest of the world.

The past instructs us about the present. Many of the contemporary efforts to "develop" and to "democratize" the Third World are really nothing more than replays of the "White Man's Burden" of a bygone era. And the proponents of democratization as represented in the mainstream literature (as discussed in the second section of this essay) are really nothing more than current versions of the Social Darwinists of the late nineteenth century, or those whose social and political writings provided the "grease" that made the engines of colonialism run more efficiently and productively.

In the same way that the altruism of the "White Man's Burden" had the reverse effect of enslaving peoples, today's well-meaningned democratization advocates are bound to provide, through their influential writings and speeches, the needed justification and validation for the perpetuation of the neocolonial relationship that has been prevalent during much of the post-World War II era. Furthermore, these advocates provide justification for conservatives who represent such right-wing "think tanks" as the Hoover Institution, the Center for Strategic and International Studies, and the National Endowment for Democracy, to "shift the meaning of democracy even further away from any concern over the failure of capitalism in most of the 'developing' countries and to push it further into a ritualized formalism concerned chiefly with elections."[8]

To believe that this is possible, one needs only to consider the *ahistorical* but very *political* character of the mainstream literature. Hardly any reference to the colonial period is made, and the present is treated in a historical vacuum. First, blame is placed on the current existence of authoritarian regimes for the lack or absence of democracy in the Third World (while long-standing U.S. support for many of these regimes is ignored altogether) so that if only these regimes could be eliminated (once they no longer serve U.S. interests) through certain "strategies" such as those described earlier, the Third World would be more democratic. Second, a premium is placed on the establishment of a constitutional framework that allows for a pluralist system of political competition as well as guarantees for personal freedoms—if democratization could be firmly rooted despite the absence of requisite socioeconomic conditions that, by their very nature, take decades to evolve.

The political nature of the mainstream literature belies its profession of objectivity. Its theorizing and application of supposedly politically sterile empirical methods of investigation could not conceal the normative (or better yet, ideological) nature of its methods and concepts and the purposes for which research results would be applied. The definition of democracy as earlier discussed, for instance, is severely limited to a political meaning, one that Diamond unabashedly claimed when he wrote, "I believe it is important to conceive of democracy *purely* as a political form of government, however much it may be enhanced by, or even to some degree depend on, particular social and economic structures."[9]

One can infer from this posture that socioeconomic development is not relevant to democracy and that democracy has no role in or contributes nothing to the enhancement of this development. Furthermore, this posture gives the impression that the masses at the grass-roots level are irrelevant to the active pursuit of and mobilization for democracy—only "prominent citizens" or "opposition leaders" are allowed the crucial role of negotiating with or prodding authoritarian leaders into liberalizing their grips on political power; the posture denies, implicitly or explicitly, the validity or even necessity of such mass actions that have led to the overthrow of tyrannical dictatorships lest these would encourage revolutionary challenges to Western, particularly U.S., interests throughout the Third World.

Throughout the mainstream literature, there is the implicit admonition—contained in the strategies suggested for democratization—that Third World elites and counterelites conserve the capitalist system of economic relations. Along with liberal guarantees for personal freedoms, it may be recalled, is the guarantee that the individual be allowed to own private property and to engage in economic activities for the purpose of accumulating profits. At the same time, Third World countries are advised to avoid anything that might scare away foreign capital; the working sectors in these countries are further advised not to engage in activities (e.g., strikes, boycotts, lockouts, and sabotage) that might jeopardize the fragile democratic institutions or invite an unwarranted military intervention in civilian politics. The implicit assumption here, bolstered by the failure of the socialist experiment in the former Soviet Union and Eastern Europe, is the inherent superiority of capitalism over any other kind of economic arrangement. This assumption is, however, blind to the failure of capitalism itself in the context of Third World experience, a subject to which we will return later. Indeed, mainstream literature assumes an affinity between the failure of socialism in the former Soviet Union and Eastern Europe on the one hand and the preferability of capitalism throughout the world, particularly in the Third World, on the other. There is, however, no affinity, and the failure of socialism in one place neither confirms the success of capitalism in another nor gives reason to foist it over those whom it has already victimized.

REVERSAL OF DEMOCRACY IN THE THIRD WORLD

It is ironic that in Third World countries where democracy was proclaimed to have returned (e.g., Argentina, Chile, Pakistan, the Philippines, Nigeria, and Uganda, among many others) democracy has, in fact, seen a reversal. What happened in these countries is merely a reflection of a persistent pattern throughout the rest of the Third World in which civilian populations are progressively marginalized and governments lose their ability to defend national sovereignty vis-à-vis powerful external forces. To understand what these forces are, it is necessary to understand some of the recent changes that have taken place in the global economy as well as some of the inadequacies of the capitalist economic system that continue to work with these forces to the detriment of the Third World. This understanding should give the practitioners of the democratization school reason to pause and ponder more deeply their stance on the meaning of democracy.

It does not require a hard-core Marxist critic to point out in a convincing manner inherent defects in the capitalist system. Herman E. Daly and John B. Cobb, two liberal thinkers who wrote the acclaimed and provocative book *For the Common Good,*[10] demonstrate how the forces at work on the basis of democratic pluralism are actually working to erode this democratic principle. The globalization of the economy, according to Daly and Cobb, has resulted in the destruction of the balances among government, market, and society; globalization has also led to the rise of institutions that have no loyalty or accountability to any nation or government. It is in this context, Daly and Cobb argue, that civil society is rendered vulnerable to or powerless to check the potential misuse or abuse by these institutions of their vast corporate power. Daly and Cobb write, "whatever form of government the state may have, its people cannot participate in the most important decisions governing their daily lives. This weakens the possibility for a nation-state to be a community."[11] Indeed, this is possible, Daly and Cobb add, because "[f]ree traders, having freed themselves from the restraints of community at the national level and having moved into the cosmopolitan world, *which is not a community,* have effectively freed themselves of all community obligation."[12]

With these trends, democracy is gradually being eroded even in a place where it is believed to have matured the most—the Western World, particularly the United States. This is not to be alarmist at all. As Daly and Cobb point out, several problems must be identified and confronted. These are:[13]

1. *The erosion of competition* because of the tendency of larger corporations to edge out of competition (such as through mergers or takeovers) their smaller competitors. The transnationalization of bigger corporations has also brought them beyond any effective and consistent regulation by their home or host governments, thus rendering any meaningful interpretation of "national competitiveness" obsolete and irrelevant.

2. *The erosion of the moral and ethical basis* of the market, which is dependent on the sharing of such values of "honesty, freedom, initiative, thrift." These values have been eroded by no less than the theoretical premise in capitalism that the individual's self-interest alone motivates him or her to undertake specific economic activities.

3. The inherent inability if not refusal of the market system to provide essential public goods and services even if it has the means because of the unprofitability of doing so. A premise of capitalism is that profits would take precedence over any other consideration; the provision of services intended for the general use of the public (e.g., highways, hospitals, and national defense) is left within the domain of the government.

4. Because of its lack of accountability, the market system allows the negative consequences of market transactions such as pollution, global warming, damage to the ozone layer, destruction of rain forests, and so on to go unabated. These "costs," which are not recognized by the market system, are ultimately paid for by the community even though culpability clearly rests with the private corporate entities that have made short-run profits from them.

5. The market's lack of or absence of concern for any distribution of resources that might be regarded as equitable or fair (e.g., wages, full employment, or benefits to employees). Its sole criterion is its efficiency in transforming a commodity into profit and in using this to accumulate more.

6. The market's lack of responsiveness to ecological concerns because of its failure to understand its position within a closed and finite ecosystem. With the market's expansion and subsequent demand for more exhaustible resources within the total system, its impact (which becomes more deleterious and less negligible with the passage of time) upon the global economy would have an unbalancing effect.

Overall, the prognosis that Daly and Cobb offer gives little comfort to those who are concerned with the globalization of the economy in the manner just described. Those who have benefited from this trend and, more specifically, from the emergence of transnational capital (e.g., the Bush administration) would continue to push for greater role for the Bretton Woods institutions—that is, the World Bank, the International Monetary Fund (IMF), and the General Agreement on Tariffs and Trade (GATT)—in the so-called New World Order. This new order ostensibly would be one in which the global economy would finally be integrated, thus fulfilling its supporters' long-standing agenda of battering down national boundaries and removing government interference and obstacles to the free operation of the market.

A look at developments in Third World economy in the last decade or so would reveal just how the path to the New World Order has been littered with the debris of failed policies and short-sighted development programs promoted by the above-mentioned institutions.[14] It must be noted that throughout most of the 1960s and 1970s, many Third World countries were showing signs of economic growth. In the last decade, however, much of this growth has been reversed. Among Third World regions, Africa has suffered the worst from a combination of factors including deforestation, desertification, drought, drop in export earnings, severe indebtedness, and civil wars. During the second half of the 1980s, nine African countries suffered shrunken economies, while eleven others registered no growth at all. Nigeria, with the largest economy south of the Sahara, suffered a precipitous drop in its annual per capita income from $800 to $380 just between 1985 and 1987.

In Latin America, even though the setback has not been as severe as that in Africa, loses are nevertheless difficult to ignore. The single greatest factor for this reversal is the crushing external debt of more than $400 billion. Even Mexico and Brazil, countries that were touted as the region's "economic miracles" during the 1970s, suffered sudden declines in their gross national products (GNPs) between 1983 and 1984. Up to 10 percent of their national incomes has been routinely transferred abroad in the form of debt-service payments, while austerity programs have cut social services that were designed for the poor. Consequently, malnutrition, infant mortality, and disease are showing unprecedented increases and, unless the trend is soon reversed, the region will suffer the type of crisis in the 1990s that Africa suffered in the 1970s and 1980s.

In Asia, the record is mixed. While the so-called Asian Tigers or new industrializing countries (NICs) of South Korea, Taiwan, Singapore, Hong Kong, and Thailand have registered respectable growth during the past decade, other countries—for example, the Philippines, Indonesia, and Malaysia—have stagnated or deteriorated. Of these countries, the Philippines suffered the worst fate, being saddled with almost $30 billion in external debt, with 10 percent of its GNP committed to servicing this debt. With price declines in the international market of sugar and coconut, two primary exports, acute unemployment, and a series of natural calamities, Filipino families who have fallen under the poverty line now make up a staggering 60 percent of the population; for this population, the threat of malnutrition and starvation increases with each passing day.

As for the two largest countries of the region, China and India, GNP growth rates of 10 percent were registered during the first half of the 1980s. This growth was due largely to both nations' strategy of limiting dependence on foreign trade as well as on minimal borrowings from foreign lenders. However, their large populations (a combined 1.8 billion people or 40 percent of the world's population), which continue to grow, are eroding whatever gains these countries have made.

Turning to the Organization of Petroleum Exporting Countries (OPEC), the organization saw a decline in both influence and revenue during the 1980s. Although OPEC was regarded as a model cartel for Third World countries to emulate during the 1970s, the drop in oil prices by approximately half since 1982 (because of alternative sources such as the North Sea and Alaska and increased use of nuclear energy and so on) has caused some (e.g., Nigeria and Venezuela) to experience negative growth rates. This in turn contributed in large measure to their mounting foreign indebtedness. OPEC's more affluent members on the other hand (e.g., Saudi Arabia, Kuwait before the Iraqi invasion in 1990, and the United Arab Emirates) have slowed down because of their programs to build a manufacturing base meant to become alternatives to the exhaustible resources of oil.

Having mapped some of the outstanding problems of the capitalist market system as well as the bleak economic scenery in the Third World in the past decade or so, the question that needs to be addressed now is: How have these imperfections and the dire economic conditions combined in such a way that democracy is actually being reversed, rather than being advanced, in the Third World?

An answer to this question must necessarily lead one to consider the role of the very same forces that many regarded as the panacea for Third World problems: international lending institutions and transnational corporations. It is postulated here that these institutions have actually been in the vanguard in eroding the sovereignty of a significant number of Third World countries. This disturbing trend is facilitated by several specific factors, including (1) the use of manufacturing technology that displaces human labor, despite the argument that transnational corporations provide employment; (2) the inability of primary products from the Third World to penetrate Western markets, despite numerous attempts to break down the barriers through North–South meetings under the auspices of the United Nations Conference on Trade and Development (UN-CTAD); and (3) persistent protectionism of industrialized countries' own industries, despite their loud rhetoric about free trade.

The role of commercial banks reached a new level during the 1980s when the presence of OPEC deposits allowed abundant loans to Third World borrowers. U.S., European, and Japanese banks posted "Open for Business" signs throughout the Third World in an effort to outdo one another. International banking competition became a "free-for-all," with Japanese banks taking the lead but followed closely by their European counterparts. For one reason or another, many Third World countries used these funds without fully realizing (or perhaps ignoring) the implications of becoming dependent on these loans.

In the early 1980s, the debt crisis intensified, and Third World countries finally realized their situation. This crisis was dramatized by the case of Brazil, which in 1983 was on the brink of default. Burdened by a price rise in its oil imports and world recession that eliminated many of the markets for its manufactured products, Brazil was no longer able to service its $90-billion foreign debt. This debt was four times as much as the country's annual export earnings, and half of its export earnings were devoted to servicing this debt. In the meantime, the inflation rate rose to 175 percent. Clearly, at this point, Brazil was unable to service its debt, let alone the principal. Only fear of repercussions prevented Brazil's lenders from declaring default. They were afraid that their own default would lead to many U.S. and European banks being unable to pay their own creditors, thus leading to an international financial crisis. Instead, a series of negotiations essentially resulted in a rescheduling of payments, and new funds were loaned to help Brazil service its debt—at least in the short run. In addition, in accepting the rescheduling scheme, Brazil had to carry out and implement a painful structural-adjustment program that included a devaluation of the country's currency, reduction of expenditures for social programs, removal of subsidies for certain domestic industries, and sharp cuts in workers' wages to far below the rate of inflation. All of these measures were needed, it was argued, to put Brazil back on track and enable it to service its debt. But these measures were so painful to the population that rioting in Brazil's principal city of São Paulo could only be quelled by the army.

At the heart of this structural-adjustment program was the IMF, which, by either design or accident, served as the commercial lenders' "negotiator, bill collector, and enforcer." The case of Brazil illustrates those of many other Third World countries in which the national governments are virtually at the mercy of the IMF and foreign lenders. As one keen observer notes, these countries have "practically surrendered the instruments of fiscal and monetary policy to fund [IMF] advisers and gave up development planning altogether as debt repayment replaced development as the *raison d'etre* of economic growth."[15]

Alongside the commercial banks were the transnational corporations (TNCs) who had more inventive ways of subverting the sovereignty of their Third World hosts. It may be noted that many authors have already documented this trend toward transnationalism and have accordingly forecast the obsolescence of the traditional Westphalian order, which promoted the primacy of the state as an actor in world politics.[16] The role of TNCs appeared to grow in importance despite their public relations setbacks in the 1970s. In the 1980s, fewer of them were nationalized not so much for fear of adverse or even hostile reaction from the United States and other Western governments but rather for fear of scaring away foreign capital for domestic investments. It is this fear of losing capital or, conversely, the need for foreign capital, that renders many Third World countries vulnerable. They realize and TNCs are aware that this vulnerability could lead these countries—as it has in many cases—to surrender their sovereignty as they become integrated in the TNCs' worldwide operations. Even a TNC's implied threat to cease operations in an area and move elsewhere is enough to make a host government tow the line. With reduced markets for many of its exports, depressed prices for its primary products, and an inability to borrow because of a lack of creditworthiness, Third World governments are all too willing to offer concessions that were unthinkable just a few years earlier. These concessions, contained in investment codes, include up to 100 percent remittance of profits abroad, tax incentives, reduced rates for electricity consumed, and access to local lenders. Even socialist countries, ironically, have begun to compete with their nonsocialist neighbors to the point that their neighbors fear them less for subsidizing local communists than for drawing capital away from them! For example, Vietnam's investment code, enacted in 1987, allows foreign investment in just about every area except national defense and prohibits nationalization of any TNC.

One inventive way that TNCs, in collaboration with commercial banks, have been able to reduce a country's sovereignty is the debt-for-equity scheme. This allows a TNC to purchase from a creditor a portion of a country's debt at a reduced price. The purchased debt is then exchanged for local currency, after which it is invested as equity. Nissan Motor Company, for instance, purchased $60 million of Mexico's debt from Citibank Corporation for $40 million. To allow this transaction, Mexico virtually had to abandon its foreign-investment regulations, including the law that required majority Mexican control over local subsidiaries of foreign companies.

TOWARD A JUST, EQUITABLE, AND DEMOCRATIC ORDER IN THE THIRD WORLD

If only practice matched rhetoric, then the Bush administration's vision of a New World Order would be more meaningful and perhaps deserving of international support. Inferred from administration statements, academic discourses, and recent trends and events, this vision for a new order may be said to contain the following elements:[17]

1. governance on the basis of dearly held moral and ethical values presumably derived from the Judeo-Christian tradition;
2. democratization along the lines of liberal democracy;
3. the precedence of nonmilitary issues over military ones;

4. greater reliance on existing international institutional mechanisms for the peaceful resolution of conflicts;
5. greater reliance on some form of collective security arrangement, such as through the auspices of the United Nations rather than on unilateral action by one or a few states in confronting acts of aggression;
6. a greater role for international nongovernmental organizations or people-oriented nonstate actors in international decision making;
7. the uniform and consistent application of existing and future rules and norms of international conduct; and
8. the reappraisal of the human rights issue so that it would no longer be regarded (by abusive regimes especially) as a purely domestic matter but rather as something of concern to the entire international community.

Ideally, this vision for a new order should also give vent to many of the aspirations of Third World peoples for justice, equity, and true democracy; it should allow for a meaningful dialogue and discussion concerning the issues affecting their development or lack of it. As earlier expressed, however, there are doubts as to whether this emergent new order is really and truly for everyone or whether it is a rhetorical shroud to conceal the hegemonic aims of one country and a host of interested individuals and groups within it. In a manner of speaking, this new order should be an ethical one concerned about issues of justice and fairness, equality and accountability—universal values with which everyone can identify. Furthermore, it should promote mutual respect for and toleration of political, ideological, and cultural differences between and among nations. Correspondingly, it should abhor intervention in the affairs of others, or the domination of one country by another either directly or indirectly, or both.

The Bush administration, however, lacks many of the qualities that would inspire sufficient confidence for it to lead others into a new international dispensation. Its selective use of military force—purportedly to check aggression as demonstrated in the recent Persian Gulf War—and its virtual domination of the United Nations on the basis of expediency as well as its single-mindedness in pursuing economic objectives abroad under the guise of free trade—all of these serve to remind us that *realism* prevails over *idealism* and is very much a part of the intellectual framework guiding this administration.

In pursing their own development, Third World countries must necessarily look to themselves—rather than to others—for mutual guidance and support. In more ways than one, their mutual plight, characterized by a depravity of material comforts and the instability of and lack of security in their political environments has also exacted from them the best of their virtues including sacrifice, hard work, conservation, and sharing. Their condition has also forced a reappraisal of the dominant modes of thinking, and has highlighted the inadequacies of traditional notions of development and democracy as they have been long pervasive in Western thinking. No longer could the processes of development and democratization be compartmentalized as if they were unrelated, and no longer could they be regarded so narrowly as to constrain action in areas beyond the narrow definitions.

Security is one instance in which reappraisal has been compelling. Traditionally, theoretical works and policy decisions have been oriented around security's military component.[18] This is reflected in the manner in which national governments, both Western and non-Western, have set their respective priorities: A hefty portion of their respective GNPs is devoted to either the production or the acquisition of military goods, and a significant segment of their respective populations is connected with the armed services as military members, employees in weapons manufacturing or distribution, or as research-and-development teams. Little or no consideration is devoted to security from the new sources of danger that, in more ways than one, are more damaging than any military threat. The realization of these new sources of danger is articulated by Lester R. Brown in the following words:

> As pressures on natural systems and resources build, as the sustainable yield thresholds of local biological systems are breached, and as oil reserves are depleted, governments can no longer boost expenditures on armaments and deal effectively with the forces that are undermining their economies.
>
> The choices are between continued militarization of the economy and restoration of its environmental support systems; between continued militarization and new initiatives to deal with the dark cloud of Third World debt that hangs over the world's economic future. The world does not have the financial resources and leadership time and attention to militarize and to deal with these new threats to security.[19]

In much the same way, the meaning of democracy has been redefined (as it is in this volume) as not merely the expansion of political rights and popular participation in government and politics but also—and perhaps more importantly so—as the empowerment of the people in the pursuit of their own economic and social well-being. Thus, the political dimension is merely one aspect of the democratization process that is understood here as a total process that integrates all aspects relevant to the improvement of the human condition. In the contemporary period, aspects that have achieved a state of urgency include the environmental condition, population growth and its attendant food situation, the distribution of scarce resources both within and between countries, human rights, the responsibility and accountability of international institutions both public and private, and underlying ethical and moral criteria in gauging public performance by both individuals and institutions. This book has been planned in such a manner as to reflect this integrated notion of democracy and to reinforce the idea that nonpolitical factors are as much a part of a comprehensive process of development as are political ones.

Having stated this, nothing here implies that this is a notion original to this book. On the contrary, it is an attempt to follow up on many earlier efforts, both at the grass-roots level and at the international institutional level, one designed to give importance to the participation of ordinary citizens in the determination and implementation of programs and decisions that affect their lives. One such grass-roots effort is the Inter-Regional Consultation on People's Participation in Environmentally Sustainable Development, which was held in Manila, the Philippines, in June 1989. From this meeting emerged a declaration that decries current development practice as being "based on a model that demeans the human spirit, divests people of their sense of community and control over their own lives, exacerbates social and economic inequity, and contributes to destruction of the ecosystem on which all life depends." Furthermore, it expresses concern that

> foreign assistance, particularly debt financing, too often has contributed more to the problem than to its solution. It places the initiative and responsibility in the hands of foreigners rather than in the hands of the people. It weakens the accountability of governments to their own citizens. It promotes and sustains an inappropriate development model driven by the export market. It primarily finances resource-based projects that destroy the natural environment and deprive the poor of access to the productive assets upon which they depend for their livelihoods. National economies remain burdened with debt. And finally it results in the imposition of policies intended to facilitate debt repayment, orienting the national economy and its resources to the needs of foreign consumers, at the expense of the poor and the environment.[20]

As a means of addressing the aforementioned problems, the declaration proposes a "people-centered development" that recognizes, among others, the need to (1) "return control over resources to the people and their communities to be used in meeting their own needs"; (2) "broaden political participation, building from a base of strong people's organizations and participatory local government"; (3) "obtain a secure livelihood based on the intensive, yet sustainable, use of renewable resources"; (4) "build within a people a sense of their own humanity and their links to the earth, its resources, and the natural processes through which it sustains all life"; and (5) engender "active mutual self-help among people . . . in their common struggle to deal with their common problems."[21]

Another effort, this time within the framework of the United Nations, is the Roundtable on Global Development Challenges held under the auspices of the U.N. Development Program. This meeting took place in Antalya, Turkey, in September 1990 with the theme "Change: Threat or Opportunity for Human Progress?" The meeting was called for the purpose of assessing the impact on human progress of the various changes that have taken place in the realms of politics, economics, demography, technology, ecology, and ethical values. Following the meeting, a statement implored that "[p]eople-centered development, the creation of productive employment opportunities, and poverty eradication should become the objectives of an effective development process."[22] The statement concurs with an underlying assumption of this volume; that is, it recognizes the interconnections "between democracy, human rights and welfare, and sustainable development, including the full involvement and participation of all, women and men, in the decision-making and development process." The statement further recognizes the necessity of striking a healthy balance between the public and private sectors so that neither grows at the detriment of the other, and it advocates free and fair trading in an "increasingly interdependent and competitive world economy" as the "main tool" for achieving development. In addressing the debt problem in the Third World, the statement does not advocate any generalized solution but rather a case-by-case solution approach in which an indebted Third World country negotiates with an industrialized country (and, by extension, with international lending institutions) for the relief of debt, poverty, and other outstanding problems. It demands that development should henceforth be undertaken in consideration of its impact on the population and the environment and regards "an all-out attack on poverty" as "the most effective way of dealing with population and environmental problems" in stressing the linkage between poverty, population, and environment. In conclusion, the statement reads in part, "Human beings must remain at the core of all development aspirations and must remain the principal agents of their own future. That future can contain all the exciting rewards, all the elements of a better life for mankind, only if we continue to think, plan and act across the traditional borders that have separated one society from another."

Although some of the terms and the objectives in the Antalya statement are similar to those found in the Manila declaration cited earlier, it must be borne in mind that many of the underlying assumptions of these two approaches are widely separated. Although the Manila declaration is unequivocal in its criticism of the type of globalism currently being promoted by TNCs, international lending institutions, and leading industrialized countries, the Antalya statement, on the other hand, is more ambivalent about the nature of this globalism. In fact, its recognition of free trade as the "main tool" for development turns a blind eye to the manner in which this principle has been applied and the consequences on the lives of Third World peoples. Its recognition of the necessity to balance public and private interests is well taken, but this recognition is undermined by its refusal to advocate a more decisive solution to the debt problem lest this would undermine the preeminent position of lending institutions. By now, it should be obvious to everyone—gleaning from the failures of socialism in Eastern Europe and capitalism in the Third World—that the problem essentially obstructing equitable distribution of resources within any society is either too much power concentrated in the state *or* in the private sector (or a segment thereof).

The differing assumptions between these two approaches may be explained by the context from which they emerged. The Manila declaration was a product of a coalition of grass-roots, nongovernmental organizations whose members join voluntarily from all sectors of society.They owe no loyalty to the government or to vested interests in society. The Antalya statement, on the other hand, was the product of a U.N.-related organization whose membership is based on supposed expertise as well as on an "old boy network." This organization acquires a corporate life and identity of its own although, ultimately, it still owes loyalty to its funding sponsors whom it cannot antagonize. The solutions it offers, therefore, may be limited and even detached from the lives, needs, and experiences of the peoples whom it purports to help.

OVERVIEW

This book consists of seven major parts, all of which are intended to reflect an underlying premise that development and democratization are intertwined processes that cannot be compartmentalized. It further reflects the premise that democracy should not be limited to a narrow political meaning. Instead, it should be regarded as encompassing a multitude of conditions that include social, economic, political, environmental, and ethical dimensions, all of which have a contribution to make in rendering greater meaning to democracy. All of these must form part of an integrated approach toward attaining the well-being of the citizenry, without whom democracy would be meaningless.

The first part, "Current Trends and New Directions in Third World Research," sets the book's tone. Aside from sifting through the fundamental assumptions of certain dominant approaches to the study of development, the two articles contained in Part I explore some of the factors that have contributed to their success or failure in explaining development or underdevelopment in the Third World. In particular, "Development Studies: Contending Approaches and Research Trends," by Kenneth E. Bauzon, broadly surveys the progress and direction of research in development studies, assessing the contributions of four contending approaches, namely, modernization theory, the developmental ethicist explanation, dependency theory, and neo-Marxist theory. Bauzon concludes that the contributions of these approaches, even though one emerged in response to the other, are limited by the narrow manner in which they define their respective problems as well as the solutions they offer. The authors further observe that these approaches essentially are propounded by "communities of scholars" (or paradigms) who share, more often than not, mutually exclusive assumptions about the nature of reality.

David C. Korten's chapter, "People-Centered Development: Alternative for a World in Crisis," is a critique of a growth-centered development paradigm that has "created a deepening global social and ecological crisis that threatens the future of life and civilization on our planet." Korten contends that foreign aid as administered by most assistance agencies and donor governments has had the opposite effect of encouraging abuse of the environment, widening the gap between rich and poor, and rendering governments vulnerable to manipulation by external forces such as the lending agencies or the transnational corporations that owe no loyalty to any people or government. According to Korten, a solution must necessarily rest with the people themselves, who must organize at the grass-roots level and spearhead a people-centered transformation of institutions and values leading toward political and economic democratization.

Part II, "Toward a Reconceptualization of Development and Democracy," explores in greater length and at the conceptual level the intertwining relationship between development and democratization. In Remigio E. Agpalo's article, "Modernization, Development, and Civilization," the ideal situation is one in which civilization prevails. As defined here, civilization is "a state of human condition characterized by political development, liberty, and democracy." The conditions needed to sustain this civilization are civility, rule of law, and social justice (all considered necessary conditions) as well as liberty and democracy (both of which are regarded as sufficient conditions). With civilization, Agpalo argues, the tendency of any modernizing efforts to become authoritarian (what he refers to as the "iron logic of modernization") could at least be "chained" or restrained to prevent it from ravaging and destroying society. The article by Edward Broadbent, "Foreign Policy, Development, and Democracy," takes the discussion to the practical level when it decries specific instances in which the "unchained" condition of authoritarian regimes—condoned and tolerated by misguided policy based on expediency—has led to grave abuses of their own citizens' human rights. Broadbent criticizes the long-prevailing assumption that economic development is incompatible with political development. "The time," Broadbent argues, "for explicitly linking economic development with democratic rights is now here." In particular, Broadbent continues, foreign policy must now be reoriented so that it would now serve as an instrument with which to pursue development and democracy, rather than continuing as a means of supporting undemocratic practices by callous dictatorships. The article by Thomas S. Axworthy, "Democracy and Development," explores further the relationship between development and democracy. Axworthy argues that "democracy and mass participation are, in fact, vital components of economic progress." He does not believe, however, that economic affluence is a necessary condition for democracy, although it is a desirable goal. What is more important, he contends, is that citizens are given the opportunity to unleash their creativity and productivity to attain the material prosperity that deserves to accompany their enjoyment of political democracy.

In Part III, "Human Rights and the Ethical Basis of Development," a consideration often neglected by development writers and practitioners—the moral and ethical basis of development—is brought forth. The traditional approach has regarded development as a technical problem. The failure of this approach, however, as reflected in the huge material costs expended to naught as well as the embarrassing ethical vacuity in the conduct of governments and corporate organizations in the pursuit of power and profits, respectively, has led to the reassertion of the belief that the pursuit of development could not and should not be regarded apart from moral and ethical guidelines. Many of these guidelines emanate from religious values, the interpretation of which identifies the mission of the church with those of the oppressed and the downtrodden.

The significance of the three articles in Part III cannot be emphasized enough. They are earnest attempts to show the importance of undergirding the public performance of governments and corporate organizations with ethical values. In more ways than one, these articles remind us that the pursuit of power and profits should not be undertaken for their own sake because of their social consequences. Too often, these consequences have proved too costly to citizens whose human rights, material well-being, and self-worth have been robbed from them.

In particular, the article by Enrique Dussel, "Theology and Economy," establishes the relevance of theology as a basis for evaluating economic activities and their consequences. Dussel argues that the oppression of peoples of the Third World is inherent in the capitalist system, which recognizes profit as the sole criterion of its performance. This system even fails to recognize the "living" nature of a product because the capital or the profit in capitalism is itself the denial of the "being" of the worker who produced it. Dussel explains: "[F]undamentally, economics deals with the calculation of the amount of profit . . . without any relationship whatsoever with the person, value . . ., or ethics. . . . The economy having been separated from 'the world of daily life' . . . comes to be set up as a system." In this context, the violation of the person by the system is an immoral one because the person is a member of the "community of life" and his product, as the "Bread of life," is being appropriated to serve the ends of a few. Dussel further explains: "If the injustice of a contract [say, between the capitalist and the worker] taken as natural . . . appropriates a part of the value produced . . ., then said profits obtained from the life of the worker should be judged as sin. Poverty, or misery (like that which is suffered in present-day Latin America because of a transfer of the value of capital from Third World countries to industrialized countries) is a wage of sin."

The article by Michael F. Czerny S. J., "Liberation Theology and Human Rights," adds another dimension by discussing human rights in the context of liberal tradition. Czerny argues that the weakness of the liberal ideology has allowed "human rights"—as a product of a particular moment in history—to be a refuge of those who abuse it in the first place. To restore human rights to their original meaning, Czerny explains, we must be clear about their *starting point* (the struggle between life and death), their subjects (the oppressed), and their goal (liberation). He also argues that the preservation of human rights should be just the minimum or basic condition that no one should be without. At the same time, he warns us about inflating them in such a manner that they are meaningless to the vast majority of the people, especially the oppressed, while they are useful—in a utilitarian sense—only to a handful whose claim to individual rights is intended to reinforce and conserve their dominant position in society. To Czerny, for human rights to be meaningful to everyone, they must be considered in the context of "what is fundamentally, essentially, and nonnegotiably necessary in order that life might be life." "From God's point of view," Czerny adds, "life is *the* gift, it is everything. Life is *the* expression of God's love." Finally, in the third article in this part, "The Human Rights Cause," George Lister discusses human rights as perceived and practiced in the U.S. foreign policy establishment. His article discusses (1) how the U.S. human rights policy evolved, (2) worldwide developments that have had an impact on human rights, and (3) observations and recommendations as to how human rights may be advanced. Lister notes that the human rights policy became firmly institutionalized during the presidency of Jimmy Carter. But perhaps one of the most salient sections of Lister's article is his discussion of the nature of this policy; that is, that it is a bipartisan policy, that is does not imply any moral superiority on the part of the United States, and that it does not give the United States any right to intervene in the internal affairs of other countries. He argues that this policy has been a useful one in strengthening overall foreign policy. He writes, "[T]he human rights factor has helped to give us a better foreign policy, one that is more compassionate, more intelligent, and more effective." With lessons learned as well as recommendations offered to strengthen human rights both in the Untied Stated and abroad, Lister is confident that a new era of peace and democracy will be upon us.

In Part IV, "Population Growth and the Environmental Imperative," the relevance of population and environment to development and democratization becomes more evident. The high population growth rate worldwide, despite arguments to the contrary, taxes the ability of the environment to sustain the population, and the progressive degradation and abuse of environmental resources threaten long-term prospects for the survival of humanity itself. The article by Deborah S. DeGraff, "Population Growth and Government Policy in the Developing World," highlights many of the factors affecting population growth rates and trends around the world, and she provides specific examples and alternative viewpoints of the relationship between development and population growth as drawn from the Asian experience. DeGraff assesses competing theories that explain the effects of rapid population growth on society and concludes that "current rates of fertility and population growth in much of the developing world have fairly strong negative impacts on socioeconomic development, the environment, and individual well-being." The alternative of reducing the birth rate suggests itself, but for many Asian countries, as DeGraff explains, government intervention has often been controversial no matter how imperative it may have been. In relating population growth to the creation of democratic institutions and conditions in the Third World, DeGraff identifies three themes: (1) population growth as an indirect agent of political change (owing to tension built when the political and social institutions are no longer able to manage an equitable distribution of scarce resources), (2) rapid population growth as a determinant of individual well-being (because, as DeGraff argues, for democracy to persist, "there must exist the social and economic conditions necessary for individuals to develop their human resource potential to the fullest"), and (3) individuals having the freedom to exercise control over reproductive behavior (especially when government limits its intervention, which in turn facilitates "the realization of reproductive desires on the part of individuals").

In "Addressing Resource Management Concerns," Marian A. L. Miller addresses an urgent topic of the global environment. Miller calls attention to the rapid rate with which the destruction by the industrialized countries of ecological resources is occurring. These resources, which include agricultural products, energy resources, forest products, and ocean resources, among others, are being depleted and destroyed. Rapid population growth also is exhibiting negative effects on the supply of these resources. In addition atmospheric pollution, owing primarily to the use of fossil fuels and chemical products such as chlorofluorocarbons (CFCs), is causing serious damage to the ozone layer that protects the earth from harmful solar radiation. Miller cites the case of the Caribbean region as one among many regions in the world that has suffered and continues to suffer form the ecological imbalance. She draws certain inferences from the environmental dilemma for democracy and concludes the following: (1) "For the world's states to address environmental issues adequately, they need to be willing to give up some measure of sovereignty." (2) "In most countries, including the industrialized democracies, popular control is, in any case, primarily a myth. Decisions are made by an elite. In developing countries, too, the environmental imperative will require dependence on a policy elite." (3) "[T]here are important economic prerequisites for democracy. . . . Without these . . ., popular control . . . can be destabilizing. On the other hand, with these prerequisites in place, the country will be more likely to have an educated populace with its basic needs met, and it will be able to rely more on persuasion and less on coercion or authority for compliance with environmental regulations."

Part V, "Distributive Justice and Equity," concerns itself with this issue at the heart of Third World peoples' struggles for betterment. Equitable distribution of resources within and between countries often is obstructed by structural barriers that may be either historically conditioned or imposed by a narrow segment whose interests may be identified with the maintenance of existing arrangements. Drawn from specific experiences in Asia, Africa, and Latin America, the articles in this part examine various aspects that are involved in attempts to achieve equitable distribution of valuable resources; the authors likewise assess some of the assumptions behind these attempts. In the process, they hope to show why these attempts have either succeeded or failed and under what conditions.

The chapter by Young J. Park, "Land Tenure and Economic Efficiency," looks at theories and empirical evidence that explain the relationship between land tenure and economic efficiency in South Korea. In the process, Park compares the owner-farmed system and share tenancy in terms of efficiency and concludes that the former is doubtless more efficient than the latter. This conclusion is supported by empirical evidence that shows that "resource allocation is inefficient in tenant farms compared with owner farms." It also recognizes the role of incentive (e.g., the promise of future land ownership) in contributing toward both inputs to be used in farming and input productivity.

In "Structural Adjustments in Sub-Saharan Africa," Gerald E.Scott touches on this region's relationship with one international lending institution—the IMF. This dimension is a significant one, especially because it sheds light on the origins and perpetuation of Africa's debt crisis throughout the 1980s. Scott explains that the debt crisis is simply one aspect, albeit a significant one, of the overall economic crisis facing all of Africa. The economic crisis was brought about by a combination of factors including balance of payments deficits, corruption, waste, high rates of inflation, low productivity, and high rates of population growth. To help alleviate these problems, the sub-Saharan countries have turned to IMF-sponsored adjustment programs. Scott examines the conditionality practice of the IMF as well as the specific reasons leading to the failure of these programs. Among his other observations are that: (1) the conditionality practice of the IMF has not been consistent with national development policies, (2) it has been based almost exclusively on Western experience, (3) it is too stringent in proportion to the amount being borrowed, (4) it all too readily prescribes currency devaluation and liberalization of payments arrangements, and (5) it is politically untenable. Scott writes, "IMF policy seems to be preoccupied with short-term economic objectives and their budgetary impacts on short-term economic conditions, ignoring the long-term factors and their impact on the government budgetary position." In the end, Scott assesses many of the arguments seeking to replace IMF programs and concludes: "In reality, most of those resources [needed by and being transmitted into the region] do not seem forthcoming; where they are, they will at least initially increase the debt burden unless they are of such long-term nature that repayments fall due only after investments have become productive."

In the third piece, "Democracy, Equity, and the Myth of the Welfare State in Developing Countries," William L. Ascher brings into sharper focus the social, economic, and political realities of Central America. In his opening statement, Ascher cautions us that in considering any program for the region's economic recovery, there is "a narrow space in which democracy, equity, and economic growth can be pursued together." However, it is his premise that democracy and equitable economic growth are equally compelling. Herein lies what he regards as "*the* essential challenge of development." Efforts to bring welfare to Central American citizens must be balanced by the development of a "just state," a conclusion that underlies the work of the International Commission for Central American Recovery and Development, a multinational group of forty-seven leaders, for whom Ascher served as project director. In describing democracy, Ascher reinforces and restates an underlying premise of this volume. "It is not enough to have formal channels for democratic participation: They are necessary, but not sufficient, conditions for true democracy. A nation also needs people who are willing and able to participate politically. To a surprising degree, democratic participation requires an *economic base.*" He further adds that "there is a critical connection between economics and democracy that goes far beyond the mere fact that democracy might provide the poor with the opportunity to press for more wealth. More wealth in the hands of the poor is a crucial requisite for sustained democratic participation." To accomplish this, however, Ascher veers away from the traditional notion of a "welfare state" and redefines it as "the role of the state." This is because even though Latin American states have claimed to intervene on behalf of the poor (i.e., as "progressives"), the reality is that "Latin America has the worst distribution of income of all regions of the world" and that whatever the governments tried to do for the poor usually ended up benefiting the wealthy class and hurting the poor because the cost of failure is ultimately passed on to the poor. Regarding efforts to end this intervention, Ascher differs from Gerald E. Scott in an earlier article on Africa in that Ascher believes that IMF stabilization programs have not been as negative as popularly believed; rather, Ascher contends, it has been the incomplete implementation of these programs, owing to the inability of the poor to organize on their own behalf to lobby for their interests, that has rendered these programs "regressive." Nevertheless, the goal remains the dismantling of the privileges of the wealthy by removing the conditions that normally lead to state intervention; here, Ascher lists at least five strategies for doing so. Ascher emphasizes the urgency of taking action *now* as well as the need for a commitment on the part of the international community to bring about the much sought-after economic recovery and development for this embattled region.

The three articles in Part VI, "Corporate and Professional Responsibility in Third World Development," examine corporate and professional responsibility in Third World development. Earlier, it was stated that neither power nor profits could be pursued for its own sake. Here, we add to this list knowledge and information; it is contended that none of these (knowledge as purveyed by professionals; information as disseminated by the media, in addition to profit as pursued by business organizations) can be pursued apart from any *motives* or *purposes,* the *choice* of means with which to pursue them, and the *consequences* that they may have on their social environment. In other words, there are normative implications to the mere existence of the various professions and corporate organizations. Through their respective activities, they may contribute to the maintenance of a given political order or to its transformation. The question now is: How do they define their respective roles and responsibilities to the extent that they affect and influence society with what they do?

The piece by Mehrangiz Najafizadeh and Lewis A. Mennerick, "Professionals and Third World Public Well-Being," confronts head on the matter on professional responsibility. Having assumed correctly that professionals could no longer remain in their "ivory tower" and profess "objectivity" by pretending to be detached from the issues of the day, Najafizadeh and Mennerick suggest that professionals must now make a conscious decision to partake in the pursuit of social change that would reflect the true needs and requirements of peoples in the Third World. This decision should be preceded by a realization that "development" as it has been pursued in the last four decades has been nothing more than a reflection of Western values and traditions detached from Third World realities. Because of the failure of the dominant models of development, Najafizadeh and Mennerick enjoin other professionals to consider the concept of "social change and public well-being." They explain: "Third World social change can take various forms, and recognition of indigenous Third World cultural values and social structures should be central to all social change activities. Of equal importance, however, is the concept of public well-being . . . [which reflects] a core of *universal* values. Public well-being consists of various components (e.g., the provision of food, shelter, health care, and education) the assurance of a nonthreatening natural environment, civil liberties, and human rights."

In their discussion, Najafizadeh and Mennerick focus largely on a central aspect of public well-being concerned with the expansion and status of education; they do so because of their belief that in the long term, education is potentially the *most* fundamental component in enhancing public well-being." With education, the citizenry would better understand various issues related to health care, the environment, and human rights.

To Najafizadeh and Mennerick, the relationships among public well-being, education,and democratization are not simple ones. This is because different forms of government (e.g., liberal democratic, authoritarian, or totalitarian) could secure varying degrees of public well-being. Cuba is cited as an example that, even though there is a lack of political freedom, has far more accomplishments toward social democratization such as the redistribution of wealth, the reduction of infant mortality, and the extension of life expectancy than, say, Costa Rica, which has a tradition of political democracy. In any case, Najafizadeh and Mennerick underscore the importance of human rights and civil liberties as well as the need to assure peoples of the Third World of their right to shape their own destinies through freedom of expression and assembly, due process, and representation in governance. In conclusion, Najafizadeh and Mennerick view the responsibilities of professionals toward democratization in two ways: first, in the promotion of further expression of educational opportunities in the Third World; and second, in the promotion of forms of schooling to enhance "personal and collective 'liberation'."

In "Business Social Policy in the Third World," Sita C. Amba-Rao deals with a topic that has long elicited spirited discussions in both academic circles and public media: the response of the multinational corporate community to criticisms about its apparent lack of social responsibility. According to Amba-Rao, three trends have impelled the corporate community to examine its responsibility and to develop an appropriate response through the codification of an ethical code of conduct that may be applied under various circumstances. These trends are (1) the worldwide expansion in activities of multinational corporations (MNCs), (2) the recognition by Third World governments of the role of private enterprise in economic and social development, and (3) the rise of Third World MNC counterparts. In addition, criticisms by social activists as well as the accumulated experiences of MNCs operating in the Third World have also contributed to the shift in corporate orientation toward committing themselves to social values.

Amba-Rao notes that theoretical works by academicians on the subject of corporate social responsibility began to proliferate only during the 1980s. Consequently, the concept of social responsibility, the explication of business ethics, and the definition of the roles of the executive, the organization, and the professional are still evolving as academicians and corporate leaders continue to debate and discuss their respective meanings, ramifications, and dimensions. The need for and the style of systemic change are also currently under discussion. Here, Amba-Rao suggests several dimensions for consideration, including (1) commitment (on the part of top management to its ethical philosophy), (2) communication (or the transmission of the top management's ethical philosophy to its members), and (3) institutionalization (which includes the integration of desired attitudes and behaviors into the system). Finally, Amba-Rao highlights the pivotal role of the subsidiary in the host country in the formulation and implementation of social policy in the Third World. She concludes by pointing out that the subsidiary could serve not only as a liaison between the parent corporation and the host government but also as a source of input for the host government in a spirit of collaboration.

In the third selection in this part, "Media Image and Development," Eronini R. Megwa and Ike S. Ndolo examine the responsibility, or lack of it, by U.S. news media in covering events in Africa. Of significance in this contribution are the inferences one may draw concerning the behavior of U.S. media beyond Africa. By using the results of content analysis of two leading U.S. news magazines from 1979 to 1989, Megwa and Ndolo confirm what has been long suspected: Objectivity in news coverage of Africa by the U.S. media is a myth. Megwa and Ndolo attribute this to the ideological framework within which media exist in American society; the authors point to the media's marketplace paradigm, in which news stories are primarily commodities to be used for "their ability to excite and entertain the audience." This results because the media are established primarily "as profit-making institutions, not as human knowledge promoters, that benefit from the production and promotion of opinions and information generated by powerful economic and political groups and institutions." In assessing the consequences of U.S. media with this kind of an ideological framework, Megwa and Ndolo assert that the negative image given to Africa has had several results, including (1) undermining the position of Africa's political and diplomatic positions at international transactions, (2) discouraging potential foreign investors from doing business in Africa, and (3) producing erroneous judgments and policy debates about Africa. This situation is compounded, according to Megwa and Ndolo, by the U.S. public's unfamiliarity with Africa, which makes the continent even less interesting as images of starvation, disease, and tribal warfare, among others, fill the pages of magazines and newspapers. The overall outlook of Africa and the rest of the developing world does not look promising insofar as the Western media are concerned. This is largely because, as Megwa and Ndolo point out in their conclusion, "[n]othing in the structure of the present international news flow ensures the promotion and protection of the interests and views of developing nations. Rather, the structure is primarily an economic arrangement designed to protect the interests of the transnational Western news agencies and to guarantee the survival of Western news media institutions." As to what can be done to alter this situation, Megwa and Ndolo suggest that U.S. media "embark on self-regulation and reeducation to sharpen critical perspectives of their international news staffs" and to "give equal attention to both the disruptive and nondisruptive aspects of development in Africa."

In "Contemporary Issues and Future Challenges for Professionals in Third World Social Change," the only article in Part VII, Lewis A. Mennerick and Mehrangiz Najafizadeh examine further the role of professionals in Third World social change and in the context of challenges that confront them in the 1990s and beyond. The traditional concept of professionals is critically examined, and the notion that professionals, as distinguished from laypeople, were unique and better suited to development work because of their positions and advanced educations is abandoned. As Mennerick and Najafizadeh point out, "formal education and professional certification are not always the only credentials needed in effective development planning." "In fact," they observe, "many professionals have come to recognize that the practical work and life experiences of Third World laypeople can provide especially important insights into alternate avenues for development."

In this emergent redefinition of professional roles, Mennerick and Najafizadeh put greater emphasis than before on the appreciation and understanding of the complexities involving social, political, cultural, organizational, and economic aspects of the environment in which development is to take place. Accordingly, they also recognize the importance and, indeed, the necessity of giving attention and consideration to the values and aspirations of the intended recipients of development assistance. In denying the traditional conception that the professional has a considerable degree of control over his or her work environment, our authors offer the sobering observation that a multitude of problems constrain the professional in carrying out his or her responsibilities. Among these are the organizational (e.g., conflicting goals or methods within or between organizations), the structural (e.g., lack or absence of infrastructure to facilitate development work), and the ideological (e.g., differences in the definition of and solution to a problem, differences that may be rooted in religion, cultural tradition, and ethnicity, among others).

Resolution of the above constraints is necessary if professionals are to move forward and to see themselves as qualified in confronting the challenges that they will continue to face well into the twenty-first century. In their concluding section, Mennerick and Najafizadeh examine certain issues that bear on the role of professionals in the democratization process: (1) the need of professionals to seek and build bridges of cooperation between and among themselves as well as between and among them and government and private development agencies; (2) the need to recognize development as relative and to consider the values, perspectives, and experiences of the peoples—especially laypeople—in the Third World; and (3) the need of professionals to be more sensitive to the pressing problems of society that affect ordinary citizens more than elites (e.g., the lack of educational facilities, high rates of population growth, environmental degradation, and maldistribution of wealth). "As manifested in these problems," Mennerick and Najafizadeh conclude, "the ultimate challenge for the coming decades is to remedy the persistent inequities that continue to characterize much of the Third World today and thereby enhance the quality of life for all segments of Third World citizenry."

NOTES

1. Probably the most prominent and representatives in this group have written the following multivolume books: Guillermo O'Donnell, Philippe Schmitter, and Lawrence Whitehead, ed., *Transitions from Authoritarian Rule: Prospects for Democracy* (Baltimore, Md.: Johns Hopkins University Press, 1986). In four volumes, namely: Vol. I, *Southern Europe;* Vol. II, *Latin America;* Vol. III, *Comparative Perspectives;* and Vol. IV, *Tentative Conclusions About Uncertain Democracies.* Also Larry Diamond, Juan J. Linz, and Seymour Martin Lipset, eds., *Democracy in Developing Countries* (Boulder, Colo.: Lynne Rienner, 1987–199-). In four volumes, namely: Vol. I, *Persistence, Failure and Renewal;* Vol. II, *Africa;* Vol. III, *Asia;* and Vol. IV, *Latin America.*

Also notable in this group are the following works: Zbigniew Brzezinski, *The Grand Failure* (New York: Scribner's, 1989); Larry Diamond, "Beyond Authoritarianism and Totalitarianism: Strategies for Democratization," paper presented at the Conference on "Pluralism, Participation, and Democracy: Prospects and Prescriptions into the 21st Century," sponsored by the Center for Strategic and International Studies, Washington, D.C., and held in Lisbon, Portugal, June 19–21, 1988 (forthcoming in *The Washington Quarterly*); Raymond D. Gastil, ed., *Freedom in the World: Political Rights and Civil Liberties, 1987–88* (New York: Freedom House, 1988); Samuel P. Huntington, "Will More Countries Become Democratic?" *Political Science Quarterly, 9* (1984): 193–218; Juan J. Linz, *The Breakdown of Democratic Regimes: Crisis, Breakdown and Reequilibrium* (Baltimore, Md.: Johns Hopkins University Press, 1978); Juan J. Linz, "The Transition from Authoritarian Regimes to Democratic Political Systems and the Problems of Consolidation of Political Democracy," paper presented at the International Political Science Association, Tokyo Roundtable, held March 29 to April 1, 1982; Brad Roberts, ed. *The New Democracies; Global Change and U.S. Policy* (Cambridge, Mass.: MIT Press, 1990); Dankwart Rustow, "Transitions to Democracy: Towards a Dynamic Model," *Comparative Politics, 2* (1970); and Tatu Vanhanen, *The Process of*

Democratization: A Comparative Study of 147 States 1980–88 (Washington, D.C.: Crane Russak, 1990).

But the most erudite in this group is Francis Fukuyama, *The End of History and the Last Man* (New York: The Free Press, 1991). Fukuyama argues that while not all countries of the world are yet liberal democratic, they are all bound to be since human nature requires it.

2. Diamond, et al. *Democracy,* p. xvi.

3. See Juan J. Linz, "Totalitarian and Authoritarian Regimes" in Fred I. Greenstein and Nelson W. Polsby, eds., *Handbook of Political Science,* (Reading, Mass.: Addison-Wesley, 1975), Vol. 3, *Macropolitical Theory,* pp. 187–192. This essay attempts to build on standard works on the subject, including Hannah Arendt, *The Origins of Totalitarianism* (New York: Harcourt, Brace & World, 1951), Carl Friedrich and Zbigniew K. Brzezinski, *Totalitarian Dictatorship and Autocracy* (New York: Praeger, 1965), and J. L. Talmon, *The Origins of Totalitarian Democracy* (New York: Beacon Press, 1952).

4. Linz, "Regimes," pp. 264–274. Other leading works on authoritarianism are T. W. Adorno and Associates, *The Authoritarian Personality* (New York: Harper & Row, 1950); Samuel P. Huntington and Clement Moore, *Authoritarian Politics in Modern Society: The Dynamics of Established One Party Systems* (New York: Basic Books, 1970), and Barrington Moore, *Social Origins of Dictatorship and Democracy* (Boston: Beacon Press, 1966).

5. Diamond, "Beyond Authoritarianism," pp. 1–2.

6. These factors were distilled from Larry Diamond, Juan J. Linz, and Seymour Martin Lipset, "Democracy in Developing Countries: Facilitating and Obstructing Factors" in Gastil, ed., *Freedom in the World,* pp. 229–258.

7. Diamond, "Beyond Authoritarianism," p. 3.

8. Robert B. Stauffer, "Philippine Democracy: Contradictions of Third World Redemocratization," *Kasarinlan; Philippine Quarterly of Third World Studies, 6* (1, 2) (1990):9.

9. Diamond, "Beyond Authoritarianism," pp. 3–4.

10. Boston: Beacon Press, 1989.

11. *Common Good,* p. 173.

12. *Common Good,* p. 234.

13. These have been distilled from Daly and Cobb, *Common Good,* particularly pp. 49–60.

14. Much of the information presented in the following discussion is derived from Walden Bello, *Brave New Third World? Strategies for Survival in the Global Economy,* Food First Development Report No. 5 (San Francisco: Institute for Food and Development Policy, February 1989).

15. Bello, *Brave New Third World?,* p. 11.

16. A seminal work on transnationalization is Robert Keohane and Joseph S. Nye, eds., *Transnational Relations and World Politics* (Cambridge, Mass.: Harvard University Press, 1972).

17. For further critical discussion, see the op-ed piece by Kenneth E. Bauzon, "The Fallacy of the New World Order," *Manila Chronicle,* May 4–10, 1991, p. 9.

18. An example of these theoretical works is Estrella D. Solidum, Roman Dubsky, and Teresita Saldivar-Sali, "Security in a New Perspective," *Asian Perspective, 5*(2) (Fall–Winter 1981). Here *security* is defined in terms of "the feeling that accompanies

actual, perceived, or sustained satisfaction of values." It is "essentially a psychological condition." *Threat,* on the other hand, is defined abstractly as a condition "perceived as constituting impairment of the enjoyment or satisfaction of values." Finally, a *strategy* designed to meet this threat is also defined in abstract terms as "a plan that is employed in order to secure far-reaching advantage for one who uses it." All of these definitions are loaded with military or political connotations, and nowhere do the authors define the above terms to account for the threat coming, say, from environmental degradation or the destabilizing debt burden of Third World countries. Thus, even as this piece was being written, it was obsolete!

19. Lester R. Brown, "Redefining National Security," in Steven L. Spiegel, ed., *At Issue: Politics in the World Arena* (New York: St. Martin's Press, 1988). This article is an abridgment of Chapter 11 of *State of the World 1986: A Worldwatch Institute Report on Progress Toward a Sustainable Society* (New York: W. W. Norton & Co., 1986). Brown is project director for the Worldwatch Institute.

20. For the full text of this declaration, "The Manila Declaration on People's Participation and Sustainable Development," see Appendix A in David C. Korten, *Getting to the 21st Century: Voluntary Action and the Global Agenda* (West Hartford, Conn.: Kumarian Press, 1990), pp. 217–221.

21. "The Manila Declaration."

22. For the full text, see *Antalya Statement on Change: Threat or Opportunity for Human Progress?* (New York: United Nations Development Program, 1991).

Part One

Current Trends and New Directions in Third World Research

Chapter 1

Development Studies: Contending Approaches and Research Trends

Kenneth E. Bauzon

This chapter broadly surveys the progress and direction of research in develop-
ment studies. This survey is done in the context of four contending schools of
thought to the study of development, namely, modernization theory, the develop-
mental ethicist approach, dependency theory, and neo-Marxist theory. Each may
be called a "paradigm" or a community of scholars who share common assump-
tions about reality and whose "objectivity" may be defined only in the context of
their respective paradigms. This chapter surveys how these paradigms define the
problem of development in the Third World, the solution they offer, the particular
tools or methods they use in solving this problem, and their general assumptions
about the nature of the political and social reality in which their respective practi-
tioners find themselves.

INTRODUCTION

The study of development in the Third World has been in a state of flux since the end of World War II. One reason for this state is the lack of a clear focus or set of common purposes among the various practitioners. But a more funda-mental reason has been the absence of a consensus among these practitioners regarding the nature and definition of the problem of development in the Third World, the solutions to it, and the tools with which to solve it. It is the assump-tion here that this lack or absence of consensus and, for that matter, commensu-rability, is traceable to these scholars' varying, often conflicting, fundamental

This is an expanded version of a paper titled "Political Leadership and Development: The State of the Discipline," which was presented at the annual meeting of the Association for the Advance-ment of Policy, Research and Development in the Third World, Mexico City, Mexico, November 14–17, 1990.

The author wishes to acknowledge with appreciation the editorial assistance of Dr. H. Monte Hill in the preparation of an earlier draft of this essay particularly in the segment on modernization theory.

presuppositions about reality itself. Reflecting this lack of consensus is the emergence of several competing schools of thought, or what Thomas S. Kuhn calls "paradigms" or communities of scholars sharing common assumptions about reality and whose "objectivity" in social research is possible only within the context of their respective paradigms.[1] It is assumed that as each paradigm attempts to explain reality, the strength of this explanation rests on its ability to account for this reality through the use of evidence, inference, or sheer logic. Otherwise, it may be rendered obsolete or irrelevant by competing paradigms or by "insurgent" groups within a paradigm that seek to modify or challenge this paradigm's standard explanation of reality.

The significance of this study is threefold: First, it brings together the dominant contending approaches to development and assesses their prospects for commensurability; second, it offers a critical perspective regarding certain prevailing assumptions on development in the Third World; and third, it offers practical suggestions to guide public policy in the Third World.

MODERNIZATION THEORY

Modernization theory was the dominant school of thought on development until the early 1960s. This theory derives from the evolutionary ideas of Charles Darwin and Herbert Spencer, and it was influenced in varying degrees by the economic ideas of Adam Smith and John Maynard Keynes. Much of the late nineteenth-century and early twentieth-century precursors of modernization theory believed in some kind of Social Darwinism in which societies, much like their biological counterparts, went through the stages of birth, maturation, and decay. Furthermore, they adhered to some kind of an international division of labor based on certain presumed endowments possessed by the inhabitants of the various regions of the world. Thus, inhabitants of the tropics, presumed to be naturally "docile, indolent, and superstitious," had to be led, educated, and administered by those of the temperate zone who were, in turn, presumed to be "industrious, creative, and culturally superior."[2]

That modernization theory flourished within the liberal democratic framework was not fortuitous. The evolutionary bent of its practitioners conformed with their belief that the democratic countries of the West have indeed attained the zenith of civilization that the rest of the countries of the world must emulate. It was further believed that the laissez-faire economic system was the driving force behind the democratic system that allowed individuals to be more productive in the pursuit of their interests. The collective progress of these individuals, it was thought, would be reflected in the overall progress of society with a little help from the "invisible hand" of individualism.

Contemporary proponents of modernization theory, while maintaining an intellectual affinity with their predecessors on the nature of social reality and human progress, have assumed an identity of their own by putting forth ideas intended to refine their predecessors' coarser beliefs. For instance, Walt W.

Rostow, perhaps the most influential—and most notorious—of post–World War II modernization theorists, argued in his landmark publication *The Stages of Economic Growth* that development occurred in five distinct phases, namely, the traditional, the take-off, the drive to maturity, mass consumption, and post-mass consumption.[3]

Several other works have been published since then. Many of these subsequent works focused on the "forces" propelling development. Gabriel Almond and Sidney Verba, for instance, stressed the value of a "civic culture" embodying democratic ideals.[4] Daniel Lerner focused on a "modern personality" who embraced science, democracy, and laissez-faire capitalism.[5] Karl W. Deutsch and Lucian W. Pye, in their respective works, asserted the necessity of an integrative system of mass communication.[6] And Seymour M. Lipset suggested a complex set of interrelated social and economic conditions.[7]

Troubled by criticisms that modernization theorists put too much emphasis on endogenous factors (e.g., culture as impediment to development) a group of "culturally sensitive" and "historically minded" scholars made a significant departure from their earlier counterparts. This group, collectively referred to here as revisionist modernization theorists, asserted that modernization was, rather, a result of interactions among multitude of complex variables that are unique to each polity. Moreover, they asserted that Third World governments can bring about "positive change" in their respective societies by intervening in the "natural" process, thereby speeding up, bypassing, or even recycling some of the sequences involved in the development process. In this context, they recognized that the problem of poverty, prevalent throughout the Third World, was more of a pragmatic managerial problem than a theoretical or ideological one. Underdevelopment, therefore, was the result of a massive failure of the essential internal political structures (both public and private), functions, and processes in solving or managing society's social and economic problems, particularly with regard to the distribution of wealth. Consequently, the revisionists thought that the best way to solve these problems, particularly poverty, was through a shift from the broad theoretical concerns to more pragmatic matters involving the implementation of development policy. As one revisionist writer explained, "the crucial factor in reform is implementation, which determines whether or not anything really takes place."[8] Bear in mind that the rise to dominance by the modernization perspective occurred within the context of a certain set of historical circumstances. After World War II, the United States emerged as a virtually undisputed world power and as a model for democracy. With this prominence, U.S. proponents of modernization theory postulated a conjunction between democracy and economic prosperity. A leading proponent of this view, for instance, asserted that the least common denominator that links political systems to other components of the society is that "democracy is related to the state of economic development. The more well-to-do a nation, the greater the chances it will sustain democracy."[9]

Upon this assumption, neo-classical economists advanced the modernization perspective by insisting that the postwar recovery of Western Europe through the Marshall Plan could be replicated with a similar plan elsewhere. Thus, the Colombo Plan was put forth and heralded as a significant milestone in Asia's postwar economic recovery. This plan called for the massive infusion of capital into the region through grants, aid, and direct investments to revitalize free enterprise and, more particularly, to rebuild the rural and agrarian infrastructure of Asian economy.[10]

By the mid-1960s and early 1970s, it had become obvious that the development strategies formulated by the modernization theorists were not working. Faced with a deepening economic crisis that exacerbated rather than reduced poverty, critics—particularly those from competing schools of thought—argued that the traditional prescriptions were not applicable in countries whose circumstances were vastly different owing to immense changes in technology, culture, and social makeup. Modernization theory, the critics further contended, was simply too static—despite efforts by the pragmatic revisionists—to account for the extraordinarily dynamic developments that were transforming social realities and how these developments were to be viewed.

A vigorous group of writers in the early to mid-1960s exhibited a unique blend of nationalism, Marxist influence, and some liberal views. They began to point out, with gradually increasing vigor and rigor, the anomalies they saw as inherent in modernization theory. Known collectively as *dependentistas,* this group had no doubt about the failure of modernization theory in achieving its stated goal of bringing "modernity" to the Third World and in eliminating the attendant socioeconomic problems that beset Third World societies. Indeed, they point out, the gap between rich and poor nations has widened rather than narrowed during the time that the developmental programs advocated by modernization theorists were being implemented and, ironically, as links between the two groups of nations intensified through trade, aid, and investments.

By and large, the failure of modernization theory is traceable to six factors, which are summarized as follows: (1) the mistaken belief that all societies follow a unilinear path to the same level of development; (2) the assumption that development is primarily a function of endogenous factors; (3) the assumption that the state is a reflection of a community-wide consensus; (4) its teleological orientation, which ignored conflictual processes; (5) the alienation and disaffection of a large segment of the population from the political system; and (6) the rise of revolutionary movements in much of the Third World that reflected the above-mentioned alienation and disaffection. In lamenting modernization theory's apparent paralysis, one of its long-time exponents, Albert Hirschman, offered a retrospective explanation. He wrote: "[T]he old liveliness is no longer there, . . . new ideas are ever harder to come by and . . . the field is not adequately reproducing itself."[11]

DEVELOPMENTAL ETHICIST EXPLANATION

The subject of development not only is controversial in terms of its theoretical and technical aspects, but also motivates a raging debate among practitioners of various persuasions regarding the role of ethics and morality.

The mainstream social science approach, to which modernization theorists adhered or professed to adhere, was to disassociate morality from any linkages to development. This approach regards ethics as some abstract set of ideals that are "nice" but irrelevant to the "real world." At its best, ethics can only assist pragmatic decision makers to choose from among lesser evils. Whoever insists on seeking the "optimum good" or the "better course" is accused by adherents of this approach as being a "softhearted idealist" or a "heretic." Development, accordingly, requires "value-free" analysis, and political choices are to be made by selecting from among morally neutral but technically differentiated options.

The development ethicists, who hold values anchored either in religion or in custom and whose discipline borrows from the works of practitioners in the various fields of social sciences and humanities, counter with the argument that there is no such thing as ethical neutrality. Like everything else in life, development choices are never made in an existential vacuum. Therefore, choosing from among alternative paths to development is as much moral as it is technical or theoretical in view of the complexity of the process of development.

Among the early proponents of development ethics were the members of the so-called French School such as Francois Perroux, Louis Lebret, and Jacques Austruy.[12] The collective works of these writers have influenced United Nations (U.N.) philosophy on development, but their greatest influence is found in such religious works as papal encyclicals, documents issued by the World Council of Churches and the Pontifical Commission on Justice and Peace, and pastoral letters issued by bishops in various countries around the world.

Analysis begins with an examination of the moral content of all aspects of political and social life. As Denis Goulet, a leading development ethicist, explains in his provocative work *The Cruel Choice; A New Concept in the Theory of Development,* development in this context may be understood as a "complex set of interrelated change processes, abrupt and gradual, by which a population and all its components move away from patterns of life perceived in some significant way as 'less human' toward alternative patterns perceived as 'more human.'[13] In more concrete terms, Goulet continues, the development process should result in (1) the creation of "new solidarities" promoting a more grass roots–oriented development; (2) the nurturing of "cultural and ecological diversity" in opposition to much of the disrespect and disregard that accompany "progress," and (3) the optimization of "esteem and freedom" at both the individual and societal levels and the corresponding rejection of abuses of human rights and personal freedoms perpetrated by the state.

In sum, the ultimate goals of development relate to the pursuit of existence itself—that is, to provide everyone with the opportunity to live fully and with dignity as a human being.

This conception of development is akin to what Brazilian educator Paulo Freire and liberation theologians call "liberation."[14] As used by these practitioners, liberation implies the empowerment of the very same people who are the object of liberation. This empowerment is an act of self-defense intended to overcome the structural vulnerabilities that result in a denial of control over the political, economic, and cultural forces that affect their existence in a very significant way. As Goulet explains, "[f]or liberationists, therefore, success is not measured simply by the quantity of benefits gained, but above all by the way in which change processes take place. Visible benefits are no doubt sought, but the decisive test of success is that, in obtaining them, a society will have fostered greater popular autonomy in a nonelitist mode, social creativity instead of imitation, and control over forces of change instead of mere adjustment to them."[15]

In responding to critics who assert that morality is relative and lacking in universality, development ethicists argue that there is, in fact, a universal value system under which development policies and practices may be evaluated. This is exemplified by the U.N. Universal Declaration of Human Rights as well as by numerous subsequent treaties and conventions that codify the protection of the rights of minorities, women, and children and specify the duties and obligations of governments as well as international organizations, both governmental and nongovernmental.[16] This codified system of values effectively renders enforcement of rights, duties, and obligations as a matter of international concern. Any protestation by a government that such issues affecting the human rights of its citizens are purely domestic or internal matters, therefore, is misplaced. The protection of human rights could no longer be left solely to the discretion of the state whose primary interest of self-preservation often runs counter to the protection of the rights of its citizens.

On the issue of foreign aid, development ethicists argue that wealthy nations have the obligation to assist poor nations in their development programs. It is argued that the wealthy nations, even out of enlightened self-interest, have the obligation to cooperate in Third World development efforts.

The ethicists caution, however, against using aid to further the donor country's ideological objectives. Aid given out of humanitarian concern should be free from political or ideological constraints or conditions. Lessons of the past decades in which donor countries, most notably the United States, selectively provided assistance to friendly regimes, even though these regimes—often authoritarian ones—have engaged in gross violations of the human rights of their citizens, are compelling enough for this position to merit consideration. Although it is true that some Third World countries in Asia, Africa, and Latin America have benefited from U.S. aid and have, in fact, become industrialized and experienced dramatic economic growth, these newly industrialized countries (NICs) essentially have not altered their exploitative class relations and the manner in which wealth and power are shared domestically.

For the past thirty years, and particularly since the founding of the U.N. Conference on Trade and Development (UNCTAD) in 1964, Third World nations have grown increasingly critical of what they call a "systematic bias" against poor societies within international economic institutions. Through the fora of the UNCTAD, Third World members have argued, and development ethicists have concurred, that it is grossly immoral for poor countries to be thrown into sudden and severe depressions because of slight changes in the international market. Simple fairness, therefore, requires that a New International Economic Order (NIEO) be established to protect poor countries against disastrous losses occurring through no fault of their own and to reform existing institutions to make them more open and equitable. Furthermore, Third World nations have demanded higher levels of resource transfers in such areas as technology, international emergency funds, debt-relief payments, grants, and low-interest loans, as well as the elimination of all strings attached to foreign aid. In general, Third World nations have called, and continue to call, on the industrialized nations to meet what they regard as a reasonable assistance target—a minimum of 1.7 percent of a donor nation's annual GNP—that was mutually agreed upon for the Second U.N. Development Decade.

The discussion thus far has concentrated on peaceful, reformist, and institutional means of achieving development from the ethicist point of view. One other area of the ethicist strategy that deserves some exploration is the question of violence. Much has been written about the notion of "just war" and how this principle, under certain circumstances, has been used to justify the use of force. Emanating largely from Western experience and tradition, this principle has been reinterpreted in the Latin American context. Liberation theologians, in grappling with Christian teachings and sociopolitical realities, have attempted to adapt the above principle to legitimize a revolutionary approach to political change. Thus, before force could be considered, six conditions must be met: (1) It must be determined that the regime that is to be the object of force shall have lost its "mission" and have degenerated into tyranny, (2) all peaceable means shall have been exhausted, (3) the anticipated outcome of the forcible action must outweigh any damage done, (4) there must be a reasonable hope of success, (5) nothing that is intrinsically evil must be used toward the goal, and (6) no deliberate act "to create an objective reality" must be done so as to justify violence.[17]

Ethicists who have resolved in their minds that the use of revolutionary force is acceptable are convinced both of its necessity and inevitability. To them, revolution has become "a symbolic redemptive act by which men purge themselves of passive complicity in the destruction of their humanity."[18]

Having said this, it is important to bear in mind that the subject of force and violence is one that continues to fuel a spirited debate within the ranks of ethicists. For one thing, there are those who worry that advocates of revolutionary violence might lose sight of their primary purpose—the attainment of peace, justice, and equity in society. And for another, once begun, revolution will have a momentum all its own that may be difficult to control, thus leading to unanticipated abuses and destruction. These concerns, real as they are, constitute the dilemma that ethicists continue to confront and must solve.

DEPENDENCY THEORY

The dependency theory emerged largely in response to the failure of modernization theory, which dominated scholarly discourse on development in the Third World during much of the post–World War II period. Dependency theory's emergency occurred at a time when changes in the world economy brought in new awareness about the impact of external factors on Third World economies.

Dependency theory has a long line of precursors, but many of its core ideas did not crystallize into a systematic form until the late 1940s when the U.N. Economic Commission for Latin American (ECLA) was established. The ECLA was designed as an implementing agency of the United Nations technical assistance program for Latin America. The work of the ECLA was guided by its first director, Raul Prebisch, who, in 1949, wrote what amounted to the ECLA's manifesto on, *The Economic Development of Latin America and Its Principal Problems.*[19]

Since then, dependency theory has gone through various stages of elaboration, refinement, and consolidation. The influence of Marxist analysis in dependency theory is evident, but to claim that the latter is a variant of the former would be a misnomer. Certainly, the core–periphery dichotomy popularized in dependency literature is reminiscent of upper class–lower class dichotomy in Marxist analysis. However, their respective foci of analysis are different: While dependency theory focuses on the problem of underdevelopment, neo-Marxism is more interested in explaining the functioning of capitalism itself along with its contradictions. In any case, dependency proponents have acquired a definite identity all their own, one that is distinct from their competitors in the marketplace of ideas.

Among the early dependency theorists, the belief was common that the periphery nations' links with the core nations were the primary cause of underdevelopment.[20] Instead of assisting in the development of periphery nations, as modernization theorists had hoped would occur, the core nations had engaged in virtual exploitation of whatever surplus might have been accumulated in the periphery. The early dependency theorists focused on the "unequal terms" of trade that characterized the relationship between the periphery as a source of raw materials on the one hand and the core as an exporter of manufactured goods on the other. This is compounded by the observation that the state has not been autonomous from external control—that is, it has been merely a "handmaiden of foreign capitalists."[21] Thus, the result is not only a retardation of economic growth but also a distortion.

The solution proposed, which later came to be known as the "ECLA doctrine," called for the diversification of the export base of the peripheral countries as well as the acceleration of industrialization through the policy of import substitution. This would allow the growth of certain domestic industries, it was thought, at the same time that precious capital is conserved for further domestic investment. It was also advocated that the state, in a manner reminiscent of state capitalism, exert more control over domestic monetary policy and assert independence from foreign aid donors and investors, the assumption being that these external actors have become too dominant in domestic policy making.

To the succeeding generation of dependency theorists writing mostly during the 1970s, however, certain anomalies in the formulations of their predecessors became apparent. These anomalies were brought on by the fact that some periphery countries were registering growth but that within others a dual economy was evolving that was characterized by the emergence of a modern sector on the one hand and a traditional sector on the other. Concomitantly, it was also observed that not all core countries appeared to be engaged in the exploitation of the periphery; some, in fact, were actively aiding the development programs of certain periphery countries.

Dissenters to the early dependency formulation suggested that external constraints to development had been overemphasized—mainly the international division of labor based on comparative advantage—and that almost no attention had been given to domestic impediments (such as unequal land-tenure systems, and inflation) that had been brought about by structural rather than monetary factors. The assumption here is that as the core countries developed and specialized in industrial production, internal political and social structures in periphery areas were simultaneously affected.

This perspective became known as "structuralism" and found articulation in the influential works of such writers as Osvaldo Sunkel, Fernando Henrique Cardoso, and Theotonio dos Santos.[22] These writers stressed the interconnectedness of both the internal and external structural factors in explaining underdevelopment.

The ascendancy of this perspective opened the door to a reinterpretation of so-called dependent development and the role that Third World elites play. "Dependent development" is the term used to describe the development of one sector of the economy. A distinct feature of this type of development is the ubiquitous role played by native elites who, more often than not, control the apparatus of the state. It is axiomatic among early dependency writers to assume that a simple inverse relationship exists between economic dependence on the one hand and political democracy on the other.[23] In other words, economic dependence is thought to "distort class structures of dependent societies, restricting the size and power of the national bourgeoisie and middle class and producing a powerful export-oriented oligarchy and a large, powerless lower class of impoverished workers and peasants."[24]

Empirical studies by later dependency writers bear out the dependent development perspective, although they criticize the simplistic and somewhat mechanistic approach taken by their predecessors. As one latter-day dependency proponent explained, "contemporary dependency studies address a situation in which domestic industrialization has occurred along with increasing denationalization; in which sustained economic growth has been accompanied by rising social inequalities; and in which rapid urbanization and the spread of literacy converged with the ever more evident marginalization of the masses."[25]

In this context, one may look at the prominent role played by the state and the emergence of the authoritarian phenomenon in much of the Third World. The role of the state has been problematic not only to dependency theory but also to competing theories. One reason for this is the complexity in which the state's ultimate course is influenced both by the elite's perception of its interests as well as by the state's own social and political environment. Nevertheless, empirical studies have been conducted investigating the patterns of state intervention in the Third World.[26] A common conclusion among many of these studies bears out the dependency assumption that "leaders pursue their political interests through policies and that patterns of state intervention often reflect the interests of the dominant classes."[27]

It is from this that "development of underdevelopment" as understood in the dependency literature gains significance. This introduces a new category of developing countries that lie somewhere between the core and the periphery. A variant of dependency theory—the world systems theory—has popularized the term "semiperiphery" to refer to countries that are located "in between the core and periphery on a series of dimensions" but which are not "an artifice of statistical cutting points" nor "a residual category [but rather] a necessary structural element in the world economy."[28]

Having now identified three parts of the world economic system (i.e., core, periphery, and semiperiphery), proponents of the world systems approach emphasize—as would dependency writers—that there remains only one world system, a total one with a single division of labor despite the diversity of its parts, in which some lose and others gain, one in which those who win and become dominant use the instrumentalities of the state to sustain their advantage. In this light, the dependency/world systems approach reminds us of a lesson that "[t]o study countries, above all perhaps to study developing societies, in a world system without studying the classes that are dominant and dominated in them is to fall into error. . . . What the world system holds together. . . is not countries or even states but economic activities and more specifically economic classes. The crucial question for us is whether these nations and classes have real possibilities of economic development."[29]

Answers to these questions are provided by several empirical studies conducted over the last decade or so that evaluate certain assumptions of dependency theory particularly with regard to the notion of dependent development. Among the developing countries, the NICs—especially those of Asia and Latin America—perhaps offer the best examples of the semiperiphery described earlier. From the modernization perspective, it may be recalled, their success appears to validate the market-oriented policies and integration into the capitalist world economy. But from the dependency/world system perspective, these countries exemplify not much more than "policy incompetence, economic distortion, inequality, and dependence."[30]

An important feature of the NICs is the apparent autonomy of their elites and, by extension, the state from endogenous forces that are potential sources of demands on them. This autonomy allows them to shape policies pertaining to land reform; the setting of wages, prices, rates, and profits; the value of the national currency; and the imposition of protection and subsidies on domestic products. This autonomy, however, stops at the water's edge, so to speak, because of the observed compliant behavior of the state toward the exogenous powers on which it depends. Dependency writers acknowledge that while some developing countries are more adept than others in turning their weakness into strength, thus appearing to challenge the compliant behavior hypothesis postulated above, by and large these countries are still subordinate to the core countries.[31]

In retrospect, the dependency theory continues to offer a viable alternative to an understanding of underdevelopment in the Third World. It addresses itself well to an anomaly that its most worthy opponent—the modernization theory—appears too paralyzed to confront. This anomaly pertains to the widening, rather than narrowing, gap between the core and the periphery as links between them intensify.[32] This is not to say, however, that dependency theory did not experience its own crises. In fact, its core assumptions have been challenged time and again, but each time its practitioners have been able to reformulate and reinvigorate it as a coherent and capable explanation to development and undevelopment in the Third World.

NEO-MARXIST EXPLANATION

The term "neo-Marxist" has come to refer to a subschool within Marxism that attempts to account for many of the anomalies that classical Marxism has proven unable to explain. Its birth may be placed in 1945 with the publication of the now classic *Political Economy of Growth* by Paul Baran.[33] Since then, neo-Marxism has evolved as it has attracted a vigorous set of adherents.

To neo-Marxists, the subject of development is of a distinctly Marxian origin. As Aidan Foster-Carter explains, "Marxism is the prototype of development theory."[34] In explaining underdevelopment in the Third World, the analysis begins with the expansionary character of capitalism. As capitalism expanded beyond European boundaries during the heyday of colonialism, the economies of the colonial areas were reshaped in a manner that rendered them subordinate to the demands of capital. One effect of this was the emergence of a kind of semipermanent international economic division of labor in which the capitalist countries of Europe and North America virtually monopolized the industries as well as the capital needed to sustain them. Much of Asia, Africa, and Latin America was regarded as a vast market for capitalist products and as a source of immense raw materials and cheap labor. A further consequence of this was the institutionalization of exploitation through various mechanisms of neocolonial control (e.g., aid, trade, and investments) so that these regions of the world would remain subordinate in their agricultural and preindustrial state.

In an apparent move to reconcile the conflicting claims of protagonists over whether the source of undevelopment and exploitation is external (e.g., "world system") or internal (e.g., "mode of production") some neo-Marxists have reinterpreted Marxist and Leninist writings in such a way to account for both sources. For instance, a leading neo-Marxist theoretician, Ernesto Laclau, has criticized Latin American Marxists for their inability to analyze Latin American conditions *"simultaneously* at the level of *modes of production* and that of *economic systems.*" Laclau further observed that their mistakes derived from a "unilateral use of one or the other of the two levels."[35]

The theme that recurs in this and in much of the current literature is the requirement for flexibility in the interpretation of and approach to the historical and social processes. The purpose, admittedly, is to enable the observer to "study the totality of all sides of the phenomenon and their reciprocal relations (or contradictions)".[36]

This leads our discussion to the nature of the relationship between the "logic of capital" on the one hand and the formation of the state on the other.[37] Contrary to the orthodox Marxist view that the historical process is reducible to economic motives, the emergent trend in neo-Marxist thought is the recognition of the primacy of the "political" as the dominant force in modern capitalism. This point was not lost on Nicos Poulantzas, who asserted early on that the intervention of the state—as a political act—has the consequence of displacing "market forces as the dominant element in the reproduction of the capital relation."[38] This theme was refined and developed by later neo-Marxists, among them Colin Henfrey. He asserted that in much of the Third World where the dominant economic forces are "external" (e.g., the metropolitan countries of Western Europe, North American, and Japan), "the ruling class rules disproportionately through the political mechanisms of its relations with other classes, rather than through economic ones, which it controls either incompletely or scarcely at all." Henfrey further asserted that social relations of production in much of the Third World have not evolved into mature capitalism; rather, these were being "reproduced largely by ideological and political rather than economic forms of coercion."[39]

On the subject of "enclave economies" or what dependency theorists refer to as "development of underdevelopment," Poulantzas's and Henfrey's accounting typifies neo-Marxist thinking on the subject. A major assumption in this regard is the "relative autonomy" of the dependent state in the Third World vis-á-vis competing domestic forces; this autonomy was seen to allow the state to better serve the interests of capitalists in the metropolitan countries. There were two elements in this autonomy, namely; control over the domestic wealth by the state and control over the political and coercive apparatus of the state by the state. These elements have the consequence of denying other sectors of society (the dominant ones included) effective access to the state because they may potentially threaten the position of the state's incumbent guardians, the ruling class. A further consequence is the inability of other sectors to influence the conditions of dependency, the distribution of the means of production, and the shape of social relations, which makes production possible. In this context, we may understand the rise of the bureaucratic-authoritarian state in many parts of the Third World. This state formation has been largely responsible in reinforcing the integration of the domestic economy into the orbit of capitalism, in enhancing the role of foreign capital, and in dictating the course of domestic production, particularly in the context of industrialization. These were made possible as the state—backed by the instruments of coercion—assumed the roles of the market in the setting of prices, profits, and wages.[40]

As a case in point, NICs of the Third World, especially the so-called Asian Tigers, are regarded by neo-Marxists and other critics of capitalism as fine examples of enclave capitalism in which a small segment of the economy develops while the rest lags behind; furthermore, this segment maintains links with, but could never compete against, its counterparts in the metropolitan countries. Despite their aggressive economic growth, they could not engage in the production, manufacture, and distribution of certain products (e.g., those deemed militarily sensitive) that could threaten or undermine the metropolitan countries' technological, industrial, and strategic advantage over the rest of the world. These nations have remained essentially assembly plant–type economies who have played hosts to Western companies fleeing unionized workers demanding high wages and benefits in their home countries. The NICs have offered abundant cheap labor, readily accessible natural resources, and conducive political climates free of worker activities that might disrupt production.

Although the NICs have attained a level of economic growth that many Third World countries find enviable, the distribution of domestic economic wealth is essentially lopsided in favor of the native capitalists who have collaborated with their counterparts from the metropolitan countries. The state, although autonomous from other sectors, remains insecure as society's repressed forces attempt to break out. Long-term political stability is sacrificed in exchange for short-term profits. Furthermore, the state remains vulnerable to outside pressures as the metropolitan countries and lending institutions, to whom it is politically indebted, seek to deepen—through various mechanisms of neocolonialism—their penetration and control of the local economy. This merely heightens the state's dependency and renders meaningless its claim to independence and sovereignty.

On the matter of strategy, neo-Marxists have taken a variety of positions. The early group of neo-Marxists—including Andre Gunder Frank arguing for Latin America,[41] Frantz Fanon taking up the case for Africa, [42] and Baran, to whom neo-Marxists owe an intellectual debt—closed the door to any peaceful and evolutionary transformation. Contending that development is about changing the world and that it is essentially a revolutionary idea, this group was convinced that any significant change in history is rarely accomplished through peaceful means. Revolutionary movements are, accordingly, seen as the preeminent instruments through which development could occur and that the barriers to development are not sociocultural patterns per se in the poor countries but rather the self-serving interests of the metropolitan countries and their native collaborators.

Some neo-Marxists writing about recent dramatic changes in socialist bloc countries have expressed reservations about the inevitability or necessity of revolution. For instance, Ernesto Laclau's and Chantal Mouffe's penetrating critique of Marxist theory and practice, *Hegemony and Socialist Strategy; Towards a Radical Democratic Politics,*[43] offers the proposition that "there are no iron laws of history, no historical necessity for a proletarian revolution, no 'special mission' for the working classes, and so forth,"[44] in an apparent effort to dismiss the popular notion that the Marxist approach to development is strictly deterministic. Nicos Mouzelis explains: "Neither the deterministic/ mechanistic nor the scientistic/authoritarian elements . . . can be considered as representing the core of Marx's thought."[45] Mouzelis continues that, on the contrary, "Marx's scheme of stages—which emphasizes the importance of class struggles as a fundamental mechanism of transition from one stage to the next—provides the conceptual means for avoiding a strictly unilinear, determinist view of development of the kind that is set out in the writings of [Auguste] Comte, for instance."[46] Thus, Marx's overall work need not entail a determinist orientation nor should it lead necessarily to an authoritarian political system.

A logical extension of this perspective has been the adaptation by socialist movements and parties to a pluralist political framework in which they find themselves; this allows them to operate by essentially the same rules as other political groups and parties that are of nonsocialist orientation. For instance, socialist parties in Great Britain, France, Greece, and Italy have obviously found a way to reconcile their existence with Marxist thought and practice in such a way that they would not be regarded as pariahs among other socialist movements. Parliamentary struggle has become the core of their approach to political power. In the Third World, the case of the Sandinista movement in Nicaragua presents an interesting example of a socialist movement that attained state power and reluctantly allowed pluralism to prevail, which led to its own ouster from power. Through the same rules by which it was defeated, the

Sandinista movement aspires to capture political power again when the time becomes propitious.[47]

CONCLUSION

This chapter has presented a survey of the literature on development in the Third World representing four of the dominant approaches to the study. Each approach claims to provide conceptual and analytical tools with which one may understand the problem of development and underdevelopment in the Third World, the general strategy or strategies with which to solve it, and the specific tools or methods that practitioners may employ in solving it.

One lesson learned from this enterprise is that, in view of the varied assumptions of the practitioners, different criteria of evaluation are used that lead to different foci of research. The method of research used is informed by the prevailing assumptions about the nature of reality—social or otherwise—within each approach. The notion of objectivity of this method of research may be understood only within the context of each approach. Otherwise, this objectivity may be regarded as mere fiction in view of the values that guide the practitioners in their choice of a subject of inquiry, defining the purpose with which the inquiry is conducted, and in shaping the conclusions that emanate from this inquiry.

It follows that the manner in which development and democratization in the Third World are defined by the various practitioners would also differ fundamentally from one approach to another. This difference is traceable to fundamental assumptions that are nurtured within each scholarly community. If one still wonders whether each of the four approaches can be reconciled, therefore, one can rest assured that commensurability—that is, fundamental grounds on which the approaches commonly agree—between and among them is illusory.

The implication of this to the more practical problem of tackling developmental problems in the Third World is indeed profound. The incommensurability at the conceptual and theoretical levels is replicated at the practical level as practitioners proceed to prescribe and implement different, and often conflicting, programs of action aimed at specific developmental issues or problems. Unless the academic enterprise itself embarks on a concerted program to de-ideologize and depoliticize itself—a program that seems quixotic—one can continue to expect problems and conflicts among the practitioners at the same time that the Third World continues to languish in its own predicament.

NOTES

1. Thomas S. Kuhn, *The Structure of Scientific Revolutions* (Chicago: The University of Chicago Press, 1970).

2. Benjamin Kidd, *The Control of the Tropics* (New York: MacMillan, 1898) p. 16.

3. *The Stages of Economic Growth: A Non-Communist Manifesto.* (Cambridge: Cambridge University Press, 1960).

4. *The Civic Culture* (Boston: Little, Brown, 1963).

5. *The Passing of Traditional Society: Modernizing the Middle East* (New York: Free Press, 1958).

6. Karl W. Deutsch, *Nationalism and Social Communication: An Inquiry into the Foundations of Nationality* (Cambridge, Mass.: MIT Press, 1966); and Lucian W. Pye, *Aspects of Political Development* (Boston: Little, Brown, 1966).

7. "Some Social Prerequisites of Democracy: Economic Development and Political Legitimacy," *American Political Science Review, 53* (March 1959): 69–105.

8. John D. Montgomery, "How Facts Replace Fads," *Comparative Politics* (January 1990): 245.

9. Seymour M. Lipset, *Political Man: The Social Basis of Politics* (New York: Anchor Books, 1963), p. 31.

10. E. Spencer Wellhofer, "Models of Core and Periphery Dynamics," *Comparative Political Studies, 21*(2)(July 1988): 285–286.

11. See Hirschman's *Essays in Trespassing: Economics to Politics and Beyond* (New York: Cambridge University Press, 1981), p. 1.

12. Francois Perroux, *L'economie du XXieme Siecle* (Paris: Presses Universitaires de France, 1964), Louis Lebret, *Manifeste pour une Civilisation Solidaire. Economie et Humanisme* (1959), and Jacques Austruy, *Le Scandale du Developement* (Paris: Marcel Riviere, 1965).

13. New York: Atheneum, 1973. p. x.

14. *Cultural Action for Freedom,* Monograph No. 1, Harvard Educational Review and Center for the Study of Development and Social Change, Cambridge, Mass.: 1970.

15. Goulet, *Cruel Choice,* p. xvii.

16. See the chapter by Sita C. Amba-Rao, "Business Social Policy in the Third World Response of Multinational Corporate Management," in this volume for codification of a set of ethical criteria governing corporate behavior.

17. Goulet, *Cruel Choice,* p. 311.

18. Goulet, *Cruel Choice,* p. 302.

19. This was subsequently published in 1950 as part of the United Nation's documents on economic development cataloged as E/CN.12/89/Rev.1. This was also published with the same title in *Economic Bulletin for Latin America, 7,* 1(1962):1–22. For a fuller discussion of the precursors of dependency theory and subsequent developments, see Kenneth E. Bauzon and Charles Frederick Abel, "Dependency: History, Theory, and a Reappraisal," in Mary Ann Tetreault and Charles Frederick Abel, eds., *Dependency Theory and the Return of the High Politics* (Westport, Conn.: Greenwood Press, 1986), pp. 43–69.

20. In this group are Raul Prebisch, cited earlier; Paul A. Baran, *Political Economy of Growth* (New York: Monthly Review Press, 1957 ed.); and Andre Gunder Frank, *Latin America: Underdevelopment or Revolution* (New York: Monthly Review Press, 1969).

21. H. Jeffrey Leonard, "Multinational Corporations and Politics in Developing Countries," *World Politics, 32*(3)(April 1980): 461.

22. See Osvaldo Sunkel, "Politica nacional de desarollo y dependencia externa," *Estudio Internacionales, 1*(April 1967); Fernando Henrique Cardoso, *Empresario industrial e desenvolvimento economico no Brasil* (São Paulo: Difusao Europeia do Livro, 1964); and Theotonio dos Santos, *El nuevo caracter de la dependencia* (Santiago: Cuadernos de Estudios Socio-Economicos, Centro de Estudios Economicos, Universidad de Chile, 1968).

23. Among the writers referred to are D. Chirot, *Social Change in the Twentieth Century* (San Diego, Calif.: Harcourt Brace Jovanovich, 1977); A. Szymanski, *The Logic of Imperialism* (New York: Praeger, 1981); and C. Y. Thomas, *The Rise of the Authoritarian State in Peripheral Societies* (New York: Monthly Review Press, 1984).

24. Mark J. Gasiorowski, "Economic Dependence and Political Democracy; A Cross-National Study," *Comparative Political Studies, 20*(4)(January 1988): 489.

25. Alejandro Portes, "On the Sociology of National Development: Theories and Issues," *American Journal of Sociology, 82* (July 1976): 75.

26. A path-breaking work along these lines is Guillermo O'Donnell, *Modernization and Bureaucratic Authoritarianism: Studies in Latin American Politics* (Berkeley: University of California Press, 1973).

27. Atul Kohli, "The Political Economy of Development Strategies; Comparative Perspectives on the Role of the State" (a review essay), *Comparative Politics, 19*(2)(January 1987): 244.

28. Immanuel Wallerstein, *The Modern World System* (New York: Academic Press, 1974), p. 349.

29. Michael Barratt Brown, "Developing Societies as Part of an International Political Economy," in Hamza Alavi and Teodor Shanin, eds., *Introduction to the Sociology of "Developing Societies"* (New York: Monthly Review Press, 1982), p. 156.

30. Stephan Haggard, "The Newly Industrializing Countries in the International System" (a review essay), *World Politics, 38*(2)(January 1986): 344.

31. See Colin I. Bradford, Jr., "East Asian 'Models': Myth and Lessons," in John P. Lewis and Valeriana Kallab, eds., *Development Strategies Reconsidered* (Washington, D.C.: Overseas Development Council, 1986),; and Robin Broad and John Cavanagh, "No More NICs," *Foreign Policy* (Fall 1988): 81–103.

32. Peter Evans, "Beyond Center and Periphery: A Comment on the Contribution of the World System Approach to the Study of Development," *Sociological Inquiry, 49*(4)(1979): 15.

33. Baran, *Political Economy.*

34. See his "Marxist Approaches to Development and Underdevelopment," *Journal of Contemporary Asia, 3*(1)(1973): 9.

35. See his *Politics and Ideology in Marxist Theory* (London: New Left Books, 1979), p. 42.

36. Ronald Munck, *Politics and Dependency in the Third World; The Case of Latin America* (London: Zed Books, 1985), p. 347.

37. B. Jessop, *The Capitalist State* (Oxford: Martin Robertson, 1982), p. 134.

38. See his *Political Power and Social Classes* (London: Verso, 1978).

39. See his "Dependent Modes of Production and the Class Analysis of Latin America," in Ronald Chilcote, ed., *Dependency and Marxism* (Boulder, Colo.: Westview Press, 1981), pp. 29–30.

40. See James Petras, "State Capitalism and the Third World," *Development and Change, 8*(1977): 1–17.

41. Representatives of Frank's works is *Dependent Accumulation and Underdevelopment* (New York: Monthly Review Press, 1969).

42. See Fanon's classic *The Wretched of the Earth* (New York: Grove Press, 1963).

43. London, Verso, 1985.

44. As paraphrased in Nicos Mouzelis, "Marxism or Post Marxism?" *New Left Review,* no. 167 (January-February 1988): 115.

45. Mouzelis, "Marxism," p. 122.

46. Mouzelis, "Marxism," p. 122.

47. For an elaboration of the neo-Marxist orientation and how its practitioners are coping with the intellectual and political turmoil in their ranks, see Kenneth E. Bauzon, "Neo-Marxism: End of a Career or Start of New One?" *Kasarinlan; Philippine Quarterly of Third World Studies,* 6/7, 4/1 (Second and Third Quarters, 1991): 113–26.

Chapter 2

People-Centered Development: Alternative for a World in Crisis

David C. Korten

Pursuit of a growth-centered development model has created a deepening global social and ecological crisis that threatens the future of life and civilization on our planet. Resolution of the crisis depends on a people-centered transformation of institutions and values to eliminate overconsumption, increase social justice, and strengthen local economic and environmental self-reliance. The policies currently embraced by most development-assistance agencies and governments are working in exactly the opposite direction: They encourage wasteful consumption and the unsustainable use of environmental resources, deepen the gap between rich and poor, eliminate the ability of governments to regulate national economies, and transfer ever-growing political and economic power to unaccountable transnational corporations that acknowledge no attachment to place or people. A global social movement in support of political and economic democratization must reverse these forces before our collective crisis passes beyond the point of no return.

INTRODUCTION

This chapter provides an overview of what many of us mean by people-centered development and why we believe it must be embraced by global society as an alternative to conventional growth-centered development thought and policy. In doing so, it is important to start with a look at our global context. This will help

This chapter was originally prepared as a summary of observations by the author at the Regional Dialogue on Governmental-Nongovernmental Relations: Prospects and Challenges for Improving the Policy Environment for People-Centered Development, sponsored by the Asia-Pacific Development Center (APDC) and the Asian Nongovernmental Organizations Coalition (ANGOC), and held in Chiengmai, Thailand in March 1991.

Many of the arguments in this chapter are developed at greater length in David C. Korten, *Getting to the 21st Century: Voluntary Action and the Global Agenda* (West Hartford, Ct.: Kumarian Press, 1990).

to establish that we are not talking about a hypothetical idealistic vision put forward by a small group of malcontents who are against human progress. Nor are we attempting to put a fancier label on the small-scale community-development projects traditionally favored by the voluntary sector. Rather our concern here is with the articulation of a vision of transformational global change addressed to the underlying problems of a world that is sinking ever deeper into crisis. We are talking about the serious business of the collective survival of a planet and its people.

GLOBAL CONTEXT: THE THREEFOLD CRISIS

Our global crisis has three basic elements: poverty, environmental destruction, and communal violence.

Poverty

In 1970, an estimated 650 million people in the world lived in absolute poverty. Currently, the number stands at 1 billion to 1.2 billion, a near doubling in twenty years. These are people who live in a desperate daily struggle for survival at the edge of subsistence and who lack the most minimal requirements of diet, shelter, and clean water. The trend toward increasing poverty accelerated in the 1980s as the gap between rich and poor grew at an alarming pace.

Environment

The pollutants with which we have loaded our atmosphere are destroying the ozone layer that protects us from the lethal rays of our own sun, as well as bringing climatic changes that threaten to melt the polar ice caps, flood vast coastal areas, and turn fertile agricultural areas into deserts. We are depleting the soils on which our growing population depends for food, destroying the regenerative capacities of the hydrological systems that provide the fresh water on which all life depends, and poisoning our surface and groundwater supplies. We are stripping our forests bare, burying ourselves in garbage, and dumping our chemical and radioactive wastes around the world wherever people are too poor to protest. We are exhausting our fossil fuels even as we continue to build economic systems that are wholly dependent on them—reassuring ourselves that some as-yet-undefined technological miracle will save us.

In the decade of the 1990s, we will add 959 million people to the world's population—the largest ten-year gain in history. The biggest increases will be in the poorest and most environmentally devastated countries. How we will feed them remains to be seen. According to the Worldwatch Institute, global per capita food production peaked in 1984. There was some recovery in 1989, a year of relatively good weather and high agricultural prices, yet per capita food production still was down 7 percent from 1984. The shortfalls are being made up by drawing from declining global reserves.

Communal Violence

The third element of the global crisis, communal violence, is a manifestation of the increasing disintegration of our social fabric. It takes many forms.

One form is organized armed violence, which has become increasingly concentrated in Southern countries, is communal in nature (confined to people of a single nationality), and now claims predominantly civilian casualties. In 1988, of twenty-five active wars in the world, twenty-four were in Southern countries, twenty-two were internal to a single country, and 80 percent of casualties were civilian. The predominant role of national armies in our "modern" world is not to protect national borders against foreign intruders but to keep dissident civilian populations in check.

Social disintegration is also manifest in:

- The random violence that has become endemic in both North and South and which is often associated with disruptive social phenomena such as religious fundamentalism and drug abuse;
- Universal patterns of family breakdown as revealed in alarming increases in divorce, abandonment, violence against spouses and children, and street children; and
- Growing numbers of refugees and international migrant workers, people who have been uprooted from communities that no longer exist or in which they no longer find a place or a means of livelihood—rootless and unwanted, sometimes without nationality, searching for an opportunity to survive.

ECONOMIC GROWTH VERSUS ECOLOGY AND COMMUNITY

Our politicians and economic planners are not unaware of the crisis, but they have not yet come to terms with its implications. All are products of an era in which human societies equated economic growth with human progress. Consequently, they persist in the belief that the resolution of the crisis depends on fine-tuning our economic systems to accelerate growth and expand the economic pie to make available the additional resources required to eliminate poverty, restore the environment, and provide more police protection.

Perhaps there was a time in our past when these solutions would have been appropriate. They are no longer. Growth will not resolve the crisis. The evidence suggests that it is our insistence on placing economic growth above all other priorities that is deepening the crisis and keeping us from finding adequate solutions. See Table 1.

Table 1
Basic Realities

Essentials of human well-being and progress	Sustained by	Threshold of tolerance has been exceeded for	Current policy recommendations call for
Life	Earth's ecosystem	The economy's demands on the ecosystem's regenerative capacity	Accelerating growth in economic output
Civilization	The noneconomic values that bind family and community	Dominance of economic over noneconomic values and relationships	Removing all constraints to economic market forces

Solution or Problem?

The data clearly do not support the growth-as-solution thesis. In 1990, annual global economic output was approximately four times higher than in 1950. This means that on average in each decade since 1950, the world has achieved a growth in annual output roughly comparable to the total increase achieved to the middle of this century since some unknown cave dweller made the first capital investment by chipping a piece of flint to form a cutting tool. No one could claim this has not been a spectacular economic accomplishment.

If growth is the solution, then we should have seen dramatic progress toward resolution of each element of the crisis during this period. In fact, during the period since 1950, we have seen dramatic increases in the numbers of absolute poor, an ever-worsening environmental destruction, and a persistent pattern of social disintegration. So far as we can tell from available data, these three trends accelerated during the 1980s. Contrary to what the experts are telling us, economic growth seems more strongly associated with a deepening of our crisis than with its solution. On its face this seems rather implausible.

Part of the explanation is found in how we measure economic output. For example, increased medical expenditures to treat cancers caused by the chemical pollutants generated by growth in industrial output count as an addition to income, as do expenditures to clean up our similarly polluted rivers and lakes, or the increased cost of commuting to work from the suburbs where we have moved to avoid inner-city crime and pollution. Increases in military and police expenditures also contribute to the growth in national product. In other words, it is quite possible for a country to grow economically, at least in the terms by which such growth is currently measured, while the well-being of its people declines.

The more fundamental explanation for the paradox that the global crisis has deepened even as growth in economic output has expanded, however, is found in the fact that we have experienced the closing of earth's ecological frontier.

The Ecological Frontier

We have long treated such ecological resources as water, air, and soil as free gifts of nature, relatively unmindful of the complex and powerful natural productive systems that continuously renew them and without accounting for the ever-growing burdens that such expansion of economic activities places on these systems' regenerative capacities. We are only dimly beginning to realize that these capacities are decidedly finite and that the demand we place on them already well exceed sustainable limits. Earth's ecological frontier has closed, forcing us to confront a new historical reality that renders traditional solutions not only obsolete, but also dangerously self-destructive.

Some of us have had our eye on the depletion of nonrenewable resources as the ultimate barrier to sustained economic growth. We now see that the first real barriers we are confronting are environmental—the limits of earth's regenerative capabilities. Thus we now find we are running out of water before we run out of oil. Indeed the immediate limit to our use of oil is not its availability so much as the limits of the planet's ability to absorb and recycle the carbon dioxide generated by its combustion.

To date, we have responded to these limits in two ways. One is to ignore them, mining nature's stored surpluses, disrupting hydrological systems and climatic patterns with consequences that are almost certain to reduce long-term productive capabilities. The other approach is to reallocate the use of available capacities away from meeting the economically low-value needs of the poor and the powerless in order to devote them to meeting the economically higher-value wants of the wealthy and powerful. In so doing, the poor have been pushed in ever-growing numbers to the outer and most fragile edges of the ecosystem in their desperate struggle for survival. The harder we push our efforts to increase total economic output as the "solution to poverty," the more the gap between rich and poor grows and the faster the pace of our collective march toward ultimate ecological disaster.

Displacement of Economic by Noneconomic Values

How does this relate to the breakdown of our social fabric? Most obvious, of course, is the growing social alienation of those who find little legitimacy in institutions that deprive them of what few resources they have to provide luxuries for a fortunate few. The problem of social disintegration, however, has deeper roots.

In our quest for economic growth, we have seen the economic values that drive our collective process of resource exploitation and wealth creation gain greater dominance over the noneconomic values that sustain the social fabric of family and community—the building blocks of human civilization. This has been an almost universal process throughout all societies of the world as the values of the consumer society have penetrated ever further into even the most remote corners of our globe. Noneconomic values have become weakened to such an extent that the social fabric is now unraveling. In place of the family, the community, and, increasingly, even the nation, the market has emerged as society's primary defining institution.

Transnationalization of Capital

Our collective acceptance of the dominance of economic values has led us to accept without question, and almost without conscious awareness, the emergence through the market's dynamics of powerful new institutional forces that are working inexorably to transfer economic and political power away from people and even governments to the impersonal and wholly unaccountable institutions that control transnational flows of capital.

The principle of private ownership is the foundation of the legitimacy of capitalism as an economic system. In the traditional formulation of the theory of private ownership, the owner, an identifiable person known to the people of his or her community, is presumed to control the use of capital and ultimately to be accountable under the law for the consequences of its use.

Over the past several decades, we have witnessed the professionalism of corporate management, a broadening of participation in stock ownership, and the emergence of investment funds and institutions that manage other people's money. Each development has contributed to separating the management of capital from its ownership.

Until recently, the institutions that controlled capital retained their national identity. They also retained a degree of loyalty to the interests of "their" nation and were subject to its laws. During the past decade, we saw an acceleration to a new stage in this institutionalization process—specifically, its *transnationalization*. This new stage has given birth to transnational capital as a largely autonomous force that transcends national interests, has allegiance to no state, and is committed primarily to the search for new profits and market share. In this search, capital scours the earth for expropriatable resources, unmindful of social or ecological consequences, to be converted into products for sale to those who have the money to pay.

Accountable only to itself, transnational capital represents free-floating economic power that is unattached to people or place, mocks the power of both state and people, and renders democratic institutions impotent as instruments of citizen control. The countries where it chooses to base its production facilities are temporary locations of convenience, of interest only so long as wages and taxes are low and environmental and health restrictions minimal. It represents the ultimate separation of power from place and people. Capital's professional managers now have no more accountability to capital's actual "owners" than to the states that issue their well-used passports. While richly rewarded for their services, these managers are in a very real sense employees of capital itself, not its owners.

Perhaps the most frightening aspect of this process is the firm belief of capital's managers that their corporations represent the vanguard of global democratization and the instruments that will ultimately drive poverty from the face of the earth through the creation of a universal consumer society that recognizes no national borders. They live an illusion in the world of capital and power, separated by their wealth from the real world of life and people, flying by helicopter and luxury jet from meeting to meeting and from office to vacation resort scarcely aware that society and the environment are crumbling beneath them and that one day they may have nowhere to land that is protected from growing devastation.

Earth's Three Socioecological Classes: Overconsumers, Sustainers, and Marginals

Previous discussions have argued that our world is divided not between the developed and the underdeveloped, but between the overconsumers and the underconsumers of earth's natural bounty. A recent article by Alan Durning of the Worldwatch Institute suggests an important refinement.[1] He divides global society into three groups, which we might label *overconsumers, sustainers,* and *marginals* (see Table 2, which was constructed on Durning's analysis). These

Table 2
Earth's Three Socioecological Classes

Overconsumers (1 billion) Cars, meat, and disposables	Sustainers (3 billion) Living lightly	Marginals (1 billion) Life at the margins of subsistence
• Travel by car and air • Eat meat-based diets • Drink bottled water and soft drinks • Use packaged foods, disposable diapers, and other disposables • Live in large, possibly air-conditioned single-family residence; many have a second home • Discard wastes • Wear clothing from image-conscious wardrobe	• Travel by bicycle and public surface transportation • Eat healthy diet of grains and vegetables supplemented by small amounts of meat • Drink clean water plus some tea and coffee • Use home-prepared unpackaged foods • Live in modest residences with extended family or multiple families relying on natural ventilation • Recycle most waste • Wear functional clothing	• Travel by foot, maybe donkey • Eat nutritionally marginal or inadequate diet • Drink contaminated water • Live in rudimentary shelters or in the open • May own a few basic household utensils and tools • Have few if any wastes other than excrement • Wear second-hand clothing or scraps

are not precisely drawn categories, but they are adequate to make several sobering points.

Most important, these three categories highlight the fact that overconsumers, who are responsible for the vast majority of our ecological damage, constitute only some 20 percent of the world's population. This is roughly the same as the population of industrial nations—which account for some two-thirds of the world's use of important metals and three-fourths of its energy use, generate two-thirds of the greenhouse gases that are altering the global climate, three-fourths of the sulfur and nitrogen oxides that cause acid rain, most of the world's hazardous wastes, and 90 percent of the chlorofluorocarbons that are destroying the ozone layer.[2]

Among the industrial nations, the United States sets the extreme standard for wasteful consumption, with each American on average accounting for the consumption of nearly his or her weight in basic materials each day—18 kilograms of petroleum and coal, 13 kilograms of other minerals, 12 kilograms of agricultural products, and 9 kilograms of other products. This contrasts starkly with the estimated 1.5 kilos of locally collected biomass consumed by each marginal consumer per day in the form of grain, fuel wood, and animal fodder.[3] Of course, it is the demand of the overconsumer's life-styles that drives the marginals to subsistence on the fringes of the environment.

Although overconsumption is concentrated in the North, some of its most extreme manifestations are found among the wealthy of Southern countries, just as we find extreme poverty among Northern populations. Indeed, we are coming to recognize that the terms North and South do not really define geography so much as class.

Our hope is found in the fact that something on the order of 3 billion people, the sustainers, are already living relatively environmentally responsible life-styles. One billion marginals would also almost surely be sustainers if given the opportunity. Responsibility for earth's crisis rests clearly with the overconsumers. Ironically, these are the very people who are currently being told by the politicians and economic planners that they must *increase* their consumption if the poor are ever to be lifted from their misery, and whose life-styles the remainder of the world is being urged to emulate.

Of course, almost without exception our politicians, experts, and other power holders are members of the overconsumer class. It is difficult for them to see themselves as being the problem rather than the solution.

This is the context of our call for a fundamental redefinition of what we mean by *development* and for a transformation of the institutions by which we seek it. Continuing on our present course would be tantamount to an act of collective suicide, an act that will leave no winners, only losers.

The survival of our civilization, and perhaps our very lives, depends on committing ourselves to an alternative development practice guided by the three basic principles of authentic development:

- *Justice:* Priority must be given to ensuring a decent human existence for all people.
- *Sustainability:* Earth's resources must be used in ways that ensure the well-being of future generations.
- *Inclusiveness:* Every person must have the opportunity to be a recognized and respected contributor to family, community, and society.

COMPETING DEVELOPMENT STRATEGIES

With this as background, we can now look at some of the major features of the growth-centered development vision that dominates the current practice of most governments and international assistance agencies. We will then contrast it with the alternative people-centered vision that many nongovernmental organizations (NGOs) and others argue is more consistent with the principles of authentic development and with the most basic of all human needs—the need for collective survival. These differences are summarized in Table 3.

Conventional Growth-Centered Development

According to the underlying theory of growth-centered development, poverty and underdevelopment result from inadequate capital investment to overcome low levels of productivity and employment.

Favored strategy. Prescriptive action therefore calls for increasing capital investment to stimulate economic growth. The capital may come from domestic savings, foreign assistance, or foreign investment. The resulting growth in economic output is expected to produce a trickle-down of benefits to the poor.

The currently favored growth strategies call for concentrating productive capacity on making products for sale abroad to foreign consumers and providing incentives to attract foreign investors. Traditionally, growth strategies have favored the industrial sector. When growth theorists direct their attention to people, their conceptual frameworks allow them to think of people's participation only in terms of their economic functions as laborers or consumers. Growth-centered analytical models tend to treat the environment as both a limitless source of free physical resources and a free waste dump.

The guiding economic principles of growth-centered development call for each nation to specialize in producing those products for which it has a comparative advantage in international markets so that economies of scale will maximize productive efficiencies. According to the theory, overall market efficiency will be maximized by removing all barriers to the free flow of goods and capital across international borders. The result is intended to be a mutually interdependent global trading system to which each country contributes according to its distinctive resource endowments and meets its own needs through purchasing from the lowest cost producers, wherever in the world they may be found.

Table 3

Competing Development Visions

Vision	Growth-centered (people in service of economics)			People-centered (economics in service of people)
		Growth with equity		
	Conventional	Basic human needs	Human resources development	
Theory of poverty	Inadequate capital investment produces inadequate growth	None	Inadequately developed human resources	Concentration and misuse of power and resources
Poverty action	Trickle-down	Welfare action	Develop human resources	Empowerment through organization and resource control
Favored strategy	Export-led growth	Supplemental services		Equity-led transformation of values and institutions
Sector focus	Industry	Services		Agriculture to industry
Advance people's participation as	Laborers and consumers	Coproducers		Holders of political and economic power
Market focus	Affluent foreigners			Consumption needs of local sustainers and marginals
Environment/ecology	Limitless source of free physical resources and waste dump			Finite, regenerative source of life
Economic principles	• Comparative advantage/free trade/mutual dependence • Specialization • Economies of scale			• Self-reliance • Diversification • Economies of community
Global linkages	Exchanging physical goods and money			Sharing information and technology
Dynamic tendencies	• Concentration of resource control and political power in institutions of transnational capital • Inability of governments to regulate national and local economies • Community and environmental degeneration • Unstable local and international economies subject to severe shocks			• Distributed power and benefits • Strong local control and accountability • Community and environmental regeneration • Resilient, self-reliant local economies within interlinked yet stable global system

Limitations. The economic theories underlying the growth models are wholly apolitical, in that they do not address the impact of differential power on market and trade relationships. Nor do they consider the depletion of nonrenewable or environmental resources, limitations to the substitutability of production factors, or the costs of economic conversion when market preferences change. In other words, the policy models of the growth vision are built on theories that bear only a passing resemblance to reality. Consequently, their application to policy formulation produces several unanticipated outcomes, including the concentration of economic and political power in the institutions of transnational capital, an inability of governments to manage national or local economies because goods and capital flow freely beyond their reach, the degeneration of community and environment, and extreme instability in the international system as shocks from a disturbance in one locality reverberate throughout the system largely beyond human control.

The free trade theory currently being promoted as integral to the growth-centered vision is a particularly important contributor to these and other negative dynamics. With the removal of constraints on trade and capital movement, capital is free to move to the lowest cost production site to produce for export from there to unprotected markets around the world. Each individual government comes under increasing pressures to keep wages and worker benefits low and health, safety, and environmental protection to a minimum, while also offering tax holidays and subsidized infrastructure if it is to compete for investment funds with every other country of the world. Small local producers are pitted in competition with powerful international giants, profits go abroad, and local markets atrophy in the absence of local purchasing power.

Growth with Equity

The growth-with-equity strategy has two variations: basic human needs and human resources development. Both are responses to the almost universal failure of growth-centered strategies to reduce poverty to socially acceptable levels. Both assume that the primary focus on economic policy will be on accelerating growth and that a portion of the resulting gains will be allocated to meeting the special needs of the poor through service delivery. Both place growth first and equity second. The main difference between them is theoretical.

Basic human needs strategies are a straightforward welfare response to the evident needs of the poor. There is no explicit effort to explain why growth does not eliminate poverty, simply a recognition that needs are not met and that the state must provide the necessary services to meet them.

Human resource development is grounded in the theoretical argument that growth has not absorbed the poor into adequately remunerated jobs because they lack the physical strength, skills, and educational attainment to have an economic value in the market. These deficiencies are to be overcome through social-investment programs aimed at developing the nation's human resources into employable commodities.

Participation takes on a different meaning in growth with equity than it does in conventional growth strategies. Because the emphasis is on service delivery, participation is commonly defined in terms of engaging beneficiaries as coproducers of the services. Mothers may be asked to volunteer time to the operation of nutrition centers or organize committees to ensure that children are in attendance at immunization clinics when the health personnel arrive. It is rare, however, that the programs in which community members are coproducers are either designed or controlled by them.

Currently, we see an interesting new twist being added to the human resource development strategies. Several people have talked of the current "economistic" thrust of many donors pushing them into basic income-generating activities. What we are seeing is an implicit recognition that the formal economy does not and will not generate the jobs even to absorb the products of successful human resource development campaigns. If most people are to have jobs, they will have to create them themselves. Not a bad idea until we realize that most of the poor have been systematically deprived of access to productive assets other than the microloans often associated with basic livelihood projects. Most such efforts at best provide the beneficiary with a means of earning a bare subsistence livelihood. Eventually, we will have to come to terms with the fact that most livelihood programs are really an unsatisfactory substitute for more fundamental structural reforms such as land reform and the breaking up of market monopolies.

In the end, without structural reform, human resource development strategies are unlikely to make any consequential contribution to breaking down the dualistic economic structures inherited from colonialism that place most productive resources in the hands of a small elite and leave the excluded remainder of the population to scrap out a subsistence at the margins of the economy and the environment.

People-Centered Development

Some NGOs have equated people-centered development with participatory village-development interventions. Such interventions are important, but in themselves are generally inconsequential. We now realize that in one respect the World Bank and other big donors are right: Policies are important. Unfortunately, however, most of the policies being promoted by international assistance agencies directly undermine most of what NGOs are attempting to achieve. Without the right policies, irrespective of how many village-development activities NGOs carry out or how many courses they offer with titles such as consciousness raising or empowerment, there will be no consequential change.

An integral part of the policy agenda of people-centered development is to reverse the tendency toward concentrating power in impersonal and unaccountable institutions, returning it to people and communities and ensuring its equitable distribution. This empowerment process is advanced in part through developing strong member-accountable institutions and strengthening local resource control and ownership. There is no question that local organizing is integral to people-centered development.

At the same time, progress toward people-centered development also requires fundamental structural reforms at national and global levels. At the national level, progress requires breaking down dualistic economic structures, integrating the modern and traditional sectors, and melding, redistributing, and reallocating the use of their assets. At the global level, such progress means breaking the unchallenged and unaccountable power of transnational capital and bringing transnational corporations under a system of controls and incentives that make them useful, accountable contributors to the creation of a just, sustainable, and inclusive human society. These are some of the issues that true empowerment initiatives must ultimately address.

People-centered development seeks to place economics at the service of people, a direct reversal of existing practice. It attributes poverty to a concentration and misuse of power and resources—especially environmental resources—in a finite world. It calls for an equity-led transformation of institutions and values to restore community, redistribute power, and reallocate earth's natural wealth to uses that contribute to sustainable improvements in human well-being.

Growth-centered development generally argues for concentrating on expansion of the economic pie on the theory that this allows everyone to gain and avoids the political resistance generated by redistribution efforts. Although there may be some implication that it would be right for the poor to receive a disproportionate share of gains of any incremental growth, the question of how this will be achieved and who will be responsible for ensuring the redistribution is generally avoided. People-centered development confronts the issue directly by pointing out that in many instances asset redistribution is needed to provide a foundation for sound growth and to increase the likelihood that resulting increases will be widely shared and contribute to the development of a strong domestic market and a local capital base.

Growth-centered development advocates commonly maintain that if one looks after growth, equity will take care of itself. People-centered development says take care of equity first, provide people the means to make productive use of their assets, and appropriate growth will take care of itself.

People-centered development gives priority in the use of local resources to developing and producing for local markets that cater to the needs of local people. The earth's ecosystem is revered as a powerful yet finite regenerative system on which all life depends. It should be nurtured, harvested, enhanced, and augmented where possible through applications of human knowledge, but above all its powerful capabilities must be preserved as a living trust in perpetuity for the continuing benefit of all generations.

People-centered development seeks to build a global system of interlinked, diversified local economies that are largely environmentally and economically self-reliant in meeting their own basic needs function as elements of a larger whole. Rather than seeking to optimize impersonal economies of scale, however, the system design seeks to optimize the release and application of the creative, social, and productive energies of people who work together with a shared sense of community and mutual contribution.

The relationships that bind these local economies into a larger global economy would be fashioned along the lines of the advice of John Maynard Keynes, the father of one of the major schools of modern economics:

> Ideas, knowledge, art, hospitality, travel—these are the things which should of their nature be international. But let goods be homespun whenever it is reasonably and conveniently possible; and above all, let finance be primarily national.[4]

This is not to argue for autarky, a closing of the borders in search of economic self-sufficiency. The self-reliant local economies of a people-centered economic system must relate to one another through trade and shared resource flows, but with careful attention to maintaining a balance between local consumption and the regenerative capabilities of the local environment, maintaining local control over productive resources, and avoiding dependent and unequal trade relationships. The primary role of the links between local self-reliant economics is to facilitate the free flow and sharing of information and beneficial technology—both of which are essential to improving the well-being of all people within the limits of a finite ecology.

GROWTH AND PEOPLE-CENTERED DEVELOPMENT

In modern society, economic growth has assumed an almost sacred quality. To be against growth is to be against all that is good and holy. Dare to suggest that perhaps aggregate economic growth must stop, and your friends back discreetly away to avoid the impact of the lightning bolt that is sure to strike the spot where you stand. Those who are antigrowth are assumed to condemn the poor to eternal poverty, to be modern Luddites who reject technology and human progress. Colleagues have suggested, "Be clear that we are not against growth. Rather we call for 'selective growth' or the 'right kind' of growth."

More Well-Being with Less Ecological Demand

It is not a simple issue. The demand for growth has become built into our collective psyche and the institutions of our economic system. Nothing predicts the fall of political empires more surely than a slacking of economic growth. Our economic systems themselves seem inclined to go into a self-propelling tailspin if growth is not sustained. Yet we must come to terms with the fact that any form of economic growth that increases aggregate demands on earth's ecosystem is suicidal over the longer term. Indeed, because the limits of tolerance have already been substantially exceeded, it has become essential that we consciously reverse such growth to reduce that demand. That is our reality—no matter how unpleasant or inconvenient it may be. The time has come that we must face and speak this basic truth. Until we do, our solutions will be half-measures at best and actively destructive at worst.

The shocked listener asks: "Does this mean I can never expect to have more than I have now? Must I abandon all hope for a better tomorrow or even for keeping what I have?"

First, it depends on who you are. Are you an overconsumer or a marginal? And second, more of what? What do you mean by "better"? An extra car? A big steak for dinner? Disposable cameras? Water in disposable plastic bottles? More vacation travel around the world by air? These you probably cannot have.

An ensured ability to meet your basic needs? A secure home? A healthy diet? Access to global communication systems? More love? More friends? More sense of spirituality? More peace? More participation in community affairs? More intellectual development? More opportunity for artistic expression? A more beautiful natural environment? These should be among our goals.

We may readily define many areas of economic activity in which sharp reductions in economic output are crucial. Military expenditures head the list. Others include the use of pesticides and herbicides, unnecessary packaging, advertising aimed at creating artificial needs, disposable and nonrecyclable products, and aggregate use of air and auto transportation.

Stocks Versus Throughput

Certainly we must define new indicators of progress that reveal actual improvements in human and ecological well-being. Some years ago, Kenneth Boulding argued that instead of measuring human progress in terms of economic throughput, as we do now, our indicators should assess the condition of human well-being and the status of the resource stocks on which that well-being depends.[5]

At its very foundation, the well-being of people depends on the sustained healthy function of our environmental and social systems. We need measures that allow us to track the health of both so that we may learn to manage our affairs against these measures. Our measures of human well-being must certainly include physical consumption as one element, but only to the point that such consumption makes a necessary contribution to a quality of life potentially available to all people within prevailing ecological limits. Important weight in such a measure should also be given to social, intellectual, and spiritual development.

Our "development" goals may then be defined in terms that clearly relate to improvements in human well-being. A great deal of attention will be needed to determining what the sustainable limits of material consumption are at both current and anticipated population sizes. The division of the world into overconsumers, sustainers, and marginals gives some clues. Marginals must be brought up to at least the level of sustainers. The adjustments required to make this possible, as well as to bring the overall load on our environment down to sustainable limits, and to give sustainers greater access to the benefits of environmentally benign or beneficial advanced technologies will have to come primarily from overconsumers.

Once we get new ways of thinking and behavior regarding resource use in place, we will find many opportunities for increasing the productive output of the ecological resource base in ways that are consistent with sustainability. Indeed, we will surely find ways to enhance substantially its regenerative capacities, providing opportunities for appropriate kinds of growth.

However, at this historical moment, we must work from the assumption that the ecological frontier is closed and that conventional growth as we have known it must end. We may then get on with the business of rethinking and reallocating our use of the ecological product in ways that will increase justice, sustainability, and inclusiveness. What happens to measures of aggregate economic output in this process is basically irrelevant because such measures tell us very little about human well-being and nothing about environmental health.

As we seek to create new models of economic organization and performance measurement, we must accept that there are no models for replication. We must create them. We must also bear continuously in mind that our current vision of people-centered development is only an incomplete approximation. A successful outcome will depend on engaging millions of people in the process of creating the new vision and recreating the structures of our society. This can be achieved only through a process of social liberation, not as an exercise in social engineering.

Prospects for Change

The changes implied would seem so radical as to lie beyond reality. That no models of a people-centered sustainable society exist seriously limits the credibility of our proposals. Keep in mind, however, that what is articulated here is a synthesis of thinking emerging from independent efforts being undertaken by thousands of people around the world in search of a way out of our self-induced crisis. This effort is born first of necessity. It is idealistic only if one views survival as an idealistic goal in our contemporary world.

Some critics say, "These are fine, even essential, ideals, but changes of the magnitude being suggested will take a long time. We must be patient." Unfortunately, we cannot be. Our ability to take corrective action depends on the vitality of our ecological and social systems. The further we move toward the collapse of these two essential systems, the greater the repair job that will be needed just to restore what was once normal functioning, the fewer the resources to be shared among a rapidly expanding population, the less slack in the system that is available for experimentation, and the fewer the social and ecological resources available to invest in change. As social and ecological break-down progresses, the more desperate and competitive people are likely to become in their independent struggles for survival in an increasingly hostile world.

We should take hope from the evidence that we live in a world in which, for the moment at least, the potentials for rapid and dramatic change are increasing. In 1988, the world suddenly came to acknowledge the reality of our environmental crisis in a mere instant of historical time. In 1989, the communist empire in Eastern Europe collapsed, resulting in a fundamental transformation of the world's geopolitical reality, again within a mere historical instant. The changes we face dwarf even these dramatic examples in their magnitude. They may not be likely. They are possible, at least for a few more years. And they are essential. The environmental crisis is the unifying political issue, as no one can escape its consequences.

INTERNATIONAL ASSISTANCE AND THE INTEREST OF TRANSNATIONAL CAPITAL

How might we assess the roles of the major international assistance agencies and their financial resources in contributing to a people-centered transformation? For most of them, particularly the multilateral development banks, there is at best a modest role.

Mandate of the Multilateral Banks

The basic mandate of the multilateral banks—the World Bank, the International Monetary Fund (IMF), and the regional development banks—comes from the Bretton Woods agreements, which established several international institutions for the purpose of expanding international trade and investment. If one believes that increasing the power of the transnationals that control this trade and investment is synonymous with development and human well-being, which the banks seem to do, then the banks have a central role to play. However, if one believes that the growing power of transnational capital is one of the single most important barriers to coming to terms with our global crisis and that the transnationalization process is undermining democratic governance and removing from people even the possibility of controlling their own futures, then one has good reason to be supremely skeptical of these institutions, their policies, and their functions.

The multilateral banks are the leading players in a global campaign to remove the final barriers posed by the nation-state to the complete free flow of trade and capital across international borders. Their success will ensure the total economic and political dominance of transnational capital over human affairs and our collective destiny. The driving vision behind this effort comes from the

U.S. government as led by an administration that has proudly demonstrated time and again that it serves first and foremost the interests of big business.

Economic efficiency and democratization, the ends that free-trade ideologues maintain their prescriptions serve, are both highly valued in people-centered development. However, neither is advanced by opening national economies to control by massive transnational oligopolies. Such action limits competition to the giants and disempowers all but a small international elite.

East Asian Models

Even the arguments of many official agencies that the efficacy of the policies they are advocating is demonstrated by the economic success stories of Taiwan, South Korea, and Japan[6] are based less on reality and more on misrepresentation to bolster an ideological position. We are told that these countries were successful because they operated by free-market principles, opened their economies, minimized government involvement, and focused on exports. In fact, their governments exerted strong leadership in the economy and provided domestic agricultural and industrial producers with substantial protection against foreign competition. Even characterizing their growth as "export-led" involves a substantial distortion. Well before the so-called Asian Tigers became successful exporters, each instituted radical land reform, made massive investments in basic education, created dense networks of rural organizations, and stabilized their populations with effective family-planning programs. These actions integrated their economies and provided the foundation for broadly based participation in the benefits of economic growth.

With a sound foundation in place, each began its economic growth spurt with a major push to increase value added per hectare based on intensive small-farm production. This produced an increase in broadly distributed rural incomes, creating a domestic market for rural industries, which in turn added to national technical and productive capacity. Urban-based export industries, with strong backward and forward linkages to the domestic economy, were built on this foundation, which was a major contributor to competitive strength in international markets.

Any resemblance between this experience and concentrating national resources on creating the supporting infrastructure for enclaves of foreign-owned factories buying cheap local labor, dumping their toxic wastes in local streams without restraint, and using imported parts and technology to produce products for reexport resembles the East Asian experience only in the minds of committed free-trade ideologues. It is evident that the policies being advocated by the multilateral banks and many other international assistance agencies have a lot less to do with replicating Asian success stories than with advancing the interests of transnational capital, which is well represented in the governments of the industrial countries that control these institutions.

Aid as a Barrier to People-Centered Development

The multilateral banks are in fact rather good at doing what they were created to do, which is to advance the international trade and investment agenda. Unfortunately, in most instances this agenda turns out to be devastatingly harmful to people and environment. Although it is tempting to applaud the many well-intentioned proposals for the reform of these institutions, these will not change the basic fact that trying to advance people-centered development with large loans of foreign currency is an inherent contradiction. We must seriously consider the possibility that the multilateral development banks have no evident role in advancing the kind of development we are discussing here and that we should be working to see them dismantled or at least reduced to a small fraction of their current size and influence.[7]

We should also note that even though the dysfunctions of international assistance are exemplified by the multilateral banks, they are by no means limited to these institutions. Overall, the North's self-proclaimed official charity has proven to be largely a deception. Presented as a gift to help the South, it has proven to be anything but a gift. It may help the South's already privileged, but it rarely benefits the South's poor. For the most part, international assistance increases Southern dependence on Northern technology, facilitates the exploitation of poorly paid Southern labor and the extraction of Southern resources, and allows the North to dictate to the South policies that open Southern markets to Northern products and Southern economies to Northern investment—and then puts the North in a position to demand repayment with interest for its loan-funded assistance and repatriation of profits on its investments. It is like dropping ten cents in the cup in a blindman's outstretched hand to distract him and win his trust while reaching around to take a dollar out of his pocket.

The established institutions to which we have long looked for leadership in development are products of the growth-centered vision. They can make adaptive changes within the basic framework of the vision's underlying assumptions, but they have demonstrated repeatedly that they lack the capability for transformational reforms that depend on questioning that vision's underlying assumptions. We cannot look to them for leadership. If change is to come, the leadership must come from elsewhere—specifically from the voluntary sector.

THE VOLUNTARY SECTOR AS AGENT FOR TRANSFORMATION

To understand the unique and centrally important role of the voluntary sector in advancing the transformation agenda of people-centered development, it is first necessary to understand the sector's distinctive nature. Such understanding is not widely shared, in part because of the mistaken tendency to treat all non-profit, nongovernmental organizations (NGOs) as though they were part of the same institutional sector.

Distinctive Competence

A few years ago, David Brown of the Institute for Development Research and I were asked by the World Bank to study NGOs and their roles in development.[8] As we reflected on the topic, we concluded that the term "nongovernmental organization" embraces such a wide variety of disparate organizations that it is impossible to identify a distinctive developmental role for an NGO. So we searched for a framework that would have more meaning in defining the distinctive nature and development roles of the organizations commonly referred to as NGOs. The result was a framework that defines three institutional sectors on the basis of their distinctive power competence.

We were led to this insight by the simple idea that every organization needs resources to function, even if it is only an informal voluntary organization sustained purely by voluntary contributions of time. We identified three basic ways by which an organization can obtain these resources: coercion, exchange, and consensus.[9] These three modes of resource acquisition in turn define three institutional sectors: government, business, and voluntary organizations. It has proven to be a highly useful framework (see Table 4).

Government. Government has the distinctive ability to demand resources through use of threat, power, or coercion. In a democratic society, it exercises this authority by mutual consent of those to whom it is applied. Government is the only institution of society that has this rightful authority. This authority is what gives government its essential and distinctive role in maintaining law and

Table 4
Institutional Sectors and Roles

Sector	Primary power competence	Priorities are determined by	Distinctive functional competence	NGO Type
Government (The Prince)	Threat (coercion)	Political markets: People who control access to political office	• Maintaining law, order, and national security • Reallocating existing wealth	Governmental NGO (GONGO)
Business (The Merchant)	Economic (exchange)	Economic markets: People who control economic resources	• Producing goods and services • Creating value added	Public service contractor (PSC)
Volunteer (The Citizen)	Integrative values (consensus)	Values consensus: People who act on value commitments	• Achieving innovations in values and institutions • Countering failures of political and economic markets	Voluntary organization (VO)

order and national security and in reallocating wealth to serve public purposes through taxation and asset reforms. It is also what makes government an inherent threat to the civil liberties of its people, because of the opportunities for misuse of this power.

In our idealized view of government, these special powers are used to defend the law and to maintain social justice through the transfer of wealth from the rich to those in particular need. In fact, the priorities in the application of government's coercive powers are determined by the political marketplace, by the people who control access to political office. Consequently, we frequently see them used to allow the rich and powerful to avoid the law and to expropriate the resources of the poor to benefit the wealthy. The cause of development has provided but one of a variety of pretexts for such action.

Business. Business specializes in the use of economic or exchange power, obtaining its resources through the sale or exchange of products and services. This special competence in the use of economic exchange power gives business a distinctive ability to create value added through the production of goods and services, an essential function in any society. Generally, business has proven far more capable in this function than either government or the voluntary sector. At the same time, the market serves only those who have money, and those who have the most money commonly gain control over the exchange process.

Voluntary organizations. Such organizations specialize in the activation and use of the power of consensus to support integrative values that motivate actions not associated with expectations of gaining personal, economic, or political power. We share a belief in something: that a child should not be forced to go to bed hungry at night or that a farmer should not be arbitrarily deprived of his land. We feel sufficiently strong about our belief that we are prepared to join forces, share our financial and political resources, and try to do something about it. We have nothing to sell, we have no ability to coerce anyone to do anything. Nor are we driven by visions of personal economic gain or political office. We seek out others who share our value commitments and engage in community education to activate similar commitments in others where we can.

Priorities in the voluntary sector are determined by those who are prepared to act on their value commitments and who are skillful in attracting similar commitments from others. Because voluntary action need not depend on consensus by a large group—it may start with only one individual—the voluntary sector is a rich source of innovative ideas and social experimentation. Driven by integrative values, it represents an important social counterforce to abuses of political and economic power. Its behavior may at times appear chaotic and its voices cacophonous, but that is the sector's nature and a major source of its creative energies. It defines a marketplace of social values and ideas. This brings us back to the issue of defining the nature of an NGO.

NGOs of Many Types

All NGOs do not necessarily belong to the voluntary sector. Indeed, each of the three institutional sectors has its own distinctive type. This is one reason that the NGO sector sometimes seems to be such a confusing polyglot.

GONGOs. Some NGOs are created by government as an extension of governmental authority to serve government's agenda and, by implication, the agenda of those who control the instruments of governmental power. Such NGOs are known by the anomalous term "governmental nongovernmental organizations" or GONGOs. Many GONGOs are a response to official donors who have announced a desire to fund NGOs. Some governments, unwilling to lose control of this foreign patronage but unable to directly deny the donor's wishes, have accommodated by creating their own NGOS.

Public service contractors. Some NGOs that are highly attuned to available funding sources function as nonprofit businesses. Such NGOs follow closely the ongoing shifts in donor funding preferences. For example, this month a particular donor is interested in buying health-service delivery, women in development, or livelihood projects. Many NGOs are quite adept at keeping abreast of such interests and packaging products responsive to them. It is a classic market response. Donors often favor this type of NGO, which are appropriately described as public service contractors, as they meet an important donor need, although the practice of delivering services for which there are long-term needs in short-term project funding bursts is generally inappropriate and should be avoided by both NGOs and funders.

Voluntary organizations. Organizations created and maintained out of a true sense of value commitment range from Mother Teresa–type charities to social activist organizations that are on the front lines of such causes as environmental protection, women's rights, human rights protection, peace, and land reform. Voluntary organizations may or may not accept official donor funding, but when they do, it is on their own terms and only to support activities integral to their self-defined mission.

The distinctions among these NGO types are important for a variety of reasons. Most NGOs are acutely aware of the special nature of GONGOs and quite quick to point out their bogus nature. Less widely acknowledged is the distinction between true voluntary organizations and public service contractors, although this distinction may have important implications for NGO coalition building. Market-oriented NGOs engaged in the sale of services generally have an inherently different view of advocacy initiatives that do true voluntary organizations. The differences in their priorities and modes of working may divide voluntary organizations and public service contractors more than either of them are inclined to acknowledge.

When donors and governments look at NGOs from the perspective of the growth-centered vision, they are usually thinking of NGOs primarily as public service contractors to deliver services in support of growth-with-equity strategies. Few donors or governments as yet have any real appreciation of the distinctive role of truly voluntary organizations. Indeed, they may see NGOs as subversive troublemakers because they set their own agendas, are wary of official influence, and may challenge official policies.

Special Role of the Voluntary Sector

The voluntary sector defines a very distinctive force in society. Part of its essential dynamism comes from its few entry barriers. One needs only a social commitment. In a democratic society, no permission is needed and no one can prevent one person or a small group of people from creating a voluntary organization around whatever set of ideas or commitments happens to motivate them. If these people are willing to volunteer their time, then even lack of money is not necessarily a barrier to entry.

One of the distinctive characteristics of voluntary action is that by definition it is not driven by expectation of economic or political reward, the two types of rewards on which the incentive systems of established institutions are most commonly built. The power of these reward systems is fundamental to the enormous resistance to any kind of fundamental change exhibited by established institutions.

People whose status and income depend on an institution's reward system become intensively threatened by questions that challenge basic premises underlying the system's logic. For institutional systems to reward behavior that potentially leads to their own dissolution and reconstruction would in itself be a contradiction. This is why we cannot look to conventional institutions to provide leadership toward transformational change, and why voluntary organizations that embody the principles of voluntary action have such a unique and central role.

A dynamic voluntary sector can flourish, however, only in political settings that respect such basic human rights as freedom of association and expression. This is why democratization is itself so central to the people-centered development agenda.

People's Organizations: The Fourth Sector

Before leaving this topic, let us specifically consider the people's sector, the fourth and most important of all the institutional sectors for people-centered development. People's organizations are membership organizations that exist to serve their members, have member-accountable leaders, and are largely self-reliant in their generation of resources. Not only are they the building blocks of a just, sustainable, and inclusive society, but they also have important distinctive qualities of their own. One of these, which makes it difficult to place them in the framework outlined in Table 4, is their ability to combine all three types of power competence.

Take a cooperative as an example. By mutual consent and through democratic processes, its members may extend quasi-governmental power to the organization's governing board to enforce agreed-upon rules, including the application of a system of fines. The organization may also serve as an instrument through which its members seek special advantages for themselves through political action relating to their industry. The organization may engage in market-oriented business activities such as marketing member produce. At the same time, the members may be bound by special social commitments that create mutual obligations of a nonpolitical, noneconomic nature among themselves and between them and the larger society.

Given the central importance of people's organizations to our undertaking, far too little attention has been given to understanding their special nature and dynamics. This is a deficiency that it is important for us to correct if we truly believe that people's organizations are the building blocks of people-centered development. So long as we fail to deepen our understanding of these organizations, we are likely to find ourselves rather consistently building the power of voluntary organizations as the voices of the people—which they are not and cannot be—rather than building the capability of the people to speak with their own voice.

BUILDING A GLOBAL PEOPLE'S MOVEMENT

Bishan Singh has a colorful way of describing the NGO experience in development. He notes that many of us began with our attention focused on the grass roots. While we were looking at the grass, larger forces were capturing control of the land and the sky.

We must not lose sight of the grass, but at the same time we must keep an eye on the land and the sky. We must develop what Bishan refers to as "helicopter vision," moving constantly between the micro and the macro and addressing the forces shaping each.

The task is daunting. Because the forces that have captured the land and the sky are global in their scope, our vision must be global as well as local. Obviously, this is beyond the capacity of any individual NGO. As individual people and organizations, we must work to meld ourselves into a global force through the formation of coalitions and alliances that ultimately meld millions of people into a global movement for change. Those of us who have defined our roles in terms of projects and the internal management of individual organizations will need to expand our perspective and become adept at new modes of working.

We must be willing to take risks, to reach out beyond the circle of like-minded organizations and individuals to build alliances with concerned citizens in business and government, to engage the mass-based social movements, religion, and the mass media. Yet when we sit with these groups to engage in dialogue on developing policy issues and opportunities for collaboration, we must also realize that many of them come to the table with quite different perspectives from our own on the nature of the development problem.

The challenge posed by our circumstances and the resulting crisis that is engulfing our world exceed any previously encountered in the course of human history. There have been past examples of great human empires collapsing as a consequence of their environmental and social follies. However, in the larger scheme of things, these have been isolated events, even beyond the knowledge of most other human societies of their day.

That no society now lives in social and environmental isolation is another of our new realities. We are not dealing here with the relatively isolated ecologies of a particular river system or mountain plateau. We are talking about the systems of our planet and about a world in which nearly all elements are in instantaneous communications with all others. This creates both a new threat and a new potential.

We must apply the newly emerged collective intelligence of human society to the re-creation of ourselves and our relationship to the ecosystem of which we are a part. It is a large agenda, but our situation leaves us little choice and little time.

We must take courage and guidance from the fact that the people-centered development agenda is a human agenda that unites the interests of all people irrespective of class, race, religion, nationality—or the institutional sector on which they depend for their daily bread. It is an agenda that must unite business people, religious leaders, newscasters, laborers, teachers, farmers, the unemployed, homemakers, politicians, bureaucrats, technicians, volunteer workers, and countless others. We have seen the potentials for building such alliances. We must act on these potentials, and we must act now.

NOTES

1. See Durning's "Asking How Much Is Enough," in Lester R. Brown et al., *State of the World 1991* (New York: W.W. Norton, 1991), pp. 153–169.

2. Durning, "How Much," p. 156.

3. Durning, "How Much," p. 160–161.

4. As quoted in Herman E. Daly and John B. Cobb, Jr., *For the Common Good: Redirecting the Economy Toward Community, the Environment and a Sustainable Future* (Boston: Beacon Press, 1989), p. 209.

5. See Boulding's "The Economics of the Coming Spaceship Earth," in Henry Jarrett, ed., *Environmental Quality in a Growing Economy* (Baltimore, Md.: The Johns Hopkins University Press, 1968)

6. Singapore and Hong Kong, which are often included in this list, have little rele-

vance to most other countries. Both are relatively small, strategically located, port cities with no rural sector. And Hong Kong remains a colony, at least for a few years.

7. *Editor's note:* This argument is further elaborated in Korten's "International Assistance: A Problem Posing as a Solution," *Development,* in press.

8. See David L. Brown and David C. Korten, "Understanding Voluntary Organizations: Guidelines for Donors." WPS 258, Working Paper, Country Economics Department, World Bank, Washington, D.C., September 1989.

9. Shortly after the first draft of this paper, Boulding published *Three Faces of Power* (Newbury Park, Calif.: Sage Publications, 1989). Here Boulding distinguished between three types of power competence—threat, economic, and integrative values— that correspond perfectly with our categories and extend our basic conceptualization.

Part Two

Toward a Reconceptualization of Development and Democracy

Chapter 3

Modernization, Development, and Civilization: Reflections on the Prospects of Political Systems in the First, Second, and Third Worlds

Remigio E. Agpalo

Modernization, development, *and* civilization *are social processes that can be distinguished from one another.* Modernization *is a term from political sociology, but* development *and* civilization *are better viewed as terms from political philosophy. The iron logic of modernization is to bring about authoritarianism in the Third and Second Worlds, and even in the First World. To chain this beast, civilization must be developed. It has three necessary conditions—civility, rule of law, and social justice—and two sufficient conditions—liberty and democracy.*

INTRODUCTION

As far back in time and as far away in various places as they could be observed by social scientists, especially political scientists, humans have been found to have wanted happiness, security, and freedom. Attempts to attain these ends were sought by humans by means of political systems such as democratic, authoritarian, and totalitarian polities; or through social processes such as modernization, development, and civilization. These political systems and social processes have been studied by social scientists, especially political scientists, with a view to discovering the most effective and the best system and process for attaining those ends.

Like all other social scientists all over the world, I too have made my attempts to understand these political systems and social processes. After some thirty-five years in academe at the University of the Philippines and De La Salle University, and having retired from these academic institutions, I now have the time, leisure, and experience to reflect on these phenomena. Perhaps owing to the fact that I have become a professor emeritus, I can be excused if I adopt in this essay autobiographical, retrospective, prospective, and reflective approaches to my topic.

Perhaps my starting point should be with the set of models of political systems that I constructed in 1977 for a valedictory lecture for the Manuel A. Roxas Chair in Political Science.[1] That set of models had two dimensions: a horizontal dimension involving the scope of democratization and a vertical dimension concerned with the stage of modernization of political systems. The ambit of the scope of democratization covered totalitarian, authoritarian, and democratic polities and the dimension on stage of modernization included traditional, transitional, and modern polities.

Totalitarian, authoritarian, and democratic polities were defined in terms of relationship of the political elite to the people or vice-versa, extent of liberty in the polity, the nature of competition in politics, and the kind of pluralism in the society. Thus, the definitions of these polities that I stipulated in accordance with these criteria are as follow:

> A democratic polity is one where control of the political elite by the people is maximum, the area of liberty of the people is extensive, politics is competitive, and society is pluralist. A totalitarian polity is one where control of the people by the political elite is maximum, the area of liberty is extremely limited, politics is non-competitive, and society is atomistic. An authoritarian polity is one where control of the people by the political elite is medium, the area of liberty of the people is neither extensive nor extremely limited, politics is semi-competitive, and society is semi-pluralist.[2]

With regard to the stage of modernization of the polity, the criterion used was modernity. If modernity is low, then the political system is traditional. If modernity is high, then it is a modern polity. And if modernity is neither low nor high—that is, moderate—then the political system is transitional. Modernity of the polity was the focus of the study, so the aspects studied were the nature of rationalization of authority, national integration, and popular participation. The greater the magnitude of these aspects, the more modern the political system.

To clearly show the set of political systems in terms of scope of democratization and stage of modernization, I constructed a three-by-three table based on democratization and modernization (see Table 1).

I would like to stress that the models specified in Table 1 do not exist in reality, they are simply ideal types. Actual polities merely approximate the models to a greater or lesser extent. With this qualification, I would like to repeat what Jean-Jacques Rousseau said about democracy, for the other political systems along the horizontal dimension of our set of models in fact are distinguishable from democracy in their proximity to the democratic polity. I agree with Rousseau's view on democracy:

Table 1
Models of Political Systems' Modernization and Democratization[3]

Scope of modernization	Scope of democratization		
	Totalitarian	Authoritarian	Democratic
Traditional	Model 1: Classical Dictatorship	Model 4: Traditional Autocracy	Model 7: Classical Democracy
Transitional	Model 2: Modernizing Totalitarian	Model 5: Modernizing Authoritarian	Model 8: Modernizing Democracy
Modern	Model 3: Modern Totalitarian Polity	Model 6: Modern Authoritarian Polity	Model 9: Modern Democracy

> If we take the term [democracy] in the strict sense, there never has been a real democracy, and there never will be. It is against the natural order of the many to govern and the few to be governed. It is unimaginable that the people should remain continually assembled to devote their time to public affairs, and it is clear that they cannot set up commissions for the purpose without the form of administration being changed.[4]

Rousseau's position, however, is correct only because his notion of democracy also is an ideal type. Actual or empirical democracies, therefore, merely approximate to a greater or lesser extent Rousseau's concept of democracy.

So that the nine models of polities included in our set of models will be clearly understood, empirical examples of such political systems should be given. A good example of Model 1, Classical Dictatorship, is the ancient Rome of Julius Caesar in 44 B.C.[5] With regard to Model 2, Modernizing Totalitarian Polity, Fidel Castro's Cuba is a good illustration.[6] As regards Model 3, Modern Totalitarian Polity, the Soviet Union during Joseph Stalin's rule serves as a good example.[7]

An actual polity that could be placed in Model 4, Traditional Autocracy, is Haile Selasie's Ethiopia;[8] Model 5, Modernizing Authoritarian Polity, is Nigeria under the military;[9] and Model 6, Modern Authoritarian Polity, is Lee Kwan Yew's Singapore.[10] A good illustration of Model 7, Classical Democracy, is the Athens of Pericles during the 5th century B.C.;[11] Model 8, Modernizing Democracy, is Indira Gandhi's India;[12] and Model 9, Modern Democracy, is the present-day United States.[13]

MODERNIZATION AND DEVELOPMENT

Having laid the foundation for discussion of our topic, we can now examine the concepts of modernization and development.

I first wrote on and advocated for modernization as development in a June 1965 paper on the state of Philippine political science, during an international conference held at the University of the Philippines at Quezon City. In that paper, I pointed out that the problem for the Philippines was "how to modernize as a nation—economically, socially, and politically."[14]

At that time, I was enthusiastic and uncritical about modernization as development primarily because my encounter with modernization was based principally on the early literature on modernization studies such as Daniel Lerner's *The Passing of Traditional Society: Modernizing the Middle East,*[15] which holds a positive perspective on modernization. Its thesis is that as countries become more modern—that is, more urbanized; more socially mobilized through such mass media as radio, newspapers, and movies; and more politically participant—the more politically developed they become. Also, during the late 1950s and early 1960s, practically all the area or country specialists were talking, writing, and publishing favorably about modernization. Jean Grossholtz, who wrote about Philippine politics in 1964,[16] for instance, was enthusiastic and favorably disposed toward modernization. When my book *The Political Elite and the People: A Study of Politics in Occidental Mindoro*[17] was published in 1972, I was no longer as enthusiastic about modernization as development as I had been in the mid-1960s. However, I still believed in modernization as both a study and a goal: As a study because I believed that it is an unavoidable phenomenon in all political systems; and hence, like it or not, we must study it to cope with it; as a goal because without some kind of modernization, the political system would be endangered and humanity would suffer. But even at that time, I already had doubts that modernization necessarily means development, for I already realized that it also brings human unhappiness as well as social and political disorganization. My misgivings on modernization were reinforced by studies by Samuel Huntington[18] and S. N. Eisenstadt[19] and by a 1971 Singapore conference on modernization at the Institute of Southeast Asian Studies. When then President Ferdinand E. Marcos declared nationwide martial law in the Philippines on September 21, 1972, I was already certain that modernization is not development.

About a year after Marcos's declaration of martial law, I was provided an excellent opportunity to articulate my thoughts on the issues of modernization and development when I delivered my inaugural lecture as the first holder of Manual A. Roxas Chair in Political Science at the University of the Philippines. In that lecture, I made the following distinction between political modernization and political development.[20] Political modernization, I said, is "a process of change from minimum to maximum level of rationalization of authority, national integration, and popular participation."[21] This definition is an adaptation of Huntington's idea of the concept.[22] Political development, I pointed out, is the higher end of humanity, "a process of change from lack to full flowering and fruition of the rule of law, civility, and social justice."[23] The former is a "new field of interest of political sociology," and the latter is "the perennial concern of political philosophy."[24] In other words, I posited that political modernization is in the realm of the empirical but that political development is in the normative.

Since 1973 I have not changed substantially my views on these two concepts, with the exceptions that (1) I have restated my idea of modernization in lexical and social science terms, and (2) I have subsumed political development to a larger normative concept, that of civilization.[25] Moreover, to summarize my conclusions on modernization after studying it since the 1960s, with special focus on the Marcos martial law regime, I have presented a thesis concerning its dynamics.[26]

Modernization may be clarified by comparing its dictionary meaning with its social science definition. According to Webster's *Third New International Dictionary, modernization* is "to make modern." Modern, it declares, is derived from the Latin *modo,* an adverb meaning "just now." Hence, modern means "of, relation to, or characteristic of a period extending from the more or less remote past to the present time."[27]

According to Dankwart A. Rustow, *modernization* is a process that "comprises many specific changes," denoting "rapidly widening control over nature through closer cooperation among men." It includes "all the specific changes such as industrialization."[28] Cyril E. Black and associates define *modernization* as "the process by which societies have been and are transformed under the impact of the scientific and technological revolution."[29]

Other definitions have been given by other social scientists. It is not necessary to examine them all, for they are only variations of those already stated. The common characteristics of these definitions, however, are (1) a *time* element and (2) the factor of *knowledge*. Of time, modern is of, about, or pertaining to the present. Thus, the old is not modern; it is traditional. The new or the recent is modern. The periodization of history into ancient, medieval, and modern follows this usage. Of knowledge, because it is cumulative, modern nations have the greatest amount of knowledge, and the traditional countries have the least. Accordingly, the best indicator of modernity of any country is the state of science and technology in that country in comparison to the most scientifically and technologically advanced nation in the world: The more developed its state of science and technology in comparison to the most advanced nation in the world, the more modern it is. In this sense, modernization is the process of attaining the level of scientific and technological state of affairs of the most advanced country in the world.

We can discern two kinds of modernization: the natural or gradual process and the forced or rapid process. Modernization in the First World (e.g., the United Kingdom and the United States) is natural or gradual, and modernization in both the Second World (e.g., the Soviet Union) and Third World (e.g., Pakistan, Nigeria, Vietnam, Cuba, Chile, and the Philippines) is forced or rapid. The natural or gradual type of modernization takes place over several generations or even centuries; the forced or rapid type is effected in only one or two decades or generations.

Having restated my idea of modernization, I now present my thesis on modernization or the iron logic of modernization. He who says modernization says tendency toward integration, which tends toward the diminution or death of individual or small-group freedom. Modernization and integration means the expansion of the power of bigger groups and the state. The polity or society that adopts and carries out a policy of or attains very high levels of rapid modernization will tend to fall into the grip of authoritarian or even totalitarian rule.[30]

MODERNIZATION IN THIRD WORLD AND SECOND WORLD COUNTRIES

The iron logic of modernization is clearly illustrated in the modernization of the countries of the Third World and the Second World, for in these nations modernization is or had been of the forced or rapid kind.[31]

Third World modernization is forced or rapid because, in the 1950s or at the time of these nations' independence, all of them had underdeveloped science and technology in comparison to those of the two modern superpowers, the United States and the Soviet Union. Because all Third World nations wanted to emulate or match the modern state of affairs of the United States or the Soviet Union so that they could cope successfully with the two superpowers' policies and politics, they all adopted policies of rapid modernization. Their attempts to modernize rapidly led to the imposition of new and strange laws, roles, and expected values for the people and sudden or drastic changes in the people's environments, life-styles, and roles. These changes eventually led to social turmoil, cultural crisis, economic dislocation, and political instability. To cope with these critical problems and to avoid anarchy, their societies or polities looked to authoritarian rule through military junta, charismatic leaders, or a predominant, hegemonic, or monolithic party or similar forceful agency.

The case of Pakistan was that of transformation from a modernizing parliamentary democracy to authoritarian rule under a military leader. The same course of change occurred in Nigeria. In Vietnam and Cuba, however, the transformation was from modernizing democracy to authoritarian rule under the hegemony of an authoritarian communist party. In the case of Chile, the story is somewhat different: Political change followed from a modernizing democracy, presidential in form, to an authoritarian rule under the military, headed by a general, Augusto Pinochet. The Philippines is the best illustration of the iron logic of modernization. I also know it best, for I have studied this polity closely for more than twenty years. Besides, I have lived in this country for most of my life. However, I shall postpone discussion of the Philippines until the next section so that I can develop a more detailed discussion. Before that, I present my assessment of the modernization process and its impact on representative countries of the Second and First Worlds.

Our Second World nation is the Soviet Union, which was born in the wake of Russia's 1917 revolution. Like the Third World countries of contemporary items, the resulting Soviet Union wanted to catch up with technological, economic, and social achievements of Western developed states. To carry out this goal, the Soviet Union adopted a policy of rapid or forced modernization, using a series of five-year plans with specific targets and quotas in the agricultural and industrial sectors. To succeed in this gigantic enterprise, the Soviet leadership centralized and concentrated the powers of the political system in a monolithic communist party and in the massive centralized bureaucracy. In the process of its rapid modernization, the Soviet Union developed a huge and modern authoritarian regime, becoming eventually a modern totalitarian polity.[32]

The iron logic of modernization apparently is not applicable to the First World countries of the United States and the United Kingdom, for these polities have not become authoritarian political systems. They are exemplary cases of vigorous democracies. It is true that during both World War I and World War II, these modern democratic polities became constitutional dictatorships but this was only temporary.[33] When the emergency conditions ended, both nations returned to their democratic ways and institutions.

The iron logic of modernization appears to be inapplicable to the United States and the United Kingdom because their modernization processes have been of the gradual type, which does not generate disorientation, disorganization, and discontent. Authoritarian power expands and concentrates gradually and imperceptively in Second World nations, but rapidly and obviously in Third World states.

A tendency toward authoritarianism, however, can be found in both the United States and the United Kingdom. Seven trends are manifest in these First World nations—urbanization, industrialization, mechanization, secularization, computerization, bureaucratization, and militarization—the seven horseman of the apocalypse of modernization. Ultimately, they will wreak havoc on American and British senses of community, civic and moral values, and traditional principles as well as on their environment's supportive roles. Perhaps by the year 2100, when these seven modernization processes have run their course and both nations have attained very high levels of modernization, they will have been plunged into social disorganization, political conflicts, and cultural malaise, among other terrible crises. Assuming that these have happened, both the United States and the United Kingdom may adopt constitutional dictatorships as they did during World Wars I and II.

MODERNIZATION IN THE PHILIPPINES

The Philippine case illustrates two aspects of the iron logic of modernization. The first was seen before the Marcos martial law regime—that is during the U.S. regime from 1898 to 1946 and the postindependence period form 1946 to 1972 or, in short, from 1898 to 1972. The second aspect could be observed in the Marcos martial law regime from 1972 to 1986.

From 1898 to 1946, the U.S. colonial government in the Philippines adopted a policy of rapid modernization so that Filipino wards should become more like Americans. This policy showed significant impact in important sectors of Philippine society, including in health, education, transportation and communications, economics, politics, and government.

In the health sector, modern medical science, technology, and facilities as well as public health programs were introduced and put into operation. Significant changes in the health sector included the eradication of such contagious epidemic diseases as cholera, smallpox, and typhoid fever and the lengthening of life-expectancy of the average Filipino, which increased from 11.54 years and 13.92 years in 1902 for males and females, respectively, to 51.17 and 55 years in 1960 for males and females.[34] As a result, the Philippine population increased tremendously, more than 7.6 million from in 1903 to 16 million in 1939.[35] This brought a proliferation of roles in society and polity, giving rise to many social and political conflicts.

In education, change during the 1898 to 1946 period of Philippine-American relations was that from elitist education to mass education. Filipino literacy rose rapidly, from 25 percent in 1903 to 48.8 percent in 1939.[36] As a result, vast numbers of people became aware of social, economic, political, and cultural issues by means of print media.

In transport and communications, the dramatic changes through modernization during the U.S. regime are partially shown in the change from the predominant use of animal power to the predominant or significant use of machine power, significant increases in the numbers of newspapers and their readers, and the introduction of the telephone, radio, and motion pictures. As a result, the people's awareness of events and developments in the country and the world was broadened and intensified, leading in turn to a revolution of rising expectations and feelings of relative deprivation.

In economics, changes from the modernization were just as dramatic. U.S. and other foreign enterprises became important to the national economy, private businesses and government corporations proliferated, cities grew, and both manufacturing and labor unions increased in the urban centers. As a result, the country's gross national product (GNP) increased significantly, the division of labor in the economy became more pronounced, the movement toward economies of scale started, government regulation of the economy gathered momentum, and centralization of the society became a salient trend even as new bases of social and political conflicts emerged.

In politics, modern changes included the rise of political parties, the proliferation of interest groups, the advent of regular popular elections of increasing number of policy-making officials, and the rapid spread of ideologies such as nationalism, democracy, socialism, and communism. As a result, politics became more dynamic, national, populistic, and even radicalized.

In government, modern changes included the Filipinization and bureaucratization of the government and expansion of its functions as it added education, social services, and the promotion and development of the economy to its traditional functions of police, war, and administration of justice. The result was Big Government.

After Philippine independence in 1946, this policy of rapid modernization was continued by the nation's political elite. As a result, from 1898 to 1972, despite improvements in the quality of Filipino life, rapid modernization caused the eruption of sociopolitical forces and events that brought political instability, social turmoil, and cultural crisis.[37] These sociopolitical forces and events ultimately triggered the proclamation of martial law by Ferdinand Marcos on September 21, 1972, and established an authoritarian regime in the Philippines.

With regard to the second aspect of the iron logic of modernization in the Philippines, Marcos, as martial law administrator, likewise adopted a policy of rapid modernization. Martial law, he said, must not only save the Republic but also reform Philippine society to attack the root causes of martial law.[38] Because Marcos had to effect his reforms within a very limited period, his modernization policy necessarily was of the rapid type.

Seven areas of reforms were to be attended to by the martial law regime. These were identified by acronym PLEDGES: Peace and order, Land tenure, Education, Development of moral values, Government, Economic development, and Social services. The end result of these reforms was expected to be Marcos's New Society. He linked his envisioned New Society to modernization and progress as follows:

> We speak of a New Society. . . . [Ours is] the dream that someday under somebody, we will be able to build a society that will give every man dignity and decency. And it shall return rationality into our political institutions, into our economy, and into our society . . . and this dream is what we are trying to implement now. It is the dream of every Filipino . . . that aspires for progress and modernization.[39]

So that the PLEDGES of the New Society could be implemented effectively, Marcos embarked on a politics of greater national unification and tighter integration of the various sectors of society. Marcos declared:

> [I]ncreasingly, we shall feel the imperative thrust towards the completion of the developments of our nation-state. . . . We shall therefore expect pressures for reforms. . . . These reforms would be directed for the most part towards the

greatest unification of the modern nation-state through the integration into the national life and polity of the various disaffected and neglected sectors of the national community.[40]

In the process of implementing the PLEDGES of the New Society, the executive's powers were greatly expanded. The president of the presidential system of government with its separation of powers and checks and balances as provided for in the 1935 Constitution (which continued as the fundamental law of the Republic after independence) became a *pangulo*.[41] As *pangulo*, Marcos under the martial law regime was chief executive, chief of state, chief administrator, commander-in-chief of the armed forces, chief legislator, martial law chief, party chief, and chief exponent of the ideology of the New Society. During the peak of his martial law regime, he was also the sole legislator. Indeed, he was superchief.[42]

What was the impact of the policy of rapid modernization that Marcos adopted during the martial law period on the people and the national government?

Many individuals lost their government jobs when their offices were abolished through reorganization. They had not been removed from their jobs without due process of law, some critics said, rather there simply were no more offices for them to hold. For example, a lawyer was disbarred after he refused to pay his dues to the Integrated Bar of the Philippines. That he had a Bachelor of Laws degree, had passed the bar successfully, and had practiced law for some time were all facts of no avail to the Supreme Court, which refused to allow him the freedom to practice his chosen profession, declaring that

[t]he integration of the Philippine Bar was obviously dictated by overwhelming considerations of public interest and public welfare to such an extent as more than constitutionally and legally justifies the restrictions that integration imposes upon the personal interests and personal conveniences of individual lawyers.[43]

Ancestral burial grounds and homes had to give way to modern hydroelectric power systems in Northern Luzon. An entire Central Luzon town, together with its ancient church, was doomed and dammed to give way to the Pantabangan power plant project. Small family enterprises of jeepney drivers started to collapse as the billion-peso metropolitan railway system went into systematic operation. These changes, of course, had a bright side: They brought happiness or prosperity to greater numbers of people or they served the public interest.

Smaller groups, both public and private, weakened or even lost their traditional freedom or authority as they struggled with the bigger groups. For instance, in the public arena, the city councils and the municipal councils of Manila, Quezon City, Caloocan City, Pasay City, Las Pinas, Makati, Malabon, Manduluyong, Marikina, Muntinglupa, Navotas, Paranaque, Pateros, San Juan, Taguig, and Valenzuela lost their freedom to engage in participatory democracy on matters vital to the Metropolitan Manila Commission. In the private realm, officially recognized groups—for example, the Philippine Chamber of Commerce and Industry (PCCI) in business and industry, the Federation of Free Farmers (FFF), and the Federation of Agrarian and Industrial Toiling Hands (FAITH) among the peasantry, and the Trade Union Congress of the Philippines (TUCP) in labor—flourished, but numerous other groups in these sectors languished because of discrimination against them.

As officially recognized or accredited groups flourished, their power also expanded. They were given sectoral representation in the interim Batasang Pambansa (National Assembly), participation in the governing boards of the Social Security System and the Government Service Insurance System, and greater opportunities to articulate their views in tripartite conferences.

Like the executive's, the power of the national government also greatly expanded. The personnel of the national government, grew from 531,059 in 1970 to 1,064,620 in 1979.[44,45] In 1970, total budget expenditures for the national government amounted to approximately 3.4 billion Philippine pesos.[46] In 1983, these expenditures had soared to the gigantic amount of 65 billion pesos.[47]

CIVILIZATION AS A RESTRAINT ON MODERNIZATION

Even if modernization does improve or advance many aspects of humans' individual and social lives, it tends to bring authoritarianism with it, whether immediate, in the case of rapid modernization or delayed in the case of the gradual variety. In the final analysis, however, modernization is a bane or a curse because it carries with it a destructive and rapacious beast—the tendency toward authoritarianism—that it sets loose to ravage and destroy the society or polity.

Therefore, the question that we cannot ignore is: What means shall we adopt to chain this beast?

My answer to this difficult question is one word: civilization. What is civilization? What are its characteristics? And what means should be adopted and what steps followed to attain it?

Civilization is both a process and the end result of a process. As a process, civilization involves the transformation of a state of human condition that can be called barbarism to another state of human condition characterized by political development, liberty, and democracy. As the polar opposite of civilization, barbarism is characterized by the absence of the minimal state of political development and the absence of liberty and democracy. Political development is a necessary condition of civilization, and liberty and democracy are its sufficient conditions.

In the second section of this essay, I wrote that the indicators of political development are the rule of law, civility, and social justice, so when I posit that political development is a necessary condition of civilization, I am also saying that the necessary conditions of civilizations are the rule of law, civility, and social justice.

The rule of law, declared former Chief Justice Roberto Concepcion, means "that law is supreme, that the rule of reason, as opposed to the arbitrary will of tyrants, should prevail, and that all men, rich or poor, high or lowly, are subject to the norms prescribed by law."[48] Without the rule of law, humans will be under the law of the jungle, the inevitable result of which will be what Thomas Hobbes described with fear and trembling: "In such condition, there is no society; and which is worst of all, continual feare, and danger of violent death; and the life of man, solitary, poor, nasty, brutish, and short."[49]

Civility is an attribute held by members of a society or polity such that each is educated in good manners and right conduct, socialized in the rights and duties of citizenship, and imbued with a commitment to defend and promote the common good. Civility is a principle of restraint or moderation that protects and promotes the general interest or the general welfare. Edward Shils said more elaborately:

> Civility is belief which affirms the possibility of the common good; it is a belief in the community of contending parties within a morally valid unity of society. It is a belief in the validity or legitimacy of the governmental institutions which lay down rules and resolve conflict. Civility is a virtue expressed in action on behalf of the whole society, on behalf of the good of all members of the society to which public liberties and representative institutions are integral. Civility is an attitude in individuals which recommends that consensus about the maintenance of the order of society should exist alongside the conflicts of interests and ideals. It restrains the exercise of power by the powerful and restrains obstruction and violence by those who do not have power but who wish to have it. Civility is on the side of authority and on the side of those over whom authority would rule.[50]

Without civility, the fate of man will be that of unendurable vexation or unending strife, the very conditions that Hobbes had feared.

Social justice, as distinguished from individual justice, is concerned with the dispensing of justice so that the society or the polity is not plunged into social turmoil, political instability, or civil war. There are both conservative-liberal and radical views of social justice. A good example of the conservative-liberal viewpoint is held by former Philippine Justice Jose P. Laurel, who declared:

> Social justice is neither communism nor despotism, nor atomism, nor anarchy, but the humanization of laws and the equalization of social and economic forces by the State so that justice in its rational and objectively secular conception may at least be approximated. Social justice means the promotion of the welfare of the people, the adoption of measures calculated to insure the economic stability of all the component elements of society, through the maintenance of a proper economic and social equilibrium in the interrelations of the members of the community, constitutionally, through the adoption of measures legally justifiable or extraconstitutionally, through the exercise of powers underlying the existence of all government on the time-honored principle of *salus populi est supreme lex*.

Social justice, therefore, must be founded on the recognition of interdependence among diverse unites of a society and of the protection that should be equally and evenly extended to all groups as a combined force in our social and economic life, consistent with the fundamental and paramount objective of the State of promoting health, comfort, and quiet of all persons, and of bringing about "the greatest good to the greatest number."[51]

A comprehensive summary of the radical position on social justice is the one articulated by A. M. Honore in a recent article:

The principle of social justice resides the idea that all men have equal claims to all advantages which are generally desired and which are in fact conducive to human perfection and human happiness. This has two main aspects: first, the equalization of the human condition as far as capital assets, human and inanimate, that is, the prerequisites of a good life are concerned. This involves equal claims to the necessities of life, to life itself, health, food, shelter, etc., and also equality of opportunity for both work and enjoyment. The second aspect of the principle of social justice consists in the principles of non-discrimination and conformity to rule. These ensure that what has been accorded under the first heading will not be taken away subsequently. There are some exceptions to the principle of social justice, in particular to the principle of non-discrimination. These exceptions fall under subordinate principles of justice such as the justice of transactions, justice according to desert, justice according to choice and justice according to need. There are no further exceptions to be found.[52]

However social justice is defined, whether from the conservative-liberal or radical viewpoints, like the rule of law and civility, it is a required condition of a civil order. Without social justice, human life will be unending torment by alienation, frustration, and anger, which in the long run will trigger an explosion of riots, rebellion, or civil war.

Having clarified the principles that are the necessary conditions of civilization, we may now explain in what sense they are necessary. Without them, civilization cannot be established, but even with their realization in the polity, it does not follow that civilization will have reached its full flowering and fruition. So that the entelechy of a civilization will be attained, there must be sufficient conditions for its full development. These are liberty and democracy.

By liberty I mean all human rights, which are civil rights, political rights, and social rights, the last including economic and cultural rights. These rights have been provided for in the Constitution of the Republic of the Philippines and in the United Nations Universal Declaration of Human Rights. Without liberty, life is meaningless. I must add, however, that liberty is equally meaningless if not understood in its social context. "It has to be thus," declares Philippine Justice Enrique M. Fernando,

for it is liberty of individuals living in groups, not in isolation, that is safeguarded. Necessarily then, one cannot simply have his way at all times. If it were
thus, given the conflicting desires of individuals in society, the result may be rank
disorder. That is as objectionable as regimentation at the other extreme. There is
need, therefore, for adjustment and reconciliation between the authority that must
be recognized as possessed by the state to be utilized for the welfare of all, and
the liberty an individual cannot be denied for his self-fulfillment as a social being.[53]

Democracy has been characterized in the Constitution of the Republic of the
Philippines: "Sovereignty resides in the people, and all governmental authority
emanates from them."[54] I had earlier defined democracy differently: "A democratic polity is one where control of the political elite by the people is maximum, the area of liberty is extensive, politics is competitive, and society is
pluralist."[55]

Whether defined in terms of sovereignty of the people or in terms of characteristics involving popular control of the political elite, extensiveness of liberty,
competitive nature of politics, and pluralist structure of society, democracy
certainly is significant to human dignity. Without democracy, human dignity
cannot be vindicated.

There remains only one question to answer: What means should be adopted
and what steps followed to bring about civilization?

I answer briefly as follows. Civilization can be made to germinate, grow,
develop, flower, and fructify *initially* by providing for the principles of the rule
of law, civility, social justice, liberty, and democracy in the constitution of the
polity, and *afterward* by educating the people and the political elite to internal-
ize, live by, and live for those principles.

Primary and secondary education should teach the principles of civilization
by means of social studies, the humanities, and selected and relevant aspects of
the natural sciences as well as through various practical or vocational courses
and extracurricular activities. Courses in civics at both levels—the primary and
the secondary—are the principal vehicles for teaching such principles.

Colleges and universities, or the tertiary level, should educate students in the
principles of civilization through a required general education program. Such a
program should educate students on those principles through relevant courses in
the humanities, social sciences, and natural sciences as well as through fora,
symposia, and extracurricular activities.

Education, however, should not be confined to the primary, secondary, and
tertiary levels of the educational system. It should also be carried out by nonfor-
mal agencies, especially by the home, the church, the government, the mass
media, mass spectacles (e.g., sports), national celebrations (e.g., national holidays), and political activities (e.g., campaigns and elections).

In brief, I posit that civilization is a strong chain that will restrain or regulate
the beast in modernization. I am not positing that this is the only chain that can

control the tendency of modernization toward authoritarianism. Certainly, external and physical chains could also be forged for this purpose, for example, various kinds of political and social institutions. But for the time being, I lay these aside, for in the last analysis, all the external and physical chains will come to naught if the principles of civilization are not made operative ideals of both the political elite and the people through education. Ultimately, the most effective defense against the beast lies in the operative internal and moral ideals forged in the hearts and minds of the political elite and the people.

NOTES

1. Remigio E. Agpalo, *Models of Political Systems and the Philippines* (Quezon City: University of the Philippines Press, 1978).
2. Agpalo, *Models*, p. 10.
3. Agpalo, *Models*, p. 4.
4. Jean-Jacques Rousseau, *The Social Contract and Discourses* (New York: Dutton, 1973), p. 217.
5. Agpalo, *Models*, pp. 15–16.
6. Agpalo, *Models*, pp. 17–18.
7. Agpalo, *Models*, pp. 19–20
8. Agpalo, *Models*, pp. 16–17.
9. Agpalo, *Models*, p. 17.
10. Agpalo, *Models*, pp. 18–19.
11. Agpalo, *Models*, p. 15.
12. Agpalo, *Models*, p. 18.
13. Agpalo, *Models*, pp. 18–19.
14. Remigio E. Agpalo, "Political Science in the Philippines," in S. S. Hsueh, ed. *Political Science in South and Southeast Asia,* Asia Political Science Association, 1966), p. 60.
15. New York: Free Press, 1958.
16. Jean Grossholtz, *Politics in the Philippines* (Boston: Little, Brown, 1964).
17. Manila: College of Public Administration, University of the Philippines.
18. *Political Order in Changing Societies* (New Haven, Conn.: Yale University Press, 1968).
19. *Modernization: Protest and Change* (Englewood Cliffs, N.J.: Prentice-Hall, 1966).
20. Remigio E. Agpalo, *The Organic-Hierarchical Paradigm and Politics in the Philippines* (Quezon City: University of the Philippines Press, 1973).
21. Agpalo, *Organic-Hierarchical*, p. 34.
22. Huntington, *Political Order*, p. 93.
23. Agpalo, *Organic-Hierarchical*, p.34.
24. Agpalo, *Organic-Hierarchical*, p. 34.
25. Remigio E. Agpalo, *"Pangulo* Regime and Civilization." *Solidarity,* no. 12(1985): 18–27.
26. Remigio E. Agpalo, "The Iron Logic of Modernization." Inaugural lecture for the Aurelio Calderon Professorial Chair in Philippine-American Relations, delivered at De La Salle University, June 10, 1985. Published in *Praxis, III* (December 198): 37–38.

27. Springfield, Mass.: G. & C. Merriam Co., 1976. p. 1452.

28. See his *A World of Nations: Problems of Political Modernization* (Washington, D.C.: The Brookings Institution, 1967), pp. 5–8.

29. Cyril E. Black, Marius B. Jansen, Herbert S. Levine, Marion J. Levy, Jr., Henry Rosovsky, Gilbert Rosman, Henry D. Smith, and S. Frederick Starr, *The Modernization of Japan and Russia* (New York: The Free Press, 1975), p. 3.

30. Agpalo, "Iron Logic," p. 39.

31. For an introduction to the dynamics of change in the Third World, see David E. Schmitt, ed., *Dynamics of the Third World: Political and Social Change* (Cambridge, Mass.: Winthrop Publishers, 1974).

32. Helene Carrere D'Encause, *Stalin: Order Through Terror* (New York: Longman, 1981).

33. Clinton Rossiter, *Constitutional Dictatorship: Crisis Government in Modern Democracies* (New York: Harcourt, Brace and World, 1963), part III, "Crisis Government in Great Britain," pp. 131–205; and Part IV, "Crisis Government in the United States," pp. 207–287.

34. Bureau of Census and Statistics, *Journal of Philippine Statistics, XXI* (2)(Second Quarter 1970): ix.

35. *Philippine Yearbook 1977* (Manila Natural Census and Statistics Office, 1977). p. 59.

36. Files of the Bureau of Census and Statistics, Manila.

37. These political forces or events were specified in Remigio E. Agpalo, *The Filipino Polity: Historical Perspective and New Goals in the 1980s* (Quezon City: University of the Philippines Press, 1976), pp. 11–12.

38. Ferdinand E. Marcos, *Notes on the New Society of the Philippines* (Manila: Marcos Foundation, 1973).

39. Ferdinand E. Marcos, *Presidential Speeches* (Manila: Marcos Foundation, 1979), vol. VIII, p. 39.

40. Marcos, *Presidential Speeches,* vol. VI, p. 206.

41. An executive more powerful than the president in a presidential system. Unlike such a president, who is *coordinate* with the legislature, the *pangula* is *superordinate* to the legislature. The term is based on the Tagalong term *ulo* (head) and the prefix *pang-* (one that is used for).

42. Remigio E. Agpalo, "The Philippine Executive," in Froilan M. Bacungan, ed., *The Powers of the Philippine President* (Quezon City: University of the Philippines Law Center, 1983), pp. 156–162.

43. Supreme Court of the Philippines, "Resolution" (with regard to Marcial A. Edillon), August 3, 1978. Full text is found in *Journal of the Integrated Bar of the Philippines, 6*(3)(Third Quarter, 1979): 229–234 (quotation on p. 231).

44. *The Philippine Civil Service: A Personal Profile* (Quezon City: Civil Service Commission, 1974), p. 8.

45. *Bulletin Today,* December 28, 1981, p. 32.

46. *1971 Philippine Yearbook* (Manila: Bureau of Census and Statistics, 1973), p. 604.

47. *Statistical Handbook of the Philippines* (Manila: National Census and Statistics Office, 1984), p. 167.

48. Robert Concepcion, "The Rule of Law: A Collective Responsibility of All Citi-

zens," in Alberto Cacnio and Guillermo Pablo, Jr., *Roberto Concepcion: Chief Justice of the Philippines* (Manila: Cacnio and Pablo Publications, 1974), p. 39.

49. *Leviathan* (New York: E. P. Dutton, 1950), p. 104.

50. "Observation on Some Tribulations of Civility," *Government and Opposition,* *15*(Summer-Autumn 1980): 528–529.

51. *Calalang* v. *Williams,* 48 O.G. 9th Supp. 239 (1940).

52. A. M. Honore, "Social Justice," in Robert B. Summers, ed., *Essays in Legal Philosophy* (Berkeley: University of California Press, 1968), p. 91.

53. Enrique M. Fernando, *The Constitution of the Philippines* (Quezon City: Central Lawbook Publishing, 1974), pp. 506–507.

54. Constitution of the Republic of the Philippines (1973), Article II, Section 1.

55. Agpalo, *Models,* p. 10.

Chapter 4

Foreign Policy, Development, and Democracy

Edward Broadbent

For some time now economic development has been understood in a manner justifying dictatorships and undemocratic practices in general. The time for explicitly linking economic development with democratic rights is now here. Environmental concerns, for instance, now arise each time an important development project, such as those now seeking funding from the World Bank, is implemented. This situation may be attributed to the work of environmental activists, who for many years seemed to speak out in a vacuum. Human rights activists now must replicate this victory. From now on, they must insist that economic development must be considered within a human rights framework, recognizing the centrality of human rights and popular participation to the notion of development. In the realm of foreign policy, development assistance must be linked on a conditional basis with human rights performance. Bilateral policies of governments as well as the policies of international financial institutions which hold development as an objective must ensure that certain human rights conditions are met if the projects are to qualify for economic assistance. In so doing, we must link survival with freedom, bread with roses.

INTRODUCTION

The positive relationship between development and democracy has often been taken for granted. In addition, the meaning of development has been seriously misunderstood by many. This twofold reality has had serious global consequences during the past four decades. The following discussion attempts to shed light on the meaning of development, on the linkages between development and

This is a synthesis of speeches delivered before the Society for International Development, Ottawa Chapter, on June 12, 1990, and the International Conference on Human Rights in the Twenty-First Century: A Global Challenge, sponsored by the Faculty of Law of the University of Calgary, Alberta, Canada, on November 9–12, 1990.

democracy, and on the global role that democratic governments should now play in securing both.

THE NORMATIVE BASIS OF DEVELOPMENT

For most of the Cold War period, the most ardent supporters of the idea of development, from both the capitalist and the so-called socialist camps, forgot that development is at its core a normative term, one founded on universal values to which humanity has always aspired: dignity, freedom, and welfare. Both Adam Smith and Karl Marx, the preeminent economic thinkers of the modern age, recognized this when they saw economies as being inextricably linked with questions of human value. To talk about development by restricting the term to quantifiable indicators—as many of their alleged followers have done in this century—would have been inconceivable to them. Where Smith regarded himself as a practitioner of a "moral science" and Marx deemed self-realization as the highest good, most Western economists today claim to avoid normative questions, and most Marxists in power have trampled over basic human freedoms.

For most of the period since World War II, whether in the West, in former Warsaw Pact countries, or amongst elites with power in the Third World, "development" as a term became virtually interchangeable with quantifiable indicators of economic growth. This idea of development, freed from any nonquantifiable considerations, has been used by many of the powerful to justify the most flagrant denial of human rights in both developed and developing nations.

At the same time, the vast army of professional planners, experts, and advisers in "developmental" work, although not seeking to obtain or preserve power themselves, have helped spread this gospel of development. By omitting human rights considerations from the definition, for example, they have produced national and international policy positions in which nonmaterial considerations appear either as secondary or even antagonistic to what they call development. In this they have been the unconscious allies of undemocratic elites in the Third World and those in the industrial world whose principal motivation has been the maximization of profit. Fortunately, this ideology of development is now under attack. The moral purposes of development—the enhancement of civilized life for human beings—is now back in the equation. From St. Petersburg to Rio de Janeiro, from Lake Ontario to the Black Sea, children and adults alike are now demanding that development must not only mean material benefits but also be consistent with the pursuit and maintenance of a quality of life that enhances, rather than diminishes their humanity. This means that development must be looked at (as it gradually is being recognized) holistically as entailing consideration of such matters as human rights, the environment, population growth, levels of literacy and health, distribution of income, and patterns of trade, to name but a few.

Although the evolution of this perception has at times been painful, at least it is now gaining currency. We may recall, for instance, that immediately following World War II, a strong prodemocracy, pro-human rights atmosphere prevailed. The creation of the United Nations itself and the promulgation of the Universal Declaration of Human Rights were greeted with enthusiasm. Alexander Solzhenitsyn has observed that the most enduring achievement of the United Nations, in fact, was the drafting of this declaration of human rights. Its universality is based on its assertion about the inherent dignity and the equal and inalienable rights of all members of the human family. Its core values are deemed to transcend all cultural and historical differences.

Regrettably, however, shortly after the adoption of the Universal Declaration, the Cold War began in earnest and lasted for four decades. A consequence of this unfortunate turn of political events in the international arena was to marginalize policy interests in pursuing international human rights standards and applications. Not only were hundreds of billions of dollars used up in armaments that could have contributed significantly to the implementation of economic rights, but also the superpowers, more concerned with gaining geopolitical advantage over their adversaries, either ignored or actively supported violations of human rights in developing countries. As long as the governing regime remained an ally, too often it could do what it wanted with its population.

The Cold War, therefore, contributed negatively to the inherently ambivalent attitude that Western democratic states have about making human rights and democratic institutions a central concern in foreign relations. This ambivalence is the result of the inevitable competition for emphasis among trade, security (defense), and human rights that democratic governments have in their foreign relations. The Cold War meant that human rights concerns did not simply take a back seat to trade and security in the crafting of foreign policy. In fact, rights were rarely in the same car.

RELATIONSHIP BETWEEN DEVELOPMENT AND DEMOCRACY

The problem has not, however, simply been a matter of competition for global power or the doctrine that development was to be seen exclusively in quantifiable terms. There also has been the view that a necessary trade-off must be made between economic growth on one hand and human rights and democracy on the other. This argument has been used by both free market and centralized planning advocates not only in Europe and North America but also in such Third World countries as South Korea, Taiwan, Brazil, Chile, and most African states.

Crudely stated, the argument is that for the Third World, more economic development requires less democracy. At a recent conference in England, this author heard a contrary variant of the same line of reasoning: democratic institutions will *guarantee* economic development.

The truth is with neither side. Historical experience in the twentieth century does not justify a global generalization linking human rights either positively or negatively with economic development. The same experience does, however, warrant the following propositions that democrats should keep in mind:

1. Although the sacrifice of human rights will not guarantee economic development, it will guarantee injustice to those whose rights are denied.
2. Although the suppression of democratic rights has been done by governments in the name of economic development, the only constant consequence has been to maintain the power and wealth of the governing party, elite, or class.
3. Although civil, political, social, and cultural liberties will not guarantee a fair distribution of economic benefits, it is unlikely that such fairness will occur when such liberties are denied.*

Advent of the New World Order

As alluded to earlier, the winds of change are blowing across the globe, sweeping away old myths that have perverted the concepts of development and democracy. Some positive prospects of this change are now discernible. The demise of the Cold War—symbolized by the collaborative rather than the confrontational relations between the United States and the late Soviet Union—provides an opportunity to elevate human rights concerns as a key component of our foreign relations.

We are now at one of those crucial moments in history when a major change in power relations enables foreign policy to be something more than the externalization of self-interest. We must seize the occasion. Without denying the existence of injustices at home, established democracies can and must play an active role in placing human rights and democratic practices on the frontburner of our external relations.

This means taking a more outspoken position on the consistent and systematic violations of human rights in other states. This important work can no longer be left solely to the courageous activists in nongovernment organizations who work so steadfastly in the face of harassment, imprisonment, or death.

For this policy to have meaning, it is imperative that democratic governments publicly launch a debate that asserts the principle that international law has precedence over domestic law with regard to human rights. In the face of arguments that human rights issues are purely domestic matters, democratic governments must insist that this is not so, that the issue is global in nature and is covered by universally accepted norms of international behavior—most spe-

---

*As one Filipino citizen once said, "Authoritarianism is not needed for development. It is needed to perpetuate the status quo."

cifically the U.N. Universal Declaration of Human Rights. In doing this, they must, of course, accept this principle as being fully applicable to themselves.

Developed democratic states should also strongly support the objectives of the 1986 U.N. Declaration on the Right to Development. Whether this declaration is a new right or simply a synthesis of the earlier human rights conventions is beside the point. What is key is the message that *all* of the family of human rights should be seen as important and that human dignity requires popular participation. Human rights, popular participation, and development should be seen and advocated by developed democratic nations as part of a desirable integrated human process.

Human Rights as a Component of Foreign Policy

If what has been said so far is acceptable, then certain related practical courses of action are essential in guiding future international development policies. The assumption of a more activist role by democratic governments in formulating a coherent policy should neither be regarded as the utopian project nor the minefield that some have suggested. This could be achieved effectively by putting the U.N. family of human rights (political, civil, economic, social, and cultural) in their rightful place in all our developmental thinking *and* by integrating human rights with our international aid, trade, and commercial policies. Democratic governments must integrate economic advancement policies with human rights and democratic practices. This is not because there is a direct causal relationship between them; rather, it is because human dignity or freedom as Aristotle, Marx, and Mill each saw require both adequate material conditions and what we in this century call human rights.

We must be insistent that the bilateral policies of democratic governments as well as policies implemented by international financial institutions whose stipulated objective is development ensure that certain human rights conditions be met if a country is to qualify for economic assistance. These conditions can be put positively and negatively; they should be applied with some degree of flexibility. However, while not absolute in application, the point is that human rights considerations must now be included in all major international development policies. It should be noted that this approach has already been advocated by members of Canada's Parliament. Several parliamentary committees have called upon the federal government to establish coherence in Canadian foreign policy vis-à-vis Official Development Assistance (ODA), trade, and commercial policies.

The most recent of these initiatives, the "Interim Report of the Sub-Committee on International Human Rights (July 1986)," states that "(t)here appears to be serious lack of coherence and consistency between many of Canada's aid, trade, and financial assistance relationships with other countries, on one hand, and our human rights commitments, on the other." "Canada," the report continues, "like most other human rights supporting nations, seems of-

ten to be in the position of piously condemning human rights abuses 'on Sun-
days' and then carrying on business as usual—including mutually lucrative
business—with human rights abusing countries, during the rest of the week."
Surely, it is time to develop and apply a coherent policy in aid, trade, and
human rights. Democratic countries must stop the practice of condemning the
brutality of Tiananmen Square in June and reestablishing bank loans in
September.*

Concern for the Environment

Turning our discussion to the environment, it is heartening to note an emergent
global movement dedicated towards its protection. This certainly did not occur
spontaneously. Rather, it was the outcome of the persistent hard work by environmental activists who for many years seemed to speak out in a vacuum. Their
numbers spread and eventually politicians responded. Although the notion of
sustainable development, given global prominence by the Brundtland Commission[1] has not yet been incorporated as a sine qua non of all economic policy
making, it has emerged as a concept with significant popular support compelling politicians in both democratic and nondemocratic societies to take it into
consideration. Now, proposals for development projects that exclude an assessment of their environmental impact will automatically generate national and
international opposition.

Not only has the notion of development been broadened by the inclusion of
the environment, but also governments now rarely dare retreat behind the hoary
national sovereignty argument to defend what they are doing. Consequently,
national governments and international lending institutions—for example, the
World Bank—now feel compelled to evaluate project proposals brought before
them on the basis of, among others, their environmental impact. A hydroelectric dam, for instance, may be a source of energy, but it also may obliterate the
housing rights of people or destroy an indigenous people's mode of existence.
A case in point was the infamous Chico Dam Project, funded by the World
Bank, which was designed to flood several valleys in the mountain provinces in
northern Philippines in the 1970s and early 1980s. Begun during the regime of
dictator Ferdinand Marcos, it would have flooded the ancestral homes of the
indigenous inhabitants in the affected areas of the region, displacing thousands
of them and yet benefiting mainly a handful of influential multinational corporations that had established plants in the Luzon area. The project was stopped
only by the loud outcry—both domestic and international—protesting its construction.

---

*This is exactly what happened in 1989.

Links in the Chain of Development

The lesson that this experience has brought home is that economics, the environment, and human rights are common links in what should be an indivisible human chain. The human family deserves not only material betterment but also a combination of clean air and safe energy with individual and cultural freedom. Any economic policy that ignores these elements is not worthy of the name.

In the fall of 1990 at the official opening of the International Center for Human Rights and Democratic Development, Canada's then-Secretary of State for External Affairs, Joe Clark, emphasized that the government of Canada would take this broad approach in its bilateral relations. He suggested that the Canadian government would be prepared to "cease to deal through the regime" in cases of the extreme abuse of human rights, although it would attempt by other means to get aid directly to those who need it. Earlier in the same year, the president of France, a U.S. undersecretary of state, and the British foreign minister indicated that their respective governments intended to make a similar link between aid policy and human rights. If followed through, this would serve notice to abusive regimes that their actions would no longer be tolerated by the international community and that normal relations with them would not be maintained unless and until they respected and safeguarded the fundamental rights of their citizens.

WHERE DO WE GO FROM HERE?

At the bilateral level, in their international aid practices and in the pursuit of trade and commercial objectives, democratic governments must ensure that treaties and agreements contain a human rights conditionality that goes beyond a simplistic proforma consideration of a country's human rights record. They must be prepared to terminate bilateral aid agreements to ODA-recipient countries whose governments persistently violate the human rights of their citizens.

At the multilateral level, concrete measures should be taken to ensure that, as a matter of routine, all aid, trade, and commercial policies include human rights and democratic practices considerations. In this, already agreed upon U.N. resolutions and covenants should be taken into account and implemented.

By extension, it is also time that national governments who participate in the decisionmaking of the World Bank and other international and regional financing institutions consider as a matter of routine the human rights impact of a proposed project, for example, the impact of an investment or debt burden decision on the civil, economic, and social rights of citizens in a developing country. Third World countries are now paying millions more in interest payments to the industrialized countries each year than they are receiving in aid. They are perfectly correct when they point out that cutbacks on medical and educational services are cutbacks on rights. It is time also that the General

Agreement on Tariffs and Trade (GATT) included provisions whose purpose would be to help prevent the exploitation of the world's poor either by multinational corporations or by governments. Such provisions would take into account existing differences in development but would obligate contracting parties to observe certain minimum labor standards based on International Labor Organization (ILO) agreements. Such standards could be worked out by an advisory committee to be established by the GATT and the ILO.

When it comes to work conditions, we must insist that international commerce regard freedom of association, the protection of children, the abolition of forced labor, and the rights of trade unionists as being just as important as the right to make a profit. What developed democracies demand for themselves as basic human rights, they must also support for others.

At home, established democracies should also demonstrate their commitment to human rights and democracy by ensuring an annual debate in their parliaments and congresses comparable in principle to the yearly budget debates. Such a debate would require the participation of senior members of government. Ministers would be expected to give a full accounting of their government's performance, including their record of votes at the United Nations, the World Bank, and the GATT. During the same debate, the whole range of human rights issues that had arisen domestically during the previous year would also receive a full discussion.

Such a debate, focusing on human rights and democratic practices at home and abroad, would be a significant contribution to the human rights education of people throughout the country. These and other fora of debate are essential elements to the involvement of citizens in all critical human rights discussions. Their consequent pressure on politicians in turn would help ensure that human rights considerations become an integral part of all government policies.

CONCLUSION

Recently, I received a letter from a man who has spent the major part of his life working on ways to help improve the condition of the poor on this planet. In this letter he offered the following judgment: In the final analysis, a more humane and just national order is achieved only by those who live within their own lands; their solutions will be based on indigenous historical imperatives. Their goals will be encouraged, and at times advanced, by foreign assistance. But essentially such people wage a solitary struggle, sustained by the strength of their commitment and the support of their fellow citizens.

The friend who wrote the letter is right. As someone who has just set out as the head of a new center for human rights and democratic development, I am aware that only vanity can make us think we either should or could reshape the destinies of others. It is essential to realize that no one model of democracy be seen or imposed as the standard. We Canadians do not have the right—nor does anyone else—to suggest our model as the standard for the world. However, when we provide some assistance to others for their choice in their struggle, we are obliged to reflect upon our own experience in the light of universal principles. We must see that all rights, economic and cultural, political and civil, be taken into account. We must see the universal linkage between bread and roses.

Whatever we do, as my friend has said, it will remain in the future as it has been in the past that a more humane and just order in any country will ultimately be created by those living within that country. What we can do is aid or hinder the process. By our action or inaction, we will take sides one way or the other. Surely we must be on the side of those favoring human rights and democracy.

NOTE

1. The Brundtland Commission, known officially as the World Commission on Environment and Development, was headed by Norway's former prime minister Gro Harlem Brundtland. In 1987, it issued an official report entitled *Our Common Future,* which called attention to the worsening environmental situation and sought to "propose long-term environmental strategies for achieving sustainable development by the year 2000 and beyond" (p. ix).

Response to this report by the international community has been characterized with approving respect and admiration. This is exemplified by a World Bank–commissioned report titled "Environmentally Sustainable Economic Development: Building on Brundtland." Its editors wrote: "Right at the outset, we want to acknowledge our major debt to the Brundtland Commission's 1987 report. . . . In particular, we greatly admire the Commission's achievement in garnering political consensus on the need for sustainable development. We use this report as our springboard" (p. 4). See World Bank Working Paper, Environmental Department. Robert Goodland, Herman Daly, and Salah El Serafy, eds. (Washington, D.C.: World Bank, 1991).

Part Three

Human Rights and the Ethical Basis of Development

Chapter 5

Democracy and Development: Luxury or Necessity?

Thomas S. Axworthy

Since the end of World War II, the world community has been perplexed by a false dichotomy between development on one hand and democracy on the other. States agonized over whether they could "afford" democracy or whether the economic price of mass participation was simply too high. This chapter argues that democracy and mass participation are, in fact, vital components of economic progress. Democracy obviously has value as a political good, but by affording the opportunity of individuals to develop their full human potential, it also unleashes economic creativity. This has always been so. But as the world economy continues to evolve from a mass industrial base to a knowledge base, the premium to be placed on human creativity grows ever more intense. In summary, a society can be democratic without being affluent, although wealth does expand the range of choice. But in the world economy of 2,000 and beyond, democracy and citizen participation in the economy will be an essential factor of production.

INTRODUCTION

There are certain years that define the age in which they fall: the Glorious Revolution of England in 1688, Colonial America in 1776, France in 1789, and now, in our time, the sequence of events in the anni mirabili, 1989–91. The Berlin Wall no longer divides. The Soviet Union no longer exists. The Cold War is over. A new world order beckons.

Debate on why the Cold War ended in a complete Western victory is only beginning.[1] Conservatives argue that containment worked, that the line drawn in Europe in 1948–49 by George Kennan, Dean Acheson, and Harry Truman

---

This chapter was based on a paper of the same title originally prepared for presentation at the "Human Rights in the Twenty-first Century: A Global Challenge" conference held in Banff, Alberta, Canada, November 9–12, 1990, sponsored by the Faculty of Law of the University of Calgary. A book based on the proceedings of this conference was published in 1991 by Martinus Nijhoff, Amsterdam.

prevented immediate Soviet adventurism and that, over time, the intrinsic economic weakness of the Soviets lessened their ability to compete. In short, the arms race bankrupted the Soviet Union into moderation. Liberals argue that detente worked: Increased contact and trade with the West gradually reduced traditional Soviet fears about attack so that in time a new leadership could take a chance on reform at home and retrenchment abroad. Both analyses ring true. Sweeping historical change is due to many causes. The important point is that our generation too can be present at the creation—the creation of a post–Cold War world order. What should be the components of that new world and, in particular, how much importance should be placed on human rights and democratic advance?

SOME BASIC PREMISES

This chapter makes a four-part argument, namely:

1. The end of the Cold War reduces most of the realpolitik constraints on placing human rights at the top of the world agenda. We are presently witnessing one of the greatest democratic explosions in world history: Our task is to consolidate the gains; fix the root of liberty solidly into the fabric of such societies as the Philippines, the former republics of the Soviet Union, and Brazil; and promote democracy in other areas such as Africa and the Middle East, which have not yet made democratic breakthroughs.
2. The nature of regimes matters. Real devotion to human rights and popular participation in government are not only essential for individual development but also form the basis of civil society. Civil societies, in turn, are usually peaceful societies. The spread of democracy and human rights across the globe will not only improve the lives of millions, but it will ensure the safety of the rest of us.
3. Despite their importance, democracy and human rights have only received lip service in development policy. The World Bank, the International Monetary Fund, and the bilateral aid programs of the West virtually ignore the nature of the recipient country's regime. Augusto Pinochet's Chile, for example, was lauded by many in the West because of its monetarism, despite its human rights atrocities. This chapter argues that ignoring the democratic dimension is not only bad politics (the second point above) but leads to bad economics. The new global economy demands intelligence, entrepreneurship, and information exchange— precisely the qualities promoted by democracy and stifled by autocracy. It is time to end the divide between economic and political development. The two must move in concert.
4. Therefore, it is time that countries such as Canada put the criteria of democracy and human rights at the center of its foreign policy. Human

rights must become a precondition for aid. This will require massive changes to existing policy. Promoting freedom rather than mouthing the rhetoric of freedom must become a compelling priority. The new world order must be a democratic world order.

Citizens who enjoy the benefits of democracy probably underestimate how difficult a system it is to create and sustain. Ancient Athens, the inventor of popular participation in government, practiced democracy for 200 years. After Phillip of Macedon conquered the city, the rule of the many vanished until the creation of the United States in 1789. American democracy has now lasted as long as the Athenian model—200 years. Throughout world history, democratic practice has always been a minority faith.

The 1990s may finally close the chapter on this sad story. Democracy is on the march: Boris Yeltsin in Russia, Corazon Aquino in the Philippines, Lech Walesa in Poland, and Raul Alfonsin in Argentina are examples of leaders who have transformed world politics. And the end of the Cold War can only hasten this process. In the era of Cold War rivalry, autocrats could play one super-power off against another: "He may be a son of a bitch," Franklin Roosevelt said of Anastasio Somoza of Nicaragua, "but he is *our* son of a bitch." Human rights were seen as a luxury that unfortunately had to be sacrificed on the altar of realpolitik. Jimmy Carter was generally derided by the foreign policy estab-lishment because he had the temerity to advocate human rights as a basic princi-ple of U.S. foreign policy. But democratic nations now hold the cards. It is Japan and the developed world that possesses the technology and wealth that the rest of the world needs. If the developed world does not make human rights and democratic rule a precondition of its aid and trade, then it is because policy makers choose *not* to do so. Arms exporters such as France and the United States may want to continue to flog their wares amongst the military regimes of the Third World, but they can no longer plead the Cold War as an excuse. For the first time since 1945, we have a real choice: Will we promote liberty or not?

GROWTH WITHOUT REDISTRIBUTION OR REDISTRIBUTION WITHOUT GROWTH?

Morality should dictate that the democratic world finally lives up to its ideals. But self-interest also should propel the world to promote a democratic agenda. In 1795, Immanuel Kant in *Perpetual Peace* made the elementary point that regimes matter. Kant reasoned that if "the consent of the citizenry is recognized in order to determine whether or not there will be war, it is natural that they will consider all its calamities before committing themselves to so risky a game." But where "the ruler is not a fellow citizen, but the nation's owner, and war does not affect his table, his hunt, his places of pleasure, his court festivities . . . he can decide to go to war for the most meaningless of reasons, as if it were a kind of pleasure party, and he can bitterly leave its justification (which decency requires) to his diplomatic corps, who are always prepared for such exercises."[2]

Since Kant wrote those words in 1795, no democracy has ever waged war against another democracy. Democracies have fought authoritarian regimes, and democratic citizens have sometimes seemed eager for war (as many appeared to be in the heady days of 1914), but no democracy has ever attacked another. Rather than spending billions or even trillions of dollars on the instruments of war, to prevent attack from former states of the Soviet Union, it would be prudent, cost effective, and morally more correct to spend millions on helping democracy to flourish in the old Soviet empire. The best guarantee of a peaceful world is a democratic world. As Kant wrote, citizens know that in war they are the losers, not their rulers. Therefore, if they have meaningful participation in their government, they will never willfully subject themselves to war's horrors.

Kant's wisdom, however, is not reflected in recent Western statecraft. Canada has spent $1 billion a year to contribute to the North Atlantic Treaty Organization (NATO) to defend Western Europe from attack from the East, but when Lech Walesa called to see what assistance we could offer to help Poland's transition to democracy, he left with a paltry $4 million. Mrs. Aquino ended the autocracy of Ferdinand Marcos, but then she was on her own. Democracy emerged in Latin America at precisely the same time that the World Bank and the IMF decreed that austerity was the way to pay back old loans. It would be laughable if it were not so tragic.

Ralf Dahrendorf captures this conundrum very well in what he calls the Martinez Paradox, named after the former Nicaraguan Minister of Foreign Trade. Under the Somoza regime, the Sandinista minister explained, the supermarkets were full, but no one could afford the goods inside. After the revolution of 1979, the shop windows were empty but everyone could afford what was there.[3] The revolution had transformed a world of plenty for the few into one of little for all. Nicaragua had gone from growth without redistribution to redistribution without growth.

Dahrendorf's point, which we must heed if we want the democratic revolution in Eastern Europe, the former Soviet Union, and Latin America to endure, is that citizens require both liberties and goods. Growth of provisions gives citizens choices. Entitlements or rights give people a claim to things. To create civil democratic societies, the Martinez Paradox must be solved: There must be access for all and plenty of goods.

This interrelationship between provisions and entitlements, between goods and rights, has been neglected in most development policies. This single-minded devotion to growth, while ignoring internal structures of power and the mechanisms of distribution, has meant that where growth has occurred, it has not contributed to the creation of civil societies. Individuals have gotten rich (usually through corruption), but the society has continued to be impoverished.

Even the most cursory look at statistics tells a depressing tale. It has been fifty years since the United States in Point IV and Canada in the Colombo Plan initiated large-scale development plans.[4] Yet of the 5 billion humans on the globe, the World Bank estimates that 1 billion are absolutely poor and live on the margin; 1 billion have increasing life chances (those who live in Organization for Economic Cooperation and Development [OECD] member countries) and the majority in between—3 billion—live in their traditional circle of poverty. For example, John Kenneth Galbraith, who helped President Harry Truman develop Point IV and was later appointed ambassador to India, concludes that despite all the effort of Western aid since 1950, "in the countries of mass poverty—India, Pakistan, Bangladesh, Indonesia, large parts of Africa and Latin American—the deprivation remains extensively unabated and unchanged."[5] Indeed, a recent report by Helmut Schmidt, the former chancellor of the former West Germany, demonstrates that in recent years the developing world has very much fallen behind.[6] Consider the following facts:

1. For the past five years, the net transfer of funds to the developing countries has been negative.
2. The level of external indebtedness in many developing countries has skyrocketed.
3. The gross national product (GNP) per capita in many developing countries has fallen.
4. Over the last twenty years, the gap between industrialized and developing countries has widened enormously: From 1965 to 1987, real per capita GNP increased from $140 to $270 for low-income countries, from $980 to $1,680 for middle-income countries, and from $8,820 to $14,550 for industrialized market economies.

Economically, the developing world is in a worsening state at the precise moment that democratic spark has finally burst into flame. This is no time for the traditional democracies to lose interest or to lose heart.

But why so little progress? The West has provided capital and technical assistance to the Third World, while ignoring the nature of the regimes. The elites and the oligarchies have spent much of the money on either the military or themselves. The trickle-down theory has not worked. Unless the traditional authoritarian structures are broken, "macro-economic growth means little for the mass, however satisfactory the International Monetary Fund may find the statistics."[7]

CONCLUSION

This is certainly the lesson of our own history. William Beveridge and John Maynard Keynes were wise enough to advance both rights and provisions at the same time. Wealth increased but was also distributed. It was distributed, not because of altruism but because democracy allowed working men and women a measure of power.

The precondition to solving mass poverty, according to Galbraith, is to break the equilibrium of poverty—the passivity or acceptance of fate that many traditional societies exhibit.[8] At a minimum, democracy is a means to stir people up. It requires participation. By giving responsibility, it demands involvement.

The first principle of development, said the Rev. Martin Luther King, Jr., is "to teach people to believe in themselves." Democracy does not assure economic advance—countries, such as Bangladesh have a myriad of problems to solve, but without democracy there will never be a fair distribution, and without a minimum level of distribution, there will never be a civil society.

So democracy is a precondition to distribution. But it has an added economic dimension that will become even more important as the world economy evolves. Peter Drucker has written most convincingly about the new realities of economic growth: information exchange, computer link-ups, and individual entrepreneurship. This transformation of the economy has, according to Drucker, as large an impact on government as it does on profits.[9]

Authoritarian societies, for example, have no way of coping with new technologies. How can you control information in the era of the personal computer, fax machine, and satellite television? The attempt to control information and to keep a society closed will inevitably have negative impact on technological development and, hence, growth. By enhancing individual capacities to create and to communicate, technology strikes a blow at autocracy. In this dimension, at least, economic progress and democratic progress run in tandem.

Analysts such Dahrendorf, Galbraith, and Drucker, then make a strong theoretical argument for the interrelationship between freedom and development. A recent study published for the United Nations Development Program, *Human Development Report 1991,* begins to make the case empirically.[10] The report develops a human freedom index for eighty-eight countries and concludes that "overall, there seems to be a high correlation between human development and human freedom."[11] Countries that rank high on the freedom index also rank more highly on the development scale. Political freedom unleashes the creative energies of people, which leads to higher levels of income and progress. "If a society is free," the report concludes, "influence does not always require affluence. Democracy is a valuable ally of *all.*"[12]

The release of this report, and especially the finding that the world's poorest nations are generally also the least free, has provoked a storm of controversy among Third World countries. Kenya's deputy minister, Robert Ramau Gathungu, for example, strongly questioned the right of the United Nations to publish the index,[13] and several Third World countries drafted a resolution to ban further publication of the human freedom index. This attempt at censorship has to be resisted at all costs. If the Third World desires assistance, then donor nations have the right to insist that aid be well spent. If freedom and a commitment to human rights is an essential component of development, then the donor country should insist upon incorporating these criteria into their aid policies. This may discomfit nations such as Zaire, China, Tanzania, or Kenya, but so be it. Such dictatorships should not be able to have it both ways: If they wish to suppress freedom, they should, at a minimum, pay the price of doing so without international assistance.

The argument can now be summarized: The world is in a democratic upsurge unprecedented in history. This upsurge not only conforms to the highest ideals of Western philosophy, but also is our best guarantee of a peaceful world. But this democratic moment will be fleeting unless the developed world helps newly emergent democracies provide both provisions and rights. And those parts of the Third World that have not yet adopted democracy must come to understand that democracy is an essential precondition to economic advance because it is necessary above all to break the traditional equilibrium or acceptance of poverty. To thrive, democracy requires growth; and to grow, economies need democracy.

The poverty implications are clear. Acceptance of human rights and democratic practice must become a condition of aid and development. The World Bank and the IMF must include political criteria in their granting policies, and rich countries such as Canada must become more generous toward newly emerging democracies such as Poland and the Philippines. The world needs more development and more liberty. We must accept the wisdom of John F. Kennedy that "if a free country cannot help the many who are poor, it cannot save the few who are rich." And we best help the many who are poor by insisting upon respect for human rights and ensuring popular participation. Our way is clear: We must put democracy first.

NOTES

1. For a spirited discussion of why Soviet communism failed, see Ralf Dahrendorf, *Reflections on the Revolution in Europe* (New York: Random House, 1990). An excellent eyewitness account of the 1989 revolution in Europe is contained in Timothy Garton Ash, *The Magic Lantern* (New York: Random House, 1990), as well as in Ash's *The Uses of Adversity: Essays on the Fate of Central Europe* (New York: Vintage Books, 1989).

2. Immanuel Kant, *Perpetual Peace and Other Essays* (trans. by Ted Humphrey) (Indianapolis, Ind.: Hackett Publishing, 1983), p. 13.

3. Ralf Dahrendorf, *The Modern Social Conflict* (Berkeley: University of California Press, 1988), pp. 7–8.

4. The Point IV Program refers to U.S. President Harry S. Truman's fourth point in his inaugural address of January 20, 1949, in which he declared: "We must embark on a bold new program for making the benefits of our scientific advances and industrial progress available for the improvement and growth of underdeveloped areas." [As quoted in W. W. Rostow, *Eisenhower, Kennedy and Foreign Aid* (Austin: University of Texas Press, 1985), p. 78.] The Colombo Plan, on the other hand, resulted from a 1954

international conference, spearheaded by Britain, Canada, and other commonwealth member countries, that sought to fashion a framework for multilateral assistance to the developing countries. The intention of this assistance was to ensure the economic rehabilitation and recovery of these countries. The plan itself was inspired by the success of the Marshall Plan for the economic recovery of Europe following World War II.

5. John Kenneth Galbraith, *The Nature of Mass Poverty* (Cambridge, Mass.: Harvard University Press, 1979), pp. 42–43.

6. Helmut Schmidt, "Facing One World." Report by an Independent Group on Financial Flows to Developing Countries, Hamburg, Germany (1989), pp. 3–5.

7. Dahrendorf, *Modern Social Conflict,* p. 14.

8. Galbraith, *Nature,* p. 61–75.

9. Peter F. Drucker, *The New Realities* (New York: Harper & Row, 1989), pp. 173–187.

10. United Nations Development Prrgram. *Human Development Report 1991* (New York: Oxford University Press, 1991).

11. U.N. Development Program, *Human Development Report 1991,* p. 21.

12. U.N. Development Program, *Human Development Report 1991,* p. 9.

13. "UN Index on Freedom Enrages Third World," *The New York Times,* June 23, 1991, p. 11.

Chapter 6

Theology and Economy: The Theological Paradigm of Communicative Action and the Paradigm of the Community of Life as a Theology of Liberation

Enrique Dussel

Take and eat, this is my body. (Matt. 26: 26)

This chapter relates the theology of communicative action—described in terms of dialogue, speeches, and texts—to the community of life as the manifestation of the human being's liberation from oppression. It critiques hegemonic "communities of communication," including those in the established church, for failing to allow the people to transcend the abstract solipsism produced by the regime of capital or the destruction of a rural community experience. Living labor, value, and cost should be central to contemporary theology; worship should be regarded not merely as an act of good faith but as both an offering and a product of human labor.

INTRODUCTION

With reason the European–North American theology has begun to give importance to the "paradigm of language," to the theory of communicative action.[1] Therefore, toward the end of the decade of the 1960s, the theology of liberation had to be delimited[2] from the theology of hope that was inspired by Ernst Bloch or the political theology that arose from the critical theory of the Frankfurt school. Today we should undertake once again the task of "delimitation" with respect to that which could be called a theology of communicative action. It is a task that is all the more urgent because at the same time it signifies for the

This chapter was based on a lecture, entitled "Liberation Theology and the Ethics of Community," delivered at Lynchburg College on April 16, 1990, as part of the Third World Lecture Series. Translated by Kern L. Lunsford, with the assistance of Vicki A. Lunsford.

theology of liberation a consciousness raising and an in-depth examination of its own development—and as a passage of the ordinary theme of faith and politics to the most current and pertinent in Latin America of praxis and economy.

By basing itself upon the paradigm of language and rational communication, the theology of communicative action (like the philosophy that inspires it),[3] has enormous resources and advantages but, at the same time, it has its limitations. If it is true that, as J. L. Austin explains it, there are ways of "doing *things* with words"[4] still those things (e.g., contracts, promises, etc.) will never be a piece of bread, a plow, or *material* instruments produced by labor. In other words, there are things that words cannot do although material things can be produced when someone orders his serf—the oppressed—to make them, but only by means of the mediation of the labor of the serf.

In the exploited and poor capitalist nations of the periphery (e.g., Argentina or Venezuela, countries that were until recently among the richest of the Third World, not to mention India or African countries, whose impoverished masses steal food so to eat and not die of starvation), a mere theology inspired in the theory of communicative action (i.e., of the language of dialogue, of words, of speeches, of texts, of conversations) is not sufficient.

THE PARADIGM OF LANGUAGE: THEOLOGY AND COMMUNICATION

In Latin America, thanks to a long experience of popular organization, there appeared at the end of the decade of the 1960s, first in Brazil (and from the movement of base education inspired in part by the pedagogical philosophy of Paulo Freire),[5] a so-called grass-roots movement[6] in which the simple people, some of them illiterate, can go beyond the situation of abstract solipsism produced by the regime of capital in the urban marginality or by the destruction of a rural community experience. This is an organization in which—thanks to dialogue, discussion, and critical reflection (using as a point of departure the biblical text, that is, an authentic, popular, and political hermeneutic)—these isolated individuals are able to constitute a community by arriving at an agreement based on their own arguments. It is a unique experience, because the members of the base communities are found outside of all of the hegemonic communities of communication in which they have not had any right to express their own voice.[7] It is in this context that the theology of liberation, since its beginning, has understood the church as a community of interpretation (to use the expression of Francis Schüssler Fiorenza), especially the base communities, as the most essential expression of the church of the poor. Thus, the entire categorical horizon of the theology of communicative action can be applied to an ecclesiology, a christology, an exegesis, and so on of a theology of Latin American liberation. The taking of the "word" of the people has been an experience on our continent by widening the horizon of argumentative critical rationality of the marginal, e.g., the working class, the rural farmer, and so on.

This fact that has been called consciousness raising, or argumentative consciousness raising of the political conditions toward a possibility of organized popular action vis-à-vis the institutions and their very essence for the purpose of structural change.

As a matter of fact, what happens is that the community of communication in the base is found in a world of daily life that seeks to be colonized by the economic system and by the state in a completely different way than in late capitalism: central, developed, and repressive. For that reason, all of the analysis should be done in a different way than it is developed in the works of Jürgen Habermas.[8]

In reality, the world of daily life suffers such a type of contradiction that the semibureaucratized state has no control over the disarticulation that the economic "system" of dependency produces on this world. Besides, there is no economic compensation that could make citizens the accomplices of a veiled but bearable system of oppression. Much to the contrary, the conditions of poverty, or horrible misery (from the nondistribution of wealth), are such that exploited members of the people have their own means to raise their consciousness to avoid being colonized so absolutely or obviously. It is on that "fissure" that the base community is established as a critical community of communicative action, and a "revolutionary consciousness" (or, at least, a deep dissatisfaction in the face of a repressive regime that has no opposing party of any type) is not impossible a priori.

Modernity, on the other hand, has not been realized since 1492 in Latin America; instead it has been a "disrealization,"[9] or the other face of modernity (like the world and system that pays for the development of European modernity). All of the Habermassian categories should be reduced to an essential reconstruction of a "world system," as Immanuel Wallerstein would say, and where "late capitalism" would be part of its system, within which it fulfills a function of a developed center of exploitation of the periphery. That categorical reconstruction would essentially, not accidentally, affect the categories because they would be redefined in their real function not only in the center, but also on the planet, which is the real concrete totality. By saying this, we wish to indicate the usefulness of such a theology of communicative action (or one that uses the Habermassian categories). However, all of them should now (and this is the first limit) be reconstructed, not only to be useful to the Third World but also to take on another meaning in the central developed world. That is, the economic system can economically compensate the salaried worker in the center, which would make the world of daily life "bearable," because the economic system is an accomplice in extracting the value of the Third World worker's salary by means of an immense exploitation of surplus value (value accumulated and stored in goods produced by human labor) and of international transference of the same. In Mexico, the so-called maquiladoras (in Santo Domingo, they are called duty free zones) pay a monthly wage of $80. Because of this, international concerns annually transfer $20 billion from the periphery to the center, and all of it coming from Mexico alone. This means that in only four years this country would pay off its foreign debt completely if this type of transference of labor could be accounted for, an impossibility in this capitalist economy.

Therefore it is difficult to affirm the following statement of Habermas for countries of the Third World:

> In the face of the pacification of class struggle carried out by the social state and the making anonymous of the structures of class, the theory of class consciousness loses its empirical references.[10] . . . Instead of anxiously pursuing the evanescent trail of a revolutionary consciousness, its objective would be to discover the conditions that would permit a reconnection of a rationalized culture with a daily communication that needs living traditions that nourish it.[11]

In the capitalism of the Third World, which is underdeveloped because of exploitation—80 percent of the world population under capitalist regimes (and from that can be diagnosed the failure of capitalism to develop in these countries)—society demands other types of analytical categories, and what in late capitalism is considered a mere juxtaposed system becomes the pertinent originating moment of human existence: the economic base (in an anthropological, ethical, and even ontological sense).

PARADIGM OF THE "LIVING CORPOREALITY": THEOLOGY AND ECONOMY

The paradigm of consciousness ("I think") was subsumed in a paradigm of language ("I speak"), which later was situated in a "community of communication" (K. O. Apel) as an *a priori* condition of possibility. As Aristotle defined it, a person is a living being (*zoon*) that has the capacity of speech (*logon*). Language subsumes all rational functions of consciousness and surpasses them, because, as Paul Ricoeur has clearly demonstrated, a concept is not the same world or discourse, and even the latter has a statute that is totally different from text.[12] The philosophy of language has made immense advances in this field, and theology cannot help but assume them. From there follows the importance and pertinence of the theology of communicative action to which we have been referring all along, above all if one bears in mind that the Bible is a text and that hermeneutics is an essential constitutive part of theology.

But what we are dealing with now—the result of an exigency that is imposed upon us by the reality in Latin America (as well as in Asia and Africa)—is that a person is not only language but also essentially and above all a living being—not merely as an irrational animal, but also as a living being always human. The logic of life becomes present in every moment of a human being. His own rationality, language, spirituality, and so on are moments of his own human life. These are functions of life. For this reason, before the person is part of a community of communication (and subjected to the same communicative action), he is already a priori a member of a community of life; and because of his being a part of it, there is a community of communication serving as a function of the community of life. It is this fundamental human level that we will call "the economic base," not as a "system" in Habermassian fashion (as a *Wirtschaftswissenschaft*) but as a practical and essential constitutive relational moment of human life in which are established the primary practical "relations," the production of the objects of life, their distribution, the exchange and consumption for human life.

The capitalist system is worldwide. The circulation of wealth throughout the world has a structure. In the analyses of the theory of communicative action, this dual aspect is not accounted for: The part (central capitalism, called "late" from an ideological point of view) is taken for the whole (the world system), which hides, first, the function of domination of the capitalist center and, second, the poverty and misery of Third World capitalism (*that should not be understood as exploited*), which cannot be explained in any way. It would seem to be a secondary question, but the capitalist system produces the ideological implantation of all of the categorical structure and, therefore, invalidates the meaning of what is analyzed in the center as well as in the periphery (that is, everywhere). We call this the fallacy of development, an aspect of "eurocentrism" that invalidates in part the Habermassian philosophy and the theology that uses these categories.

The first practical human relationship is person to person,[13] and it is the economic moment par excellence.[14] The economic is not only a question of market or money, but also one of corporeality, or the practical relationship of bodies (the master exploits the slave or serf, and the capitalist exploits the salaried employee) and the consumption or material reproduction of life ("lesser circulation" or *kat,exokhén* as Karl Marx said).[15] "Hunger" as necessity is the point of departure of economy with respect to the essence of the market. And in capitalism, "hunger without money is not a market, because it is not solvent." On this rests the problem: If the hungry have no money because the system does not permit them to work and therefore earn a salary, how can they be fed? And the system of Third World capitalism, because it is a system exploited by central capitalism (that is, the latter transfers value in a structural way)[16] and unable to accumulate sufficient value, has only "weak" capital. That is, it cannot absorb the totality of the population as salaried; as a consequence, it overexploits [17] by the force of labor with very low salaries that do not create a sufficient national market. The result is a capitalist economy of misery to which the Habermassian categories cannot be applied (because the world of daily life and the systems respond to a logic and to a crisis that are completely different from those of central capitalism, which is euphemistically described as "late").

The second relationship of the economic base is that of person to person nature by means of labor. In this case, living labor is subsumed in the institutionalized totality of capital.[18,19] Only in this case can the worker work because other possibilities for exercising that right have been taken away. The process of labor is the second moment of transformation (change of form) of nature as a product (the "bread" to which we will refer later).

The economic statute of the product can be described in many ways. In the first place, living labor materializes part of its life (the objectified value) into the product, a property of capital by means of the same process of production (that equally subsumes technology and competition among capital, which determines the obsolescence of the worst technologies and allows to stand only the most productive ones and, thence, the permanent technological revolution of capitalism). In the second place, because of the competition among capital, and also among nations, a transfer of value can be produced, which, in fact, it is. This phenomenon of impoverishment of Third World national capital is of the greatest importance and can be discovered only if one takes into account the Marxist category of value, which is so essential for the underdeveloped countries. It is here that a theology of communicative action remains limited to the region known as the United States and Europe, including Eastern Europe emancipated from Stalinism (13 percent of the present world population). A theology of liberation that strives to place repression in its world context cannot be circumscribed *only* by the paradigm of communicative action or by communication in general (and in view of this, merit cannot be denied to this progressive and very important theology).

LIVING LABOR, VALUE, AND COST

Living labor, value, and cost should be a central aspect of contemporary theology. The question of the "theory of value"[20] is not only a theoretical problem, but also the necessary categorical mediation to connect the capitalist market, which has shown itself to be very efficient but not necessarily moral with human life and personal dignity. In effect, their market is the place where products are transformed into merchandise and where they acquire their cost that will be the determination of value in money for an anthropological and ethical doctrine like that of Marx.[21] Even for the marginalists (William Jevons, Karl Menger, or Leon Waldras), cost would be simply that which is valued according to how much it is desired or needed by the buyer (although this need is not that of the producer). For a theory in which a human being is the absolute (and to transform or use him as a thing or merchandise is considered a fetishistic inversion that constitutes sin from a theological point of view),[22] it is important to reconnect the market, that is, the cost of merchandise to the human subject (living labor). The only way of articulating the relationship of labor to the cost of merchandise is by the mediation of value. The value is in the product (and in the merchandise and therefore in the cost), which is the same objectified human life. The central question in the intent—and this is my interpretation—of the author of *Das Kapital* (an economist who, as we will prove in a future work, developed a negative or metaphorical theology in its strong meaning, as

Ricoeur would say) was Marx being able to articulate the exchange of goods or market matters or the subjectivity of the producer (that is, the worker)[23] by basing each category or moment of method on a previous one, and all, lastly, on living labor. Not until 1872 did Marx distinguish value in general from the concept of value of exchange when he prepared the second edition of *Das Kapital.* For his concept of value, the essential distinction is not between concrete and abstract work but between living labor and objectified (dead) labor. Living work is not valuable because it is the "creative source of value from the nothingness" of capital (a creationist position of Schelling[24]). The force of labor indeed has value because it assumes the means of subsistence that the worker consumes for the reproduction of his capacity for labor. Value is then life, but *objectified* life. It is not life itself as subjectivity but as an activity that, nevertheless, is found in absolute poverty.

In an anthropological view—and beyond the humanist view—of Marx's position, it can be discovered that in reality the latter analyzed the totality of the moments of economy as an unfolding of the human being. Capital (in the anthropological and ethical view of Marx) is the fruit of accumulation, whose being is the nonbeing of the worker, whose reifying realization is human "disrealization," death, perversion, and ethical injustice (not merely moral):

> This process of realization [of capital] is at one and the same time the process of disrealization [Entwirklichungs] of labor. Labor is given objectively, but it posits this objectivity as its own Non-being or as the Being of its Non-being: capital.[25]

In 1871, Jevons published *The Theory of Political Economy,*[26] only four years after the appearance of Marx's *Das Kapital.* The former work produces the beginning of the "inversion" that is at the base of all contemporary capitalist economics—of "marginalism" and of the theologies that follow. Jevons says:

> The science of Political Economy rests upon a few notions of an apparently simple character. Utility, wealth, value, commodity, labor, land, capital are the elements of the subject. Value depends entirely upon utility. Prevailing opinions make labour rather than utility the origin of value; and there are even those who distinctly assert that labour is the cause of value.[27]

The determination of value has as its base pleasure or pain,[28] the feeling[29] of the buyer of the merchandise; for greater pleasure or feeling (or necessity but in a subjective sense and bound to the market, fashion, etc.), merchandise has a greater utility, that is, value for me, for us, here and now. If there is a variation in the feeling, then that determines a certain variation in the value (determined for its part of supply and demand and by the abundance and scarcity of merchandise). For this reason, "pleasure and pain are undoubtedly the ultimate objects of the Calculus of Economics,"[30] and "the degree of utility" determines that of value (especially the "final or ultimate degree of utility"[31]). Therefore, Jevons believes Adam Smith is wrong when he thinks that "labour was the first price, the original purchase-money that was paid for all things."[32]

Thus, a complete inversion has been produced. From living labor and the person as a point of departure, we pass now to the market or to capital as said foundation. This fetishistic inversion (theologically it is the idolatry and the atheism of the living God and his creatures: the human being as the absolute criterion of all economics) is consummated when one thinks that to still talk about value is to unnecessarily complicate things. With Marshall, Hayek, and Friedman, it is only necessary to refer to cost; the fetishization is complete. The last of the above authors says to us in the chapter entitled "The Power of the Market" in his work *Free to Choose:*

> Costs play three roles in the organization of economic activity: first, they transmit information; second, they provide stimulus to adopt more cost-efficient means of production; third, they determine who obtains the different quantities of the product—the so-called income distribution.[33]

Now the whole discourse (and also the theological discourses that depend on this type of analysis)[34] begins from its only founding principle: the market, capital. Science—which in Max Weber received absolute independence from anthropology, from the person, and from ethics[35]—begins from the horizon of capital and the market as something already given and as natural facts as we saw in Smith[36] and in Rawls. For Friedman, inequality (the most serious problem for Marx to resolve, because of the rationality of the economy, in order to determine the foundation of injustice or of unpaid labor) is now a matter of simple chance (the purely irrational and contradictory to all reason):

> Chance determines our genes. Chance determines the type of family and cultural context into which we are born, and consequently, *our opportunities to develop our physical and mental capacities.* Chance fixes equally other resources that we may inherit from our parents or other benefactors.[37]

As we have already expressed with respect to Rawls and equally with Friedman, it is pure chance that one person is born the son of a New York millionaire and another the child of a New Delhi beggar. Theologically, there exists an ethical exigency with respect to whether that historical initial difference should later be remedied. Chance does not justify that the differences ethically should be maintained (of course, their elimination is concomitant with new difficulties, such as duty to create new types of differences in the new social organization). At any rate, chance should not be confused with nature (nor believed to be irremovable, immutable, or untouchable, as are the pariahs of India).

THE "WORSHIP" OF THE FETISH
AND EUCHARISTIC SACRAMENTALITY

Because we have dealt with this question of the worship of the fetish and eucharistic sacramentality in other works,[38] we will not devote much space to this topic.

In reality, Hegel writes in his *Lessons on the Philosophy of Religion* that for worship to exist, it is necessary "for me to be separate from God,"[39] and this is imperfect worship. On the other hand, perfect worship is "for me to be in God and for God to be in me."[40] This concrete unity can be realized only with "the certainty of Faith and Truth,"[41] remembering that the Truth is the All and that the All is God. Faith for Hegel is an act by means of which representation—not like thinking—affirms the believed object as the absolute idea—that is, the Being of God that is only represented objectively and not speculatively. This supreme act of belief, of which representation is the idea (very superior to the act of esthetics, but inferior to absolute knowledge is perfect worship):

> Worship is an act that has a purpose in itself, and this act is the Faith that is the concrete Reality of the Divine and consciousness in itself.[42]

This perfect worship, a moment of our understanding that approaches reason, is the central moment of the Kingdom of the Son whose supreme (and Eurocentric) expression is Germanic-European culture and the Christian religion, that which is the foundation of the state as one and the same thing.[43] In this case, worship (the liturgy) is an intellectual act and faith, understanding, representation, certainty, reason, and knowledge are all moments of knowledge.

Once the market or capital has been disconnected from living labor, the science of economics concerns itself essentially with fetishized problems within the horizon of said market (or exclusively from capital). Fundamentally, economics deals with the calculation of the amount of profit (the determining of value) without any relationship whatsoever with the person, value (as an objectification of life), or ethics (as a judgment on unpaid labor). The economy having been separated from "the world of daily life" (*Lebenswelt*) comes to be set up as a system.[44] In that case, culture and religion constitute moments of said *Lebenswelt*, and it is in relationship with the latter that theology effects its reflection. At any rate, the narrow horizon of the community of communication where communicative action is fulfilled cannot be avoided.

Much to the contrary, our intent is to show that worship or liturgy demands an objective material moment, a product of work as a relationship of carnality or corporeality, the Hebrew *basar* or the Greek *sarx* that was not the mere body (*soma*) opposed to the soul whose statute is, in a precise sense, *economic*. That is, it is a practical relationship (among the celebrant community and with God) a person-to-person relationship and a productive one (person-to-nature relationship through work). The person is not only a member of a community of communication, but also previously and radically of a community of life:

> They were steadfast in hearing the teaching of the apostles and in the community (*koinonía*), in the breaking of bread and in prayer. . . . The faithful lived together and they held everything in common (*koiná*); they sold their possessions and goods and divided them according to the needs of each one. . . . They broke bread in their homes and ate together (Acts 2:42-46).[45]

In this description we have all the elements of a theology of the community of life (as a subsumption of a community of communication), a community in which they ate together. Eating is neither an act of language (texts are neither lived nor eaten, as Ricoeur knows, although eating is celebrated with beautiful symbols) nor an act of communication (discourse is not eaten; Habermas cannot deny it, even though all discourse is always related to life, human life, and its reproduction). In this case, religion is not a mere moment of *Lebenswelt* (with its own intentionality), but it should be situated in an even more radical level of human life,[46] in a level appropriately called "economic" (that is, of practical relations, of work, bread, consumption, and the satisfaction in which consists the Kingdom of God).[47] Therefore, worship or the liturgy is not an interior act of good faith; it is an objective act that should count on an offering, a material of sacrifice, a product of human labor: "We offer you this bread, the fruit of labor and of the earth" says the celebrant in the offertory of the Catholic Mass. The sacramental bread—about which Feuerbach talks to us in the text cited at the beginning of this chapter—that can be eaten is material in the sense of the material of human labor.[48] Worship then requires a "pro-duct" (*Her-stellt*) of labor because of a transformation (change in form) of nature. That labor objectifies human life in the product and, therefore, said bread is already sacred at the outset. Biblically, objectified life was symbolized with blood[49] (which we call value in anthropological and ethical economy).

If the injustice of a contract taken as natural (Rawls gives salary as an example) appropriates a part of the value produced (as surplus value), then said profits obtained from the life of the worker should be judged as sin. Poverty, or misery (like that which is suffered in present-day Latin America because of a transfer of the value of capital from Third World countries to industrialized countries) is a wage of sin.[50] But this sin is invisible to the one who does not possess the categories that would lay bare this social relationship of repression (a relationship of capital as such and the relationship of dependency between global national and capital of the periphery and that of the center). In this case, the worship of God is as the prophet expressed: "I want compassion and not sacrifices." To deny the denial (i.e., negation) of the poor person, who in his flesh suffers sin (in his cold, in his thirst, in his sickness . . . all of which the Latin American, African, and Asian peoples suffer under Third World capitalism), is the worship desired by God—who has an economic objective, material sacramental statue such as bread, wine, oil, salt, water: the material of the sacraments that reproduce carnal and spiritual life.

On the other hand, the Devil (Satan, the Antichrist) lives off the lives of the poor, and the economic structures control the poor the same way as "the princes of the nations control them and the powerful oppress them" (Matt. 20: 25):

> These [the powerful] have the same purpose, and will deliver their power and their authority to the Beast. . . . And that no one could buy nor sell, but he who had the sign or the name of the Beast, or the number of his name (Rev. 17:13 and 13:17).[51]

By obtaining an economic perspective one is allowed to obtain a sufficient level of reality in which religion becomes sacramental, and corporeal; where practical concepts such as grace or sin determine the relationship between persons and of production with nature, and where the liturgical bread can be the bread of life. For this reason, by placing themselves in this concrete, real level, the poor suffer persecution and death—like Ignacio Ellacuría and his companions in November 1989 in the moment of the fall of the Berlin Wall:

> The hour is coming in which those who murder you will think to worship God (John 16:2).

In reality, the "worship" of Satan is consummated by the accumulation of the blood of the poor (because the poor must sell their bodies for a salary, and their objectified life, value, is accumulated as the profits of capital) or the blood of the martyrs who fight concretely to free them from the (practical-productive, economic) "social relationship" that controls them. Those "structures of sin" are historical; in them consists the essence of the Devil, the Antichrist. But a theology of economy is necessary—in its strong meaning—to be able to bring about a hermeneutic of this invisible being that is not apparent in the world of merchandise, the market, or capital as seen from itself and not from living labor.

This chapter serves an introduction to a more extensive work now in preparation.

NOTES

1. See Helmut Peuckert, *Wissenschaftstheorie, Handlungstheorie, Fundamentales Theologie* (Frankfurt: Patmos, 1976). Also see Edmund Arens, *Habermas und die Theologie* (Düsseldorf: Patmos, 1989); especially the following pieces: H. Peuckert, "Kommunikatives Handeln, Systeme der Machtsgteigerung," pp. 39–64; Francis Schlüssler Fiorenza, "Die Kirche als Interpretations—gemeinschaft," pp. 115–144; and Matthew Lamb, "Kommunikative Praxis und Theologie," pp. 241–270.

2. This task was realized especially by Hugo Assmann in his work *Teología desde*

la praxis de la liberación (Theology from the Praxis of Liberation) (Salamanca, Spain: Sigeume, 1973), particularly in his essay "Confrontaciones y similitudes" ("Confrontations and similarities"), pp. 76–89.

3. On Jürgen Habermas, we believe that the most important works for our purposes are *Erkenntnis und Interesse* (Frankfurt, Germany: Suhrkamp, 1968); *Theorie Des Kommunikasten Handelns* (Frankfurt, Germany: Suhrkamp, 1981), vols. I–II; *Moral Bewusstsein und Communikatives Handeln* (Frankfurt, Germany: Suhrkamp, 1983). Also see R. J. Siebert, *The Critical Theory of Religion* (New York: Mouton de Gruyter, 1985).

4. We are referring to Austin's *How To Do Things With Words* (Oxford: Oxford University Press, 1962).

5. See Dussel, *La pedagógica latinoamericana* (Latin American pedagogy) (Bogotà, Colombia: Nueva American, 1980).

6. See Dussel, "La base en la teología de la liberación. Perspectiv latinoamericana" ("The base in the theology of liberation: A Latin American perspective"), *Concilium, 104* (1975): 76–89.

7. As Otto Apel would call them in his *Transformation Der Philosophie* (Frankfurt, Germany: Suhrkamp, 1973), vols. I–II.

8. About his 1989 trip through Latin America, some have said that Habermas probably would have expressed confusion in the face of the reality of this continent. No wonder! His categories were thought out for "late capitalism," but not for an exploited and peripheral capitalism like ours.

9. See Dussel, "Comentario a al *Introducción* de la *Transformación de la Filosofía*" ("Commentary on the *Introduction* of the *Transformation of Philosophy* of K. O. Apel from Latin America"), In Ethik und Befreiung (Augustinus-Buchhandlung, Aachen, 1990).

10. See Habermas, *Theorie des Kommunikativen Handelns* (Spanish ed.) (Madrid: Taurus, 1987). v. II, pp. 497–517ñ.

11. Habermas, *Kommunikativen,* pp. 522, 502.

12. See, for example, Ricouer's "Qu'est-ce qu'un 157" in *Du texte a l'action. Essai d'hermeneutique,* (Paris: Seuil, 1986), Vol. II, pp. 137.

13. See Dussel, *Ética comunitaria* (Community ethics) (Dümusseldorf, Germany: Patmos, 1988), Chapters 1, 4, and 5. & English edition, *Ethics and Community* (Maryknoll, N.Y.: Orbis, 1988).

14. For Karl Marx, capital is essentially a "social relationship," fundamental practical question forgotten by those who criticize his putative "productivist paradigm." See Dussel' *El Marx definitivo (1863–1882). Un comentario sobre la tercera y cuarta redacción de "El Capital."* The definitive Marx, (1863–1882). A commentary on the Third and Fourth editions of *Das Kapital*) (Mexico City: Siglo XXI, 1990), Chapters 9 and 10. That is to say, "the practical" is the essential constitutive part of "the economic" (that can be relegated because of this to a mere "system" that is connected by means of "money" to the "world of daily life," as Habermas repeatedly states).

15. See Marx's *Grundrisse* (Berlin: Dietz, 1974), B. 570: "The small circulation between capital and the capacity of labor. . . . The part of capital that enters into this circulation—the means of subsistence—is circulating capital *kat,exokhén.*"

16. See Dussel' *Hacia un Marx desconocido (1861–1863). Comentario a la segunda redacción de "El Capital."* (Toward an unknown Marx (1961–1863), Commentary on the second printing of *Das Kapital*) (Mexico City: Ciglo XXI, 1988), Chapter 15 on the "Concept of Dependency" (with a copious bibliography and debate).

17. Thesis of Mauro Marina in *Dialéctica de la dependencia* (Dialectic of dependency) (Mexico City: Era, 1973).

18. There would much to correct here in the well-expressed thesis of Martin Jay, *Marxism and Totality* (Berkeley: University of California Press, 1982).

19. The subsumption of the capital of living labor from the outside is grounded in a contract, which is established by two sides: a violent situation (the part of living labor) and repression (the part of the owner of capital). In *Theory of Justice* (Cambridge, Mass.: Harvard University Press, 1971) John Rawls takes as his point of departure a formal and abstract situation but never descents to the real level of capitalism, where essentially the two parties of the contract are in unequal positions. Marx emphasized this point even in *Das Kapital*, when he writes: "A true Eden of innate human rights. What reigned there was liberty, equality, prosperity, and Bentham. Freedom!" (1873, ed. cap. 4; MEGA II, 6, p. 191).

20. See how Habermas treats this question in *Kommunikasten*, vol. II., pp. 477, 496. In reality, Habermas has only a "sociological" and never, properly, an economic interest. Therefore, he cannot enter into the present line of thinking we are introducing. The same will apply to the post-Marxist theology of those who follow in his steps.

21. When value and cost are disconnected, all of the scientific intent of Marx's theoretical work is destroyed. See Piero Sraffa, *Production of Commodities by Means of Commodities; Prelude to a Critique of Economic Theory* (Cambridge: Cambridge University Press, 1960). See also Ian Steedman *Marx After Sraffa* (London: Verso, 1981). The polemic of Ian Steedman, Paul Sweezy, Anwar Shaikh, and others, *The Value Controversy* (London: Verso, 1981), attempts to adequately show this disconnection. Franz Hinckelammert answers in his unpublished *La coherencia lógica de la construcción de una mercancía patrón* (The logical coherence of the construction of a merchandise pattern) (San José, Costa Rica: 1988), especially Chapter 12, "Las posiciones ideológicas de Sraffa" ("The ideological positions of Sraffa"). In addition, see Roy Bhaskar, *Scientific Realism and Human Emancipation* (London: Verso, 1986), especially Chapter 3, "The Positivistic Illusion, Sketch of a Philosophical Ideology of Work," pp. 224ff; George McCarthy, *Marx's Critique of Science and Positivism* (Boston: Kluner Academic Publishing, 1987), or Paul Rojas, "Das Unvollendete Projekt. Zur Entstehungsgeschichte von Marx *'Kapital'*," *Argument* (Hamburg) (1989), where the value and cost transformation problem is studied (pp. 208ff).

22. See Dussel *Ética comunitaria*, Chapters 2, 3, and especially 12 on capital as a structural, institutional, and historical "social relationship" of sin.

23. On this topic, see Dussel, *El Marx definitivo*, Chapter 10, pp. 2–4.

24. Defining living labor as a creative source rather than as a foundation of value created from nothing is a position of the definitive Schelling of the *Philosophie der Offenbarung* of 1841—a matter that I believe would have given Habermas another completely different interpretation of Marx.

25. Marx, *Grundrisse*, pp. 345–358, 411.

26. We will cite from fifth edition (New York: Kelly and Millman, 1957).

27. Jevons, *Political Economy*, p. 1.

28. Jevons, *Political Economy*, p. 28.

29. Jevons, *Political Economy*, p. 29.

30. Jevons, *Political Economy*, p. 37.

31. This "final degree of utility" (Jevons, *Political Economy*, p. 52) is the point of departure of the future "marginalisms."

32. Jevons, *Political Economy,* p. 167, cites Smith in *The Wealth of Nations,* Book I, Chapter 5. Evidently, Marx does not accept Smith's definition either because "cost" determines "value," and the latter is that which determines "cost." This criticism is found repeatedly in Marx (see Dussel, *Marx desconocido,* Chapters 1, 2, and 6), who writes : "A. Smith [. . .] confuses at times and at others displaces the determining of the value of merchandise for the quantity of necessary labor [and he confuses it [. . .] with the quantity of living labor." [See his *Theories of Surplus Value,* Spanish ed. (Mexico City: FACE, 1980), Vol. 1; Mega II, 3, 2, pp. 364–365]. The value produced in the "necessary time" is part of the value of the merchandise (because it would be necessary to add to it the surplus value); the "quantity of merchandise" that is bought with a salary (value of the capacity of labor) includes surplus value that now the worker pays for with his salary. That is, the value that is produced in the "necessary time" is less than the value of merchandise; the money that is obtained by a salary is equal to the cost-value of the merchandise. (In other words, the worker can buy less value with his salary than the value he produced to obtain his salary.) In this lies the theological question par excellence. If a human being is not the substance (effecting cause) of the foundation of the determination of value, then all economics become fetishized, that is, they are founded on capital and not on the human being.

33. Milton Friedman and Rose Friedman, *Free to Choose* (New York: Avon Books, 1979), p. 6. See also Friedman's *Capitalism and Freedom* (Chicago: University of Chicago Press, 1982) or his teacher Friedrich Hayek's *The Road to Serfdom* (Chicago: University of Chicago Press, 1976).

34. See, for example, the work of Michael Novak, *The Spirit of Democratic Capitalism* (New York: American Enterprise Institute, 1982), especially Chapter 2: "Theologically speaking, the free market and the liberal polity follow from liberty of conscience. . . . In this sense, a defense of the free market is, first, a defense of efficiency, productivity, inventiveness and prosperity. It is also a defense of the free conscience" (p. 112). See the work of Hugo Assmann and Franz Hinckelammert, *Teología y economía* (Theology and economy) (Petrópolis, Brazil: Vozes, 1989).

35. See the excellent critique of the thoughts of Max Weber in Franz Hinckelammert, *Las armas ideológicas de la muerte* (The ideological weapons of death) (San José, Costa Rica: DEI, 1977), pp. 64ff (English ed. Maryknoll, N.Y.: Orbis, 1987) This is all the more important because Weber certainly is under the analyses of Habermas (and therefore the theology that is constructed on his thought). In Habermas's *Economía y sociedad* (Economy and society) (Mexico City: FACE, 1984), we read: "We purport to speak here of economy in another sense. . . . We have, on the one hand, a necessity or groups of necessities and, on the other, according to the subject's evaluation, a scant supply of means. . . . It is necessary that the specific attitude of economic come into play: *scarcity of means* in relation with *what is desired*" (pp. 273–274). The coincidence with Jevons can be seen: The economic part is the relationship of merchandise with pleasure, feeling the "necessity" of the buyer in the market (it is not the "necessity" of the worker or producer, who was at the origin of the "producing" that which, because of not existing, came into existence by means of labor).

36. Smith says to us naively: "In that early and rude state of society which precedes both the accumulation of stock [capital] and the appropriation of land, the proportion between the *quantities of labour* necessary for acquiring different objects seem to be *the only* circumstances which can afford any role for exchanging them for one another . . . *As soon as stock* [capital] has accumulated in the lands of particular persons, *some of*

them [why?] will naturally employ it in setting to work industrious people . . . in order to make a profit . . . by what their labour *adds* [from where?] to the value of the materials" [*The Wealth of Nations*, I, 6 (New York: Penguin, 1985), pp. 150–151]. The only question that should be put to Smith would be: That "as soon as stock . . .," is it a state of *nature* or is it a moment and product of a historical institution? And if it is a historical institution, the problem of a priori "effect" that has no "cause" should be studied; said "effect" should not simply be accepted as an a posteriori fact of natural reason. On this rests the entire problem of a "critical" economy—that of the Theology of Liberation—because this "historical" fact is a historical and originating "structural sin." (See Dussel, *Ética comunitaria*, Chapters 2.2–2.6 and 12.4–12.10.) I think that this is the essential problem of all contemporary theology.

37. Friedman, *Free to Choose*, p. 13. "Chance" is the concept that replaces the "rationality" to which Marx aspired.

38. See Dussel, *Ética comunitaria*, Chapters 1.6–1.8, 6.3–6.7, 11, and 12; Dussel, *Herrschaft und Befreiung* (Freiburg, Switzerland: Exodus, 1985); and especially Dussel, "Christian Art of the Repressed in Latin America," *Concilium*, *15*(2) (1980): 215–231; and Dussel, "Le pain de la célébration: signe communautaire de justice," *Concilium*, *17*(2) (1982): 89–101. This is a theme dealt with at length in the Introduction to Dussel, *Historia general de la Iglesia en América Latina* (General history of the Church in Latin America) (Salamanca, Spain: Sígueme, 1983), Vol. I, pp. 6ff, starting with the theme of the "conversion" of Bartomé de las Casas. Also, in Dusell, *Para uma ética da Libertacâo Latino-americana* (Toward and ethic of Latin American liberation) (São Paulo, Brazil: Loyola, 1984), Vol. 5, "Archeological Economy," pp. 87–99; or in Dussel, *Filosofía de la liberación* (The philosophy of liberation), Chapter 3.4.8, "Critical Materialism and Worship as Economy" (an idea that was equally inspired by Emmanuel Levinas and Karl Marx and, of course, by the New Testament), English ed. (Maryknoll, N.Y.: Orbis Books, 1985).

39. Hegel, *Religionsphilosophie,* in Werke (Frankfurt, Germany: Suhrkamp, 19), Vol. 16, p. 202.

40. Hegel, *Religionsphilosophie,* p. 202.

41. Hegel, *Religionsphilosophie,* p. 203.

42. Hegel, *Religionsphilosophie,* p. 218.

43. Hegel, *Religionsphilosophie,* p. 236.

44. For Habermas, the economic, like "money" or like "power" on another level, colonizes the *Lebenswelt*. (See the *Theorie Des Kommunikativen Handelns*, Vol. II, "Entkoppelung von System und Lebenswelt," pp. 229–294, and "Marx und Die These der Inneren Kolonisierung," pp. 489–547, in Spanish ed., Vol. II, pp. 215–280 and 485–501).

45. See the way in which we treated this text in Dussel, *Ética comunitaria*, Chapter 1, pp. 11–10. Equally, for what follows, keep in mind the work cited in note 9, especially point 4: *"The community of life* and the *interpolation of the poor. Liberating praxis"* (and even 4.3 of "the community of communication of *language* to the community of communication of *life"*), where we confront the position of K. O. Apel with that of Marx—reinterpreting the latter in light of his four unknown editions of *Das Kapital*.

46. Years ago, this question was raised in Dussel, *Religión* (Mexico City: Edicol, 1977), where we spoke of "religion as infrastructure." By not being able to attribute to Marx himself that type of categories (as "supra-" and "infrastructure")—or at least, they were not fundamental categories of his thought as we have proved in our commen-

tary on the "four versions" of *Das Kapital*—we should put the problem better at a purely "economic" level (but as *Oekonomie,* anthropological, ethical ontological, and not only as *Wirtscharfseissenschaft*).

47. See the concept of the Kingdom of God as "satisfaction" (in its carnal and spiritual sense, at one and the same time) in Dussel, *Ética comunitaria,* Chapter 1.7–1.10.

48. Marx has a productive meaning of "matter" (the theologian would call it sacramental). That is, the "cosmic" matter of a putative "dialectical materialism" (to which Marx never referred) is not what is important, but a constructing of nature as a matter of labor. [See Dussel, *La producción teorética de Marx* (The theoretical production Marx) (Mexico City: Siglo XXI, 1985), pp. 37ff]. "This nature prior to human history is not the nature that lives in Feuerbach, but a nature that, might be of one of the Australian coral reefs of recent formation, does not exist now today anywhere nor does it exist either, therefore, for Feuerbach" [Dussel, *La ideología alemana*] (German ideology) (Barcelona: Grijalbo, 1970), p. 48: MEW 3, p. 44). Marx is not interested in the "A priority of external nature" (Dussel, *Ideología alemana,* p. 48). He says to us: "This is the matter [material] in which his [man's] work is realized, in which he works, with which and by which he produces." (*Manuscript I 44;* MEW EB 1, p. 512).

49. "He who does not pay a just salary sheds blood." BenSira, Eccles.

50. See Dussel, *Ética comunitaria,* Chapter 2.7–2.8 on "the poor" and "death."

51. It is well known that Marx quotes this text of the Apocalypse in Chapter 2 of Vol. I of *Das Kapital* (Spanish ed.), (Mexico City: Siglo XXI, Mexico, 1979), p. 106; MEGA II, 6, pp. 115–116. This, and hundreds of other Biblical texts [see Reinhard Buchbinder, *Bibelzitate, Bibelanspieulungen, Bibelparodien, Theologische Vergleiche und Analigien bei Marx une Engels* (Berlin: Erich Schnidt Verlag, 1976)] show that, for Marx, capital was the "Antichrist," Mammon, Moloch—that is, the Demon. We will show in another work that this metaphor opens, by the semantic confusion that it produces, a "new world" (as Ricoeur would say) of unexpected meaning for theology.

Chapter 7

Liberation Theology and Human Rights

Michael F. Czerny, S.J.

The idea of human rights emerged out of the liberal tradition. Its starting point is the struggle between life and death. Those who are oppressed are its subject, and its goal is their liberation. The rights of the poor and the oppressed form the basis for a human community. In Christian terms, this community based on respect for life becomes God's expression of love. Although only God has the infinite capacity to love, only He has the unlimited imagination to foresee how systemic violations of the rights of the poor can give way to a society of justice, security, and peace. The role of liberation theology is to make sense of what seems contradictory and impossible; it sheds light on our task in the work for human rights and in the defense for life.

INTRODUCTION

I was born in what used to be called the Second World. I grew up, was educated, and formed in the First World, and now I live and work in the Third World. I am here from El Salvador, tiny and poor, its only claim on world attention being the decade-old agony of civil war through which it is living, indeed, dying. I speak to you out of deep concern that, as the Second World joins the First, the Third World is assimilating to the Fourth, and soon we will end up with no world at all.

This chapter was originally prepared for presentation at the conference entitled "Human Rights in the Twenty-First Century: A Global Challenge" held in Banff, Alberta, Canada, November 9–12, 1990, sponsored by the Faculty of Law of the University of Calgary. A book of the same title based on the proceedings of this conference, of which the original version of this chapter is a part, was published in 1991 by Martinus Nijhoff, Amsterdam.

THE RELATIONSHIP BETWEEN LIBERATION THEOLOGY AND HUMAN RIGHTS

The Liberal Heritage

Human rights and liberation theology should shed light on each other. Human rights has come out of the liberal heritage or tradition. Where the weakness of liberalism prevails and where economic and Social Darwinism is the only real law of the land, one gets the impression that human rights is yet another marketplace of so-called free competition, "a hidden way of protecting what has been achieved or what could be achieved by the more powerful."[1] But this fundamental treachery is the product of a particular history, limited to one part of the world, whereas human rights at its best enjoys a universal basis and expresses common desires of all peoples of the world.[2]

The splendid achievement and constant developments in human rights might nevertheless remain at the level of a false universality, abstract and absolute, insofar as discourse and even practice occur at a distance from the real conditions, circumstances, and history in which people live.

Human rights can be effective if, and only if, we are clear about their starting point, their subject, and their goal. The starting point is the struggle between life and death. The subjects of human rights are those who are oppressed, the great majorities, the repressed minorities. The goal is their liberation.

The Case of El Salvador

El Salvador covers an area of 21,041 square kilometers. Of its small but overcrowded population, nearly 2 million people "manage": They live the sort of security that one might call middle class, and a small pocket within them have great wealth and luxury. Another 2 million live in technical poverty—that is, despite all the work they do, they are able to earn just enough to ensure the minimum basket of basic goods and services and nothing more. It is the poverty of day-to-day survival. And another third, another 2 million, live in absolute poverty, unable to earn the minimum basket of goods and services. Yet El Salvador is internationally notorious; not for its poverty but for its war. And although we work very hard to bring that conflict to an end, I speak to you out of the fear that the war is our last link to the world and, once it is over, El Salvador will sink into the oblivion of an indistinguishable poverty in which all human rights are abused.

The Latin American Economic Council has predicted that in the year 2000, less than ten years away, the population of Latin America will be approximately 500 million persons. Of those, roughly one-third will manage to be "middle class." Another third will struggle in average or technical poverty. And another third will suffer critical or absolute poverty.

Time magazine's business section, in this case a reliable source, has predicted that 80 percent of Latin America is heading toward a poverty characterized simply as "Bangladesh." And yet in all of the Americas, only Haiti is listed by the United Nations Development Program as belonging to the world's forty-four poorest countries![3]

Both technical and especially absolute poverty generate the cycle that obtains major human rights violations in every circumstance. This cycle is one of exploitation, misery, protest, repression, violations, and often violence. Such poverty, which is the fate of vast numbers of people, needs to be turned into *the* priority in human rights and *the* starting point of our reflection. It does not mean that it is the only problem. It does not mean that the violation of other rights, not directly connected to poverty, should be tolerated. But it does mean that poverty is *the* starting point and thus *the* priority.

Human Rights as the Minimum

Human rights is only a minimum. Lawyers, philosophers, and practitioners perhaps have a tendency to inflate human rights into a world view, a way of life, a vision, a mystique. Human rights may become any of these, but essentially and primarily it is a minimum. A legal and constitutional minimum about which, after all, people should *not* have to worry. And were this a more just world, a minimum that should not have to be the subject of law and coercion. Let us not inflate human rights into a maximum that, it turns out, is only another masquerading form of individualistic, Western-style liberalism.[4] Of human rights, therefore, the fewer the better. Let the declaration wither away. Let the conventions and the treaties become obsolete. Let the courts go out of business. The best future for human rights is to become the real minimum that everyone can, literally, take for granted.

In privileging the rights of the poor, we bring human rights back to the minimum they ought to be—a minimum of us all. The rights of the poor many do not turn into injustice for the few. The rights of the poor do not turn into the exploitation, the persecution, the torture, the disappearance, the summary execution of the few. Quite to the contrary, the rights of the poor form the basis for a human community for us all. In privileging the rights of the poor, there need be no conflict either within the hierarchy of human rights or between generations of human rights.[5]

Discourse on human rights must begin with the right to life, *the* right precisely of the poor. "This is the basic intuition in Latin America with regard to human rights. To see them in the perspective of the right to live of the poor, and not the other way around."[6] In Christian terms, Archbishop Oscar Romero emphasized this more than ten years ago when he said, "In my country cruel death is an everyday occurrence. The poor are being murdered. Peasants (*campesinos*) are being tortured, day in and day out, with the most extreme violence. What must be defended is the minimum. God's maximum of Life."[7]

The relationship between human rights and liberation technology is the relationship between this minimum and the maximum.[8] Human rights considers the human condition in terms of what is fundamentally, essentially, and nonnegotiably necessary so that life might be life. So that life might begin, grow, and develop in all of its dimensions. The minimum. The least we can and must do.

From God's point of view, life is *the* gift, it is everything. Life is *the* expression of God's love. God's gift to the poor is life.

Perhaps the best known and most oft-quoted theme of liberation theology is the notion of "preferential option for the poor." Only God can really exercise a preferential option for the poor and yet treat all with justice and with love. Only God has the infinite love to love the poor preferentially but not exclusively, and to treat each man and each woman on earth as a unique and beloved child of God. Only God has the unlimited imagination to foresee how systemic violations of the rights of the poor—that is, the many, the majority, more than two-thirds of the world's people—will give way to societies of justice, security, and peace. But the fact that on our own we cannot muster the love does not exempt us from the task that God gives us, which is to struggle to defend the rights of the poor.

The role of liberation theology is to coordinate or harmonize the divine maximum with the human maximum. Liberation theology sheds the light of Jewish and Christian revelation and, by extension, the light of all divine revelation on these unabsorbable facts of life for the majority of humankind.

Liberation theology makes sense out of what seem contradictory and impossible, what seems surely beyond all strength and all our resources. For liberation theology sheds light as well on our own task in the work of human rights. We are all called to take up this defense of the right to life even though it brings us into confrontation with the powers of this world and with the forces that tend to annihilate it.

CONCLUSION: THE HUMAN RIGHTS STRUGGLE AS A VOCATION AND A MISSION

On November 16, 1989, six of my brothers and their two coworkers at the Central American University were murdered by members of the Salvadoran armed forces for believing in human rights and the preferential option for the poor, and for living their faith to the full. Their vocation as human beings, as priests, and as intellectuals was to convert this truth—the facts of life and death for the people of El Salvador—into the truth and meaning in the university and in the society.

One cannot speak about human rights without speaking about a vocation and a mission. In the Christian tradition and in many others, too, to lay down one's life for the life of the poor can be expressed in one word only—Love. The defense of the life of the poor is love. The defense of their life, at the risk and the price of one's own, is love to the divine limit.

NOTES

1. Ignacio Ellacuria, "Historizacion de los derechos humanos desde los pueblos oprimidos y las mayorias populares," *Estudios Centroamericanos*, 45(502)(Agosto 1990): 590.

2. V. Ramaswamy, "A New Human Rights Consciousness," *IFDA Dossier*, 80(January-March 1991): 3–16.

3. United Nations Development Program, *Human Development Report 1990* (New York: Oxford University Press, 1990), p. 185.

4. Human rights confined to liberalism assumes that "liberty has as its proper subject each individual; each person is who can be free, and freedom is predicated formally only of individual person. Liberalism and individualism thus seem to be mutually inclusive." Ignacio Ellacuria, "Entorno al concepto y a la idea de liberacion." *Implicaciones sociales y politicas de la teología de la liberación.* (Madrid: Escuela de Estudios Hispanoamericanos, Instituto de Filosofia, 1985), p. 99.

5. Such conflict may be taken as further evidence of marketplace "competition" within a narrowly liberal idea of human rights.

6. Jon Sobrino, "The Divine Element in the Struggle for Human Rights," in *Spirituality of Liberation: Toward Political Holiness* (Translated by Robert R. Barr) (Maryknoll, N.Y.: Orbis Books, 1988), note 44.

7. Sobrino, "Divine Element," note 44. For a discussion of the meaning of the life and death of Archbishop Romero, see James R. Brockman, S. J., *The Word Remains: A Life of Oscar Romero* (Maryknoll, N.Y.: Orbis Books, 1990).

8. "The fact that philosophy or theology do not talk about the violation of human rights diminishes the importance of this question and at the same time makes their violation easier; the fact that the institutional Church does not do it brings about the same result. If, on the other hand, philosophy and theology took human rights as a relevant issue of social praxis (a redundant expression), they give this historical reality a relevance which would otherwise remain concealed to the benefit of the dominant groups or class." Ignacio Ellacuria, "Funcion liberadora de la filosofía," *Estudios Centroamericanos, 40* 435–436 (Enero-Febrero 1985): 58.

Chapter 8

The Human Rights Cause:
How We Can Help

George Lister

The United States' human rights policy as based on the United Nations Universal Declaration of Human Rights has become institutionalized and thus has improved the nation's overall foreign policy performance. Human rights progress in Eastern Europe, particularly in the last few years, has been astounding. News from South Africa is encouraging, but black Africa remains neglected by the media. Chile and Nicaragua moved toward democracy. Cuba continues under dictatorship. Guatemala and El Salvador have severe human rights problems. U.S. human rights policy can be improved by constructive, accurate criticism. Human rights advocates should oppose violations by both the left and the right. The human rights cause has become a peaceful democratic world revolution.

INTRODUCTION

We could hardly find a more appropriate moment to discuss the subject of human rights. The events of the past few years and the progress achieved in human rights in some parts of the world have been breathtaking and unbelievable, and they hold much promise for further progress. For one who has been an active supporter of the human rights cause for many years and participated in the development of our human rights policy for more than fifteen years, these achievements are most encouraging.

The discussion that follows consists of three parts, namely: (1) the origins of our human rights policy, or how things got started in the United States Department of State; (2) some human rights developments in a few specific countries; and (3) some concluding observations and recommendations as to how the human rights cause can be advanced. In so doing, it is hoped that interest in the

This is based on a lecture of the same title delivered at Lynchburg College in Lynchburg, Virginia, February 20, 1990, as part of the College's Third World Lecture Series.

subject can be stimulated and others will be encouraged to become actively involved in human rights work.

ORIGINS OF U.S. HUMAN RIGHTS POLICY

The current U.S. human rights policy may be traced back to the period of 1973–74 and a series of congressional hearings on the subject. After 1976, during the Carter administration, the policy was firmly institutionalized, and the human rights priority was injected into the State Department's bloodstream, as it were. During both the Reagan and Bush administrations, the policy and its implementation have continued to develop, with growing experience and expertise, building on past achievements and failures. Today, our Human Rights Bureau is alive and well, led by Assistant Secretary Richard Schifter. One of the most insightful things Karl Marx ever said was: "We are all accidents of history." In that connection, you may wish to read a copy of a 1988 speech by Ambassador Schifter in which he tells of his boyhood in Vienna under the Nazis. Dick Schifter has dedicated his work in our bureau to the memory of his parents, victims of the Holocaust.

Now, a few points as to what our human rights policy is and is not. First, our policy is bipartisan, receiving support from both the Republicans and Democrats. Second, our human rights policy does not imply any moral superiority on the part of the United States, which has plenty of human rights violations of its own. Nor does our policy imply any God-given right on our part to intervene in the internal affairs of other nations, although we certainly do have the right, indeed the duty, to include human rights considerations in the conduct of our relations with other governments. And, lastly, the human rights cause is universal, based on the Universal Declaration of Human Rights, applying to everyone regardless of race, nationality, color, religion, sex, or age. That brings me to one main point that I wish to emphasize: That our human rights policy has been institutionalized has improved our overall foreign policy. Obviously, we do not have a perfect foreign policy. But the human rights factor has helped to give us a better foreign policy, one that is more compassionate, more intelligent, and more effective. It has also become clear that an *honest* human rights policy can exert a powerful political influence in the international arena. And in an effort to establish honesty and candor in this policy, we prepare an annual human rights report on every country in the world, as mandated by law.

In recent years, many other governments have established human rights bureaus or sections, and the subject of human rights has become a daily topic of discussion and debate in the United Nations and in other international fora.

HUMAN RIGHTS DEVELOPMENTS ABROAD

We will now look at the human rights situation in specific countries. Of course, this is a subject that cannot be covered adequately in a few sentences. For those who wish a more detailed discussion, the State Department's annual reports are recommended.

First, a look at Eastern Europe and the former Soviet Union. For one who has spent many years working on East European affairs, including five years in the Soviet Union and Poland, the events of the past few years are astounding if not miraculous. Poland, Hungary, Czechoslovakia, East Germany, Bulgaria, Romania, Lithuania, Latvia, Estonia, and the Soviet Union—a cascade of surprises beginning with the morning newspapers, continuing with the hundreds of cables pouring in from our embassies, and then still more sensational news on evening television. The years 1989 may well go down in history as more significant date than 1789, the year of the French Revolution. And some of the vivid pictures that have come with these changes are unforgettable: the demolition of the Berlin wall; in Prague, the State Department interpreter for Secretary of State James Baker breaking down in tears as he translated the secretary's promise to support freedom in Czechoslovakia, the country from which the interpreter had escaped in 1973; and the failed military coup that led to the rapid collapse of the Soviet Union under Mikhail Gorbachev. And some personal experiences have certainly been memorable. Now it is possible to talk candidly with visitors from the former Soviet Union, in conversations that would have been impossible four or five years ago. In the year before the Soviet collapse, a People's Deputy from Moscow was describing the economic problems of his country. Talking about the rate of exchange between the dollar, the pound, and the ruble, he said, in jest, that "it takes a pound of rubles to buy one dollar." Incredible. And then, a joke from the ranks of the Soviet proletariat: "We pretend to work and they pretend to pay us." For an old Soviet hand, it is very good to have lived to see these times.

Of course, one does not wish to imply that these dramatic changes in Eastern Europe are solely the result of our human rights policy. Obviously not. The main credit for this progress goes to such heroic giants as Andrei Sakharov and Lech Walesa, as well as to those countless others who struggled courageously and died in oblivion. But certainly our human rights policy has made a significant contribution to this breakthrough, and that should give us quiet satisfaction.

Obviously, no one knows what the future will bring in Eastern Europe, and the former Soviet states, which are faced with urgent, monumental, and complex problems. Let us hope fervently that the coming years will see still further democratic progress, accompanied by the consolidation of friendly relations with all of the governments and peoples of the area.

Turning to Africa, there, too, the latest news is most encouraging: for example, the release of Nelson Mandela following twenty-seven years of prison. This is another triumph for the human rights cause, one that is being celebrated by friends of racial equality around the world. Let us hope and continue to work for further progress toward democracy for all in South Africa. Once again, that will not be easy. Many difficulties and problems lie ahead.

From the human rights viewpoint, so-called black Africa is one of the most neglected areas of the world. For example, if a human rights activist were to be killed tomorrow in Belfast, or in the West Bank, in Cape Town, Warsaw, or Santiago, Chile it would probably be front-page news. Unfortunately, the same does not hold true, for example, for human rights violations, say, in Central Africa. The reasons for this are not entirely clear. Of course, with only twenty-four hours in a day and some 170 countries, a great deal depends on how much interest Washington has in a specific area of the world. Certainly, our annual human rights reports give equal treatment and attention to black Africa, and dedicated human rights groups, such as Amnesty International and Africa Watch do so as well. However, the area may be somewhat neglected by the media and the general public in the West. Also, there may be reluctance on the part of some to criticize black governments.

Shifting to Latin America, Chile is a country that has long been a center of world human rights attention. After the Pinochet military dictatorship had established itself, the Chilean Communist party did its best to show that the only possible course of action was violence—the overthrow of the dictatorship. And, as our human rights policy developed, both Moscow and Havana made frequent broadcasts to Latin America claiming that our support for human rights was simply imperialist propaganda, because we were allegedly keeping the Pinochet regime in power. There comes to mind a personal experience during one visit to Santiago a few years ago, while walking through a slum area with a human rights activist of the Chilean Catholic church. After some minutes of strolling past the humble dwellings of those who live their lives in quiet desperation, we came to a large sign, painted on a wall with the hammer and sickle of the Communist party. The sign read, "La Unica Solucion—Revolucion" ("The only solution—Revolution"). It turned out that the sign was wrong, fortunately. There was a much better solution than revolution. The State Department worked hard, in cooperation with human rights activists in Chile, to make clear our strong support for human rights and a democratic solution. And, in 1988, a plebiscite indicated the Chilean people's wish for fair elections. In December 1989, those elections were held and a democratic government assumed power shortly thereafter.

Before we leave Chile, let us return to the Santiago slums. Does the inauguration of a democratically elected government solve the problems of the miserable and underprivileged? Of course not. But it certainly does offer more hope for progress than does violence or dictatorship, right wing or left wing.

Another Latin American country that has had many human rights problems is Cuba, but thus far there has been no democratic solution there. For a long time, the Castro regime survived through massive Soviet economic and military assistance, estimated to have been $5 billion and $1.5 billion, respectively, as recently as 1988. The Cuban dictatorship is certainly the most repressive in this hemisphere, and there are no indications that Castro intends to permit either perestroika or glasnost in Cuba. Indeed, if anything, there has been a crackdown in recent years. Moreover, Cuban propaganda has been hostile toward what it sees as a betrayal of socialism in Eastern Europe and the former Soviet Union. Of course, a plebiscite and honest elections are just as important in Cuba as they were in Chile, but thus far the Castro response has been to circle the wagons and to remain in growing isolation. Some now refer to Cuba as "the Albania of the Caribbean."

Still another country with severe human rights problems is Guatemala, a beautiful land with a tragic history. In January 1986, the Guatemalan government invited me to the inauguration of President Vinicio Cerezo, the Christian Democratic candidate who had won in fair elections, following twenty years of military rule. We had been friends for several years prior to his victory, cooperating on human rights problems. While in the capital city, I had the opportunity to meet with an elderly Guatemalan woman whose son had "disappeared," as they say. We had long been in contact but had never met. During our conversation, she suggested that it might be helpful for her to introduce me to a Guatemalan woman active in human rights. Within a short time that woman came to my hotel room. I greeted her warmly and expressed the hope that now, with the election of Cerezo, our two democratic governments could cooperate closely on human rights problems. My visitor eyed me coldly and asked me to identify the second democratic government. I explained that I was with the U.S. State Department and working on human rights. Whereupon the woman responded: "Your President Reagan is a fascist." I stared at the woman for some seconds and then inquired as to whether she had ever been to the United States. She said she had not, but that she hoped to do so soon. I urged her to stay as long as possible, and I predicted that she would then discover that we have many shortcomings, and certainly many problems, but that fascism is not one of them. After another minute of conversation, the woman simply turned away and left the room. My elderly friend was dismayed and, of course, I was surprised and disappointed. But, obviously, not everyone welcomes the opportunity to cooperate with us on human rights. Unfortunately, human rights violations continue to be a major problem in Guatemala as set forth in detail in our human rights report.

Concerning Nicaragua, as you know, elections in February 1990 led Violeta Chamorro to become the new president, marking the end of more than ten years of Sandinista rule. The people of Nicaragua have made their decision on the basis of what they wanted, not on the preferences of Havana, Washington, or Moscow. The whole Nicaraguan tragedy of the past ten years could have been avoided if the Sandinistas had lived up to their promises, when they came to power in 1979, to hold fair elections. The Carter administration was eager to cooperate with the Sandinistas but was soured by the latter's manipulation of control, which resulted in the entrenchment of a small clique of leaders. The 1990 elections were generally regarded by international observers as fair and honest and a step toward genuine democracy. That was the wish of the majority of the Nicaraguan people and certainly the objective of the State Department.

Lastly, a brief comment on El Salvador. Many of you know of the November 1989 murders of Father Ignacio Ellacuria and five other Jesuits in San Salvador. Father Ellacuria was a friend, and it is deeply troubling to reflect on how many friends of mine have been assassinated by the right and the left. El Salvador is a country with a tragic history and severe political, economic, and social problems. There are many human rights violations by the right, including right wing death squads, and the judicial system is very weak. However, there has been considerable political progress since 1982, there have now been several honest elections and a peaceful accord was reached in late 1991 between the government of Alfredo Christiani and the Farabundo Marti National Liberation Front (FMLN). The United States is seeking the development of genuine Salvadoran democracy, based on the free choice of the Salvadoran people.

The FMLN long sought to impose a Castro-type dictatorship. But the human rights answer to right-wing oppression and injustice is not left-wing dictatorship. The answer to right-wing death squads is not left-wing death squads. It was the FMLN that broke off 1989 negotiations with the Salvadoran government, tried to assassinate government leaders, and launched another bloody offensive. In an article appearing in the January 1990 issue of *30 Days,* a Catholic monthly published in Italy, Salvadoran Archbishop Rivera Damas was quoted as questioning FMLN sincerity in the negotiations. Also on page 12, Father Ignacio Baro, one of the above-mentioned Jesuit priests subsequently murdered, was quoted as asserting that the Salvadoran people saw the FMLN as the side more opposed to ending the war. And it is also relevant to mention the fate of Roque Dalton, the guerrilla leader who wrote the very moving *Poem of Love,* which described the tragic plight of the Salvadoran people. Dalton was executed in cold blood, not by a right-wing death squad but by a guerrilla faction currently represented in the FMLN's top leadership.

Finally, as recommended reading, there is the 1989 Congressional testimony on El Salvador by Bernard Aronson, Assistant Secretary for Inter-American Affairs, and our 1990 human rights report on El Salvador.

SOME LESSONS AND RECOMMENDATIONS

What are some of the lessons we can learn from the human rights experience of the countries discussed? How can we help the human rights cause? The following are a few thoughts and recommendations.

1. One can give careful attention to the State Department's's human rights performance. And, presumably, we all agree that there is nothing wrong with criticizing our government. But that criticism should be as accurate and as constructive as possible. The criticism should not be based on one's political preference, be it democrat, republican, or other, but should instead have a single purpose: to help the cause of human rights.
2. All forms of human rights violations should be opposed, regardless of

whether they are committed by the right or the left. We should all apply the same standard that we demand of our government. And, of course, we should be just as critical of human rights violations in our own country as those abroad.

3. All human rights advocates should oppose right-wing and left-wing dictatorships. And we should also oppose those political groups and alleged human rights organizations that support such dictatorships.

4. We should distinguish between the democratic left, or those who advocate profound political, economic, and social reforms to strengthen democracy, and the antidemocratic left, which seeks to impose left-wing dictatorship.

5. Lastly, those seriously interested should consider becoming active in human rights work, inside or outside the government or both. Sometimes such work can be difficult. When one is needed urgently on the phone, the news is almost always bad. And if one really cares about the work, it can be heartbreaking. But the human rights cause needs and deserves all the help it can get.

CONCLUSION

In conclusion, reflecting on the collapse of Communist dictatorships during the past few years, it seems clear that Lenin's "world revolution" of violence and dictatorship has failed. But it now may well be that another world revolution—the peaceful, democratic revolution of human rights—is on the march. And with the events of 1989–91 still ringing in our ears, and despite all the difficulties and problems that still lie before us, perhaps we would be justified in borrowing a line from the old leftist song "The Internationale" and proclaim, "A better world's in birth."

Part Four

Population Growth and the Environmental Imperative

Chapter 9

Population Growth and Government Policy in the Developing World: Lessons from Asia

Deborah S. DeGraff

This chapter examines the relationships between population growth, development, and government policy in Asia. It begins with an overview of population growth rates and trends throughout the world, presenting alternative viewpoints concerning the linkages between population, growth and development. Given this background, the chapter pursues the discussion within the Asian context, providing examples from individual countries. Emphasis is placed on the effects of population growth on development and of government policy on population growth. The chapter concludes by relating these issues to the process of democratization in Asia.

INTRODUCTION

This chapter examines the interrelationships among population growth, development, and government policy and draws implications concerning linkages between population growth and democratization in the developing world. The relationships between population dynamics and political processes and institutions have received very little attention in the demographic literature. Research in this general area has focused largely on characteristics of governments and political systems that render the effective implementation of population policies more likely. There has been a significant lack of interest in examining the effects of population growth and policy on political processes. The underlying theme of this chapter is that population growth and related dynamics have sufficient impacts on social and economic conditions to warrant serious atten-

This is a revised version of a lecture of the same title delivered as part of the Third World Lecture Series at Lynchburg College on March 5, 1990.

151

tion in discussions of the evolution of democratic institutions in the developing world.

The next section provides an overview of population growth rates and trends throughout the world and then focuses on fertility as the component of population growth that differentiates the demographic situations of developing countries. The third section presents alternative viewpoints on the linkages among population growth and development, the environment, and individual well-being. Given this background, the discussion is pursued within the Asian context, with examples from individual countries. Emphasis is placed on the effects of population growth on development and on the role of government policy in influencing fertility and population growth. The fourth and final section distills some implications concerning possible linkages between population growth and democratization in developing countries.

POPULATION GROWTH: DEFINITION AND TRENDS

To discuss population growth and government policy aimed at influencing population growth, it is first necessary to define population growth. A brief explanation of its components will facilitate the understanding of the phenomenon's causes and consequences. Population growth consists of three components: births, deaths, and migration. The change in population size of any given region or country over a specified time period is simply the number of people born during the period, minus the number of people who have died during the period, plus the number of immigrants minus emigrants. At the country level, in most cases the net number of migrants is very small and attention is focused on fertility and mortality as the primary components of population growth.[1] Migration often plays a significant role when analyzing the population growth of various regions within a country, such as rural versus urban areas in many developing countries or the Midwest versus the Southwest in the United States. At a global level, migration is not a factor; total population growth consists entirely of numbers of births and deaths. This chapter does not explicitly consider migration trends or policy issues related to migration.

Typically, in addition to considering the absolute change in population size, *rates* of population growth are derived, usually on an annual basis. Population growth rates provide an indication of the extent that the population is growing relative to population size. For example, an absolute increase in population of 100,000 people over a year, given an initial population of 10 million, has very different implications than would the same absolute increase in population if the initial population size were only 1 million. A population growth rate of zero percent indicates that births and deaths (ignoring migration) are just balancing each other out and that the size of the total population does not change. A population growth rate of 3.0 percent is considered very high and would lead to a doubling of population size in approximately 23 years if it were to persist. A negative population growth rate indicates that births are fewer than deaths and that the population is getting smaller.

Currently, the world is experiencing a population growth rate of approximately 1.6 percent per year, which, although substantial, is significantly lower than the historically unprecedented population growth rate of 2.0 percent obtained in 1965.[2] However, this global rate of 1.6 percent masks a great deal of variation by region and country. The population growth rate of the industrialized countries stands at 0.5 percent. In contrast, the developing world as a whole has a growth rate of approximately 2.0 percent.[3] At these rates, the population of the industrialized countries, which currently constitutes only 20 percent of the total world population, would double in about 140 years, while the population of the developing world would double in just 35 years. A few country-specific examples, shown in Table 1, further illustrate the extent of variation in population growth rates. Germany is experiencing population decline with a growth rate of −0.1 percent. At the high end of the spectrum, Kenya and the Ivory Coast are growing at the rate of almost 4.0 percent per annum, which would double their populations in a mere eighteen years. In between these extremes are the United Kingdom, the United States, and France, with positive but relatively low population growth rates; China, with a moderate rate of growth; and India, Mexico, Bangladesh, and Nigeria with ever-larger population growth rates.

There are two points to emphasize from the examples cited here. First population growth rates are substantially higher in the Third World than in the industrialized countries. Second, even among developing countries, there is a

Table 1
Selected Population Growth Rates, 1990

Country	Population growth rate (% per year)
Industrialized countries	
Germany	−0.1
United Kingdom	0.2
France	0.4
United States	0.9
Developing countries	
China	1.3
Mexico	2.1
India	2.1
Bangladesh	2.6
Nigeria	3.2
Kenya	3.8
Ivory Coast	3.9

Source: *World Development Report,* 1990.

great deal of variation in population growth rates. This variation across countries and regions can be more easily understood if placed within the context of demographic transition theory. Demographic transition theory is a conceptual framework developed to explain the emergence of high rates of population growth and the evolution from high rates to low rates of population growth. It is largely based on the historical experience of Western Europe but has relevance for today's developing countries.[4]

Briefly, the theory suggests that the demographic history of a population consists of three stages. The first stage, which covers the majority of human history, is characterized by high birthrates and death rates that result in minimal or no population growth. Death rates are high because living conditions are extremely harsh, and birthrates are high to ensure the perpetuation of the population. A Malthusian equilibrium is maintained in which short-term increases in population are quickly offset by greater mortality as the social, economic, and natural environments are unable to sustain a larger population.

In the second stage, a variety of forces, including enhanced knowledge and technology in the health field and improved methods of agricultural production, lead to a relatively rapid decline in death rates. With birthrates remaining at the high levels of the first stage, the population begins to grow fairly rapidly. The countries of Western Europe experienced this second stage in the 1700s and 1800s.

The third stage of the demographic transition is characterized by declining birthrates from factors associated with modernization such as a greater emphasis on the education of children and a reduction in child labor, increased costs of raising children, changing roles of men and women, and declining expectations for children to support elderly parents. All of these influences, along with reduced infant and child mortality, motivate parents to have fewer children. The fall of the birthrate, coupled with low mortality rates, eventually results in very low and sometimes negative rates of population growth.

The industrialized countries have generally completed the demographic transition and have relatively low rates of population growth, but the countries of the developing world are at various points of evolution in the transition. Although mortality rates on average continue to be higher in the Third World than in the industrialized world, the change from the extremely high mortality rates of the first stage to the markedly lower mortality rates of the second stage is already underway throughout much of the developing world. Furthermore, because the reduction of mortality rates in developing countries has resulted largely from the application and adaptation of already existing knowledge and technology from the industrialized countries, the change in death rates has occurred much more quickly than in the historical experience of Western Europe. This has led to a much more rapid increase in population size in this century than has been experienced previously.

This description of the demographic evolution of contemporary developing countries suggests that the most important factor contributing to differences in population growth rates and in the position of countries along the demographic transition is the level of fertility. Although substantial variation remains in mortality rates across developing countries, the extent to which fertility has declined is the key determinant of population growth rate differentials in the developing world.

To illustrate this point further, Table 2 examines the fertility rates that correspond with the population growth rates of the developing countries listed in Table 1. The ranking from the lowest to highest fertility rate is the same as the ranking from lowest to highest growth rate. The average number of children born per woman reaches a low of 2.3 in China, and a high of 7.2 in the Ivory Coast. In the absence of reliable historical data on fertility before 1960 in most developing countries, the high fertility rates in the Ivory Coast can be viewed as roughly indicative of pretransition fertility levels in the developing world. This provides an idea of the extent to which fertility has declined elsewhere. In contrast, the average number of children born per woman in the industrialized countries is approximately 1.8, well below the lowest fertility rate in the developing world.

The discussion thus far has established the following: (1) that population growth rates and fertility rates are generally considerably higher in developing countries than in industrialized countries, (2) that at current growth rates the size of the population of the developing world will double from slightly more than 4 billion to more than 8 billion in just 35 years, (3) that the strongest force behind this increase is continued high levels of fertility, and (4) that there is substantial variation across developing countries in these measures. The next section considers the implications of these trends for economic development and the standard of living of the peoples of the developing world.

THE IMPLICATIONS OF RAPID POPULATION GROWTH

The primary reason for interest in population growth is the potential for interrelationships between population growth and conditions that influence the welfare of current and future generations. One motivation for focusing on population growth is to understand the consequences of high rates of growth for economic development, social change, and the environment. There is a long-standing debate among population scientists as to whether the overall effects of rapid population growth are beneficial or detrimental to society.[5] Those who argue for net gains to rapid growth put forth hypotheses such as the following: (1) A larger population promotes a higher degree of labor specialization, which results in more efficient production; (2) greater population density induces agricultural innovation and increases food output per input of land, labor, and capital; (3) a larger population encourages efficient organization of markets; (4) a larger population contains more extremely talented people; and (5) population pressure itself induces advancements in knowledge and technology that are

Table 2
Selected Total Fertility Rates, 1990

Country	Total fertility rate
China	2.3
Mexico	3.4
India	4.0
Bangladesh	5.2
Nigeria	6.4
Kenya	6.8
Ivory Coast	7.2

Source: *World Development Report,* 1990.

required to overcome any potential detrimental effects of rapid population growth.

Although those who maintain the opposite viewpoint generally do not deny the potential benefits of population growth, they assert that such benefits do not outweigh the costs of the current rapid growth of population. Arguments concerning the negative effects of population growth include the following: (1) Increasing population density in rural areas may actually lead to less efficient agricultural production if plots of land are divided into smaller parcels through inheritance or household partition; (2) population growth rates in many countries are currently too high for agricultural innovation to keep pace with food needs, while more intensive and extensive cultivation leads to soil depletion, erosion, and lower productivity in the long run; (3) high fertility results in an ever-younger population with a growing percentage of very young children dependent on a shrinking percentage of working-age individuals; (4) with rapid population growth, cohorts entering the working ages are growing in absolute numbers and may experience increasing difficulty in securing adequate employment; (5) population growth requires increasing government expenditures to maintain social services and infrastructure, such as schools, hospitals, and roads, let alone improve the availability and quality of such basic amenities; and (6) rapid population growth is considered at least partially responsible for the severe environmental degradation that the earth is experiencing.

Although the arguments presented above are couched primarily in terms of detrimental macrolevel interrelationships, a second set of reasons to be concerned with high rates of population growth involves the potential effect on individual welfare. Reducing illness and mortality is a positive objective in its own right, so we focus here on the effects of high fertility on individual welfare. It has been fairly firmly established that maternal illness and death increase with frequent births, and births early and late in the reproductive life cycle. Similarly, closely spaced births have a negative impact on the health of infants.

Somewhat less firmly established is the idea that a large family size results in fewer resources per child (such as food, medical care, parental time, and schooling) and greater demands on children to contribute economically at an early age. Furthermore, the macrolevel effects previously discussed have indirect impacts on individual welfare as well. These factors can impair the development of children, both physically and mentally, thereby reducing their own welfare and limiting their ability to contribute to the overall development of their country.

A great deal of research over the past three decades has been devoted to understanding the consequences of rapid population growth for socioeconomic development, the environment, and individual welfare and to provide some sort of tally of the positive and negative effects. However, the issues are very complicated and difficult to quantify, and the answer to the question remains somewhat a matter of opinion. The perspective of this chapter is that current rates of fertility and population growth in much of the developing world have fairly strong negative impacts on socioeconomic development, the environment, and individual well-being. This perspective underlies the discussion in the following sections on population trends and interrelationships in Asia, the role of government policy directed toward population growth, and the implications of these for democratization.

POPULATION GROWTH AND DEVELOPMENT ISSUES IN ASIA

The discussion so far has painted a fairly general picture of the current population growth situation and its implications for development in the Third World. This section now considers Asia and examines some of these issues in more detail for selected countries. Perhaps more so than any other region of the world, Asia stands out for its size and diversity. The region constitutes 60 percent of the current total population of the world with slightly more than 3 billion people. Six of the world's ten most populous nations are in Asia—namely Pakistan, Bangladesh, Japan, Indonesia, India, and China. The populations of these six countries range from 108 million in Pakistan to 1.1 billion in China; thus, approximately one-fifth of the world's population lives in China. The remaining four largest countries in the world, as measured by population size, are Nigeria, Brazil, the United States, and the states of the former Soviet Union, with populations ranging from 110 to 285 million. The smallest country in Asia is Singapore, with a population of approximately 2.7 million.[6]

In terms of population growth, Asia is also characterized by a wide diversity. The population growth rate for Asia as a whole is approximately 1.7 percent per year, which on average places Asia further along in the demographic transition than Latin America or Africa.[7] The lowest growth rate in Asia of 0.6 percent is experienced in Japan, an industrialized country that has completed the demographic transition. The next lowest population growth rates are for

Singapore, Taiwan, Hong Kong, South Korea, and China, all with growth rates ranging from 1.0 to 1.3 percent per year. With the exception of Sri Lanka and Thailand, the remaining countries of Asia have population growth rates of 2.0 percent or more, with a high in Pakistan of 3.1 percent.[8]

It is also important to note the extent to which population growth rates have declined in Asia over the past three decades. All of the countries mentioned above with current population growth rates in the range of 1.0 to 1.3 percent were experiencing growth at the rate of 2.0 percent or more in the mid-1960s. This is a remarkably rapid transition relative to the historical experience of most industrialized countries. Furthermore, almost all Asian countries have experienced some decline in population growth rates over this period, although the extent of decline varies widely, and many countries continue to grow at a fairly rapid rate. India provides a good example. Even though the population growth rate has declined from approximately 2.3 percent to 2.1 percent since the mid-1960s, its population size will still double in approximately thirty-three years given the current growth rate. Similarly, the Philippines' population growth rate has declined from 3.0 percent in the mid-1960s to approximately 2.4 percent currently; but nonetheless, population size will double in just twenty-nine years if the current rate persists.[9] Thus, although the increase in population has slowed in most of Asia, and rates of growth are lower than in much of the developing world, many Asian countries still experience rapid increases in population size.

The declines in population growth in Asia have been fueled by declining birthrates. In 1965, the average number of births per woman in most Asian countries was 6.0 or greater. Currently, the only Asian country with a fertility rate this high is Pakistan. Since the mid-1960s, fertility has fallen from 6.4 to 2.3 average births per woman in China, from 6.2 to 4.0 in India, from 6.8 to 5.2 in Bangladesh, from 6.3 to 2.4 in Thailand, and from 4.9 to 1.8 in South Korea.[10] These figures suggest that even though fertility has declined substantially in several Asian countries, much of Asia is still experiencing moderate to very high fertility rates.

The variations in population growth rates and extent of fertility declines make Asia a particularly interesting region for studying population growth dynamics. Asia is also highly diverse in terms of the level of economic development, political structure, and culture. The majority of Asian countries have a per capita income of less than $1,000 per year, with a range from less than $200 in Bhutan, Nepal, and Bangladesh to more than $6,000 in Hong Kong, Taiwan, and Singapore. The percentage of total national income that derives form agriculture is as high as 50 percent in Bangladesh and Nepal, and as low as 10 percent in South Korea, with virtually no agricultural production in Hong Kong and Singapore. Several countries, including South Korea, Thailand, Indonesia, Pakistan, and India, have experienced a substantial restructuring of their economies away from agriculture and toward industry and services since the mid-1960s. Similarly, the extent of urbanization ranges from less than 10 percent in

Nepal and Bhutan to 70 percent in South Korea, while Hong Kong and Singapore are almost entirely urban.[11]

Asia also possesses a rich and diverse cultural heritage. Many different ethnicities and languages and most of the major religions of the world are represented throughout Asia. These factors, along with differences in historical circumstances and local conditions, combine to weave a multifaceted cultural tapestry with substantial variation in customs, beliefs, and practices within and across countries. Similarly, the political and institutional landscape is equally heterogeneous, with systems of government ranging from democratically elected officials, to military dictatorships, to authoritarian bureaucracies. These differences in culture, political situation, and level of economic development must be borne in mind in any discussion of population issues in Asia.

Before examining the population dynamics of selected Asian countries in more detail, we return for a moment to the general discussion of whether the overall effects of population growth are beneficial or detrimental. A very simple examination of population growth rates, fertility rates, and rates of economic growth in Asia indicates that those countries with the largest reductions in fertility and population growth since the mid-1960s have also experienced the greatest degree of economic growth as measured by increase in per capita gross national product (GNP). The increase in GNP per capita in China, Singapore, Hong Kong, South Korea, and Taiwan (and to a lesser extent in Thailand, Malaysia, and Indonesia) has been substantial, averaging 4.0 percent or more per year. The remaining countries of Asia have experienced a much more modest or a zero rate of economic growth over this period.[12] This ordering of countries by degree of economic growth corresponds fairly well with the ordering of countries by extent of decline in population growth and fertility. One cannot conclude that the lower population growth rates contributed to economic growth because the relationships are highly complex and it is difficult to establish cause and effect. Nonetheless, this simple example is suggestive.

Given this background on Asia, it is useful to focus briefly on two specific countries and describe their population situations and related conditions in more detail. Bangladesh is the first country to be examined, one of the poorest countries of the world.[13] As already noted, the population growth rate and the fertility rate remain relatively high, with only limited declines over the past three decades. Although Bangladesh is the ninth most populous nation in the world, in terms of land area it is quite small, with less than 2 percent of the land size of the United States. This leads to an extremely high population density and very intensive use of land for habitation and cultivation.

Bangladesh is largely rural, with only 20 percent of the population living in the urban areas. Levels of infrastructure and standards of living in general are very low. The majority of the population does not have access to electricity or clean water for drinking and cooking. Sanitary systems for waste disposal are almost nonexistent, roads are few and of low quality in rural areas, and housing conditions are poor. Infant and child mortality rates are high, and education levels are very low, particularly for women.

Bangladesh is also a very resource poor country, its only notable natural asset being fertile soil well-suited for rice production. Even so, the country has not been self-sufficient in food output for thirty years. In addition to this chronic condition of food shortages, Bangladesh is frequently plagued by episodes of weather-induced famine. However, the devastating floods that periodically besiege Bangladesh and contribute to major food shortfalls are not entirely natural forces. To some extent they are the products of human interention. Bangladesh is a low-lying delta area formed by the Himalayan watershed. Deforestation and soil erosion in the foothills of the Himalayas, have increasing population density, and expansions and intensification of agri-cultural production have reduced the capacity of these areas to absorb and retain rainfall. The result is an increase in the frequency and destructiveness of floods in Bangladesh.

Many government officials in Bangladesh, as well as others knowledgeable about population and development issues in the country, believe that the high rate of population growth is exacerbating an already difficult situation. Ever-larger cohorts are entering the labor force, making it increasingly difficult to generate sufficient employment. Agricultural expansion reached its limit many years ago and the contributions of improved agricultural technology have not been able to keep pace with the growing population. Social services provided by the government, such as education and health care, are barely able to main-tain existing coverage, let alone expand coverage or improve quality. The same holds for the development of infrastructure. Even a tremendous influx of for-eign assistance has not been able to significantly improve standards of living in Bangladesh in the face of the rapidly growing needs of the population. Although the causes of Bangladesh's impoverishment are many and complex and cer-tainly cannot be attributed to high rates of population growth alone, the rapid growth of the population clearly renders the improvement of living conditions a much more formidable task.

China's population situation provides another interesting example, one quite different from that of Bangladesh. China has experienced a remarkable fertility decline and reduction in the population growth rate since 1970. Before that time, the demographic profile of China was similar to that of Bangladesh, although the problems were not quite as extreme because population density was not as high and there was a greater endowment of resources. However, the absolute size of the population posed significant challenges to development, and the prospect of a doubling in size in thirty years was alarming. The decline in population growth over the past two decades has been associated with improve-ments in living conditions. As noted previously, the rate of economic growth has been fairly high over the past decade. Similarly, even though China remains predominantly rural, improvements and expansion in government health care and public health measures have contributed to a reduction in infant and maternal mortality, and life expectancy has increased to a level comparable to that of the industrialized world. Per capita food production has increased by approximately 50 percent since 1970, while average daily calorie consumption has also experienced a substantial increase.[14] Few would argue that these improvements in the standard of living are not to some extent attributable to the decline in the population growth rate.

The slowing of population growth in China, however, is not without problems of its own. The extremely rapid transition from very high to relatively low fertility, combined with the increase in life expectancy, is, in the short-run, producing an age structure with a growing proportion of elderly people. The implications of change in age structure are many.[15] For example, in the absence of a formal social security system, elderly parents traditionally depend on children for support. This will become increasingly difficult as the ratio of elderly parents to children increases. Similarly, there will be an adjustment period in which the percentage of the population in the labor force will be abnormally low, which may put stress on the economic system and on government revenues. Also, the type of health services required by an aging population are markedly different from those needed by a younger population, suggesting that a transformation of China's health care structure may be necessary. Furthermore, there have been social costs associated with the reduction in fertility that will be discussed below in relation to the role of government policy.

POPULATION GROWTH AND GOVERNMENT POLICY IN ASIA

Thus far, the analysis has not explicitly addressed the question of how fertility decline in Asia has been achieved. We have discussed potential consequences of high fertility and rapid population growth and have looked at specific examples of population and development issues in Bangladesh and China, but we have not yet examined how fertility decline has come about. Given that marriage is almost universal in Asia and that extramarital fertility is negligible, there are two avenues through which substantial fertility reduction can occur. The first is by delaying marriage, and the second is by reducing births within marriage. Although both of these have played an important role in fertility decline in Asia, the focus here is on the latter.

Demographic transition theory discusses factors associated with modernization that alter the costs and benefits of children and change people's attitudes toward childbearing. The theory views such factors as being responsible for declines in the number of children that couples desire. Such influences are certainly evident in many Asian countries. However, *actual* reduction in fertility from the pretransition average number of births requires the use of effective contraception or abstinence. Modern contraceptive methods, while by no means the only options available for fertility regulation, are largely responsible for the rapid reduction in marital fertility throughout Asia.[16] The use of such methods is much lower in those Asian countries with continued high fertility and population growth. For example, the percentage of women of childbearing age using modern contraceptives is 60 percent or greater in China, Thailand, Taiwan, Hong Kong, Singapore, and South Korea. In contrast, the comparable percentage is 26 in Bangladesh, 22 in the Philippines, 15 in Nepal, and 7 in Pakistan.[17]

Note that the rise of contraceptive use in Asia has not taken place in a political vacuum. Without fail, in those countries where the use of contraceptives is widespread, the government has adopted strong policies aimed at reducing fertility and population growth, including the provision of modern contraceptives and the promotion of their use. Almost all Asian governments have expressed a concern about rates of population growth over the past two decades and have furthermore expressed a desire to reduce these rates, but generally there has been a weaker political commitment and a lower allocation of government resources to this objective in those countries where contraceptive use is limited.[18]

Although government policy is not the only factor responsible for fertility decline in Asia, its role has been fairly well established. Thus, it is important to consider whether government intervention in fertility behavior is justified. Should governments have the right to adopt policies that are specifically aimed at influencing fertility? If so, to what degree should governments be able to intervene?[19] The question of degree is important. The provision of contraceptives and education about their use is a fairly nonintrusive and direct form of policy, although it is not the only type of policy that can be adopted. Other possibilities include advertising campaigns to promote a small family norm, pressure on couples to adopt contraceptives, tax incentives for small families, higher costs of education and health care for children beyond some limit, financial penalties for exceeding a specified number of births, and incentive payments for the adoption of contraception. Each policy departs to some extent from voluntary control of fertility, and each has been enacted in various countries of Asia.

The question of whether governments should intervene in fertility behavior with the express purpose of influencing the number of children that women bear is subject to substantial debate. We argue that if there are detrimental effects of high fertility on society as a whole or on individual children through the fertility behavior of their parents, then governments have the right to intervene. Given the previous discussion regarding the effects of rapid population growth on socioeconomic development, the environment, and individual welfare, it is argued that government intervention of some form is warranted in most developing countries. In theory, the appropriate degree of intervention depends on the extent of the costs imposed on society by high fertility and on the costs of the proposed interventions, both financial and social. In practice, however, it is not easy to determine where to draw the line between appropriate and inappropriate government policy. Most population specialists and policymakers agree that the provision of contraceptives and related family planning services to promote voluntary contraception is appropriate, while coercion to use contraception is not. However, the gamut of potential government policies in between these two extremes is open to considerable controversy.

To obtain a better understanding of the range of population policies in Asia, we can briefly review selected policies for a few countries.[20] In Bangladesh, government policy consists primarily of the provision of contraceptives and information, with limited propaganda promoting a small family size and the acceptability of contraceptive use. In contrast, government policy in China has consisted not only of the provision of contraceptives and related family planning services, but also of a wide range of incentives and disincentives, some of which are fairly coercive.[21] In the early 1970s, government policy was adopted in China that provided financial incentives for having few children. In 1978, the one-child policy was enacted that incorporated financial disincentives for having two or more children and brought extreme public pressure to adopt contraception and rely on abortion in the case of contraceptive failure. The 1980 marriage law *required* couples to use contraception. Since 1984, there has been some relaxation of the one-child policy, allowing for two or more children under certain circumstances. Although these policies have been highly effective in reducing population growth, the costs in terms of individual freedom have been quite high. Even though population policy in China has clearly been more effective in reducing fertility than in Bangladesh, some population researchers believe that an alternative mix of policies with lower social costs would have been equally as effective in China.[22]

Singapore is another interesting case. Since independence in 1965, the government has provided contraceptives and family planning services along with financial incentives and disincentives to limit births. By 1975, fertility had fallen so much that population size was projected to decrease if the trend continued. Government concern about the age structure, with a growing percentage of elderly people and a potential decline in the working-age population, led to the closing of the government family planning association in 1986 and the adoption of a pronatalist population policy in 1987. This policy incorporated financial incentives to promote fertility.[23] Similar but less extensive policies have recently been enacted in Malaysia with the objective of slowing the decline in fertility. It is too early to tell whether such policies will achieve the desired results.

The degree of success of government policies in reducing fertility in Asia has undoubtedly been conditioned by several factors other than the content of the specific population policies. For example, the status and roles of women in society are very important influences in determining the effectiveness of family planning programs. The low status and restricted activities of women in Bangladesh are clearly obstacles to reducing fertility. Similarly, religious attitudes toward birth control can play an important role. The reduction of infant and child mortality may also weaken one motivation for high fertility as parents need not compensate in their reproductive behavior for actual or antic-ipated child deaths. Furthermore, the extent to which population policy is consistent with and supported by other development objectives and policies can influence the effectiveness of the population policy itself. For example, policies that encourage people to remain in rural areas may undermine efforts to reduce fertility if land is abundant and children contribute labor to cultiva-tion.

The characteristics of political structures and the political environment in general can also have an impact on the effectiveness of population policy.[24] For example, political instability and strong opposition to the government may di-vert government resources toward consolidation and undermine the implemen-tation of population policy. Also, the degree of professionalism and cohesion within government bureaucracies will influence their capability to implement effective policy. The degree of autonomy of the government is also an important factor. The extent to which the government is controlled by a dominant elite may detract from its ability to formulate and implement policy aimed at larger social objectives. More generally, the ability of the government to penetrate society, both in terms of tax-revenue generation and influencing individual be-havior, is a determinant of the effectiveness of policy implementation. This is particularly important in the context of policy aimed at reducing fertility be-cause the behavior in question is so personal. The egalitarian character of politi-cal institutions is also important because this may influence the position of women in society, access to health care and education, and the degree of partici-pation in and interaction with the government. These conditions are all likely to have a direct bearing on fertility behavior as well as an indirect effect by conditioning the response to government intervention.

CONCLUSION

Considerable research has focused on documenting and understanding popula-tion dynamics in the developing world and exploring the interrelationships be-tween population growth and development, but little attention has been given to the role of population growth in the process of democratization. The discussion in this chapter points to at least three themes that relate population growth to the creation of democratic institutions and conditions in developing countries. Al-though these themes will not be fully developed here and are somewhat specula-tive in nature, it is hoped that a brief outline of the ideas will engender further thought along these lines.

The first theme views rapid population growth as a potential indirect agent of change of established political systems. The argument, very briefly, is as follows.[25] A high population growth rate, as this chapter has argued, may contribute to a situation in which a large proportion of a country's population perceives that a scarcity of resources is available to them. To the extent that political and social institutions are unable or unwilling to address such concerns about resource scarcity and allocation, internal conflict may arise between the people and the government or external conflict may arise as governments attempt to acquire more resources through expansion. Although the result of such conflicts cannot be determined a priori, one possible outcome is that confrontation between the governed and the institutions of government, or between national governments, may lead to the establishment of more democratic political systems. Within this context, rapid growth acts as a catalyst for democratic reform.

The second theme to consider is the role of rapid population growth as a determinant of individual well-being and the associated implications for democratization. The connection between individual welfare and democracy is a dominant theme of this volume, but it is not discussed in detail here. However, it is important to note how population growth can be viewed within this perspective. Stated simply, democracy involves more than political rights such as freedom of speech, the right to vote, to assemble, travel freely, and so on. In addition to this political dimension of democracy, there is also an equally important socio-economic dimension. For democracy to develop and persist in the long run, it is argued, there must exist the social and economic conditions necessary for individuals to develop their human resource potential to the fullest extent desired. Such individual development is considered a prerequisite to the establishment of democracy and the effective exercise of political rights.

As discussed throughout this chapter, rapid population growth may have detrimental effects on socio-economic development, the environment, and individual well-being and may therefore undermine the ability of individuals to realize their human resource potential. As such, rapid population growth acts as a deterrent to sustained democratization. Somewhat ironically, the alternative scenario discussed above, in which population growth is a catalyst for political change through conflict, can be viewed as the eventual outcome of population growth as deterrent to democratization if governments do not respond effectively to the demands of the people.

The final area in which population growth and democratic processes are clearly related concerns the freedom of individuals to exercise control over reproductive behavior. This topic has been discussed in some detail in the previous section on population policy. However, it is worth reiterating the basic concepts here. Limited government intervention in the realm of fertility behavior often serves to facilitate the realization of reproductive desires on the part of individuals. In such instances, efforts to influence population growth enhance individual freedom. In contrast, after some point, the greater the degree of government intervention in fertility behavior, the further removed is the population from a situation of free choice. Once again, the costs of intervention, which may include the loss of individual reproductive rights, must be weighed against the benefits in terms of socioeconomic development and individual welfare. And here it is important to note that the valuation of the costs and benefits of population policy is ultimately determined largely by the existing political system, which may or may not hold the creation of democratic institutions as a desirable objective.

These three themes are not exhaustive in terms of potential relationships between population growth and democratic processes, but they provide a useful foundation for further thought. This chapter has demonstrated the importance of population growth and population policy to economic development and to the improvement of individual well-being in contemporary developing countries. As such, it is argued, the role of population growth and policy should be incorporated into discussions of democratic processes in the Third World. The three themes outlined above are intended to promote the further consideration of these linkages by population specialists and analysts of democratization alike.

NOTES

1. Clearly, there are exceptions to the generalization that net migration is a trivial component in a country's population growth. For example, certain oil-exporting countries in the Middle East have experienced very large increases in population size because of immigration.

2. See Ghazi M. Farooq and Deborah S. DeGraff, *Fertility and Development: An Introduction to Theory, Empirical Research and Policy Issues* (Geneva: International Labor Office, 1988).

3. See World Bank, *World Development Report 1990* (New York: Oxford University Press, 1990).

4. For a more thorough discussion of demographic transition theory, see, for examples, John C. Caldwell, "Toward a Restatement of Demographic Transition Theory," *Population and Development Review, 2* (1976): 3–4; Thomas McKeown, *The Modern Rise of Population* (New York: Academic Press, 1976); T. Paul Schultz, *Economics of Population* (Reading, Mass.: Addison-Wesley Publishing, 1981); and George J. Stolnitz, "The Demographic Transition: From High to Low Birth Rates and Death Rates," in R. Freedman, ed., *Population: The Vital Revolution* (Garden City, N.Y.: Anchor Books, 1964).

5. Within the vast literature on this topic see, for example, Ester Boserup, *Economic and Demographic Relationships in Development* (Baltimore, Md.: Johns Hopkins University Press, 1990); Lester R. Brown, *State of the World 1984* (New York: W.W. North & Co., 1984); Ansley J. Coale and Edgar M. Hoover, *Population Growth and Economic Development in Low-Income Countries* (Princeton, N.J.: Princeton University Press, 1958); Geoffrey McNicoll, "Consequences of Rapid Population Growth: Overview and Assessment," *Population and Development Review, 10* (2)(1984); National Academy of Sciences, *Rapid Population Growth: Consequences and Policy Implications* (Baltimore, Md.: Johns Hopkins University Press, 1971), 2 vols.; National Research Council, *Population Growth and Economic Development: Policy Questions* (Washington, D.C.: National Academy Press, 1986); Julian L. Simon, *The Ultimate Resource* (Princeton, N.J.: Princeton University Press, 1981); Julian L. Simon and Herman Kahn, *The Resourceful Earth: A Response to Global 2000* (New York: Basil Blackwell,

1984); and World Bank. *World Development Report 1984* (New York: Oxford University Press, 1984).

  6. See *World Development Report (1990)*.

  7. See Farooq and DeGraff, *Fertility.*

  8. See Population Reference Bureau, *World Population Data Sheet* (Washington, D.C.: National Academy Press, 1986).

  9. See *World Development Report 1990.*

 10. *World Development Report 1990.*

 11. *World Development Report 1990.*

 12. *World Development Report 1990.*

 13. For a more thorough discussion of population and development issues in Bangladesh, see Brian W. Arthur and Geoffrey McNicoll, *"An Analytical Survey of Population and Development in Bangladesh," Population and Development Review, 4* (1)(1978); Mead T. Cain and Samuel S. Lieberman, "Development Policy and the Prospects for Fertility Decline in Bangladesh," *Bangladesh Development Studies, 11* (3)(1983); Rafiqul H. Chaudhury, "Population Pressure and Its Effects on Changes in Agrarian Structure and Productivity in Rural Bangladesh," In G. Rodgers, ed., *Population Growth and Poverty in Rural South Asia* (New Delhi: Sage Publications, 1989); and M. R. Khan, "Economic Development and Population in Bangladesh," *Bangladesh Development Studies, 12* (3)(1984): 1–18.

 14. See *World Development Report 1990.*

 15. See Linda G. Martin, "Emerging Issues in Cross-National Survey Research in Aging in Asia," in *IUSSP International Population Conference* (New Delhi: IUSSP, 1989); and Zeng Yi, "Aging of the Chinese Population and Policy Issues: Lessons from a Rural-Urban Dynamic Projection Model," in *IUSSP.*

 16. See East-West Population Institute, "Policies for Fertility Reduction: Focus on Asia," *Asia-Pacific Population and Policy,* no. 9 (1989): 1–4.

 17. See Population Reference Bureau, *World Population.*

 18. Rodolfo A. Bulatao, "Fertility Targets and Policy Options in Asia," *Asian and Pacific Census Forum, 11* (2)(1984): 1–4,8.

 19. See Bernard Berelson and J. Lieberson, "Government Efforts to Influence Fertility: The Ethical Issues," *Population and Development Review, 5* (4)(1979); Partha Dasgupta, "The Ethical Foundations of Population Policy," in D. G. Johnson and R. D. Lee, eds., *Population Growth and Economic Development; Issues and Evidence* (Madison: University of Wisconsin Press, 1987); and Ronald G. Ridker, *Population and Development: The Search for Selective Interventions* (Baltimore, Md.: Johns Hopkins University Press, 1976), for further discussion of the ethics of population policy.

 20. We restrict the discussion here to policies aimed at influencing fertility. Many other dimensions of population policy are possible, including those directed toward population distribution, mortality and morbidity, and other aspects of population quality.

 21. For detailed discussion of China's population dynamics and policy, see Judith Banister, *China's Changing Population* (Stanford, Calif.: Stanford University Press, 1987); John Bongaarts and Susan Greenhalgh, "An Alternative to the One-Child Policy in China," *Population and Development Review,11* (4)(1985): 585–617; Susan Greenhalgh, "Shifts in China's Population Policy, 1984–86: Views from the Central, Provincial, and Local Levels," *Population and Development Review, 12* (3)(1986);

and Karen Hardee-Cleveland and Judith Banister, "Fertility Policy and Implementation in China, 1986–88," *Population and Development Review, 14* (2)(1988): 245–286.

22. See Bongaarts and Greenhalgh, "An Alternative."

23. See Paul P. L. Cheung,"Recent Changes in Population Policies," in *IUSSP International Population Conference.*

24. Alwyn R. Rouyer, "The State and Fertility Decline in Low-Income Countries," in *IUSSP International Population Conference, 1989.*

25. See Nazli Choucri, *Multidisciplinary Perspectives on Population and Conflicts* (Syracuse, N.Y.: Syracuse University Press, 1984) for a further development of this theme.

Chapter 10

Addressing Resource Management Concerns: The Third World in Global Environmental Politics

Marian A. L. Miller

The global environment has, over the last 200 years or so, sustained significant damage. To reverse this situation and to maintain ecological balance, crucial decisions and actions concerning the environment need to be taken simultaneously and urgently by both industrialized and less developed countries. This chapter evaluates the global environment's current condition and the attempts to redress past mistakes through on-going negotiations in various international organizations and agencies. Issues in these negotiations (e.g., debt-for-nature swaps, technology transfer, and the toxic waste trade) are discussed and the respective positions of the industrialized and less developed countries are highlighted and elaborated. Finally, the implication of these issues on democratization in the Third World are discussed and illustrated.

INTRODUCTION

In less than two centuries, aggressive exploitation by the industrialized nations has destroyed significant ecological resources in both the developed and the developing world. Decisions affecting the environment are now ever more crucial. To restore the balance that will keep the planet habitable, circumstances demand action on several fronts simultaneously.

As actors in global environmental politics, the developing countries face a dual task. First, they have to protect themselves from developed countries who try to pass some of the costs of their development on to the developing coun-

This is a revised version of a paper of the same title presented at the annual conference of the Association for the Advancement of Policy, Research and Development in the Third World, held in Mexico City, Mexico, November 14–17, 1990.

tries. Second, as the developing countries continue to develop, they need to carefully address the option of choosing a less aggressive development path to slow or reverse environmental damage. They have to resolve the tension between development and conservation. Many threatened resources are important to their development process. These countries will repeatedly have to decide whether they are willing to forgo particular development options to protect the environment. This can be a difficult choice when the benefits of doing the latter are not necessarily immediately apparent.

This chapter begins with an overview of global environmental and resource issues, illustrating some of the development questions facing Third World countries. It then focuses on the oceans, particularly the Caribbean Sea. The issues involved in dealing with the ocean environment are illustrative of some of the concerns to be addressed and the trade-offs to be made in other environmental policy areas. The article ends by addressing the implications of these choices for democracy.

ENVIRONMENTAL OVERVIEW

The term "developing countries" implies that these countries are involved in the process of growth. Some of the citizens of these countries aspire to a level of development that will provide them with the standard of living enjoyed by the industrialized West. Various economic and political strategists point the paths to this goal. These strategists imply that the growth process is infinite and conveniently forget the price paid by the environment to support the development of industrialized countries. They believe that advancing technology can take care of any temporary problems. On the other hand, ecologists take account of resource and environmental constraints. They see growth as a finite process, because of the limits of the earth's ecosystem. The following summary illustrates these concerns.

Population

The global population doubled between 1950 and 1987, reaching approximately 5 billion. Another billion will likely be added by 1998. The United Nations estimates that by the year 2025, global population will exceed 8.2 billion: 90 percent of this growth will occur in the developing world. Population growth rates have been falling in many developing countries for more than a decade, but these nations still have relatively high fertility rates, and a large proportion of their populations is in the reproductive years.[1]

Although a country's population is an important potential development asset, that potential cannot be tapped if the resources to support the population are unavailable. Developing countries can draw on two generations of international family-planning experience. Countries such as China, India, Mexico, and Thailand can serve as models for different approaches. They can offer important lessons regarding what should be avoided and included in designing effective programs and in creating a social environment that is receptive to smaller families.

Food and Agriculture

Food and agriculture are related to population, because a rapidly increasing population exacerbates the problem of hunger. Global food production has increased over the past few decades. But because of rapid population growth and the inequitable distribution of food, hunger still threatens millions throughout the developing world. Over the past twenty years, per capita food production has increased in every region except sub-Saharan Africa, where it fell 13 percent, largely because of rapid population growth, unfavorable environmental conditions, and ineffective agricultural policies. By contrast, over the same period, food production per capita rose 23 percent in Asia as a whole, and more than 45 percent in China, Indonesia, and Malaysia. In spite of the success in increasing global food production, the number of hungry people is growing. In 1988, it was estimated at 950 million. Nations with a per capita income of $400 or less account for approximately 80 percent of the undernourished. Most of them live in South Asia and Africa. High population growth rates in these regions ensure that hunger will continue in the coming years.[2]

Having reliable access to food is an aspect of national security that is often overlooked. Developing countries need to rely less on surplus U.S. grain stocks, which may not always be available. They need to focus on making a transition from the colonial cash crop–based economy to an agricultural strategy that will allow them to feed a greater portion of their populations. There might be transitional costs resulting primarily from worker dislocation and infrastructure development. But the people employed in producing the cash crops could be shifted to production for local consumption. The experience of some agriculturally productive countries suggests that much of the dislocated labor force could be absorbed in producing for local consumption.[3]

Energy

The demand for commercially traded energy has continued to grow, although the growth rate has declined. Oil is the main commercial fuel in Western Europe, Australia, North America, and the developing countries. More than half the developing countries rely on imported oil for more than 75 percent of their commercial energy needs.[4] Renewable energy sources are unlikely to become major alternatives to fossil fuels in the next few decades.

Energy security is a major concern today; this issue is highlighted by events in the Middle East. As developing countries attempt to implement growth strategies, there is concern that the cost and availability of energy will be a major constraint. Economic growth does not necessarily mean a commensurate increase in energy consumption. Several developed countries have realized gains in energy efficiency, and a few developing nations are investigating ways of doing so. Understanding energy use patterns is essential for promoting efficiency and ameliorating energy-related environmental problems. Oil accounts for 43 percent of global commercial energy production, solid fuels 31 percent, natural gas 21 percent, and primary electricity 5 percent.[5] Approximately half the world's population, however, relies on noncommercial fuel wood as its sole energy source. Most fuel wood is collected on a noncommercial basis for domestic heating and cooking, so it is not usually included in official energy statistics. A shortage of fuel wood is the most important energy-related problem for many developing countries.[6] In some cases, fuel wood can no longer be regarded as a renewable resource because consumption rates exceed sustainable yields.

Forest and Rangelands

The use of wood for fuel is one major reason for the loss of tropical forests and woodlands. The other factor is clearing for agriculture. Every year, some 11 million hectares of tropical forests and woodlands are lost. In the temperate north, damage from air pollutants affects an estimated 15 percent of the total timber volume in seventeen European countries. In most regions, the area of land in permanent pasture is shrinking because of conversion to cropland.[7]

Temperate forests account for approximately 57 percent of the world's closed forest area, and they are expanding slowly with the establishment of plantations.[8] By contrast, tropical moist closed forests are being rapidly destroyed. They cover only 7 percent of the earth's surface, but they contain at least half of the earth's species.[9] In addition to the 7.3 million hectares of tropical closed forests cleared each year for agriculture, another 4.4 million hectares are selectively logged.[10] This is an area of concern because of the high rates of loss as well as the value of these forests in terms of biological diversity, wealth of timber and other products, and environmental functions.

Wood is the most important commercial product from forests. Nearly half of the wood is used for industrial purposes and the rest is used as fuel. Despite the low value of wood relative to its bulk, wood products are the third most valuable commodity in world trade after petroleum and natural gas. World trade in wood and wood products is projected to grow for the next 50 years. However, recent projections of trade in tropical hardwoods suggest that these timber resources will become depleted by deforestation and the slow regeneration of logged forests. Therefore, global trade in tropical hardwoods is expected to peak just after the turn of the century and then to drop significantly.[11]

Concerns about deforestation have been voiced by leaders throughout the Caribbean region and Latin America. Jamaica's minister of development, planning, and production warned that if the current rate of deforestation continued, Jamaica's forests would disappear within thirty years.[12] Jamaica's 67,000 hectares of forest are disappearing at the rate of approximately 3 percent per year.[13] President Carlos Salinas of Mexico has launched a program to plant at least 5 million trees throughout Mexico; however, ecologists have complained that massive deforestation is continuing unabated in the Lacandona Forest, the largest tropical rain forest in southern Mexico. Experts say that it is being destroyed at a faster rate than the Amazon rain forest and is threatened with disappearance in the next five to ten years.[14] Millions of acres of forest have also been destroyed by fire in the Yucatan Peninsula.[15] Brazil has begun to draft bills dealing with deforestation, the invasion of Indian reservations, and the activities of mineral prospectors in the Amazon River basin. The country is seeking support from Bolivia, Colombia, Ecuador, Guyana, Peru, Surinam, and Venezuela, its neighbors in the Amazon Pact.[16]

Atmosphere and Climate

Atmospheric pollution is increasing in many parts of the world. Pollution contributes to unhealthy air in cities and damages crops and natural ecosystems. Burning fossil fuels and clearing tropical forests are altering the global climate, and these activities are likely to cause severe disruptions through regional climate changes, rising in global sea levels, and unpredictable weather patterns. Depletion of the earth's protective ozone layer, already well advanced over Antarctica, may damage both human health and delicately balanced natural systems.[17] Some Third World cities such as Mexico City have significant air pollution problems. The Mexican government's "Day Without a Car Program," aimed at reducing car traffic in the city by one-fifth on workdays, has kept Mexico City's smog problem from worsening significantly since the project started in November 1989, but dangerously high levels of ozone, lead, and other pollutants continue to be recorded routinely.[18]

The world's nations are working together to try to halt the damage to the ozone layer. In June 1990, ninety-three nations agreed that, by the end of the century, they would halt the production of chemicals that destroy the ozone layer. This agreement went far beyond 1987 Montreal Protocol, which involved fifty-seven nations, and called for a 50 percent reduction by 1998. China and India, which had refused to accede to the 1987 treaty, were satisfied by this later agreement. The agreement gives the poor nations a ten-year grace period, requiring them to halt production before the year 2010, rather than 2000. A fund will be set up to help the poorer nations make the transition to technologies that do not use chlorofluorocarbons.[19]

Oceans and Coasts

Available data indicate some decrease in ocean dumping, oil spills, land runoff, and atmospheric deposition in the oceans. Oil spills, for example, have been declining in frequency and volume for fifteen years.[20]

The world fish catch has increased steadily, reaching 90 million metric tons in 1986, up from 30 million metric tons in 1958. But some experts believe that continued large increases are unlikely because the annual catch is approaching the maximum sustainable yield. Regionally, several fisheries have been either overfished or reduced by a combination of overfishing and environmental factors, with substantial harvest declines.[21]

Coral reefs off the coast of more than 20 countries are suffering from increasingly severe human and natural assaults. Overfishing, coral harvesting, vessel groundings, widespread chemical pollution, sewage and deforestation, and such natural phenomena as sharp swings in water temperature have threatened the corals. Beginning in 1987, Caribbean corals have suffered from widespread bleaching from a blight that kills or impairs corals. This was a particular problem in the waters off the north coast of Jamaica, off Martinique, and off St. Croix. Scientists blame rising water temperatures, which sensitive corals cannot withstand. The bleaching occurs when the algae on which coral organisms depend die.[22] The bleaching phenomenon seems to be over, and most of the corals show signs of recovering. Other factors causing damage to the coral reefs in the Caribbean include hurricanes, disease, loss of sea urchins, and overfishing.[23]

FOCUS ON THE CARIBBEAN SEA

The ocean is a global resource as well as a national and local one. But a marine region such as the Caribbean Sea presents special problems because it is semi-enclosed. Its health depends on policy coordination among the coastal states. They need to adopt a common, consistent strategy to reverse the current damage and to avoid further significant damage. Twenty-eight states in the region are signatories to the Convention for Protection and Development of the Marine Environment of the Wider Caribbean, but this accord should be seen merely as a starting point. The treaty does not regulate such critical land-based pollution sources as soil and sewage runoff.[24]

Kingston Harbor illustrates the existing damage to the marine environment. It is heavily polluted, and if environmental management is not put in place soon, the progressive decline will be difficult to control.[25]

Marine resources are usually managed by regulating fishing, shipping, oil drilling, and other individual activities. A newer approach involves designating a coastal or marine area for special management as a marine protected area. This may involve strict protection, development for tourism, or a zoning approach that allows different activities in different zones. Marine protected areas vary in size from less than a hectare to hundreds of thousands of square kilometers, and they may include coastal areas, small islands, coral reefs, estuaries, seagrass beds, historic shipwrecks, and open water areas. A 1988 International Union for Conservation of Nature and Natural Resources (IUCN) survey lists 820 marine and coastal protected areas, some 400 of which have a significant marine component.[26] A 1986 literature survey showed approximately 1000 coastal and marine protected areas in eighty-seven countries.[27]

Designation of a marine area as protected is the first step in the management process. However, actually providing a protected area with a staff and budget may be more difficult. The Greater Caribbean Basin, which includes the Gulf of Mexico, has 112 legally established marine protected areas. Most of them were so designated in the past twenty years. They are recognized by country governments, the IUCN, and the Regional Seas Program of the United Nations Environment Program (UNEP). But an Organization of American States (OAS) assessment indicates that most of them are without management or enforcement. Only twenty-eight have budgets, staffs, management plans, and institutional support.[28]

The establishment of these protected areas was an important first step for the governments involved. Management plans can focus on specific areas, and the protected areas can serve as barometers for the health of the entire marine region. In the Caribbean, virtually no pristine reefs remain. Coral reefs are especially important to the economies of Caribbean island nations, many of which depend on tourism for a large portion of their gross national product, employment, foreign exchange, and government revenue. In addition, shallow-water fisheries are seriously depleted in most Caribbean countries.

The major uses of Caribbean marine protected areas are recreation (67 areas) and wildlife habitat (78 areas). Other uses include fishing, research, designation as important ecosystems, and as habitat for endangered and threatened species. The most significant problems stem from urban, agricultural, and industrial development (45 areas) and direct physical damage from boat anchoring and sediment loading (37 areas). Direct damage by tourists is a problem in 34 areas, overfishing in 30, and hunting in 25. Of concern in fewer areas are solid waste disposal (15 areas), nutrient loading (11 areas), natural stresses, such as hurricanes (6 areas), and introduction of exotic species (2 areas). Most protected areas suffer from development pressure caused by growing local populations and development of tourist facilities.[29] Artisan-like fisheries can be enhanced by protected areas that preserve a breeding ground for fish. Unchecked fishing pressure on many reefs has caused severe depletion. For example, in the Tobago Cays area of St. Vincent and the Grenadines, overfishing caused a decline in the fish catch from 83 metric tons in 1974 to 25 metric tons in 1987.[30]

Lack of funding is a major obstacle to effective management of these marine protected areas. Caribbean Basin countries, with their restricted budgets and heavy debts, may find it difficult to set aside funds for marine protection. But so many of them are dependent on the sea for their survival (from tourism, fishing, and so on) that such perspective would be short-sighted indeed. Marine protected areas range from parklike areas to reservelike areas. In the former, management of resources can be coordinated with tourism to generate income. Fees can be charged to people using parklike protected areas. In order not to encourage a situation in which the country pays for goods that are reserved primarily for the use of foreign visitors, a nominal fee can be charged to locals and a higher fee to foreign visitors or tourists. Of course, there is the possibility that the money gained from this activity would go into the central treasury and not be reinvested to benefit the marine protected areas. A mandatory requirement for success is the political will to make protection of the sea a central concern.

The reservelike areas, which should be preserved for scientific study or as breeding sites for marine organisms, usually have little potential for generating income in the short term, though they may be valuable long-term assets. Several strategies can be implemented to raise funds at the national and international levels. At the national level, special taxes can be used to set up an environmental fund. For example, taxes could be placed on certain categories of boats. It may also be possible to generate donations from the private sector. In many countries, the private sector earns considerable economic benefit from biological resources and may be able to provide voluntary support to conserving those resources. Such voluntary support may be particularly appropriate where a number of tourist enterprises rely on protected areas for their livelihood.

Funds generated at the national level will probably need to be supplemented by funds from international sources. Some international conventions provide funding. For example, several of the Regional Seas conventions established by the UNEP involve trust fund agreements that provide significant funding to conservation activities. Direct support can also be sought from international conservation organizations. People living in industrialized countries earn considerable benefits from biological resources in tropical countries, and they often express their interest in conservation through donations to conservation organizations.

A third approach to seeking funding at the international level would involve a debt-for-nature swap. This method attempts to deal with the problem of Third World debt as well as that of ecosystem destruction. In debt-for-nature swaps, nongovernmental Western conservation organizations buy up developing country debt at a discount and then arrange to write off the debt in exchange for the debtor country putting some effort and local currency into conservation. Three widely publicized agreements were reached in 1987, involving the countries of Bolivia, Costa Rica, and Ecuador. In the Bolivian case, the government had created the Beni Biological Reserve of 134,000 hectares, but it lacked the funds to develop and safeguard it effectively. A U.S. foundation, Conservation International, wanted to make this reserve workable. In 1987, the foundation acquired a Bolivian debt of $650,000, which was discounted to $100,000, from a Swiss bank. Conservation International then canceled the $650,000 debt, in exchange for which the Bolivan government set up a zone of 1.4 million hectares around the reserve and a $250,000 endowment to be managed by a Bolivan foundation.

OAS studies suggest that marine parks can be good investments. The studies, by a team that included an economist, a biologist, and a park management specialist, resulted in funding proposals for parks in the Caribbean islands of St. Vincent and the Grenadines, Jamaica, and St. Lucia.[31]

A strategy to deal with the problems of the Caribbean Sea cannot be long delayed, as the environmental degradation of the Mediterranean has illustrated. If the countries of the region do not act to reverse environmental decline before it has significant effects on their health and economies, they will have to spend decades trying to regenerate regional waters.

IMPLICATIONS FOR DEMOCRACY

In the original Greek concept, *democracy* was rule by the people and by this was distinguished from monarchy or oligarchy. Democracy now has almost as many definitions as it has definers. Based on these, democracy could be distinguished by several factors, including the following: (1) rule by a majority, (2) the existence of institutions allowing elections and other means of political participation by citizens, and (3) economic and social participation by the majority of the citizens.

As we look at democracy, we will focus not only on political or institutional democracy, but also on social and economic democracy. Political democracy is clearly compatible with significant inequality in both wealth and income. But it can also be used to attempt to transform society and achieve justice and therefore affect social and economic democracy. Defined in this way, democracy is divisible. Sometimes there is tension between political democracy and social and economic democracy. In such cases, the former has to be bypassed to serve the latter. An examination of some of the issues related to the environmental dilemma illustrates how democracy is affected.

Collective Interest Versus Individual Interest

The environment is a finite common property resource. The rational action is to maximize individual interests. But in such a situation, this is usually done at the expense of the collective good. As a result, there is a conflict between collective and individual interests at the international, regional, national, and local levels. A focus on individual interests, then, is clearly detrimental. For the world's states to address environmental issues adequately, they need to be willing to give up some measure of sovereignty. This dilemma is also reflected at the regional level in a semienclosed area such as the Caribbean Sea, where a common strategy among the littoral states will be important. At the national level, citizens may need to surrender some individual liberties to serve the common good. In no society are these freedoms totally unrestricted. But environmental concerns are likely to demand further restrictions on freedoms such as the following: freedom to engage in trade and establish certain enterprises, freedom of movement, freedom of occupational choice, and freedom to use private property as one likes. These freedoms are generally regarded as an intrinsic part of the framework of liberties provided by a democracy. International treaties and local laws instituted to serve the collective interest will temper the discretion of individual state actors at the global level and constrain the discretion of citizens at the local level.

Popular Control

A related issue is that of popular control. For some people, a major basis of democracy is majority control. They believe in the wisdom of the majority. But dependence on this wisdom can be dangerous. In matters of collective interest versus individual interest, it is possible that the majority choice would weigh on the side of serving individual interests. Majority opinion may also be an inadequate basis for choosing between short-term and medium- or long-term interests. In the example of the oceans, this can be illustrated by the conflict between the need to replenish almost-depleted fish stocks and the need to obtain today's meal. For a poor fisherman, opting for the short-term benefit is a rational decision. Developing countries will need material help to enable them to meet short-term needs without sacrificing medium-term benefits. For this, assistance from the industrialized world or from some of the newly industrializing countries may be necessary. This might be difficult to obtain, because some industrialized country leaders believe that the environmental problem is a divisible one.

In most countries, including the industrialized democracies, popular control is, in any case, primarily a myth. Decisions are made by an elite. In developing countries, too, the environmental imperative will require dependence on a policy elite.

Economic Growth Impacts

Those who emphasize the social and economic dimensions of democracy believe that there are important economic prerequisites for democracy. Developing countries need an economic infrastructure that is sufficient to provide basic needs such as health services and education. There is some concern about how much environmental constraints on development will impede or delay the achievement of the economic prerequisites for democracy. This is likely to be a short-term result in countries that make the hard choice to forgo a development option that could have negative consequences for the environment. Without these economic prerequisites, popular control, which is seen as an important feature of democracy, can be destabilizing. On the other hand, with these prerequisites in place, the country will be more likely to have an educated populace with its basic needs met, and it will be able to rely more on persuasion and less on coercion or authority for compliance with environmental regulations.

AN ARGUMENT FOR SEIZING THE INITIATIVE

Developing countries have borne some of the development costs of industrialized countries. One area in which this has occurred is that of toxic waste disposal. In 1988, increased attention began to be paid to the practice of dumping toxic waste in the Third World. In particular, Africa, the Caribbean, and Latin America had become the preferred dumping grounds of waste peddlers from industrialized countries. As awareness of the dangers of this practice increased in developing countries, ships sailed from one Third World country to another trying to unload waste.[32] Deals to accept toxic waste from developed countries were uncovered, and the task began of cleaning up waste that had already been dumped.[33] Monitoring by Greenpeace identified more than 3.6 million tons of waste shipments from industrialized to underdeveloped countries between 1986 and 1988 alone.[34] More than 17.4 million tons per year were proposed for export to developing countries but then refused permission.[35] The Basel Convention on the Control of Transboundary Movement of Hazardous Wastes and their Disposal was approved by 117 countries in 1989. The convention is aimed at preventing the export of hazardous waste to unsafe, inadequate sites by requiring waste exporters to notify and receive consent from receiving countries before shipping the waste. In addition, the treaty requires the countries exporting waste and those receiving it to ensure that the waste is ultimately discarded in an environmentally sound manner.[36]

With regard to the toxic waste trade, Third World countries were forced into a reactive mode. They were not prepared to address the situation with a coherent strategy. As they formulate development plans, it is important that they adopt an activist strategy and that they not wait for the industrialized countries and Western environmental groups to plan their development and environmental future. Their efforts have to be coordinated at the local, regional, and international levels.

The argument for an activist rather than a reactive role also relates to Third World strategies for dealing with the environment as a whole. Developing countries can benefit from the mistakes of the industrialized world. They should recognize that there is no need to slavishly imitate the development process of the industrialized world, especially with regard to the use of energy-intensive and nature-destroying technology.

In 1992, the World Conference on Environment and Development will be held in Brazil. As developing countries prepare for the conference, they need to formulate their own vision of environmentally responsible development. One issue that needs to be addressed is the placing of environmental conditions on the disbursement of badly needed development funds. Developing countries are likely to find that development decisions are increasingly taken out of their hands. When there is the perception that certain national actions have global repercussions, the international community might want the right to interfere in order to mitigate the consequences of such actions. This raises concerns about the sovereign rights of nations. And it may suggest that, with regard to certain issues, the concept of sovereignty needs to be redefined. These important concerns make it mandatory that developing countries enter the debate prepared. They should not be content merely to respond or react to the demands or decisions of the industrialized countries and the development agencies they control. Developing countries have demonstrated the ability to seize the initiative with regard to environmental issues, as shown by their sponsoring of "The World Charter for Nature," which passed the General Assembly of the United Nations in October 1982. They should demonstrate similar initiative and creativity as they try to formulate an environmentally responsible development path.

NOTES

1. World Resources Institute, *World Resources 1988–89* (New York: Basic Books, 1988), p. 2.

2. *World Resources 1988–89,* p. 3.

3. Institute for Food and Development Policy, *Food First Resource Guide* (San Francisco: IFDP, 1979), p. 10. Agriculturally productive countries in Asia without a hunger problem such as Japan employ twice as many workers per acre as countries with low productivity and much hunger such as India or the Philippines.

4. *World Resources 1988–89,* p. 110

5. *World Resources 1988–89,* p. 5.

6. *World Resources 1988–89,* p. 5.

7. *World Resources 1988–89,* p. 4.

8. *World Resources 1988–89,* p. 4.

9. Jeffrey A. McNeeley et al., *Conserving the World's Biological Diversity* (Washington, D.C.: International Union for Conservation of Nature and Natural Resources), p. 44.

10. McNeeley et al., *Conserving,* p. 44.

11. *World Resources 1988–89,* p. 44.

12. "News in Brief," *Jamaican Weekly Gleaner,* November 5, 1990, p. 22.

13. McNeely et al., *Conserving,* p. 45.

14. William Branigan, "Mexico Adopts Campaign to Save the Environment," *Washington Post,* June 6, 1990, p. 18.

15. William Brenigan, "North America's Largest Rain Forest Faces Destruction," *Washington Post,* July 17, 1989, p. A17

16. Richard House, "Brazil Declines Invitation to Conference on Ecology," *Washington Post,* March 4, 1989, p. A20.

17. *World Resources 1988–89,* p. 8.

18. Branigan, "Mexico Adopts Campaign," p. A18.

19. Malcolm W. Browne, "93 Nations Move to Ban Chemicals that Harm Ozone," *The New York Times,* June 30, 1990, p. 1.

20. Browne, "93 Nations," pp. 7–8.

21. *World Resources 1988–1989,* p. 7.

22. "Coral Reefs off 20 Countries Face Assaults from Man and Nature," *The New York Times,* March 27, 1990, p. C4.

23. "Coral Reefs," p. C4.

24. William J. Orme, Jr., "Treaty to Protect Caribbean Advances at Mexico Conference," *Washington Post,* April 27, 1985, p. A10.

25. "News in Brief," *Jamaican Weekly Gleaner,* November 5, 1990, p. 22.

26. International Union for Conservation of Nature and Natural Resources, Conservation Monitoring Centre (IUCN/CMC), unpublished data, IUCN/CMC, Cambridge, UK, 1988, cited in *World Resources 1988–89,* p. 149.

27. *World Resources 1988–89,* p. 150.

28. *World Resources 1988–89,* pp. 150–151.

29. *World Resources 1988–89,* pp. 150–151.

30. *World Resources 1988–89,* p. 152.

31. *World Resources 1988–89,* p. 152.

32. "Ship Heads for West Africa with Cargo of Unwanted Ash," *Washington Post,* June 12, 1988, p. A10.

33. James Brooke, "African Nations Barring Foreign Toxic Waste," *The New York Times,* September 25, 1988, p. 18; Blaine Hardin, "Outcry Grows in Africa over West's Waste-Dumping," *Washington Post,* June 22, 1988, p. A15; Blaine Hardin, "Africans Turn to Hostages in Battle Against Foreign Waste," *WAshington Post,* July 16, 1988, p. A19.

34. Greenpeace International, *The International Treade in Toxic Wastes* (Washington D.C.: Greenpeace International, 1988–89), cited in Bryan Wynne, "The Toxic Waste Trade: International Regulatory Issues and Options," *Third World Quarterly,* July 1989, p. 120.

35. Wynne, "Toxic Waste," p. 120.

36. Steven Greenhouse, "U.N. Conference Supports Curbs on Exporting of Hazardous Waste," *The New York Times,* March 23, 1989, p. 1.

Part Five

Distributive Justice and Equity: Lessons from Asia, Africa, and Latin America

Chapter 11

Land Tenure and Economic Efficiency

Young J. Park

Despite numerous investigations, both theoretical and empirical, opinions still vary widely on the effects of share tenancy. While one school of thought contends that share tenancy promotes inefficiency, the bulk of literature takes the contrary position. This debate is significant in that, first, it sheds critical light on the assumption that land reform may not be as compelling as it has been made out to be, and that, in cases where land reform has been introduced, the system of tenant farming—with its consequent absentee landlordism—has persisted. Using data collected on the Korean land reform experience, this chapter assesses these assumptions with particular emphasis on the role of incentives and their effects on resource allocation and farm productivity. It is contended here that incentives—a subject neglected by most contemporary analyses—have actually been among the most important offshoots of land reform, contributing to more efficient resource allocation and enhanced productivity in postreform agriculture. This conclusion has significant policy implication for the rest of the Third World where allocative efficiency and consequent farm output are top priorities: The owner-farmed system is clearly more efficient than share tenancy.

INTRODUCTION

The neoclassical marginal productivity theory has long been used to demonstrate that share tenancy was not as efficient as owner farming in terms of resource allocation and, thus, output. But this conclusion has been challenged by other models over the years.[1] A recent study of Keijiro Otsuka and Yujiro Hayami again attempts to cast further doubt on the conclusion reached by the marginal productivity models.[2] The debate on land tenure and economic efficiency is important in at least two ways.

First, if it can be decisively shown that share tenancy is not inefficient when

This is a revised version of a paper presented at the annual meeting of the Association for the Advancement of Policy, Research and Development in the Third World held in Mexico City, Mexico, November 14–17, 1990.

compared with owner farming, this might have adverse effects on future land reforms because many previous reforms used the inefficiency of share tenancy as an important rationale.

Second, even in many countries where land reforms have taken place, share tenancy has reappeared, often illegally. Any attempt to eliminate or prevent it may be hampered if it is theoretically and empirically proven that equal allocative efficiency exists in both tenant and owner farms.

This chapter attempts to examine the issue of land tenure once again. After a theoretical analysis, data from the Korean land reform program will be used for empirical verification.

SUMMARY OF THEORIES

A share contract means that the tenant farmer pays the landowner a specific proportion of total crop. The marginal productivity theory postulates that both income-maximizing owner farmer and tenant farmer will employ units of input up to the point at which the value of marginal product (VMP) of input equals the price of that input.[3] In Figure 1, because the tenant farmer has to pay $r\%$ of his total crop as share rent, his VMP lies below that of the owner farmer.

Thus, as long as the price of input is positive at either w or i, the amount of input used by the tenant farmer is less than that of the owner farmer. The tenant farmer uses OQ units of input while the owner farmer uses ON units of input. The resource allocation is, therefore, inefficient in tenant farms.

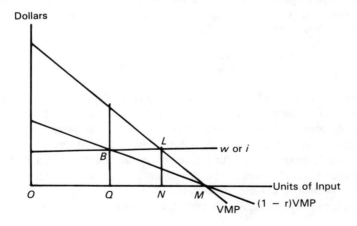

Figure 11-1 Comparison of the value of marginal product of tenant farmer to that of owner farmer.

Mathematically, let the production function of a farm be $X = f(L,C,1)$, where L is the size of land per farm, which is given; C is the amount of capital input used per farm; and 1 is the amount of hired labor used per farm. Then the owner farm's income equation is $Y = XP - w1 - iC$, where P is the price of farm output; the tenant farm's income equation becomes $Y = XP - w1 - iC - rXP$.

For income maximization, $w = p\ \partial x/\partial l$, and $i = p\ \partial x/\partial C$, in the owner farm and $w = (1 - r)p\ \partial x/\partial l$, and $i = (1 - r)p\ \partial x/\partial C$, in the tenant farm. Thus, as long as r is positive, the amount of input used per farm is less in tenant farms than in owner farms.

The resource allocation is also considered to be more inefficient under share tenancy than under fixed-rent tenancy, as long as the cost of farming is shared between landowners and tenants.[4]

The inescapable conclusion reached by the marginal productivity theory is that share tenancy prevents efficient allocation of resources in agricultural production and that its existence implies exploitation of tenants by land-owners.

The average productivity model contends that the amount of input used in farming will be the same among different forms of land tenure because of both competition among tenants and landowners and enforceable contracts between landowners and tenants.[5] Stephen N. C. Cheung presents this point in Figure 2, using labor input as an example.[6]

Cheung states that

> Given $\partial q/\partial t\ (1 - r)$ as drawn, and assuming that the landowners contractually accept any amount of labor, competition among tenants will push labor input on each farm to $t3$. The resulted [*sic*] overcrowded tilling implies that rental shares are not at maximums. Competition again prevails. Given homogeneous factors of production, wealth maximization implies that the landowner will choose among tenants who offer rental percentages as high as r^*, while competition among landowners implies that it will not be any higher. Given r^* which defines $\partial q/\partial t\ (1 - r^*)$, the amount of tenant labor competitively offered and contractually accepted for each farm will be $t2$. The market equilibrium reached occurs when the marginal product of tenant labor in each farm equals the marginal tenant cost [point B in Figure 2].[7]

At equilibrium point B, resource allocation under share tenancy is as efficient as under owner farming under the given production function. The average productivity model rejects the neoclassical assumption that share tenancy is regulated by custom. Instead, it maintains that tenancy occurs where utility maximization by both tenants and landowners exists. Furthermore, share contracts are affected by the factor prices, although indirectly and through several dimensions. The average productivity model finds no strong evidence that share tenancy results in allocative inefficiency when compared with both owner farm-

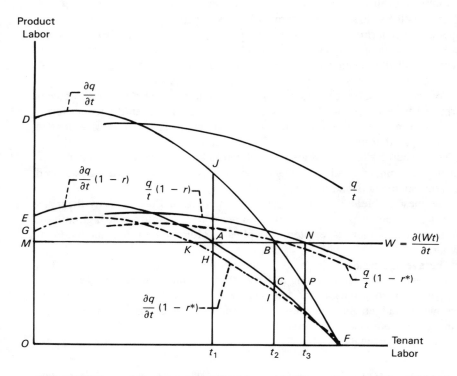

Figure 11-2 Comparison of marginal productivity model with average productivity model to share tenancy. $\partial q/\partial t$, marginal product of tenant labor; q/t, average product of tenant labor; $\partial q/\partial t$ (1 − r), marginal tenant receipt net of rent; q/t (1 − r), average tenant receipt; $W = \partial Wt/\partial t$, prevailing wage rate or marginal tenant cost; r, original rate of rent, 40% of total product; r*, raised rate of rent; t, amount of tenant labor input per farm. Source: Steven Cheung, *op. cit.*, p. 52.

ing and fixed-rent tenancy. And the existence of share tenancy is justified as a device of risk sharing between landowners and tenants under the condition of uncertainty.[8]

EVALUATION OF THEORIES

The question of whether share tenancy results in inefficient allocation of resources is an empirical one. Both the marginal productivity and average productivity theories have important shortcomings, however.

First, there is no differentiation between the use of hired workers and family workers. In subsistence agriculture, farming is mostly done by family workers. The wage constraints that affect the labor resource allocation in the case of hired workers may not be applicable when family workers are primarily used. Both the marginal productivity and average productivity theories assume that labor supply is unlimited at the prevailing wage rate. But the labor supply curve of family workers should be different.

On the one hand, the labor supply curve may be horizontal at zero because of the lack of employment opportunities outside the family farm. With the zero opportunity costs of family workers, both tenant and owner farms will use labor input up to M in Figure 1. Then the amount of labor input used is the same regardless of types of land tenure. This is the same conclusion reached by the average productivity theory but for different reasons.

On the other hand, the labor supply curve of family workers may be upward sloping from the origin, although it may still lie below the prevailing wage rate. This is because even in highly overcrowded subsistence agriculture the opportunity cost of using family workers may not be zero. In this case, difference in terms of labor input allocation will be observed between tenant and owner farms in the framework of marginal productivity theory. However, the difference in labor input use between tenant and owner farms will be less in the case of an upward sloping curve than it is in the case of a horizontal labor supply curve at the prevailing wage rate.

Second, both the marginal productivity and average productivity theories fail to include the role of incentives in their models. While the marginal productivity theory implies the lack of incentive on the part of tenants as a possible explanation for inefficiency of share tenancy, the average productivity theory simply ignores the role of incentives in farming. If resource allocation is indeed the same among different forms of land tenure, as is postulated by the average productivity theory, then there would be no difference between tenant and owner farmers in terms of incentives. In other words, different forms of land tenure do not affect incentives. Even if they do, according to the average productivity theory, tenant farmers' low incentives can be brought up to owner farmers' levels by enforceable contracts.

Even when differences in farm input use and, thus, output are observed between tenant and owner farms, attempts are made to explain away the phenomenon in terms of differences in production function rather than in incentives. For example, Otsuka and Hayami state that the observed differences in output between tenant and owner farms seems to reflect differences in production functions resulting from differences in crop mix between sharecropping and owner-farming areas.[9]

Although the traditional allocative efficiency theory recognizes incentive as a factor in production, including farm production, it is not clear about the source of incentive. Producer incentives may be treated as part of entrepreneurial ability. In this sense, the farm output differences between tenant and owner farms simply results from difference in specific inputs, incentives manifested in differences in entrepreneurial capacity. But where did incentives come from?

It is difficult to accept that farmers' incentives are not affected by land tenure or that they can be manipulated by enforceable share contracts. The analysis of land tenure and resource allocation should include the role of incentives.

LAND TENURE AND INCENTIVES

Land reform typically brings about changes in land tenure from tenant-farm status to owner-farm status. If such a change results in increased input use and output in the new owner farms, then it can be said that the change in land tenure produces positive incentive effects. It is possible, however, that the change in land tenure may result in the decreased input use and output, especially in the short run, "if [the former] tenants prefer to take out the windfall gain partly or wholly in the form of more leisure."[10] But this should not be used as an argument that the change in land tenure produces negative incentive effects. This is merely the case when the increased income from the elimination of rent causes new owner farmers to curtail the amount of work voluntarily, in much the same way as the big lottery winner decides to quit his job. The real issue is whether there is a difference in terms of input use and output between tenant and owner farms, ceteris paribus.

In reality, the change in land tenure is expected to result in heightened interest and incentive on the part of operators.[11] Incentives brought on by the change in land tenure will affect farm production in two ways.

First, landownership gives the former tenant farmers inducements to increase labor and capital inputs used in farming.[12] This can be termed the "static incentive effect of landownership" that gives rise to the marginal productivity theory of resource allocation under share tenancy. As the new owners of land they cultivate, former tenant farmers no longer have to operate on the value of marginal product of input curves that lie below those of the owner farmers.

Second, landownership means more than simply putting more inputs in farming. It also means improvement of the quality of inputs put into farming by the new owner farmers. Improvement of input quality may come as a result of farmers' actions of thinking more deeply, putting technology into land utilization, and improving crop cultivation.[13] Although improvement of capital input means the use of high-yield crop seeds, fertilizers, and pesticides, improvement of labor input also means the farmer's willingness to learn and acquire new knowledge and skills about modern capital inputs and new farming techniques. This can be termed as the "dynamic incentive effect of landownership" that increases productivity of inputs. The value of the marginal product of input curve shifts upward. As Hla Myint notes:

> Economic incentives should be regarded not merely as the method of inducing the peasants to sell the food surplus obtained with their existing agricultural techniques, but more importantly as a method of inducing them to adopt better methods of production which will raise the food surplus in [the] future.[14]

The existence or development of improved capital inputs and farming techniques is important to produce more output, but farmers' willingness and ability to take advantage of them is essential for increased output.[15]

The combination of static and dynamic incentive effects of landownership should be such that owner farms have not only more efficient allocation of inputs but also higher productivity of inputs than do tenant farms. Owner farms operate on the improved production function compared with tenant farms, not because of different crop mix but because of incentives associated with the newly acquired ownership status. As a United Nations' report concludes:

> Over and above those results of land reform which can be recorded concretely and even statistically, there are intangible results which can best be sensed by the observer on a visit to land reform areas. Appreciation of those intangible results is deeper and more securely based if the observer has also had the opportunity to know the same area before the reform. In addition to the visible signs such as better kept fields, improved crops, more and finer livestock, and better infrastructure facilities, there are evident also the pervading spirit of optimism, will to progress, and even enthusiasm—assets which are valuable for output and productivity as well.[16]

LAND TENURE AND CAPITAL INPUT USE: THE KOREAN EXPERIENCE

In 1950, Korean land reform brought about drastic changes in the farmers' land tenure. In 1945, owner farms represented only 14.2 percent of all farm households, but in 1963 more than 83 percent of all farms were owner farms.[17] The Korean land reform, however, did not significantly affect the size of landholding per farm. In 1947, 74.5 percent of all farm households cultivated less than 1 chongbo (or 2.45 acres) of land; the comparable statistic was 73.3 percent in 1963.[18] Furthermore, the distribution of farms by the size of cultivated land was the same before and after land reform (see Tables 1 and 2). In other words, Korean land reform changed the landownership status for the vast majority of farmers but not the size of landholding per farm. Neither did it change the crop mix in the new owner farms after land reform. Thus, Korean land reform offers an opportunity for empirical verification of the theoretical analysis of the effects of land tenure on input use and output. Because the positive effects of landownership on labor input use have been discussed elsewhere,[19] the Korean data on capital input use are presented here.

Capital inputs in agricultural production include fertilizers, seeds, farm tools, domestic animals, farm buildings, and other material inputs. Among them, fertilizers are the single most important input in Korean agriculture, because soil fertility must be constantly maintained by application of manures and chemical fertilizers for successful crop growing. Farmers use fertilizers

Table 1
Number of South Korean Farm Households by Cultivated Land Size
Before and After Land Reform

Size (chongbo)	1947		1963	
	No. households (1000)	Percent of total	No. households (1000)	Percent of total
<0.5	895	41.2	1,009	41.8
0.5–1.0	724	33.3	761	31.5
1.0–2.0	409	18.8	497	20.6
2.0–3.0	113	5.3	139	5.7
>3.0	31	1.4	9	0.4
Total	2,172	100.0	2,415	100.0

Source: National Agricultural Cooperative Federation, *Twenty Years of Korean Agricultural Policy* (Seoul: NACF, 1965), p. 99; and NACF, *Agricultural Yearbook, 1970,* pp. IV-14–15.

almost without exception, and their cost is significant. In 1933, for instance, more than 50 percent of total expenditures on capital inputs was on fertilizers in all farms regardless of landownership status, and it was more than 40 percent in 1968.[20]

Fertilizer consumption in Korean agriculture has generally increased since 1919.[21] There is, however, a big difference in terms of fertilizer consumption per tanbo (or 0.1 chongbo) between farms of different land tenure and between farms of different size of landholding. In prereform agriculture (Table 3), tenant farms used the least amount of fertilizers per tanbo. On the other hand, fertilizer consumption per tanbo is greatest in the small new-owner farms (which are

Table 2
Number of South Korean Farm Households by Ownership Status
Before and After Land Reform

Type	1945		1963	
	No. households (1000)	Percent of total	No. households (1000)	Percent of total
Owner	285	14.2	2,006	83.0
Owner-tenant	716	35.6	367	15.2
Tenant	1,010	50.2	43	1.8
Total	2,011	100.0	2,416	100.0

Source: NACF, *Twenty Years,* p. 103; and NACF, *Analysis of Korean Agriculture* (Seoul: NACF, 1963), p. 175.

Table 3

a. Total Production Expenditure and Fertilizer Consumption per Tanbo, 1933 (in Yen)

Ownership status	Total production (yen spent per tanbo)	Fertilizer consumption (yen spent per tanbo)
Owner	36.67	5.74
Part owner	35.26	5.39
Tenant	33.83	4.31

Source: Chōji Hishimoto, *Study of Chōsen [Korean] Rice Production* (Tokyo: Chiguru Shobō, 1938), p. 235.

b. Fertilizer Consumption per Farm and per Tanbo, 1936 (in Yen)

Ownership status	Size of cultivated land per farm (in tanbo)	Fertilizer consumption (in yen) Per farm	Per tanbo
Landlord	17.4	48.63	2.8
Owner	5.9	16.37	2.7
Part owner	10.8	36.87	3.4
Tenant	6.2	14.69	2.3

Source: Japanese-Manchuria Agricultural Policy Association, *Survey of Chōsen [Korean] Agriculture* (Tokyo: JMAPA, 1941), pp. 62–63.

Table 4

Size of Landholding per Farm, Fertilizer Consumption per Farm,
and Fertilizer Consumption per Tanbo in Selected Postreform Years

Farm size (chongbo)	No. of tanbo (L)		Fertilizer consumption per farm in won (K)		Fertilizer consumption per tanbo in won (K/L)	
	1967	1968	1967	1968	1967	1968
<0.5	3.4	3.5	3,472	3,787	1,052	1,082
0.5–1.0	7.3	7.2	6,725	7,147	921	993
1.0–1.5	12.1	12.2	11,507	10,964	951	899
1.5–2.0	17.5	17.6	14,171	15,152	810	861
>2.0	25.8	26.3	19,767	19,945	766	728

Source: Ministry of Agriculture and Forestry, *Yearbook of Agriculture and Forestry,* 1970, and NACF, *Agricultural Yearbooks 1968, 1969,* and *1970.*

mostly the former tenant farms) after land reform (Table 4). Two factors may explain this postreform phenomenon.

First, tenant farmers in prereform agriculture were the poorest lot. After paying rent ranging from 20 to 90 percent of total output, tenant farmers simply lacked the financial ability to purchase high-priced fertilizers. They were also discouraged from borrowing the necessary funds from landlords because the rate of interest on borrowed money often ran as high as 40 percent or 50 percent.[22] On the other hand, new owner farmers, who on average retained more than 75 percent of total farm output as net income, could afford to use more fertilizers.[23]

Second, the new owner farmers had stronger incentives (both static and dynamic) after land reform. The significance of static incentive becomes clearer when the fertilizer consumption pattern is compared between the new small-owner farms (the former tenant farms) and the large owner farms (the former landlords or owner farms). The fertilizer consumption per tanbo has been con-sistently greater in the new small owner farms than in the large farms in postre-form agriculture (Table 5). The implication is that changes in land tenure gave new landowners stronger desires for and more interest in engaging in more intensive farming.

The dynamic incentive effect of landownership may be manifested in in-creased land productivity (measured here by farm income per tanbo). Although land productivity was lowest in tenant farms before land reform, it has been highest in the new small-owner farms in postreform Korean agriculture (Tables 6 and 7). The value of marginal product of input curves appear to be the highest in the new small-owner farms. Land productivity is determined by many factors such as availability of improved farming techniques and physical inputs, weather conditions, soil fertility, and so forth. Because any changes in these factors following land reform are likely to have affected all farms regardless of the size of landholding, the highest land productivity in the new small-owner farmers can be attributed to changes in land tenure in these farms.

The existence of dynamic incentives among the new owner farmers after land reform can be seen in several areas. One is increased education among farmers. Children in owner farms are willing and able to receive more education than those in tenant farms.[24] There was a marked change in the rate of illiteracy among farmers after land reform. In 1931, 43 percent of male farmers and 77.5 percent of female farmers could not read, while those who could not write were 48.7 percent and 83.6 percent of male and female farmers, respectively.[25] In contrast, only 10 percent of farm family members were completely illiterate in 1969. Even in the new owner farms, those who could not read or write were only 12.3 percent of farm family members.[26]

Increased education among the new owner farmers suggests that their knowledge of outside events increased and that they were more apt to take advantage of technological progress. There is ample evidence that farmers in general made conscious efforts to increase production in postreform Korean agriculture: New high-yielding rice seeds, called IR–5 and IR–8, were used, and new farming techniques—improving land utilization and mixing fertilizer inputs and pesticides—were also used.[27] Loans and discounts extended to the farm sector also have been increasing since land reform. This suggests that farmers' demand for production capital increased after land reform (Table 8).

Table 5
Total Capital Input per Farm and per Tanbo

Farm size (chongbo)	Capital used per farm		No. of tanbo per farm		Capital used per tanbo	
	1960 (1000 hwan)*	1967 (1000 won)	1960	1967	1960 (1000 hwan)*	1967 (1000 won)
<0.5	56.4	12.1	4.0	3.4	14.1	3.6
0.5–1.0	84.0	20.0	8.0	7.3	10.5	2.7
1.0–1.5	123.8 {	31.5	14.1 {	12.1	8.8 {	2.6
1.5–2.0		38.9		17.5		2.2
>2.0	179.8	52.2	22.7	25.8	7.9	2.0

*Before June 10, 1962, the hwan was the unit of Korean currency. On that date, the third currency reform changed the unit to the won; the value of the hwan was reduced to one-tenth of the new won. See Bank of Korea, *The History of Korean Money* (Seoul: Bank of Korea, 1969).

Source: National Agricultural Cooperative Federation, *Korean Agriculture Yearbook, 1961*, p. I-97; Ministry of Agriculture and Forestry, *Yearbook of Agriculture and Forestry Statistics, 1971*, pp. 156–159.

Table 6

a. Gross Income (in Yen) per Farm by Size of Cultivated Land (in Acres) and Ownership Status, 1928*

b. Gross Income (in Yen) per Farm by Size of Cultivated Land (in Tanbo) and Ownership Status, 1936‡

a.

Ownership status	Land size (in acres)			
	>0.735	0.735–2.45	2.45–7.35	<7.35
	Income (in yen)			
Landlord	—	—	—	2,236†
Owner	314	441	732	1,237
Part owner	241	381	595	1,015
Tenant	215	333	591	824

b.

Ownership status	Gross income per farm (yen)	Cultivated land per farm (tanbo)	Income per tanbo (yen)
Landlord	2,111.25	17.4	121.3
Owner	469.42	5.9	79.5
Part owner	496.90	10.8	46.0
Tenant	159.60	6.2	25.7

*Figures for 1928 represent the average income per farm. However, because farming brought the most income to most farms, it is plausible to assume that average income per farm represents total farm income per farm.

†Because of lack of data, the income per landlord farm is based on a size of 12.25–12.49 acres.

Source: Lee, *Land Utilization*, pp. 267–272.

‡Figures for 1936 are from a sample village in Kyong-Sang Province.
Source: JMAPA, *Chōsen Agriculture*, p. 63.

Table 7

Agricultural Productivity by Landholding Size per Farm in Selected Postreform Years

Farm size (chongbo)	Total income per farm			No. tanbo per farm			Total income per tanbo		
	1958 (1000 hwan)	1960 (1000 hwan)	1962 (1000 won)	1958	1960	1962	1958 (1000 hwan)	1960 (1000 hwan)	1962 (1000 won)
<0.5	255	256	32	4.3	4.0	4.0	59	64	79
0.5–1.0	365	409	54	8.1	8.0	8.1	45	51	67
1.0–1.5	544	} 564	} 80	12.9	} 14.1	} 13.5	42	} 40	} 59
1.5–2.0	784			17.4			45		
>2.0	1,001	911	105	24.8	22.7	22.4	40	40	47

Note: The multiplication of number of tanbo and total income per tanbo may not equal total income per farm because of rounding.
Source: NACF, *Agriculture Yearbook*, 1959–1971.

Table 8
Outstanding Loans and Discounts by Banking Institutions Extended
to the Farm Sector, 1956–1969

Year	Amount (million hwan)	Year	Amount (million won)
1956	29,900	1963	—
1957	68,600	1964	17,129
1958	78,700	1965	18,491
1959	82,200	1966	20,971
1960	115,400	1967	25,547
1961	—	1968	38,367
1962	—	1969	62,910

Source: Bank of Korea, *Economic Statistics Yearbook, 1960*, pp. 41–63, and *1970*, pp. 124–125.

CONCLUSION

Although its reasoning is not complete, the traditional marginal productivity theory clearly demonstrates that resource allocation is inefficient in tenant farms compared with owner farms. And there have been numerous empirical studies that lend support to that conclusion. The average productivity models argue that efficient resource allocation can be found in farms regardless of land tenure forms. But these models have not presented convincing empirical evidence that showed equal allocative efficiency between tenant and owner farms. Instead, it appears that they try to explain away the existing discrepancies between tenant and owner farms in terms of factors other than differences in land tenure. This is done to provide support for these models' theoretical analyses.

This chapter has attempted to do two things. First, it has recognized land ownership as the source of incentives for former tenant farmers. This appears to be a common sense conclusion, but various theories of land tenure have failed to account explicitly for this. This chapter attempts to establish a clear linkage between landownership and stronger incentives. And the effects of incentives are analyzed for two aspects: one causes more inputs to be used in farming and another causes productivity of the given input to improve. Second, the Korean data are drawn to support the theoretical contention. Despite their general paucity, the Korean data before and after land reform are very useful for empirical verification.

The analysis in this chapter leaves no doubt that landownership enhances allocative efficiency in farming and increases productivity. In many underdeveloped countries, increasing allocative efficiency and thus farm output are of overriding importance, so the policy implication is clear: The system of owner farms is favored over tenant farms.

NOTES

1. D. Gale Johnson, "Resource Allocation Under Share Contracts," *Journal of Political Economy, 58*(2) (April 1950): 111–114; Stephen N. C. Cheung, *The Theory of Share Tenancy* (Chicago: University of Chicago Press, 1969).

2. See their "Theories of Share Tenancy: A Critical Survey," *Economic Development and Cultural Change, 37*(1) (October 1988): 31–68.

3. Johnson, "Resource Allocations," pp. 111–114; Cheung, *Share Tenancy,* pp. 30–51; Rainer Schickele, "Effects of Tenure Systems on Agricultural Efficiency," *Journal of Farm Economics, 23*(1) (February 1941): 185–207; and Earl O. Heady, "Economics of Farm Leasing Systems," *Journal of Farm Economics, 29*(3) (August 1947): 599–678.

4. Charles Issawi, "Farm Output Under Fixed Rents and Share Tenancy," *Land Economics, 33*(1) (February 1957): 74–77.

5. Johnson, "Resource Allocation," pp. 111–125; Cheung, *Share Tenancy.* Because both Johnson and Cheung apply the average product of input curves in their analyses, their approach to theory of share tenancy is called the "average productivity model."

6. Cheung, *Share Tenancy,* p. 52.

7. Cheung, *Share Tenancy,* pp. 54–55.

8. Otsuka and Hayami, "Theories," pp. 32–53.

9. Otsuka and Hayami, "Theories," pp. 50–51.

10. Peter T. Bauer and Basil S. Yamey, *The Economics of Under-developed Countries* (Chicago: University of Chicago Press, 1926), p. 212.

11. United Nations, *Progress in Land Reform, Third Report* (New York: United Nations, 1962), p. 32.

12. A. Y. C. Koo, *The Role of Land Reform in Economic Development: A Case Study of Taiwan* (New York: Praeger, 1968), p. 64.

13. Koo, *Land Reform,* p. 74; Martin C. Yang, *Socio-economic Results of Land Reform in Taiwan* (Honolulu: East-West Press, 1970), pp. 163–169.

14. Hla Myint, *The Economics of Developing Countries* (New York: Praeger, 1966), p. 88.

15. Koo, *Land Reform,* p. 64.

16. United Nations, *Progress,* p. 50.

17. National Agricultural Cooperative Federation, *Twenty Years of Korean Agricultural Policy* (Seoul: NACF, 1965), p. 103; and NACF, *Analysis of Korean Agriculture* (Seoul: NACF, 1963), p. 175.

18. NACF, *Twenty Years,* p. 99; and NACF, *Agricultural Yearbook, 1970* (Seoul: NACF, 1970), pp. iv; 14–15.

19. Young J. Park, "The Effects of Land Reform on Labor Input Use: Theory and a Case Study of Korean Agriculture," *The Korean Economic Journal, 15*(2) (June 1976): 214–235.

20. Choji Hishimoto, *Study of Chosen [Korean] Rice Production* (Tokyo: Chiguru Shobo, 1938), p. 235; and Korean Ministry of Agriculture and Forestry, *Yearbook of Agriculture and Forestry Statistics* (Seoul: KMAF, 1970), pp. 287–289.

21. NACF, *Korean Agricultural Problems* (Seoul: NACF, 1969), p. 200; and NACF, *Yearbook, 1970,* p. 27.

22. Hoon K. Lee, *Land Utilization and Rural Economy in Korea* (Chicago: University of Chicago Press, 1936), p. 215.

23. NACF, *Agricultural Yearbook, 1957* (Seoul: NACF, 1957); and NACF, *Yearbook, 1970.*

24. Jin Whan Park, "The Comparison of Farm Income and Land Productivity by the Landownership Pattern," *Agricultural Economy,* Ministry of Agriculture and Forestry (December 1965): 114.

25. Lee, *Land Utilization,* pp. 52–53.

26. NACF, *Yearbook, 1970,* p. 147.

27. NACF, *Yearbook, 1970,* pp. 74–75.

Chapter 12

Structural Adjustments in Sub-Saharan Africa: A Review of IMF Stabilization Programs

Gerald E. Scott

This chapter reviews the experiences of sub-Saharan African countries with fund-assisted structural adjustment programs in the 1980s. It begins with a review of the theoretical aspects of the international adjustment to a payment problem and with an examination of the specific reasons for the failure of the international adjustment mechanism to achieve desirable results in sub-Saharan Africa in the 1980s. The second part examines the role of the fund, including an appraisal of its conditionalities on the use of its resources. The standard International Monetary Fund stabilization and standby model is appraised against the peculiar structural characteristics of sub-Saharan African countries. Finally, there is a general evaluation of several studies of IMF structural adjustment programs, including some of the suggested alternatives. This chapter echoes the suggestion that the adjustment problems in the region need to be tackled with significant internal changes in sub-Saharan Africa, in addition to assistance that may come from the international community.

INTRODUCTION

The economic crisis in sub-Saharan Africa (SSA) continued with unrelenting intensity in the 1980s, with food supplies for minimum levels of subsistence falling below critical levels. This serious food shortage has resulted in massive starvation, extensive malnutrition, and misery, and it has been attributed largely to problems in the agricultural sector. Other analysts have argued, however, that it is one component of a more widespread crisis resulting from a lack of coordination in economic decision making and management, a crisis that is manifested in severe balance-of-payments deficits, unsustainable debt service, high rates of inflation, low productivity, inefficiency and antiquated conditions in public services, corruption, waste, rapidly deteriorating infrastructures, and high rates of population growth. A clear manifestation of the crisis today has been the decline in standards of living to levels below those of the 1970s.

In searching for solutions to their varied problems, SSA countries have increasingly resorted to International Monetary Fund (IMF) adjustment programs. This chapter will examine current IMF conditionality and discuss alternatives that would help the region to overcome some of its problems. The chapter will be divided into four parts. The first will briefly review economic problems in SSA in the 1980s and assess prospects for the 1990s. The second part will examine the general and specific reasons for the failure of the international adjustment mechanism to promote adjustments in SSA. The third part will examine IMF conditionality on the use of its resources and, in particular, assess the stabilization and stand-by package in the context of SSA. The fourth part will review certain studies of stabilization and adjustment programs and discuss alternative approaches that would lead to more favorable conditions for economic, social, and political development in the region.

THE ECONOMIC CRISIS IN SSA

Of the forty-five countries classified as low income by the World Bank, 75 percent are in SSA. Today, the region faces a most devastating economic crisis, with all key economic variables (e.g., per capita GNP growth, food production, exports, terms of trade, balance-of-payments and budget deficits, inflation, external debt, and reserve losses) indicating that the region has been moving backward at an accelerating rate. Because the continent as a whole has never benefited from any high and sustained levels of development and lacks economic resilience, the deterioration in economic conditions has been particularly devastating.

Between 1980 and 1989, with population growth of 3.2 percent per annum, per capita GDP declined by 1.1 percent. Export receipts declined from $57.8 billion in 1980 to $39.7 billion in 1989, and the terms of trade have deteriorated steadily for many countries. Thus, balance-of-payments deficits remained large and persistent throughout the 1980s. The developments in external indebtedness have also been discouraging. At the end of 1989, total external indebtedness stood at $150 billion, and for many countries, debt represented more than 100 percent of GNP and more than 500 percent of exports. The obligation to repay debts has imposed a severe strain on economic performance because developmental resources are diverted into debt service. Further, with food production on the decline, basic needs fulfillment is constantly jeopardized as debt repayments fall due.

The fundamental reasons for the economic malaise in SSA include a combination of basic structural problems, adverse external conditions, high rates of population growth, drought, and political problems, all of which have been aggravated by policy mistakes and massive corruption. The prospects for the

1990s appear grim, especially because redemption seems to rest on a large-scale inflow of resources, an eventuality that also seems very unlikely in view of recent trends.

The process of promoting economic development, however, is very complicated and will entail a massive restructuring of economic systems, the rehabilitation and development of basic infrastructure, and the establishment of a climate that is conducive to efficient resource allocation. The key ingredient is the mobilization of resources to initiate and sustain self-reliant economic development in the region. This requires that corruption institutional distortions and other forms of inefficiencies must be eliminated.

FAILURE OF THE INTERNATIONAL ADJUSTMENT MECHANISM IN SSA

The international adjustment mechanism as it relates to SSA has been undermined by the structural characteristics of the SSA economies, as well as by several unfavorable events in the international and domestic economies.

With regard to the structural factors, first, there is typically a heavy dependence on exports of primary commodities for foreign-exchange needs. However, inadequate or negative growth of demand in the developed countries coupled with unfavorable prices have in the past created secular balance-of-payments difficulties for SSA nations.

Second, the physical and financial infrastructures are rudimentary. With limited infrastructures, productive investments, even when soundly based, encounter serious limitations that inhibit their effectiveness.

Third, there is limited domestic production of manufactured goods, so an increase in income is immediately translated to an increase in demand for industrial imports. Because these imports are usually not readily available as a result of controls, the immediate effect is inflation. Local manufacturing industries are limited not only by inadequate infrastructure, but also by lack of foreign exchange, skilled technicians, and managers.

Fourth, government and public sectors are sometimes very poorly managed by incompetent and corrupt officials who not only are incapable of formulating and implementing development projects, but also operate within a political and administrative structure that is devoid of coordination in economic decision making.[1]

Apart from these structural factors, which have undermined the international adjustment mechanism, the specific reasons why this mechanism has failed to achieve the desired results include oil shocks, exchange rates and real interest rates, deteriorating terms of trade and protectionism in developed countries, asymmetry in the adjustment mechanism, and various domestic factors.

Oil Shocks

Following dramatic increases in oil prices, the low elasticity of SSA demand resulted in major increases in oil imports and thus very serious deterioration of current account balances. Furthermore, the oil shocks caused serious recessions in the developed countries, which ultimately depressed demand for SSA exports. Thus, while oil imports could not be readily reduced, export receipts dwindled, resources for adjustment and growth became even scarcer, and countries had to squeeze out development expenditures.

Exchange Rates and Real Interest Rates

The international adjustment mechanism in SSA has been adversely affected by flexible exchange rates and high real interest rates. The steep rise in the value of the dollar through the mid-1980s resulted in rising expenditures on debt service and imports. Furthermore, foreign-exchange earnings and developmental projects that once seemed feasible ceased to be attractive once the dollar and other non-African currencies had appreciated. The dearth of domestically produced industrial goods means that most of the needed capital and consumer goods have to be imported. The unavailability of foreign exchange and the need to curtail imports have led to a situation in which the bulk of uncommitted foreign exchange is increasingly allocated to goods needed for survival. Thus, the process of adjustment is considerably undermined.

The adjustment process has also suffered as a result of high real interest rates. From previously low or negative levels in the 1970s, real interest rates increased to more than 8 percent in the 1980s. The increasingly common practice for interest on debt to be indexed to inflation, coupled with high average levels, increased payments burden for debtor countries, thereby reducing the resources available for adjustment and growth.

Deteriorating Terms of Trade and Protectionism in the Developed Countries

For SSA as a whole, the terms of trade fell sharply in the 1980s, although they remain higher than the levels reached in the early 1970s. This unfavorable development has been aggravated by increased protection, recession, and the use of contractionary monetary and fiscal policies in the developed countries. The ultimate effect is a reduction in demand for SSA exports and a loss of potential foreign exchange that is required for adjustment and growth.

Asymmetry in the Adjustment Mechanism

The burden of adjustment has always been placed squarely on the shoulders of the deficit countries. A good and effective international monetary system should more evenly distribute the burden of adjustment irrespective of the nature of the disequilibrium. Although the deficit countries in SSA face the most serious need for resources, they are rarely the recipient of such resources, even though they are badly needed for orderly adjustment and growth.

Domestic Factors

Adverse weather and internal political and ethnic conflicts have undermined efforts at adjustment and economic development. Diversity and heterogeneity in ethnic and cultural backgrounds creates divisions within the political systems, resulting in nepotism and massive corruption (somehow an acceptable practice), which fosters misallocation of resources and underdevelopment. The mode of governance that has been described as "personal rule" is a "response of political leaders to their central conundrum: How to hold together unintegrated peasant societies in the absence of legitimate authority. However this mode of governance, although permitting regime survival and advancement of political insiders, has an economically destructive tendency."[2] Those problems have been compounded by policy mistakes and various institutional distortions.

IMF CONDITIONALITY

Overview

Before resources can be released, conditionality spells out the types of policies that the IMF expects a member to follow. The member must agree to follow those policies as specified in the agreement, and the IMF adopts safeguards to ensure that the member continues to adhere to the agreed-upon policies. The IMF certainly lacks unlimited resources, and conditionality seeks not only to protect against misuse, but also to ensure that the use of such resources is maximized for the benefit of all members.

One of the purposes of the IMF as outlined in the first of its Articles of Association is "to give confidence to members by making the Fund's resources available to them under adequate safeguards, thus providing them with opportunity to correct maladjustment in their balance-of-payments without resorting to measure destructive to national and international prosperity." This article contains four important elements, namely (1) resources are to be provided on a temporary basis, (2) resources are to be provided under adequate safeguards, (3) resources are for correcting members' balance-of-payments disequilibria, and (4) the IMF frowns on the use of measures it considers to be destructive to international prosperity.

The IMF is regarded as custodian of a reasonable order in the international monetary system. As an important administrator of international liquidity, it has developed policies that are clearly manifested in the types of conditionality it imposes on members requested the use of its resources. The essence of conditionality is that the member must endeavor to undertake an adjustment process, because financing alone fails to correct the basic problem of disequilibrium in the external sector.

The term "conditionality" does not appear in the IMF's original Articles of Association or in any of the subsequent amendments. Nevertheless, conditionality has evolved as an important ingredient in the IMF's lending policies. Although the articles fail to provide explicit guidelines on the types of policies the IMF would expect a member to follow, the member is expected to follow policies that would help the member not only to correct the balance-of-payments problems, but also prevent its recurrence, as well as ensure that the member avoids measures that are harmful to international prosperity. Thus, in the final analysis, the policies pursued must be likely to result in an augmentation of the country's resources so that it can repurchase its currency and satisfy the requirements of temporariness and the revolving nature of the use of IMF resources.

The IMF's conditionality is a safeguard that protects resources; furthermore, the fund usually is convinced that its conditionality—because it is based on sound theory—is the most feasible way to ensure a favorable turnaround in economic conditions. Because the members who have increasingly sought the IMF's assistance have been poor and underdeveloped nations who usually lack the expertise to present well-developed feasible strategies, the IMF's philosophy tends to prevail. In addition, members hardly ever present well-developed feasible alternative strategies. It is no secret that many members who seek the IMF's conditional assistance have been guilty of economic and financial mismanagement, much of it resulting in the serious misallocation of resources, persistent balance-of-payments deficits, inflation, and high external debts. They generally resort to the IMF's discipline when all else has failed. The IMF is usually anxious to carry out its rescue operations, but only on its own terms and condition. The emergency character of such rescue operations usually call for dramatic changes. The IMF does not usually compromise on the core aspects of its conditionality even if the problems were caused by events that were completely beyond the members' control.

Criticisms and Responses

The most criticism of conditionality has come from developing countries who have pleaded for less stringency and more flexibility. Several years ago, Pakistan's minister of finance and coordination contended that "the use of Fund's resources by developing countries is being seriously inhibited because the conditions set are not easy to fulfill in the context of the socio-economic conditions prevailing in these countries."[3]

One major criticism of conditionality is that it conflicts with the primary objectives of national development policies—for example, encouraging growth, eliminating poverty and unemployment, and ensuring a more equitable distribution of income—because of its primary emphasis on demand management. With low levels of capacity utilization, employment, and investment, there seems to be need for expansionary policies not only to stimulate growth, but also to reduce the reliance on protectionist trade policies. In the IMF's view, restricting demand, curbing inflation, sacrificing growth initially, and eliminating the balance of payment deficit are more desirable actions. Thereafter, the IMF argues, a solid foundation would be established for healthier and sustained growth. In the short run, the key is to keep aggregate demand in line with the economy's productive capacity. Besides adequate financing is usually not available for expansionary policies.

A second criticism of conditionality is that it is too standardized and based almost exclusively on traditional Western economies, with institutional and structural assumptions of well-functioning commodity, factor, and money markets.[4] Even in these types of economies, market imperfections of various kinds sometimes prevent the price mechanism from efficiently allocating resources. This problem is exaggerated in the SSA economies with their limited production possibilities and shortages of essential factors of production, raw materials, skills, capital, and foreign exchange.[5] However, reliance on physical controls for the allocation of resources is an inferior alternative because the efficient administrative machinery necessary for its effective functioning is usually lacking in many countries. In addition, a proliferation of controls, usually breeds corruption, which is a most undesirable eventuality, especially for countries with very unequal distributions of income. Given their structural characteristics, most SSA countries feel that the effective implementation of a development strategy inevitably requires some degree of state intervention in the economy. The market cannot be relied on to reach certain desired outcomes.

A third criticism of conditionality is that it is too stringent in the higher credit branches and that the major policy changes advocated by the IMF take much longer to yield results than the three to five years within which repurchases have to be made.[6] The IMF responded by introducing some two-year standby facilities and an extended fund facility that provides medium-term loans over a period of three years that are repayable within four to eight years. A supplementary financing facility was also introduced in response to the complaint that members are forced to comply with the IMF's recommendations on a wide range of policies in return for only a tiny fraction of their financing needs.

A fourth criticism is that the IMF too often and too readily recommends a devaluation and liberalization of exchange and payments arrangements.[7] Many studies (such as those by R. N. Cooper and Sweder van Wijnberger) have pointed to the contractionary effects of a devaluation on output.[8] This devaluation effect imposes very serious damage on countries experiencing very low rates of economic growth. Further, rather than solve the payments problem, the devaluation worsens it because of its immediate inflationary impact. At the same time, because export bases are undiversified and resource mobility is limited between sectors, trade flows are not very responsive to the relative price changes brought on by a devaluation. The supply response necessary for import substitution and export expansion do not materialize in the short run. Thus, specific measures aimed at improving domestic production would improve the balance-of-payments rather than the relative price changes that come with devaluation. The IMF responds that a devaluation is the least painful of all policy alternatives to revitalize the export sector, whose development has been stifled as a result of costs and prices becoming uncompetitive relative to those of trading partners.

Another criticism of conditionality relates to the asymmetrical nature of the adjustment process. The burden of adjustment rests squarely on the deficit countries with no pressure on surplus countries. Thus, it is argued, conditionality has a deflationary bias in the world economy. Although economically strong countries have extensive access to resources for financing, weaker countries can only resort to the IMF and its rigid discipline. The IMF, however, has maintained that poor domestic management is the chief cause of balance-of-payments problems. Indeed, generally it is these economically weak countries who have poorly managed their economies and who have the greatest need for IMF's guidance and direction in the running of their economic affairs.

A final criticism of conditionality is that it is politically unsustainable.[9] When conditionality is accompanied by greater economic hardship—especially for the mass of poor who lack the resilience to reduce the adverse effects of conditionality—it becomes politically unacceptable. Many SSA governments have had to deal with a variety of civil disturbances as a result of pursuing policies under IMF conditional assistance. In addition, conditionality has been attacked for its nonneutrality, because it is favorable to and supportive of socioeconomic groups who control capital and financial resources and thus are well poised to take advantage of the price and market mechanism. Inevitably, there will be further entrenchment of those groups within the economic and productivity structure.

The New Guidelines

In response to criticisms, the IMF in 1979 attempted to make its conditionality more flexible with a view to expanding access to its resources under easier terms. Although hailed as a major improvement, the new guidelines have neither eliminated nor reduced conditionality to any significant degree. What the new guidelines do is merely create an easier and more flexible base of the application of basically the same patterns of conditionality. The heart and spirit of conditionality have not been compromised; the new guidelines have only fiddled with its peripheries.

The IMF is probably unwilling to compromise because of the apprehension that once it starts to do so, the diverse nature of SSA and its problems would require so many exceptions that it would be extremely difficult to apply the rules in a nondiscriminatory manner. Instead, the IMF has endeavored to broaden the base within which the rules are applied. Some new provisions include encouraging members to seek assistance at the early stage of their problem, agreeing to consider standby arrangements of more than one year's duration, agreeing to "pay due regard" to the domestic social and productivity objectives of members, and omitting phasing and performance criteria in the first credit tranche. In sum, the changes are superficial and certainly have not compromised on the essential aspects of conditionality. Based on the IMF's record in SSA, there is a very strong case for the new guidelines to be amended. The new amendments should recognize rigidities such as resource immobility and shortages of essential inputs (e.g., foreign exchange, capital, and skilled personnel) that thwart adjustment efforts in low-income countries. Furthermore, the commodity composition of exports, the extent of poverty, and productivity fragility must be duly regarded in the design and implementation of the IMF's conditionality.

THE IMF STABILIZATION STANDBY MODEL

The stabilization program was designed to tackle several economic problems in countries of diverse institutional setting. Increasingly, however, countries seeking IMF assistance under a stabilization program not only are usually afflicted by balance-of-payments problems, but also are experiencing the scourge of inflation and very unsatisfactory rates of growth.

Although the policy measure included in a stabilization program will vary depending on the cause and magnitude of the payments problem, the IMF has a standard prescription for problems of balance-of-payments deficits and inflation. The basic feature of the IMF package would include an exchange-rate devaluation, demand restraint, and liberalization of foreign trade and payments.[10] The IMF position is that because the problems typically result from a persistent balance-of-payments deficit, fiscal deficits, and high inflation, policies should be designed to curb demand and promote efficient reallocation of resources into the traded goods sector.[11]

IMF policy seems to be preoccupied with short-term economic objectives and their budgetary impacts on short-term economic conditions, ignoring the long-term factors and their impact on the government budgetary position. The emphasis on demand restraint and cuts in government expenditure has a negative effect on the quality of infrastructure, capital stock, and administrative efficiency in the public service. Thus, the deflationary package undermines the prospects for growth by reducing investment and creates additional unemployment in a situation in which severe underemployment and unemployment are quite common. Further, as expenditures on education, health, and nutrition programs are reduced, long-term growth is again seriously undermined.[12]

Because monetary expansion results from government's deficit financing and credit creation by the banking system, the answer to the problem of inflation is to reduce credit to government and to cut government spending. Consequently, in the pursuit of antiinflation policies, wages that are already very low are held down, government subsidies are eliminated, taxes and prices of public utilities are increased, and massive retrenchment takes place. These measures depress real income and welfare of the average citizen, whose standard of living is already deplorably low. Thus, even though the policy prescriptions make sense, they also have undesirable consequences that may be hard to swallow. Rather than insisting on a drastic reduction in government expenditure, the emphasis should be on a redirection of expenditure into the most productive areas. Government spending does indeed promote economic growth.

The commodity composition of exports from SSA has not been favorable for the region to benefit greatly from devaluations. Trade flows have not been very responsive to the relative price changes that a devaluation brings about. This is partly because export bases are undiversified, production is generally dependent on imported inputs, and resource mobility is limited between sectors. The elasticity of export supply tends to be low at least in the short run because of the nature of exports (agricultural and with a long gestation period), and import elasticity is also low because imports have generally been squeezed down to bare essentials of food, intermediate goods, and capital goods.[13] A further reduction in these imports can only have even more disastrous consequences. The elasticity of demand is also low because of the characteristics of African products. Typically, these products are not consumed domestically and foreign buyers are not quite responsive to price reductions for these goods. Even when goods may have a potential, protectionist trade barriers in the industrial countries make it difficult for African countries to penetrate those markets.

Because of a serious shortage of foreign exchange, most countries utilize exchange and trade controls to ration scarce foreign exchange among the various competing alternatives.[14] By liberalizing exchange and trade, scarce foreign exchange is not likely to be allocated in a manner that is consistent with the long-run best interest of the African countries. Liberalizing imports and prices with a view to fostering efficient resource allocation may not be desirable when markets are not structured in a perfectly competitive way. In short, the frequent advice to get prices right may not be desirable when there is a wide divergence between social costs and benefits and when the distribution of income is so highly unequal.

EVALUATION OF IMF STABILIZATION PROGRAMS

A program should be assessed against the background of the primary objectives of a nation's development policies—that is, to encourage growth, eliminate poverty, ensure equity in the distribution of income, and maintain political stability. Assuming the political system has not been disrupted, if the general economic situation has improved and is sustainable, then the program was undoubtedly successful. A general criterion should stress the effect of the program on the objectives of national development policy. However, even if these objectives were not fully realized, the program could still be regarded as successful if it has laid a sound base for the future realization of these objectives or if only some of them were achieved. Surely, if the program led to massive starvation while the key economic indicators improved significantly, then it would be a pyrrhic victory. How much economic hardship can a program bring, and are the expected benefits worth the sacrifices? Could a program have been modified so that improvements in the key indicators could have been realized at lower costs to the average citizen? Did a program arrest a deteriorating situation even if conditions did not improve? These questions cannot be easily answered; therefore, it is somewhat more difficult to assess IMF programs.

A variety of studies have attempted to assess SSA performance under IMF stabilization programs. Several studies performed by IMF staff have concluded that the results have been "mixed"; for example, see the study by Justin Zulu and Saleh Nsouli.[15] Other IMF staff studies have emphasized some of the limitations in attempting to assess IMF programs. The bulk of studies outside the IMF have consistently indicated that performance under IMF programs have been very disappointing; see those conducted by John Loxley, Tony Killick, Frances Stewart, and the United Nations Economic Commission for Africa (UNECA).[16] In a 1987 study, Stewart concluded that "after undergoing tough programs, many countries found themselves with reduced growth potential and often with no significant improvement in their external accounts."[17] Admittedly, conditions in the international economy have been subversive to adjustment efforts, but this does not seem to be the primary reason for disappointing performance.

IMF programs have been criticized for their excessive preoccupation with short-term economic objectives and their effect on short-term economic conditions. Long-term factors such as declining infrastructure and capital stock and the existence of massive unemployment should be taken into account before prescribing drastic reductions in government expenditure, particularly in economies in which government spending contributes significantly to the volume of economic activity and economic welfare. When development expenditures are cut, then unemployment and economic hardships are made worse.

Because of its concern for stability in the international monetary system, the IMF has appealed to a philosophy that stresses monetary and financial stability as its main concern and which is less favorable to policies that would facilitate and accelerate economic growth. The attitude of the IMF is that the pursuit of sound monetary and financial stability policies is a necessary requisite for meaningful economic growth. Others have argued, however, that the priority attached to monetary stability is too extreme and that there is a strong case for change where the policies do not contribute significantly to or are in conflict with the objectives of national development policies. SSA countries are usually faced with the central dilemma embodied in the conflicting nature of monetary stability on the one hand and economic growth on the other. However, they usually have little alternative but to adopt the IMF's conditionality if they are to gain access to foreign exchange and increase their prospects for aid from Western banks and multilateral institutions through loans, grants, or debt relief. No doubt, the monetary problems of SSA nations are strongly connected with the fact of underdevelopment. Therefore, attempts to solve the monetary problem, independent of the developmental problem, would be futile or at least will encounter serious obstacles. The IMF has argued that it is not a development institution. However, since the fund's inception, it has done well in terms of institutional innovations designed to meet the changes and challenges of a dynamic world. It could use such ingenuity to provide development assistance in addition to its current functions.

Conditionality certainly is too stringent in the upper credit branches, but no one questions the need for the IMF to safeguard its resources. Therefore, the point that has been emphasized is not whether there is need for conditionality, but rather which specific type and nature should be imposed. Conditionality that increases the economic hardships of the poor is as unacceptable as it is inequitable. Conditionality that reduces a government's scope and ability to develop and manage the economy, and which further entrenches powerful socioeconomic groups within the economy, must also be avoided. Conditionality that threatens the survival of a legitimate government is also unacceptable at least to that government even if it is guilty of gross mismanagement. Conditionality should be altered so that it not only addresses the issue of balance-of-payment adjustment, but also complements a long-term strategy of economic, social, and political development that strengthens and consolidates the ability of a government and a people to successfully implement adjustment programs.

ALTERNATIVES TO IMF PROGRAMS

There is unanimity that, during the past decade, SSA nations have failed to reach adjustments that are required for sound economic development. Indeed, countries that have been assisted by the IMF performed just as poorly as those who received no such assistance.[18] Although the international environment has been recognized as somewhat hostile to adjustment efforts, the IMF typically blames lapses in implementation for failure of programs. Other observers have attributed blame to the inappropriateness of conditionality. In reality, these two apparently different views are merely different expressions of the same thing: When conditionality is inappropriate, it is unlikely to be implemented; thus, a failed program can be traced ultimately to an inappropriately designed program. For example, to the extent that a deficit in the budget stems from overexpenditure by government and finance of this expenditure was effected by borrowing from the banking system, then it is reasonable to expect that part of the return to stability and normalcy should take place through spending and bank loan cutbacks. In practice, the optimum rate of deflation that is consistent with the restoration of equilibrium in the balance of payments and the maintenance of respectable levels of growth and employment is difficult to determine. When conditionality leads to what is perceived as a too-rapid reduction in government expenditure, and a government realizes the political and welfare implications of such cutbacks, then it may become less willing to implement a program. Thus, when conditionality if perceived as inappropriate, there tends to be a lapse in implementation.

Several arguments have been made for changes in conditionality to foster adjustment and growth. Daniel Schydlowsky argues that the need for alternatives arises because the usual applied techniques seem to yield a mix of balance-of-payments improvement that is based far too little on growth of exports and far too much on the reduction of imports.[19] Sidney Dell points to the low capacity to adjust as a good reason for change.[20] Although G. K. Helleiner, John Loxley, and the United Nations Economic Commission for Africa emphasize SSA structural characteristics, Tony Killick suggests that the IMF should adopt its conditionality to correspond with the changing geography of its clients—that is, the poorer less-developed countries.[21] The main philosophy of the structuralist approach as outlined by Loxley is that programs should be tailored to the structural characteristics of the country in question and with the specific economic problems being faced at a particular time, rather than being applied as a standard deflationary package. Killick recommends that the World Bank, which is more development-oriented and sympathetic to poor countries, absorb the IMF.[22] Stewart advocates certain changes in international environment, especially in the areas of international demand, trade, commodity prices, and flows of finance.[23] Further, she emphasizes that countries should devise their own conditionality that reflects their own objectives and political, social, and economic circumstances.[24] Other alternatives have recommended the introduction of more symmetry in the adjustment process, extending stabilization programs and repurchases, increasing the political power of poor countries to give them a bigger voice in the decision-making process, increasing IMF resources, and so on.

The main case for change rests on the claim that the IMF does not adequately take into account the basic structure of African economies; for example, the commodity composition of exports, the long gestation period of exports, the dependence of productive capacity on imported inputs, the shortage of essential inputs, the largely undiversified export base, the limited infrastructure and resource mobility, the fluctuations in commodity prices, the political power of urban workers, the diversity of tribes and cultures, the rudimentary financial infrastructure and the highly imperfect capital markets, and the fragility of the governments.

One common denominator to most of the suggested alternatives is that more resources should be provided to SSA nations. The reality is that the amount of resources needed from outside do not seem forthcoming. In the past, SSA nations have been too dependent on foreign aid, and the region can ill afford to continue to wait and hope for foreign assistance. No doubt there is need for changes in both the international environment and within SSA; however, the major emphasis should be directed at meaningful changes in structure, policies, and attitudes within the region. The international community is more likely to be more responsive to pleas for additional resources from a region that is making genuine efforts at adjustment.

Assuming, therefore, that help is not forthcoming from the richer nations and that the impetus for adjustment and growth should originate from within the region, what can SSA nations do? This chapter suggests a sacrifice approach to adjustment and growth in the region. In this approach, the major initiative should come from within the individual countries, with officials being urged to abandon their personal and selfish interests for the common good. No doubt a wide variety of problems in the region impeded the drive toward rapid and sustained development and some of these problems are outside the region's control. However, it is my firm belief that a sizable proportion of the problems could be eliminated if there is the political will to do so. Much too often governments adopt policies that are obviously unprogressive and detrimental to national development. This inexcusable practice predominates largely because governments do not feel accountable to the people. There is little doubt that SSA countries can improve performance by making desirable internal changes; the degree of improvement will depend on the extent to which those changes are successfully implemented. It would be silly to pretend that such changes will eliminate all problems or that they will transform African into a North American or Europe in a short period of time. However, they would represent a significant contribution toward encouraging growth, eliminating or reducing poverty, and ensuring equity in the distribution of income.

There is no doubt that the main problems of persistent balance-of-payments and fiscal deficits, inflation, and external debt service could be traced to inadequacies in the productive sectors. The obvious answer, therefore, is to correct these inadequacies and extend production possibilities. Any package of measure designed to achieve this goal should strike a proper balance between "appropriate" market prices and regulation. The primary emphasis should be self-sufficiency in food so that, at the minimum, each country can provide its basic food requirements. Next, production for exports should be encouraged. There are many major advantages to achieving self-sufficiency in food: Basic needs would be more fully satisfied, the demand for imports would fall, inflation would decline, the balance of payments would improve, there would be less pressure on such government resources as food subsidies, more resources would be released for development, a vibrant and well-nourished pool of potentially productive workers would become available, the manufacturing sector would be given a boost, and political stability would tend to be greater. One problem is that the resources required to initiate production usually are not available. Indeed, in SSA nations there is a serious foreign-exchange shortage that has undermined the growth and adjustment prospects. Faced with huge external debts and balance-of-payments deficits, countries have been forced to curtail imports to the detriment of production. Because production is somewhat dependent on imported inputs, and given that nonessential imports have in general been eliminated, the axe falls on essential inputs. If self-sufficiency in food production is realized, much needed foreign exchange would become available for other ventures such as the rehabilitation of existing infrastructure and raising productive capacity.

One major inadequacy in the productive sector is the low productivity of investments. This can be traced partly to the inadequacy of infrastructure. The region is in serious need for basic infrastructure, including roads, transportation systems, vocational and technical schools, hospitals, water-supply systems, and agricultural extension services. Again, substantial resources are needed to provide these basic infrastructures, and the question of resource availability emerges once more. The resource constraint can be met in part if local governments in consonance with national governments can mobilize the mass of people for self-help projects. If the authorities can impress upon local communities the need for communal effort in social overhead construction and also emphasize the link between the community's efforts and the rewards, then more and more people would be inclined to participate. It is highly essential, however, that the leaders set a good example in terms of both commitment and conduct. Thus, by encouraging mass participation and utilizing labor-intensive techniques, some of the resources needed can be tapped from within the local economies.

To rehabilitate and develop basic infrastructure and initiate and expand production with a major emphasis on food self-sufficiency, many inputs would have to be purchased with resources that seemingly are unavailable. A major portion of these resources can come from eliminating administrative inefficiency provided the political will exists to do so. The term "administrative inefficiency" refers to fraudulent conversion and embezzlement of a state's resources, overinvoicing of government purchases, and simple waste of government resources. Of these three forms of administrative inefficiency, the main culprits in SSA nations are the first two. These have tended to be downplayed, thereby giving the impression that the problem lies with the third, the result of inefficiency. In fact, with the exception of opposition groups in SSA nations (when they are allowed to operate), important groups such as multilateral agencies, international organizations, developed countries' governments, international banks, and even educated elites within SSA nations have failed to seriously condemn the rampant practices of overinvoicing and embezzlement of state resources. Corruption has impoverished the peoples of Africa for too long, and all concerned should take the responsibility of attempting to reverse the undesirable situation.

Robert Klitgaard attributes incompetence and corruption to low public-sector salaries.[25] I would argue that low salaries are not the primary cause of corruption, at least in the lower and middle levels of public administration. Corruption is encouraged within an economic system if it is pervasive within the upper echelons of public administration; and the more offenders go unpunished, the greater the tendency for officials to be corrupt. Corruption has become "so regularized and institutionalized that organization[s] support wrong-doing and actually penalize those who live up to the old norms."[26] Throughout SSA, there have been numerous reports of improprieties continuously and consistently perpetuated by public officials and private individuals to the detriment of national well-being. Thousands of cases are well known to Africans, especially, with many individuals' wealth and life-styles exceeding the budget allocation for an entire ministry. It is not uncommon for some public officials to possess wealth that exceeds the total value of their lifetime income, assuming that they saved all their incomes and worked for a hundred years. Sandbrook reports that a good share of the spoils of office are wasted on such things as conspicuous consumption, real estate speculation, and foreign holdings.[27]

In countries in which the topmost leadership has established a reputation as dedicated, honest, intolerant of corruption, and eager to severely punish offenders, there tends to be less corruption or at least fewer reported cases—for example, Guinea during the period of president Sekou Toure and Gambia during most of President Jawara's rule. Also, Rawlings of Ghana has (among other things) made considerable efforts to wipe out corruption, and the country has reversed its downward slide into economic decay, partly as a result of curbing corruption. On the other hand, in Sierra Leone, Zaire, Nigeria, and Liberia, where top leaders have been corrupt or have paid only lip service to reform, corruption has continued to loom as a potent evil that has destroyed the foundation for reasonable levels of economic development. It seems therefore that the extent to which corruption and administrative inefficiency exists is a function of the degree to which it exists or is encouraged at the top levels. During the brief regime of Juxon-Smith in Sierra Leone, administrative efficiency reached its highest level ever. The main reasons were the serious commitment on the part of the leadership, its exemplary conduct, and the sanctions imposed on offenders.

Chief offenders in the area of fraud and embezzlement of government resources and overinvoicing are politicians and public-sector officials. In the area of overinvoicing, the same offenders join forces with multinational firms, private contractor financiers, private individuals, and domestic firms. The amounts involved are certainly not trivial, and cases abound in which governments have had millions siphoned away through these very common and somewhat acceptable practices. In the adjustment process, the leadership must be committed to eliminating corruption and fraud, especially within the government and public sectors.

Furthermore, politicians, top civil servants, and other top public officials must be prepared to alter their behavior radically by committing completely to adjustment and growth. They have been entrusted with the difficult tasks of designing and implementing appropriate programs, and they also have to assume the role of convincing the mass of poor that more sacrifices must be made for the common good. In setting the pace, a government can start with a rationalization of its foreign-exchange budget. Expenditure on government imports, embassies, diplomatic missions, and foreign travel must be subjected to serious cost-and-benefit evaluation. Even in the face of serious foreign-exchange shortages, some government officials continue to be accompanied by huge delegations to useless trips to foreign countries and Central Banks, usually under political pressure, allocate foreign exchange for absolutely inessential expenditures. Serious foreign-exchange savings can come from this area. It is indeed scandalous for government officials to drive the latest models of luxury automobiles through unpaved and pot hole-infested streets, and when people face starvation less expensive cars would be equally useful and far less costly. When leaders can be seen to be making sacrifices themselves, it becomes easier to mobilize the mass of people into providing infrastructures and other self-help communal projects that utilize labor-intensive techniques.

Another major component of SSA adjustment and growth should be the formation of regional and economic unions or customs unions that would closely integrate economies in the region. The advantages of economic integration that fosters inter-African trade will include greater economies of scale, foreign-exchange savings, increased production efficiency, and better terms of trade especially through the monopolistic pricing of their products. SSA should start producing the goods that would lead to flourishing inter-African trade. The Linder thesis, which has received substantial empirical verification, suggests that trade will flourish between countries with similar per capita income. This has not been true for SSA, largely because of the absence of the institutions and other structures that promote trade. When customs unions are established, there may be some initial disruptions as existing trade patterns are altered, but the gains are likely to be worth the sacrifice.

A final component of adjustment is the adoption of a zero-debt policy. Countries that have been caught in a debt trap should refrain from debt that further increases the debt burden. All foreign exchange and government budgets must be based on availability of domestic resources, realistic forecasts of export earnings, commitments for long-term loans, and legitimate access to international sources of soft loans. Countries have to become very selective in seeking or accepting capital from abroad; therefore, contractors' finance, suppliers' credit, Eurocurrency credits, and commercial bank credits all have to be removed from the region's repertoire as sources of foreign exchange. Sacrificing these sources of credits is in the long-term interest of an economy: They only tide a country over for a short period before the problem reemerges with greater intensity.

CONCLUDING REMARKS

SSA nations have performed very poorly with or without IMF programs. Although IMF programs emphasize structural adjustments in their design and implementation, they somehow do not adequately take into account the economic, political, and social structures of SSA. For instance, the nature of SSA's exports and the limitations of intersectoral resource mobility are ignored in determining the nature and magnitude of exchange-rate adjustments. Also, the political structure and influence of urban workers are ignored in conditionalities relating to prices, taxes, and subsidies.

Many alternatives have been suggested, but they mostly emphasize the role of the international community and call for more resources to be transmitted into the region. In reality, most of those resources do not seem forthcoming; where they are, they will at least initially increase the debt burden unless they are of such long-term nature that repayments fall due only after investments have become productive. A feasible alternative is what has been described as the sacrifice approach,which takes into account availability and access to resources and urges officials to become more responsible and accountable to the public. The sacrifice approach will succeed only if there is genuine commitment and willingness to make sacrifices, especially on the part of leaders. A key ingredient in any package of measures is the elimination of corruption and the presence of a strong democratic process. The issue is much more a question of political will than of economic capacity. A political will of sufficient intensity can galvanize authorities and the mass of people into formulating, adopting, and implementing the structural changes that would lead to rapid and self-sustaining economic growth.

NOTES

1. Robert Klitgaard, "Incentive Myopia," *World Development, 17*(4) (1989): 447–459.

2. Richard Sandbrook, "The State and Economic Stagnation in Tropical Africa," *World Development, 14*(3) (1986): 319–332.

3. International Monetary Fund, *IMF Survey* (Washington, D.C.: IMF, 1980), p. 344.

4. Cheryl Payer. *The Debt Trap: The IMF and the Third World* (New York: Monthly Review Press, 1974).

5. John Loxley, "Alternative Approaches to Stabilization in Africa," in G. K. Helleiner, ed., *Africa and the IMF* (Washington, D.C.: IMF, 1986), p. 134.

6. Loxley, *Africa* p. 121.

7. Louka T. Katseli, "Devaluation: A Critical Appraisal of IMF's Policy Prescriptions," *American Economic Review* (May 1983): 359.

8. R. N. Cooper, "Currency Devaluation in Developing Countries," *Essays in International Finance No. 86,* International Finance Section, Princeton University (1971); and Sweder van Wijnberger, "Exchange Rate Management and Stabilization

Policies in Developing Countries," *Journal of Development Economics, 23* (1986): 227–247.

9. Loxley, "Alternative Approaches," p. 125.

10. Payer, *Debt Trap*; and Daniel M. Schydlowsky, "Alternative Approaches to Short Term Economic Management," Center for Latin American Development Studies, Discussion Paper No. 50 (Boston: Boston University, 1981), p. 105.

11. Manuel Guitan, "Economic Management and International Monetary Fund Conditionality," in Tony Killick, ed., *Adjustment and Financing in the Developing World* (London: IMF, 1982), p. 77.

12. Frances Stewart, "Should Conditionality Change?" in Kjell Havnevik, ed., *The IMF and the World Bank in Africa: Conditionality, Impact, and Alternatives* (Uppsala, Sweden: Scandinavian Institute of African Studies, 1987), p. 39.

13. Loxley, "Alternative Approaches," p. 119. See M. E. Bond, "Agricultural Responses to Prices in Sub-Saharan African Countries," IMF Staff Papers 30, No. 4, Washington, D. C. (Dec. 1983): 703–26, for empirical estimates of supply elasticities in Africa.

14. Payer, *Debt Trap*, p. 33.

15. See their "Adjustments Programs in Africa: The Recent Experience," IMF Occasional Paper, No. 34, Washington, D.C. (April 1985). See also Alhasane Outtara's "Design, Implementation and Adequacy of Fund Programs in Africa," in Helleiner, *Africa,* 86.

16. Loxley, "Alternative Approaches"; and Loxley, "The IMF, World Bank and Sub-Saharan Africa: Policies and Politics," in Havnevik, *World Bank in Africa*; Tony Killick, ed., *The Quest for Economic Stabilization: The IMF and the Third World* (London: Heinemann Educational Books, 1984); Stewart, "Change?," p. 33. and United Nations Economic Commission for Africa (UNECA), *Alternative Framework for Structural Adjustment Programmes for Socio-Economic Recovery and Transformation,* E/ECA/CM/15/6Rev.3.

17. Stewart, "Change?," p. 33.

18. Stewart, "Change?," p. 33.

19. Schydlowsky, "Alternative Approaches, p. 106.

20. See his "Stabilization: The Political Economy of Overkill," World Development, 1982, *10*(8)(1982): 597–612.

21. Tony Killick et al., "The IMF: Case for Change in Emphasis," Richard E. Feinberg and Valeriana Kallab, eds., in *Adjustment Crisis in the Third World* (Transition Books, 1984) p. 31; Loxley, "Alternative Approaches"; and UNECA, *Alternative Framework.*

22. Killick, *Quest.*

23. Stewart, "Change?," p. 40–41.

24. Stewart, "Change?"

25. Klitgaard, "Myopia," p. 447.

26. G. E. Caiden and N. J. Calden, "Administrative Corruption," Public Administration Review, *37*(3)(1977): 306.

27. Sandbrook, "Stagnation."

Chapter 13

Democracy, Equity, and the Myth of the Welfare State in Developing Countries: The Case of Central America

William L. Ascher

Democracy, equity, and growth must be pursued together for sustained develop-ment in Central America. Economic justice and political stability cannot succeed through the standard recipe of statist regulation masquerading as "progressive reform," which has often resulted in greater inequality. Certain policy reforms can both dismantle the privileges for the wealthy embedded in governmental inter-vention and improve the efficiency of Central American economies. The direct economic role of Central American governments should be to oversee a strong human resource strategy.

PROLOGUE

In thinking about the redevelopment of Central America, we have to realize that there is a narrow space in which democracy, equity, and economic growth can be pursued together. The narrowness of this space is sometimes taken as an argument against trying to pursue democracy in cases of compelling economic growth needs or even in cases such as South Korea and Taiwan where the government proposes to pursue both growth and equity at the cost of democ-racy. The premise of this chapter, however, is that pursuing democracy and *equitable* economic growth is both normatively compelling and, in many cases, essential for sustained economic growth. In Central America, at least, it is very easy to argue that the economic boom of the 1950s and 1960s was untracked by

This is a revised version of a lecture delivered on March 26, 1990, at Lynchburg College in Lynchburg, Virginia, as part of the Third World Lecture Series.

disruption that was fueled by dissatisfaction with dictatorship and maldistribution of income, wealth, and land.

Therefore, the emphasis ought to be on how to find and occupy this space, even if it is narrow. Is it difficult to pursue growth, equity, and democracy simultaneously? Of course. But it is not just "worth doing"—it is *the* essential challenge of development.

Exploring the prospects for Central America can help to develop a conception of a just state that looks out for the welfare of its citizens, particularly its currently poor citizens; such a conception will be appropriate for developing countries in general. In particular, this is the model underlying the recommendations made by the International Commission for Central American Recovery and Development,[1] an independent group of forty-seven leaders from twenty countries who are organized to write a blueprint for equitable and democratic development for Central America now that the civil wars in Nicaragua and El Salvador have subsided. Now that the armed conflicts in these countries apparently have ended, the chances for the commission's recommendations to play a major role are extremely high.

As have many other regions in the Third World, Central America has experienced a combination of extreme poverty and, except for Costa Rica, a dramatic lack of democracy by any reasonable definition of the word. Yet Central America experienced rather impressive economic growth from the late 1950s to the mid-1970s. Some of the governments took on the mantle of champions of the poor. But even though economic growth did take some of the poor up the economic ladder, many were left behind. The past decade of war and economic collapse has made practically everyone worse off.

Therefore, the economic recovery process again holds the danger of repeating an economic growth process that addresses neither equity nor democracy. To ensure that Central America's short-term economic recovery can contribute to long-term, equitable, democratic development, we have had to find a different role for government and its associated institutions. For convenience, we call this "the role of the state." The conception of the appropriate role of the state outlined here will be unorthodox, inasmuch as its bears little resemblance to what currently passes for a "welfare state" in less developed countries.[2] First, however, it is important to clarify why a new conception is required.

REQUISITES OF DEMOCRACY

We must begin by meditating on what democracy requires. It is not enough to have formal channels of democratic participation: They are necessary, but not sufficient, conditions for true democracy. A nation also needs people who are willing and able to participate politically. To a surprising degree, democratic participation requires an *economic base*. Thus, while the commission's plan has called for the development of democratic political institutions, it also has emphasized the crucial importance of providing the poor with the economic where-withal to take advantage of those institutions and to do so responsibly.

The key to effective democratic participation is the capacity to organize, and the key to organization is to have the economic resources and skills necessary for people, including and especially the poor, to get themselves organized. Organization requires resources: time, money, and skills. In developed countries, it is often taken for granted that innumerable political groups—existing apart from government—allow our citizens to participate in deliberations over policy without control by the government. These include labor unions, business associations, civic organizations, and other voluntary associations. In the typical developing country, the unorganized participate in a sporadic, often chaotic, and easily manipulated fashion.[3] Often they are too easily mobilized by populist leaders who so often end up abandoning the truly poor.

When the extremely poor, unorganized masses do participate in opposition to the government, it is typically in a highly polarized, confrontational, untempered mode that leads to uprisings, retaliatory massacres, and then renewed repression. Authoritarian leaders feel vindicated when democratic openings end in violent confrontation, and the government sends in troops to put down the rampaging masses.

Thus, there is a critical connection between economics and democracy that goes far beyond the mere fact that democracy might provide the poor with the opportunity to press for more wealth. More wealth in the hands of the poor is a crucial requisite for sustained democratic participation.

Now, the so-called welfare state that has become so prevalent in advanced industrial societies provides benefits to a very large proportion of our population, although even in these cases there are inequities. First, the benefits are based on an economy that can afford to extend them rather broadly; second, they have been *won politically* by those who receive them. When the government of a developing country, with a much poorer economic base and more unbalanced political power, claims that its interventions are to the benefit of the poor, we are justifiably suspicious, particularly in Latin America, where the state plays the largest role in the economy outside of the former Soviet-bloc countries. Here the claim that governmental intervention is progressive clashes strongly with the fact that Latin America has the worst distribution of income of all regions of the world.

The problem is that when there is little political pressure from the poor themselves, governments that set out to formulate policies ostensibly designed or intended to help them often end up constructing policies whose benefits are instead captured by the wealthy. This is because of the two different paths to helping the poor: One is the path of least resistance for financially strapped governments, and the other has often been rationed in favor of the nonpoor.

The first path is the policy-oriented, market-distorting state. This arises when governments act in the name of the poor by setting prices and manipulating regulations as the basic means for determining who gets what. This is in contrast to the approach of providing goods and services directly. For example, if the government wants to provide cheap food to the poor, it can either prohibit high food prices or it can sell or give food to the poor. When the government takes the tack of manipulating prices and regulations, it requires the constant attention of a large cadre of bureaucrats, and the system usually does not work very well. The most dangerous side effect is that the government or the state itself benefits from this kind of intervention, by increasing the number and importance of state officials. Therefore, even if the system is not working effectively, the state has a vested interest in its continuation.

The second path is that of the state as direct provider. The state can provide education, housing, food, health services, modest loans, family-planning assistance, and so on directly to the poor. Of course, the state can also pay the private sector, or the nonprofit segment of the private sector, to provide these benefits to the poor. Unfortunately, where the poor have not had much political power, these benefits have often been steered to the nonpoor.

Historical experience in Latin America has shown that the first path is disastrous because the likelihood that regulation and market distortion will truly be used to benefit the poor is low—*and* this path can easily kill the country's economic growth prospects. The second path is more viable, but it requires strong supportive mechanisms to ensure that the direct provision of goods and services are not drained off by the nonpoor.

THE NATURE OF POVERTY

On the most fundamental level, poverty means a large segment of people with extremely low productivity. Poor people remain poor when they lack the capacity to increase their productivity. This premise does not depend on assuming that people are typically entrepreneurial or like to work especially hard, but rather that when the opportunity arises to get richer, most people will take it.

This can be shown by many rather surprising examples. In El Salvador, the economic basket case of Central America, one will nonetheless find that many people who own small shops or drive taxi cabs are from peasant families. *Their* children—if peace truly has been restored to their country—may end up as professionals. In Guatemala, Mayan-speaking women, whom one would think are very far from modernity, produce beautiful handicrafts that find their way to the shops of Miami and Washington.

What these examples show is that the poor are not always, or even typically, the pathetic creatures that we see on well-intentioned documentaries. The poor can be very hard-working and enterprising—*when given the incentives*. The key issue, then, is why the incentives are so often lacking.

So the question becomes, "What accounts for the fact that such large segments of the populations of poor countries lack the opportunity to increase their productivity?" In some cases, the natural resource endowments of the country are so limited or the physical conditions so daunting that opportunities are simply lacking. However, in most poor countries, the resource endowment would permit greater productivity—or the resources could be brought to the people from abroad. Therefore, the question that should be raised is whether the resources for greater productivity—land, labor, capital, skills, and technology—are being withdrawn or withheld in any particular case.

Many studies have demonstrated that the poor often lose out because of a series of policies that are—ironically but not accidentally—portrayed as *progressive*.[4] This is a very surprising result that requires careful explanation.

It is often assumed that efficiency and equity are opposites and correspond to their associated ideological positions. It is tempting to link the leftist political and economic agenda to both a very strong economic role for the state and progressive income distribution, thereby linking statism to progressivity. But this is often a projection of the ideological assumptions of industrialized societies onto less developed countries.

In less developed countries, governments often expand their roles by claiming that they are reaching out to help the poorest of the poor. But when their reaches fall short, *the resources to finance the governments' expanded roles are extracted, in large part, from the poor themselves.*

This occurs through at least the following ten mechanisms.

1. The rural poor suffer when the government enforces low food prices as a benefit to the urban population. Low food prices also keep down government spending, inasmuch as soldiers are usually fed directly by the state and bureaucrats' wages have to cover their food purchases as well as other necessities.

   The cost of artificially low food prices is borne by the rural poor, who lose the opportunity to earn a decent income. Some produce food for the urban market but get less for it; others cannot even get returns that make it worthwhile to produce beyond their own subsistence needs.

   Note here that there are other ways to make food more affordable to the *urban* poor. The government could buy food at the market farmgate price and sell it at lower prices, provide cash or food stamps to the poor, or invest in agriculture to make farming more productive and food more abundant. However, these alternatives require government spending and thus are constrained by the limitations on taxing capacity. The one way to make food more affordable without penalizing the small farmer is to eliminate the policy distortions that, in many cases, have already pushed up food prices.[5]

2. Even a policy as seemingly esoteric and unconnected to poverty as the official *currency exchange rate* typically discriminates against agriculture, from which the poorest populations make their living. Many developing countries rely on the export of agricultural or other raw commodities. A higher exchange rate that yields fewer units of local currency per

dollar earned will provide lower returns for those who are involved in agricultural export (e.g., banana or coffee growers), while it will make urban consumers better off insofar as they can buy imported goods.

3. When government provides *credit,* even when it claims that cheap credit is intended to help the poor, all too often the poor cannot qualify. They typically lack the collateral, the standing in their communities that is associated with "creditworthiness," the literacy required to fill out forms, the personal connections with the bureaucrats who *ration* credit when it is in short supply, or the capacity to travel to the cities and towns where the lending agencies are situated.[6]

4. When government performs *services* for its population, the greater access of the nonpoor often leaves the poor with a disproportionately small share. Having a well-educated population is wonderful, but the free or nearly free university educations provided in many countries rarely benefit the children of the very poor, who are thus deprived of additional resources for the primary, secondary, and vocational educations that could improve their productivity.

5. The same holds when the government tries to provide the income-maintenance schemes successfully utilized in developed nations, such as *social security* and *unemployment insurance.* To qualify, one must have an income that is already above a certain minimum or one must work in an enterprise large enough to be covered by social security and unemployment insurance programs. In most poor countries, the bottom half of the population simply does not qualify.

6. Because all of these programs require administrators, the interventionist state employs increasing numbers of *government employees,* who in turn absorb an increasing amount of the resources that the government has at its disposal. In this respect, the state sector becomes an economic interest group in its own right, one with an obvious access advantage over the poor when it comes to fighting over who should get the benefits. In the Philippines, for example, the National Food Authority does not do a good job of distributing inexpensive rice to the most nutritionally needy population—although it has very nice discounts for its own employees.

7. The interventionist state can only regulate a limited number of economic actors. These are typically the larger, more modern businesses involved in what we think of as "modern" activities or the so-called formal sector. Inasmuch as most regulation has the effect of improving the status of workers in that sector, *regulation of the formal sector* benefits the workers of that sector, although this comes at the cost of the typically lower-wage workers who toil away in small sweatshops or go unemployed. This is because employers consider all benefits going to their employees as their wages; as these increase, the employer is more disposed to use more machinery and hire fewer workers. Ironically, good treatment of employees by formal sector businesses—when forced

by the government instead of being voluntary actions by the businesses to attract labor—is a major contributor to *unemployment*.

8. The financial support for bureaucrats and what they do, of course, is derived largely from *taxation*. In most developing countries, tax systems are regressive. That is, the rich actually pay a smaller proportion of their incomes than do the nonrich. This is true even when the tax system seems to be based on *progressive* rates of income taxation. The problem, of course, is that some people evade their taxes. A slightly more subtle but equally important problem is that many of the wealthy legally move their economic activities into areas that offer tax exemptions. Such exemptions have often been put on the books to stimulate investments in various areas, but in effect they distort investment flows into areas that do not warrant the investments in terms of society's returns and they naturally reduce the amounts of tax revenues that the government collects. Therefore, governments in developing countries tend to devote their effective revenue-raising efforts where they can collect the money: taxing wages, which must be reported; and taxing cigarettes and other so-called luxury items that constitute a larger proportion of the family budget of the poor family than of the wealthy family.

9. In lieu of normal taxation, governments develop other mechanisms to provide benefits. It has been widely recognized that *inflation* can serve this purpose: Printing more money allows the government to spend, although at the expense of those whose incomes, savings, or purchasing power is reduced through subsequent inflation. This has even been called the "inflation tax." Inflation hurts the poor in several ways. It denies them the opportunity to prosper along with the rest of the economy, because inflation compels investors into investments that protect the value of their money but do not necessarily contribute the most to the productivity of the economy. Inflation also erodes the savings of the poor, who tend to have less flexibility to protect their savings from inflation. It even sometimes allows the government to dilute the benefits it has promised the poor. Witness how in the United States, the *real* value of welfare payments under the Reagan administration dropped dramatically.

10. When the partial welfare states of developing countries run into financial crises—which has been all too often in the last decade because of the debt crisis—the economic stabilization policies that they typically choose or are forced to accept typically exact more sacrifice from the poor than from the nonpoor for two reasons. First, when governments are compelled to reduce spending to bring down inflation, budget deficits, and spending on imports, the better organized groups can more easily fight politically to maintain their benefits. Second, the wealthier the economic actor, the more flexibility that actor typically has to

change economic activities to avoid making the sacrifice. Therefore the so-called austerity packages seen all over Latin America, and in much of Asia and Africa, have typically been devastating to the poor. That is why there has been so much talk about the necessity of "adjustment with a human face."

But here is the biggest surprise. The policy reforms required by institutions such as the International Monetary Fund (IMF) seem very harsh and are usually criticized by governments as damaging to the poorest segments of their securities. These packages typically call for the dismantling of government interventions in the economies. But what makes their impact regressive is not the general thrust of dismantling the government's interventions, but rather the *partial* dismantling of those interventions that do not have strong political support by powerful groups.[7] In other words, it is often the *incompleteness* of the implementation of IMF packages that makes them regressive. The more stringently they are implemented and the harsher the penalties for noncompliance, the more complete their implementation would be and the more progressive they could be.

This seems totally contradictory with the image of the IMF in developing countries, where it is usually cast as the bogeyman bringing sacrifice and inequity against the will of the government that is forced to abide by its cruelty to get essential loans to service the foreign debt. In reality, the IMF generally insists that the government does what the IMF analysts believe that the country needs in the long run; however, this is precisely what is unpopular among those who have political clout—otherwise, the reforms would have been willingly adopted by the government even without the IMF's insistence.

Those who still advocate the classic welfare-state approach are not unaware of these problems. But they argue that we have to start somewhere; that the *coverage* of these policies and programs can be extended, gradually or even rapidly, until it covers virtually all of the population. Was this not the way currently rich and equitable countries, such as Great Britain and Germany, ended up with the entire population enjoying the fruits of the nation's wealth?

The alarming truth, however, is that developing countries such as Brazil and Mexico can become richer on an overall (or aggregate) basis but still not be willing or able to extend the coverage of government benefits to the lower-income segments of the population. Moreover, even aside from the enormous debt burden that so many developing countries face, the maldistribution of income becomes an *obstacle* to further economic growth. The population in a country with severely uneven income is less capable of learning the skills necessary for high productivity, less able to contribute to the demand for domestically made products, and less willing to tolerate economic reforms, even if they are needed.

In addition, the nonpoor who benefit from the privileges embedded in such policies also become less productive. The very distortions that provide them with virtually guaranteed benefits make it more difficult for them to earn bigger profits from true risk taking, which is the essence of capitalism. *Thus what seems to explain the lack of economic growth in so many countries of Latin America, Africa, and Asia—especially when compared to apparent economic miracles such as Taiwan and South Korea—is the absence of risk taking entrepreneurship.*[8]

Therefore, the classical welfare-state model has fared very poorly in developing countries. What are the alternatives?

At this point, one might be tempted to give way to despair. If the rich can so easily take advantage of the poor, and the rich have the power to maintain the current system, then why should we expect any improvements? Fortunately, however, the rich are also dissatisfied with this typical state of affairs. First, it is clearly far better to be a rich person in a growing economy than a rich person in a declining economy. The stagnation of economies hemmed in by the rigidities of special privileges is typically denounced even by those who benefit from the privileges—although they would certainly not be willing to see their own benefits cut back while the government continues to provide benefits for the rest of the nonpoor.

Second, the rich have shown a strong preoccupation with "horizontal equity"—that is the fairness of benefits and burdens for people of roughly the same income levels. Oftentimes, the rich businessman will be more conscious that someone else of the same earning capacity is receiving greater benefits or, even worse, is paying less in taxes! Our studies of efforts at tax reform in developing countries show that the appeal to horizontal equity can gain political support for a fundamental tax reform that also helps to make the tax system more just in terms of the vertical distribution of benefits and burdens.

The solution, then, is to dismantle the privileges for the rich by freeing the economy of many state interventions. Therefore, the key question is, Under what circumstances do "market-freeing" reforms have a net progressive impact? Under what circumstances can "liberalization" mean dismantling the economy-distorting privileges of the wealthy?

It is crucial to bear in mind that the idea of liberalizing the economy in this way has been the darling of groups that would be labeled "conservative" in this country. These are reforms that are rarely viewed by anyone outside of the economics profession as even having the capability to be progressive. Therefore, to espouse this strategy automatically makes one sound like a defender of the right-wing economic approach.

Indeed, policy makers espousing neoclassical positions have not always, or even usually, imposed progressive policies. Surveys of Latin American neoliberal approaches during the 1970s and 1980s show that the "typical" package was the reduction of social services and the suppression of labor movements but not of business associations.[9] The former is typically regressive in terms of overall income distribution; *if* the distributive effects are confined to the modern sector, then the latter also may be. However, neoclassical[10] prescriptions *can* be more progressive than the status quo.

The second problem is that espousing a free market sounds like saying that laissez-faire establishes the optimal distribution; in fact, it only says that the current distribution of benefits and opportunities does not even do as well as laissez-faire.[11] We must therefore go beyond the neutrality of distribution of the free market, as long as economic growth is not jeopardized.

Indeed, there is a way to justify direct benefits for the poor that, far from being an obstacle to economic growth, are essential for long-term growth. This is the *human resources strategy.*[12] To the degree that the economic growth of developing countries depends on improving the skills and robustness of workers, there are substantial gains to be made by *investing in people* as "human capital." For example, the phenomenal economic growth rates of South Korea and Taiwan were *preceded* by huge government investments in *rural* development targeted to the lowest-income populations. Neoclassical economists such as Arnold Harberger have often been the first to see the *economic* benefits of investing in education and health.

How can the dismantling of the market-distorting state and the installation of a human resources strategy be accomplished? There are at least five promising initiatives.

1. *Dismantling in the name of horizontal equity.* At the end of the day, we still have to ask how the nonpoor can be expected to take the risks presented by this bold new strategy. In this regard, it is important to remember that the nonpoor are not unified. They have their own divisions and their own worries about benefits going to others. The limitations of invoking horizontal equity to dismantle only the privileges for the wealthy are (1) that the partial dismantling will still leave room for some privileges and thus threaten those who were willing to forgo theirs only if an empty slate were maintained, and (2) that the remaining benefits could still be stolen away by some of the rich.[13]

2. *Decentralization of decision making.* Some of the most mundane measures, such as decentralizing the budget process so that local governments are in charge of taxation and budgeting, can make a very significant difference.

3. *Organizing the unorganized.* This obviously requires providing them with certain resources: the skills that are necessary to be politically participant. Interestingly, these correspond to many of the same attributes that make people more productive: education, good health, and a bit of surplus cash. This also calls for the *human resource strategy* that emphasizes the importance of making people more productive in order to make the economy more productive and which *also* makes politics more egalitarian.

4. *Reducing other risks.* It is crucial to recognize the relationship between rents and risks. It is true that rents may be sought after because they

provide both benefits and safety. Yet the difficulty of trying to dismantle rents seems to hinge on the problem of security. Many of the societies most beset by economic inefficiency and inequity have become rigid precisely because it is feared that changes would expose currently protected groups to unaccustomed risks. For example, why is credit "rigged" in Guatemala? It is not so much because the rich believe that they have to squeeze every quetzal out of the economy for their own benefit; after all, some of the wealthy in Guatemala are philanthropists of considerable magnitude. This is not so much to gain more power as it is to gain security in an otherwise unstable and unpredictable environment. To have a guaranteed loan for a business venture is the best hedge against disaster if the economic context changes to the point where what would have been a wise business deal turns out to have been totally impractical.

Economic groups will resist policy reforms when the magnitude of costs that they might have to endure cannot be anticipated. Certainly no representative of an economic interest group is going to expose his or her group—and job—to open-ended risk. One prominent member of the Central American Commission, when he was the finance minister of Guatemala, tried to enact a tax reform in his country only to become the target of assassination attempts. But sometimes policy reforms can be linked so that risks are reduced even if costs must still be incurred. The classic case was the 1974 announcement by the president of Colombia that, for the first time, wealthy landowners would be taxed on the basis of the value of their land. However, he also announced that, for the foreseeable future, the government would not pursue the *land reform* that landowners feared even more. The reform was successful.[14]

5. *Conditionality.* Left to their own devices, most governments of developing countries would bow to the power of the wealthy in the absence of other factors. Another major factor, however, is the potential for foreign donors and lenders to insist that the aid they are providing be used to promote equitable development. Thus far, bilateral and multilateral sources of finance—whether the U.S. government, the IMF, or the World Bank—have been quite willing to impose economic reform packages that, in their *partial* implementation, have placed the burden on the poor while many of the rich have wriggled out of their sacrifices.

A POLITICAL-ECONOMIC MODEL FOR CENTRAL AMERICA

How do these insights relate to Central America? Here again, the question is whether these societies can enjoy "growth with equity"—distributive justice and economic efficiency—on a sustained basis. Pessimists with respect to Central America have typically assumed that efficiency and equity are opposites or trade-offs. This view rests on the assumption that the state interventions designed to help the poor (e.g., minimum wages, subsidized loans, make-work jobs) detract from an economy's capacity to respond efficiently to market forces. Similarly, it is often assumed that the wealthy can better afford to save and that these savings go into productive investment. Finally, many people presume that resources devoted to helping the poor are being diverted away from building the nation's productive capacity.

The Central American Commission's "development strategy" focuses on greater overall economic efficiency. This is to be brought about by dismantling the state intervention that provides risk-stifling benefits for the wealthy and by revitalizing the most dynamic source of potential growth—Central American exports. These changes are in turn designed to finance the best long-term approach to making the poor more productive: human resource development.

Where do assumptions underlying the growth-versus-equity trade-off go awry? First, although it may be true that tinkering with the economy to subsidize the poor would detract from market efficiency our background studies revealed that most distortions in Central American economies entailed embedded privileges for the rich rather than the poor. Therefore, the movement toward greater efficiency—by dismantling the rules and programs that distort the economy *to benefit the rich*—can redress inequality as well.

Second, although rich people may be more capable of saving and investing, they may very well not do so in their own domestic economies. Capital flight out of Central America results not only from fear of instability, but also from the lack of attractive investment opportunities, which in turn rests on the small size of consumer markets where large segments of the population are too poor to purchase much beyond the bare necessities. In other words, in the long run, the poverty of millions of Central Americans—currently, 40 percent cannot even afford their basic food needs—is as much an impediment to growth as is the lack of investment capital.

Third, the idea that benefits for the poor detract from economic productivity proves to be a very short-sighted view in the Central American context. Development economics increasingly recognizes the importance of human capital as an essential component of economic growth. Healthier, better-educated workers are more productive. Education and health are also correlated with lower birthrates and therefore could reduce the population pressures that hamper efforts to improve the well-being of each Central American citizen. Therefore, if the benefits going to the poor come through improved education, medical care, nutrition, sanitation, family planning, housing, and community services, then productive capacity can be improved rather than sacrificed for greater equity.

Nonetheless, an existing "motor of growth" must be triggered *now* for economic recovery and development to get started. Poverty alleviation and greater economic justice are the destinations, but a path for arriving there must be found. Except in the most drastic revolutionary circumstance, redistribution does not occur without a growing economy.

Particularly for small economies, the best prospect for growth is in the promotion of *exports,* both traditional exports such as coffee, sugar, and bananas and nontraditional exports such as flowers and light manufactured items. Of course, this requires that Central America's trading partners, including the United States, open their markets to Central American exports.

However, the export-promotion strategy has long been criticized by the left as an inequitable approach to economic growth. If the wealthy economic groups that engage in the export activities are capable of capturing and retaining the lion's share of the export earnings, then why should such activities be promoted? Two points must be clarified. First, "export promotion" does not require subsidizing the groups engaged in export industries. Currently, export production in Central America is actively *discouraged* by economic policies. Exports are disadvantaged by specific taxes, currency-exchange controls, and tariffs against goods from other countries. Thus, once again the improvement in economic policy can be secured by removing existing distortions in the economy—which are not currently benefiting the poor. Second, the wealth coming from exportation can be channeled into human resource development without discouraging export production, as long as exportation is not taxed more heavily than other potential sources of income.

This leads to what may seem an obvious—but also ominous—point. To link the export promotion strategy with the human resource development strategy requires *tax reform* so that at least a moderate amount of surplus generated from revitalized activities (such as exportation and production for the domestic and regional markets) can be directed through government to the poor. With the partial exception of Costa Rica, the tax systems of Central America are woefully inadequate. On the one hand, too few people are subject to the existing income taxes; on the other hand, there is rampant evasion by high-income families and businesses. Efforts at tax reform have often provoked literally violent reactions.

The rechanneling of hard-earned profits from exportation and domestic recovery to human resource development must be deliberate and gradual. The economies must not be starved for investment or more vulnerable to capital flight. As essential as it is, tax reform must leave some incentive for businesses to invest. Redistribution during depressions or even fragile recoveries is politically and economically infeasible. For now, Central America's domestic policies will have to focus on tighter "targeting" of human resource investments for the poor, and greater efficiency in providing these services, until stronger Central American economies can produce significant surpluses.

Clearly, this requires patience, a commodity in understandably short supply in Central America. Only the support of the international community can hasten the implementation of a human resource strategy. This can be done in several ways. First, foreign assistance can focus directly on providing the social services that promote human resource development, particularly of the more than 1 million refugees and internally displaced persons who will require repatriation or resettlement now that peace has been restored. Without such help, Central America will be in grave jeopardy of losing an entire generation to illiteracy and debilitating disease. The collapse of health and education facilities, particularly in Nicaragua and El Salvador, has been extremely alarming.

Second, the governments and international organizations that provide aid, loans, and trade concessions can *condition* these benefits on whether Central American governments adopt policy reforms to make their economies (and political systems) more equitable. To some, this may sound like economic imperialism. However, in signing the Esquipulas Peace Accords in 1987, the Central American presidents committed all five governments to the pursuit of peace, democracy, and equitable development. Therefore, when the International Commission for Central America, with twenty of its forty-seven members from Central America, calls upon the international community to apply progress toward meeting these objectives as the criteria for such *conditionality,* it is reinforcing the values expressed by the Central Americans themselves and holding the five governments to their own commitment.

How does risk reduction figure into planning the recovery of Central America? Perhaps the most likely scenario for Central America is that there will be at least a short-term recovery, during which the economic groups still receiving benefits from as-yet-unreformed policies will argue against further policy changes on the grounds that such changes would "rock the boat." That will be the critical juncture, because it is rather clear that such recovery without reform would lead to a repeat of the dissatisfaction–disruption cycle that has been so costly for the region. It seems that the willingness to go along with reform and all of its risks will depend on whether those who have to acquiesce to the reforms view them as the lesser of the evils. And indeed, there are two possible greater evils, depending on how the wealthy see the world and on how we act toward Central America. First, the wealthy may see another cycle of violence unless the reforms are made. It is impossible to say how many will view the world this way. How chastened is the Central American business sector, or the landowners, or the military that seems, in Guatemala at least, to be taking over much of the land that ought to be better distributed?

Second, virtually every Central American economy would collapse if it were not for U.S. support. Nicaragua is not an exception: Its economy *did* collapse, which explains the Sandinistas' loss as much as anything else. This means that if the United States could credibly signal that its economic assistance were contingent upon continued policy reforms, then the wealthy would have to contrast accepting the reforms with suffering from a potentially devastating withdrawal of economic aid to their countries. Unfortunately, the U.S. record in upholding policy-reform conditionality in Latin America has not been very impressive. During the 1960s and even into the 1970s, the U.S. aid plan for Latin America, known as the Alliance for Progress, formally required land reform, tax reform, and greater equity, but settled for pretty plans that said that these reforms would be undertaken, although they rarely were.

This is a good place to end: The changes and commitments that have to be made in developing countries, such as those in Central America, turn out to require policy changes and commitments on the part of the international community. Is the rest of the world willing to do anything to increase the chances that these will occur?

NOTES

1. *Poverty, Conflict, and Hope: A Turning Point in Central America (The Report of the International Commission for Central American Recovery and Development)* (Durham, N.C.: Duke University Press, 1989).

2. The rather misleading rhetoric provided by defenders of the Latin American welfare state is explored briefly in William Ascher, "On the Convergence of Efficiency and Equity via Neoclassical Prescriptions," *Journal of Interamerican Studies and World Affairs, 31*(1–2) (Spring–Summer 1989): 49–62.

3. This argument was made most eloquently by William Kornhauser, *The Politics of Mass Society* (New York: Free Press, 1959).

4. A good example of this literature is Ian Little, *Economic Development: Theory, Policy, and International Relations* (New York: Basic Books, 1982).

5. For a thorough analysis of these problems, see C. Peter Timmer, Walter P. Falcon, and Scott R. Pearson, *Food Policy Analysis* (Baltimore, Md.: Johns Hopkins University Press for the World Bank, 1983).

6. This issue is evaluated in detail for Central America by Claudio Gonzalez Vega and Jeffrey Poyo, "Central American Financial Development," in William Ascher and Ann Hubbard, eds., *Central American Recovery and Development: Task Force Report to the International Commission for Central American Recovery and Development* (Durham, N.C.: Duke University Press, 1989), pp. 181–211.

7. See Raymond Mikesell, "Appraising Fund Conditionality: Too Loose, Too Tight, or Just Right," in John Williamson, ed., *IMF Conditionality* (Washington, D.C.: Institute for International Economics, 1983), pp. 47–62.

8. A strong formulation of this argument can be found in Anne O. Krueger, "The Political Economy of the Rent-Seeking Society," *American Economic Review, 64*(3) (1974): 291–303.

9. Alejandro Foxley, *Latin American Experiments in Neo-Conservative Economics* (Berkeley: University of California Press, 1983).

10. See Little, *Economic Development,* for a simple definition of "neoclassical," based essentially on "a concern for prices and their role" (p. 26). In essence, neoclassical prescriptions are typically based on a presumption that deviations from market mechanisms, because of price distortions, will do more harm than good.

11. Moreover, neoclassical, market- and price-sensitive development policy is "in." Anyone sympathetic with equitable distribution has an interest in pushing neoclassical prescriptions toward the convergence of efficiency and equity.

12. Paul Streeten's more recent formulations of an economic rationale for basic needs—for example, *Development Perspectives* (London: Macmillan, 1981), which goes beyond his earlier arguments of humanitarian concern—converge with Arnold Harberger's emphasis on the development of human capital, as expressed, for example, in "Investment in Men Versus Investment in Machines: The Case of India," in C. Arnold Anderson and Mary Jean Bowman, *Education and Economic Development* (Chicago:

Aldine, 1965). This is remarkable in light of the presumed antithesis between Streeten's leftist reputation and Harberger's rightist image.

13. This appeal was quite effective in the successful tax reforms in Colombia. See William Ascher, "Risk, Politics and Tax Reform: Lessons from Some Latin American Experience," in Malcolm Gillis, ed., *Tax Reform in Developing Countries* (Durham, N.C.: Duke University Press, 1988).

14. See Ascher, "Risk."

Part Six

Corporate and Professional Responsibility in Third World Development

Chapter 14

Professionals and Third World Public Well-Being: Social Change, Education, and Democratization

Mehrangiz Najafizadeh and Lewis A. Mennerick

Rather than focusing solely on economic development indicators, this chapter elaborates a broader conception of development that draws explicit attention to the central issue of public well-being. First, we critically examine the concept of "development" and argue that professionals should focus instead on the concept of "social change and public well-being." Second, we analyze Third World educational change as potentially the most fundamental component in enhancing well-being. We focus on the inadequacy of Third World educational expansion, variations in expansion, the relationship between education and public well-being, and the relationship between population growth and future educational expansion. Third, we elaborate on education and on other indicators of well-being in relation to democratization, and we explore how various sociopolitical contexts can enhance or hinder particular components of public well-being. We conclude by identifying two specific areas in which professionals who are engaged in activities related to Third World education bear special responsibilities in fostering the well-being of the Third World citizenry.

INTRODUCTION

By virtue of their specialized knowledge and expertise, professionals hold unique positions in the occupational and social hierarchy. Professionals possess the potential to play dynamic roles in shaping Third World social change, and because of their expertise and privileged positions, they also bear special responsibilities in efforts to enhance the well-being of Third World citizenry. Such professionals include government and international-development agency offi-

This is a revised version of a paper presented at the annual meeting of the Association for the Advancement of Policy, Research and Development in the Third World, which was held in Mexico City, Mexico, November 14–17, 1990.

cials who formulate development policies, social scientists who conduct research on and theorize about the Third World, specialists from various disciplines who devise development projects, and practitioners who implement
projects.

In this chapter, we examine the concept of *development* and argue that professionals should focus instead on the alternative concept of *social change and
public well-being*. This latter concept is less Eurocentric and less politically
grounded, while at the same time more immediately central to meeting the
needs of the Third World citizenry. Next, we concentrate extensively on Third
World educational change as a major component of public well-being. Finally,
we elaborate on education and Third World public well-being in the broader
context of democratization, and we identify issues that must receive greater
attention from professionals.

DEVELOPMENT VERSUS SOCIAL CHANGE
AND PUBLIC WELL-BEING

Conceptions of development and the actual activities of professionals engaged
in Third World development programs have varied historically. Before World
War II, development activities of professionals were largely the province of
colonial government officials, Western religious missionaries, and limited numbers of Third World professionals. Throughout this period, development activities primarily reflected the political and economic goals of the colonial powers
and the religious goals of Christian missionary groups, frequently to the detriment of the well-being of indigenous Third World citizens. The 1950s brought
the emergence of the broad concept of development as we know it today. Third
World development activities gained scholarly legitimacy among social scientists through the formulation of modernization theory. By the late 1960s and
early 1970s, dependency theory provided alternative perspectives on development, as did world systems theory. The 1980s brought what some view as a
trend toward convergence of these theories of development and increased attention to comparative historical political economy theory.[1]

During the past four decades, Third World development activities also
gained political legitimacy as governments of the industrialized North—the
United States, Western Europe, and the former Soviet Union—sought to influence the development process. Development activities became intertwined with
competing economic and political ideologies: capitalist economic and democratic political systems stood at one end of the continuum, and socialist or
communist economic and political systems stood at the other end. As such,
development activities have reflected a complex mixture of humanitarian concerns, economic self-interests, and foreign policy objectives of the industrialized North. Throughout, the North has attempted to shape Third World development through various forms of economic and technological assistance, while
on particular occasions also using covert and overt political or military inter-

vention. Development has reflected Northern values and traditions wherein Northern industrialized nations have portrayed themselves as models for the Third World to emulate. And quite often development has been used by the industrialized North as a euphemism for the "Westernization" or the "Sovietization" of the Third World—for Third World social change consistent with Western or Soviet global self-interests and political and economic agendas.

The main shortcoming of such politicization of development is that Northern governments frequently have failed to acknowledge and respect the historical integrity and cultural diversity of particular Third World nations and regions. Perspectives on how Third World nations *should* develop are not value-free. Rather, conceptions of what constitutes appropriate development vary not only between the industrialized North and the Third World but also among Third World citizens. Historically, Third World citizenries have been caught between conflicting and contradictory forces: The United States and Western Europe in relation to the Soviet Union, and the industrialized North as a whole in relation to the Third World. Such forces frequently have been viewed as reflecting the political, economic, and cultural imperialism or hegemony of the industrialized North. However, politicization, corruption, and self-interests associated with development activities also have characterized particular Third World governments (both socialist and democratic) and some segments of the Third World elite, to the detriment of the well-being of the Third World citizenry as a whole.

Given this backdrop, we argue that the concept of development, if not obsolete, is of limited utility. This concept, with its numerous sociopolitical overtones, historically has implied that Third World nations should imitate the sociopolitical systems of *either* the Soviet Union or the West. However, recent events in Eastern Europe and the former Soviet Union, as well as in particular Third World nations, reveal quite clearly that sociopolitical experiments with socialism and communism have not provided promised levels of public well-being. At the same time, it is also evident that, in many instances, efforts by the West to promote democracy and Western-oriented development within the Third World have not always achieved their intended goals.

Therefore, we maintain that professionals should concentrate less on development and more on the concept of *social change and public well-being* and on various types of social transformation that may contribute more effectively to the enhancement of the well-being of all Third World citizens.

Third World social change can take various forms, and recognition of indigenous Third World cultural values and social structures should be central to all social change activities. Of equal importance, however, is the concept of public well-being. While acknowledging the integrity and uniqueness of various Third World cultures, the concept of public well-being also must reflect a core of *universal* values. Public well-being consists of various components, most notably, the provision of food, shelter, health care, and education as well as the assurance of a nonthreatening natural environment, civil liberties, and human rights. In the following analysis, we focus extensively on social change as related to a central aspect of public well-being: the historical expansion and current status of education in the Third World.

EDUCATION AND PUBLIC WELL-BEING IN THE THIRD WORLD

We emphasize education and indicators of educational expansion in this chapter because, in the long term, education is potentially the *most* fundamental component in enhancing public well-being. In addition to its potential to contribute to economic productivity and the provision of adequate food and shelter, education provides the intellectual foundation for increased understanding of matters related to health care and physical well-being, to the prudent use of natural resources and the remedying of environmental problems, and to increased respect for human rights and the implementation and maintenance of civil liberties. The following analysis focuses on the inadequacy of Third World educational expansion, variations in expansion, the relationship between education and public well-being, and the relationship between population growth and future educational expansion. However, before proceeding, it is extremely important to elaborate major limitations of available data.[2]

Third World Educational Data

Central to our analysis of educational expansion is the percentage of youth enrolled in both primary and secondary schools. As the major source of international educational data, the United Nations Educational, Scientific, and Cultural Organization (UNESCO) provides two types of student-enrollment percentages: gross and net. Given that UNESCO calculates gross-enrollment percentages by dividing the total number of students (including older youths and adults who are attending school) by the total number of school-age youths, these percentages frequently exaggerate the actual extent of educational expansion. Indeed, because such older individuals are sometimes included, gross enrollments can exceed 100 percent. As but one example, the African nation of Lesotho has a gross primary school enrollment of 111 percent and a net enrollment of only 71 percent. Thus, net-enrollment percentages exclude older youths and adult students from the calculation and thereby provide more accurate indicators of school expansion.

However, gross-enrollment percentages are available for more countries than are net percentages. Further, only gross percentages are available for combined primary and secondary school enrollment. Therefore, gross percentages are routinely included in various development-related documents: The World Bank's *World Development Report,* the U.N. Population Fund's *The State of the World Population,* The U.N. Development Program's *Human Development Report,* and UNICEF's *The State of the World's Children,* as well as the widely utilized *World Military and Social Expenditures.* The inadequacy of gross percentages is especially noteworthy because, despite their tendency to exaggerate school enrollments, many professionals—including scholars, development specialists, and policy makers—often use such data without qualification in assessing educational change.

Given this cautionary note, we identify enrollment as either gross (G) or as net (N) percentages in the following analysis.

Educational Expansion in the 1980s

Many Third World nations demonstrated major educational expansion during the past several decades. For example, the gross percentage of combined primary and secondary school enrollments increased from an average of 16 percent in 1950 to 51 percent in the 1980s in Africa, from 48 percent to 82 percent in the Caribbean and Latin America, and from 30 percent to 73 percent in Asia. Nonetheless, numerous variations in school enrollments still existed in 1980, both among and within Third World nations, and large numbers of Third World youths still lacked access to schooling. This pattern continued during the decade of the 1980s with some Third World nations experiencing modest increases in school enrollments, while other nations experienced declines.

To provide greater detail, Table 1 includes countries that we refer to as "Less Educationally Developed." These are countries that *enroll less than 50 percent of their youth in primary school or in secondary school.* Because of the inadequacy of available data noted previously, we use the dividing line of 50 percent as a broad (and somewhat arbitrary) indicator of the insufficiency of educational expansion that continues to exist in the Third World today.

Primary school enrollments. Primary schooling is the most fundamental component of formal education; therefore, nations that enroll less than 50 percent of their primary school-age youths in school manifest the most extreme educational insufficiency. Seventeen nations continued to be less educationally developed on the primary school level during the 1980s: Fourteen in Africa and three in Asia (in Table 1, the names of these countries are shown in italics). Overall, enrollments range from only 11 percent (N) in Somalia to 49 percent (N) in both the Central African Republic and Malawi and 49 percent (G) in Sudan. The average enrollment for all seventeen nations is only 34 percent. Thus, the decade of the 1980s has *not* produced major expansion in primary schooling. Indeed, since 1980, enrollments in nine of these seventeen countries have *declined:* Central African Republic, Ethiopia, Guinea, Guinea-Bissau, Liberia, Mali, Somalia, and Sudan in Africa and Afghanistan in Asia. Only five nations—Gambia, Mauritania, Senegal, Haiti, and Yemen—that were less educationally developed in 1980 have since increased their primary school enrollment to 50 percent or more.

Table 1

Selected Educational and Social Indicators for Less Educationally Developed Nations: 1980s

Region and countries	Secondary school enrollment	Students per teacher		Female students per 100 males		% Grade 1 students completing primary school	Percent literate adults		Access to health service (%)	Access to safe water (%)
		Primary	Secondary	Primary	Secondary		Male	Female		
Africa										
Angola	13 G	46	NA	NA	NA	NA	49	33	30	30
Benin	13 N	33	28	51	41	36	37	16	18	52
Botswana	25 N	32	19	107	107	89	73	69	89	54
Burkina Faso	6 G	65	NA	59	46	74	21	6	49	67
Burundi	3 N	62	15	75	52	87	43	26	61	26
Cameroon	26 G	50	26	85	64	67	68	45	41	33
Cape Verde	9 N	34	23	NA	NA	NA	NA	NA	NA	NA
Central African Republic	12 G	63	55	62	37	17	53	29	45	NA
Chad	6 G	71	NA	40	18	17	40	11	30	NA
Comoros	30 G	35	NA	NA	NA	NA	NA	NA	NA	NA
Equatorial Guinea	9 G	68	NA	NA	NA	NA	NA	NA	NA	16
Ethiopia	15 G	49	NA	61	63	41	NA	NA	46	NA
Gambia	16 G	28	17	NA	NA	NA	NA	NA	NA	56
Ghana	40 G	24	16	80	66	NA	64	43	60	56
Guinea	9 G	40	20	45	31	70	40	17	32	19
Guinea-Bissau	7 G	25	8	NA	NA	NA	NA	NA	NA	NA
Ivory Coast	19 G	36	NA	70	44	68	53	31	30	19
Kenya	23 G	34	21	93	70	62	70	49	NA	30
Lesotho	13 G	53	20	125	153	52	62	84	80	36
Liberia	18 G	NA	NA	NA	NA	NA	47	23	39	55
Madagascar	21 G	40	27	94	85	30	74	62	56	32
Malawi	4 G	63	21	80	60	33	52	31	80	56
Mali	6 G	38	NA	59	42	39	23	11	15	17
Mauritania	16 G	50	21	70	44	92	NA	NA	30	NA
Morocco	29 N	26	19	63	66	69	45	22	70	60
Mozambique	5 G	63	33	78	54	39	55	22	39	16

Country										
Niger	6 G	38	NA	56	42	75	19	9	41	47
Nigeria	29 G	44	36	79	NA	63	54	31	40	46
Rwanda	3 N	57	14	97	35	49	61	63	27	50
Senegal	12 N	54	32	69	51	83	37	19	40	53
Sierra Leone	17 G	34	NA	NA	NA	NA	38	21	NA	25
Somalia	4 N	20	15	52	58	33	18	6	27	34
Sudan	20 G	35	24	68	76	61	33	14	51	21
Swaziland	32 N	34	NA	NA	NA	NA	NA	NA	NA	NA
Togo	24 N	52	26	63	32	59	53	28	61	55
Tunisia	40 N	31	17	81	75	77	68	41	90	68
Uganda	13 N	30	21	82	54	76	70	45	61	20
United Republic of Tanzania	4 G	33	17	99	66	76	93	88	76	56
Zaire	23 G	37	20	75	40	60	79	45	26	33
Zambia	17 G	47	NA	90	58	91	84	67	75	59
Zimbabwe	46 G	39	28	95	68	74	81	67	71	NA
North America										
Costa Rica	35 N	31	18	94	105	81	94	93	80	91
El Salvador	29 G	45	24	102	92	31	75	69	56	52
Guatemala	21 G	35	15	82	NA	36	63	47	34	38
Haiti	17 G	38	24	87	88	15	40	35	70	38
Honduras	21 N	39	26	100	NA	43	61	58	73	50
Mexico	44 N	32	18	94	88	71	92	88	45	77
Nicaragua	43 N	32	NA	107	168	20	NA	NA	83	49
Panama	48 N	22	19	92	105	82	89	88	80	83
South America										
Bolivia	27 N	27	22	87	86	NA	84	65	63	44
Brazil	15 N	24	15	NA	NA	22	79	76	NA	78
Paraguay	25 N	25	NA	92	98	50	91	85	61	29
Surinam	40 N	25	15	NA	NA	NA	NA	NA	NA	NA
Venezuela	44 N	26	17	96	119	73	88	85	NA	90

Table 1

Selected Educational and Social Indicators for Less Educationally Developed Nations: 1980s (*Continued*)

Region and countries	Secondary school enrollment	Students per teacher		Female students per 100 males		% Grade 1 students completing primary school	Percent literate adults		Access to health service (%)	Access to safe water (%)
		Primary	Secondary	Primary	Secondary		Male	Female		
Asia										
Afghanistan	7 G	37	NA	50	49	63	39	8	29	21
Bangladesh	18 G	59	28	66	45	20	43	22	45	46
Bhutan	5 G	37	10	54	31	NA	NA	NA	65	NA
China	42 G	24	17	83	69	68	82	56	NA	NA
Democratic Yemen	19 G	26	18	36	48	40	59	25	30	54
India	39 G	46	NA	64	48	NA	57	29	NA	57
Indonesia	36 N	28	15	93	79	80	83	65	80	38
Iran	48 G	26	21	80	68	83	62	39	78	76
Iraq	41 N	25	23	82	62	71	90	87	93	87
Laos	23 G	25	11	78	73	14	92	76	67	21
Myanmar	24 G	45	28	NA	NA	NA	NA	NA	NA	NA
Nepal	26 G	35	28	41	30	28	39	12	NA	29
Oman	38 G	26	14	85	65	89	47	12	91	53
Pakistan	19 G	41	18	49	39	49	40	19	55	44
Saudi Arabia	31 N	16	14	80	66	90	71	31	97	97
Thailand	28 G	20	17	NA	NA	64	94	88	70	64
Turkey	36 N	31	23	89	60	85	86	62	NA	78
Viet Nam	42 G	34	NA	91	90	50	88	89	80	46
Yemen	26 G	54	24	29	12	15	42	7	35	42
Oceania										
Papua New Guinea	12 G	31	22	79	57	67	55	35	NA	27

Source: School enrollment data from UNESCO, *Statistical Yearbook 1989* (Paris: UNESCO, 1989). NA = data not available, G = gross-enrollment ratio, and N = net-enrollment ratio. The names of countries with less than 50 percent total primary school enrollment are shown in italics. Numbers of female students per 100 males from World Bank, *World Development Report 1990* (New York: Oxford University Press, 1990) and *World Development Report 1989* (New York: Oxford University Press, 1989). Percentage of grade 1 students completing primary school from UNICEF, *The State of the World's Children 1990* (New York: Oxford University Press, 1990). Male and female adult literacy rates and percentage of population with access to health services and safe water from Nafis Sadik, *The State of World Population 1990* (New York: UNFPA, United Nations Population Fund, 1990); also see UNICEF, *The State of the World's Children 1990* (New York: Oxford University Press, 1990).

Secondary school enrollments. Table 1 also includes seventy-four Third World countries that enrolled less than 50 percent of their youths in the secondary school level during the 1980s: forty-one countries in Africa, eight in North America, five in South America, nineteen in Asia, and one in Oceania. Only seven Third World nations that were less educationally developed in 1980 have since increased their secondary school enrollments to 50 percent or more: Algeria, Mauritius, the Dominican Republic, Colombia, Malaysia, the Philippines, and Syria. Six of these seven countries, however, experienced only modest increases and still enroll only 50 percent to 59 percent of their youths in secondary schools. The sole sizeable increase—from 42 percent (G) to seventy-four percent (G)—was in the Dominican Republic.

Overall, secondary school enrollments in twenty-two of the seventy-four less educationally developed nations either *did not change* or *declined* during the 1980s. Table 1 also reveals continuing intercountry differences. Secondary school enrollments range from only 3 percent (N) in Burundi and Rwanda to 48 percent (N) in Panama and 48 percent (G) in Iran. The average enrollment for these seventy-four countries is only 22 percent.

Variations in Educational Expansion

In addition to documenting continuing problems of educational insufficiency, these data raise numerous issues regarding variations in educational expansion in the Third World during the 1980s. Here we briefly focus on only four points to illustrate the range of salient issues.

1. Compared with other Third World regions, Africa continues to demonstrate the lowest levels of educational expansion. Of the forty-one less educationally developed African nations, thirteen enroll *less than 20 percent* and fourteen enroll *less than 10 percent* of their youths in secondary schools. Major differences also exist among African countries; secondary school enrollments range from 3 percent (N) in Burundi and Rwanda to 46 percent (G) in Zimbabwe.

2. All Latin American nations from Mexico to Panama continue to be less educationally developed on the secondary school level. Mexico, for example, continues to enroll only 44 percent (N) of its youths in secondary schools. Similarly, despite major educational changes following the overthrow of the Somoza dictatorship in 1979, Nicaragua continued during the 1980s to enroll only 43 percent (G) of its youths in secondary schools. Further, for several decades, Costa Rica has been a symbol of political stability and of democracy in Latin America. Yet, despite its democratic heritage, secondary school enrollments in Costa Rica actually have declined from 39 percent (N) to 35 percent (N).

3. Many less educationally developed countries also manifest gender inequities in school enrollments. Table 1 provides one indicator of gender dif-

ferences: Numbers of female students per 100 males, both in primary and secondary schools. The average number of female students per 100 male students is 76 in primary schools and 64 in secondary schools. Only in Botswana and Lesotho in Africa and Costa Rica, El Salvador, Honduras, Nicaragua, Panama, and Venezuela in Latin America do the rates of female student enrollment equal or exceed those of males.

4. Although professionals frequently use gross national product (GNP) as an indicator of development, GNP and educational expansion are not always positively related. For example, during the 1980s, Zimbabwe, with a per capita GNP of only $620, experienced sizeable educational expansion. Primary school enrollment increased from 85 percent (G) to 128 percent (G), and secondary enrollments increased from 8 percent (G) to 46 percent (G). In contrast, Saudi Arabia, with a per capita GNP of $6,950, experienced quite modest educational expansion. Primary schooling increased from 50 percent (N) to 56 percent (N), and secondary school enrollments increased from 22 percent (N) to only 31 percent (N).

Educational Expansion and Public Well-Being

Traditionally, professionals have placed major emphasis on the links between educational expansion and economic development. However, we maintain that the goal should be much broader. The ultimate goal of educational expansion should be to increase directly the well-being of Third World citizenry. Rather than viewing education as an isolated social institution, we suggest the importance of viewing education as both one indicator of public well-being and as a social institution that has the potential to contribute to the enhancement of still other aspects of public well-being.

However, in this context, serious questions remain regarding not merely the availability of schooling in the Third World but also the *quality* and *effectiveness* of such schooling. Table 1 provides three indicators. First, although there are exceptions, less educationally developed nations tend to exhibit relatively high student-to-teacher ratios. In these seventy-four countries, the average primary school ratio is thirty-eight students per teacher, compared with a ratio of twenty-one in the United States. And the average secondary school ratio is twenty-one students per teacher, compared with a ratio of thirteen in the United States. Second, these countries also vary markedly in the percentage of grade 1 students who actually complete primary school. The range is from 14 percent to 92 percent, with an average completion rate of only 57 percent. Third, histories of inadequate formal schooling for youth, coupled with inadequate educational programs for adults, have resulted in a legacy of continuing problems of insufficient *adult* literacy. In these seventy-four nations, literacy varies from a low of 6 percent for women in Burkina Faso and Somalia to a high of 94 percent for men in Costa Rica and Thailand. Overall, the average adult literacy rate is 61 percent for men, but only 44 percent for women. Yet, even for countries that indicate relatively high "official" adult literacy rates, available data do not reveal the percentages of adults who actually are functionally literate.

In addition to confronting major educational problems, many of these seventy-four nations continue to lack other basic facilities that would enhance public well-being. Table 1 reveals that access to health services, for example, varies from 15 percent of the population in Mali to 97 percent in Saudi Arabia, with an average of only 56 percent. Further, access to safe water supplies ranges from 16 percent of the population in Ethiopia and Mozambique to 97 percent in Saudi Arabia. The average is only 47 percent. In turn, both health problems and educational problems often are interrelated. Inadequate access to health services and safe drinking water, as well as insufficient nutrition, are directly detrimental to physical well-being and ultimately lead to reduced educational performance by many Third World youths. At the same time, increased education tends to lead to improved health and life expectancy, and the educational levels of parents influences both the physical well-being and the cognitive development of their children.[3]

Population Growth and Educational Expansion

Prospects for increased public well-being are tempered by high fertility rates and population growth rates that exert severe pressures on various elements of public well-being, including the ability of Third World nations to provide adequate access to education. The seventy-four countries, which are already less educationally developed, also tend to have relatively high fertility rates and population growth rates.[4] Fertility rates range from a low of 2.2 in China and Thailand to a high of 8.0 in Rwanda. Whereas the fertility rate in the United States is only 1.9, the rate of these seventy-four nations averages 5.5. Indeed, high fertility rates are quite prominent in those nations that have the lowest levels of educational expansion. Fertility rates in the seventeen countries that enroll less than 50 percent of their youths in primary schools range from 5.5 to 7.0, with an average of 6.3.

Likewise, projected population growth rates for the period 1990 to 1995 range from 1.0 percent in Tunisia to 4.1 percent in Kenya. The average is 2.8 percent, compared with only 0.7 percent in the United States. In fifty-three of these seventy-four less educationally developed nations, including all seventeen nations that enroll less than 50 percent of their youth in primary schools, the population is projected to *at least double* by the year 2025. The dilemma for professionals is significant. Generally, as the level of education for women increases, fertility declines. Yet, for countries where the percentage of youths—including females—currently enrolled in school already is so low, education professionals and policy makers confront a difficult task in expanding educational opportunities to meet projected population growth.

PUBLIC WELL-BEING, EDUCATION, AND SOCIAL CHANGE

Regardless of the sociopolitical labels—socialist, communist, authoritarian, democratic—that are attached to particular Third World nations, the political leaders of these countries often publicly claim that their goals include the *enhancement of their citizens' welfare*. Yet political labels, rhetoric, and revolutionary slogans often have not translated into the fulfillment of such goals. Differences exist about the meaning of "public well-being," and numerous Third World leaders have been notorious for their use of the media, secret police, and the military to control segments of the citizenry that disagree with the leaders' definitions of well-being. Further, certain other countries that are usually regarded as democracies have only one dominant political party, thereby concentrating control over how public well-being is defined. Indeed, for many Third World nations, distinctions among socialism, democracy, and authoritarianism frequently are blurred, and a mixture of political ideologies, self-interests, and corruption influences both sociopolitical structures and programs oriented toward public well-being.

Therefore, it is the *actual* well-being of the citizenry, not sociopolitical labels and rhetoric, that is relevant. Further, the relationship between public well-being, education, and democratization is neither simple nor straightforward. Particular forms of authoritarian governance, for example, can provide certain components of public well-being. Indeed, some authoritarian governments, such as that in Cuba, have emphasized public welfare and have viewed educational expansion as a mechanism that would contribute to social democratization: To the redistribution of wealth, to the reduction of the power of the elite, and ultimately to increased public well-being more generally.

Similarly, Third World democratic governments, such as in Costa Rica, also emphasize public well-being and access to education. Yet democratic governance does not guarantee that every citizen will equally share all aspects of well-being. For example, despite its democratic tradition and relatively stable political structure, Costa Rica enrolled only 35 percent (N) of its youths in secondary schools in the late 1980s. This stands in contrast to Cuba's secondary school enrollment of 70 percent (N). And Cuba's primary school enrollment exceeded Costa Rica's by 10 percent. Yet other indicators suggest that overall public well-being is roughly equal in these two contrasting nations. For example, whereas Cuba has more physicians per capita and a slightly lower infant mortality rate, Costa Rica has a slightly longer adult life expectancy and a higher percentage of citizens with access to safe drinking water. Ultimately, however, the pendulum shifts when international human rights treaties and other human rights indicators are incorporated as an additional measure of public well-being. Although authoritarian governance in Cuba has improved certain elements of public well-being, the historical trade-off has entailed the lack of human rights protection and civil liberties.[5]

Efforts to assess social change and public well-being, then, must extend to human rights and civil liberties, as well as to assurances that Third World citizenries shape their own destinies through freedom of expression and assembly, due process, and representation in governance. This does not mean, however, that all Third World nations must adopt sociopolitical structures that mirror Western-style democracies. Conceivably, various forms of culturally compatible structures might be utilized. Regardless, in the end, democratic governance in any form can be viewed as only a necessary but not a sufficient condition for Third World public well-being. Democratic sociopolitical structures establish the fundamental foundation for public well-being, but efforts then must be made to ensure the fulfillment of this goal. Such efforts require that Third World citizenries share representation in the political, economic, and cultural agendas of their nations. Increased access to formal education, in turn, is fundamental to such democratization and to the fulfillment of the various other components of public well-being.

CONCLUSION

Education is both a central component of and contributor to Third World public well-being. Professionals who are engaged in activities related to Third World education are quite varied: social scientists engaged in education-related research and theory construction, social scientists and educators engaged in the formulation and evaluation of educational programs, government leaders and technocrats engaged in formalizing educational policies, and school administrators and teachers charged with the implementation and oversight of educational programs on a day-to-day basis. Given the expertise and privileged position of these various professionals—and given the centrality of education to public well-being—these professionals bear special responsibilities for attempting to foster such well-being.

When we view education and public well-being in the broader context of democratization, these responsibilities become manifest in two major ways. First, these professionals must promote further expansion of educational opportunities in the Third World and understand the complex sociopolitical and cultural settings in which such expansion will occur. The lack of educational expansion, as reflected in dramatically low levels of primary and secondary school enrollment, is central to various forms of Third World social inequality. Restricted educational opportunity leads to the concentration of relative political and economic power among those who have access to education. Restricted educational opportunity also relates directly to other aspects of public well-being including knowledge of matters pertaining to health care and physical well-being. And it leads further to the perpetuation of inequality between women and men, between urban and rural citizenries, and frequently among various religious, linguistic, and ethnic groups.

Second, these professionals are responsible for promoting forms of schooling for personal and collective "liberation" that contribute to the realization of intellectual potential and, in turn, ultimately contribute to the well-being of the citizenry more generally. Again, in the context of democratization, professionals should abandon education that merely encourages rote memorization and the blind acceptance of knowledge that is found in many Third World nations. Instead, professional responsibility lies in fostering schooling that rewards not only the mastery of fundamental knowledge but also the ability of students to think critically, creatively, and independently. Only the latter will provide Third World citizens the basis upon which to exercise informed choices and to make informed judgments about current and future political leaders and government policies that directly affect the various components of the citizenry's well-being.

NOTES

1. See Peter B. Evans and John D. Stephens, "Development and the World Economy," in Neil J. Smelser, ed., *Handbook of Sociology* (Newbury Park, Calif.: Sage Publications, 1988); Alvin Y. So, *Social Change and Development: Modernization, Dependency, and World Systems Theories* (Newbury Park, Calif.: Sage Publications, 1990).

2. Our analysis of educational expansion elaborates and updates our previous work: Mehrangiz Najafizadeh and Lewis A. Mennerick, "Worldwide Educational Expansion from 1950 to 1980: The Failure of the Expansion of Schooling in Developing Countries," *The Journal of Developing Areas, 22* (April 1988): 333–358. The present analysis uses data from UNESCO, *Statistical Yearbook 1989* (Paris: UNESCO, 1989); for most nations, available data for the 1980s is for 1986 and 1987.

3. See UNICEF, *The State of the World's Children 1990* (New York: Oxford University Press, 1990); World Bank, *World Development Report 1990* (New York: Oxford University Press, 1990); and Nafis Sadik, *The State of World Population 1990* (New York: UNFPA, United Nations Population Fund, 1990).

4. Population data compiled from Sadik, *World Population 1990.*

5. See, UNICEF, *World's Children 1990,* p. 77; Ruth L. Sivard, *World Military and Social Expenditures 1989* (Washington, D.C.: World Priorities, 1989), pp. 50–51; Amnesty International USA, *Amnesty International Report 1990* (New York: Amnesty International Publications, 1990), pp. 75–78, 284–289.

Chapter 15

Business Social Policy in the Third World: Response of Multinational Corporate Management

Sita C. Amba-Rao

The growth in the number of multinational corporations (MNCs), their worldwide scope, and economic and political power draw attention to corporate social responsibility. This chapter examines the role of the MNC in the social concerns of Third World nations. The MNCs' cumulative experience worldwide—in particular, with Third World host countries—leads to an understanding of the needs and expectations of the peoples of these countries and a commitment to their development socially as well as economically. Three concepts provide the framework for this chapter: Social contract, business ethics, and corporate systemic change and transformational leadership. Implications for corporate role will be discussed.

INTRODUCTION

At least three forces concerning the business world gave impetus to examining the issue of global multinational social responsibility in the Third World: (1) the spread and influence of multinational corporations (MNCs) from the developed nations worldwide, (2) the awareness and recognition by Third World governments of the role of private enterprise and free trade in economic and social development as well as their sophistication with regard to business transactions, and (3) the rise of modernized MNCs from Third World countries.[1] These forces tend to balance the power among the parties. In this process, people of the Third World have experienced benefits in improved standards of living. However, such benefits have not been equitable within each society. Furthermore, sever harmful effects were widely experienced because of technological

This chapter is based on a paper prepared for the annual meeting of the Association for the Advancement of Policy, Research and Development in the Third World, which was held in Mexico City, Mexico, November 14–17, 1990.

advancements and their modes of transfer. Many environmental disasters attest to the ill effects of technology. And certain marketing and employment practices, such as infant-formula marketing and workplace practices based on apartheid in South Africa, also illustrate the social inequity.[2]

MNCs failed to recognize the need to manage adverse social impacts because they operated largely under traditional capitalist ideology. Consequently, MNCs have been governed by economic goals with market and legal constraints. In their view, social effects were the responsibility of host governments. Further, any direct concerns such as legal enforcement were within the domain of the decentralized local subsidiary management, which lacked a corporate monitor or guidance. In turn, local management followed a similar path in failing to establish and manage a social policy as it would an economic or market policy.[3]

Parallel to this traditional corporate behavior, however, pressures from social activists and the MNCs' own cumulative experience in the Third World led to an awareness of the needs and expectations of Third World peoples. Consequently, corporations have begun to address their commitment to social values both internally and externally. Internally, they began to incorporate social goals in their business strategy and policy, and they implemented these goals by means of operational adaptations. Externally, commitment was manifested through cooperative overtures, particularly with host governments.

The need for and legitimacy of corporate social responsibility in the international arena have been theorized and advocated by management scholars only recently, particularly in the 1980s.[4] Furthermore, the response of MNC managers to the development and implementation of social policies began to be examined by critical observers.[5]

This chapter will examine the relevance of social responsibility to MNCs and their managements' responses in fulfilling their social commitments. First the concept of social responsibility, including business ethics, will be clarified, and then leadership roles and corporate systemic change will be discussed.

CORPORATE SOCIAL RESPONSIBILITY AND BUSINESS ETHICS

Social Responsibility

The social responsibility of business, which has been popularly referred to as corporate social responsibility (CSR), has been defined variously in different sources. The definitions range from the classical economic sense of increasing shareholder wealth to considering broad social interests within a society.[6] The dimensions of this argument have been extended to the international sphere. The explanations of S. P. Sethi, W. C. Frederick, D. Windsor and L. E. Preston, T. Donaldson, and S. P. Sethi and P. Steidlmeier will be used to clarify the rationale for MNC social policy in their operations in the Third World.[7]

The scope and meaning of business's social responsibility was based historically on views of corporate legitimacy and the prevailing values of management. The development of the concept ranged from perceiving business obligation as being based on minimal legal and economic criteria and maximal accountability to stockholders to the inclusion of broad social goals. Sethi explained three phases of responsibility: social obligations, social responsibility, and social responsiveness.[8] Social obligation limits itself to stockholder interests and legal compliance and, as such, holds a defensive stance. Social responsibility moves beyond a legal consideration to a more accommodative, yet reactive, approach toward stakeholders—that is all other constituents, such as consumers or the general public. Finally, social responsiveness spurs the corporation to interact with stakeholders and to take anticipatory actions with commitment toward both social and economic goals. Frederick categorizes similarly, except his "CSR3" refers to a social rectitude for business activities and their negative consequences.[9] Other analysts have observed that this historically developed view of business's concern with societal interests involves groups beyond its direct business constituents and includes issues of social values and expectations—in short, all those issues affected by its decisions and actions.[10] Furthermore, business and society are interdependent and coexist, with business using society's resources and in turn fulfilling economic needs and changing social goals.[11] Thus, business and society are bound by a reciprocal "social contract" that is considered to be the "core idea of corporate social responsibility."[12]

This view of the relationship between business and society has been recognized and extended to the international context. Windsor and Preston argue that MNCs and the nation-states (as stakeholders) are equally independent entities attempting to maximize their self-interests;[13] therefore, their collaborative relationship is based upon mutually acceptable rules fostering social justice with or without ethical considerations. Windsor and Preston label this CSR4, refinement of Frederick's CSR3. Donaldson, however, adds the ethical element as an imperative in MNC activities.[14] He suggests three conditions of conduct under the social contract for an MNC operating in a host country: (1) enhancing the welfare of consumers and employees, (2) respecting the rights and justice of the people in the society, and (3) minimizing harm and other negative effects such as misuse of power or depletion of natural resources. Donaldson also emphasizes these as "minimal duties" as distinguished from a "maximal duty," which may be an act of corporate good citizenship such as supporting Third World development program or economic aid. Such acts may be desired but not required. Meanwhile, one interest group that has emerged and has attempted to redirect MNC policy in the Third World is that of religious activists. The most visible of these is the liberation theology movement. The implication of liberation theology for MNC activities was examined by Sethi and Steidlmeier, who compared the theology with liberal capitalism.[15] In essence, the latter focuses on individual freedom and rights with regard to property ownership and its use, is utilitarian by its emphasis of the social contract, and is represented by institutions. The former is communal by its emphasis on egalitarian outcomes, is based on a religious covenant, and emphasizes government by the people rather than by autocratic or elitist groups. The implication of liberation theology for MNCs is that they ought to recognize the role of such a representative government in economic and social development. Further, MNCs are under a fiduciary duty to society; as such, their mission ought to be wealth creation as well as satisfaction of social values. The latter concept involves reinvestment of profits within the host nation, adopting human resource management practices including employee participation, and satisfying consumer interests in safe and efficient products that are fairly priced. These ideas have also been identified in management literature in different forms, such as trusteeship and quality-of-life management.[16] Thus, the concept of social responsibility involves decisions, actions, and outcomes regarding the issues, the stakeholders, and the society at large.

Business Ethics

Although most explanations of CSR provide the relevance for MNCs' social policy, the moral basis or standard for corporate decisions and actions in meeting social expectations should be made explicit.[17] Several ethical theories have been proposed.[18] Of these, four key principles are most relevant: Utilitarian, rights, justice, and cultural relativism. The utilitarian approach evaluates a decision in terms of its consequences; that is, does it satisfy the greatest number? This may be evaluated in economic or noneconomic terms, be applicable to any stakeholder, and be measured by net costs and benefits.[19] The principle of justice incorporates an equitable means by which the benefits and costs of a corporate action are borne by different segments. The bases of equity may be needs, efforts, contributions, and equal distribution of positive or negative effects.[20] The rights principle calls for preventing harm or protecting the rights of others who are affected by the corporations, along with the responsibility of the host government or any other entity.[21] The rights and justice principles form the deontology philosophy.[22] Thus, the utilitarian approach covers societal interest, while deontology is concerned with individual interests.

The fourth principle, that of cultural relativism, is directly applicable to MNC practices in the Third World. According to this view, practices and customs abroad should be respected even though they may conflict with home country norms.[23] Examples abound, as with cases of bribery, levels of environmental pollution, and consumer safety standards accepted by the host country. When the standards under each of the above issues, for example, are lower in the host country than in the MNC decision makers' country of origin, then a question arises as to whether the manager should follow the higher home country norms and whether doing so will imply an attitude of ethnocentric superiority and disrespect for cultural diversity.

Several authors have contributed to the understanding and managing of corporate social responsibility and ethical considerations by examining how ethical standards or decisions are influenced and how decisions are made.[24] The various *influences* are individual or institutional and include individual socialization and personal factors and external forces such as stakeholders, social institutions, and organizational factors (e.g., managerial influences and reinforcement systems). In contrast, the decision-making *process* is explained by ethical theories and models. Relevant factors that influence ethical standards will be discussed in the next section, while discussion of ethical theories follows.

Kohlberg proposed that individuals progress through different stages of moral development, the highest being that of individual conviction without self-interest, which is based on the moral principles of utilitarianism or deontology.[25] Kohlberg proposed that individuals' behaviors differ in similar ethical situations over time as they progress toward their moral ultimate, but the "situationists" believe that each situation should be considered individually, based on the most appropriate course of action that should be chosen.[26] At the group level, a similar argument posits that moral principles cannot be universally valid and that groups may differ in their values. Hence, individuals in a group would follow group norms; thus, moral standards are culturally specific. This argument forms the basis for the theory of cultural relativism referred to earlier. Donaldson, among others, argues against this inevitability of cultural relativism.[27] He analyzes international business operations that have been complicated by conflicts between home and host country norms. A set of ten fundamental international rights were developed (e.g., the right to subsistence and political participation) that corporations should respect as a "universal objective minimum."[28] Donaldson explains how many of these rights are violated indirectly in the routine course of business in host countries. For example, the bribery of elected officials undermines public trust and hence is a violation of the right to political participation. Although he recognizes cultural differences (such as in the case of political participation), Donaldson asserts that these rights warrant certain minimum consideration on the part of the MNCs irrespective of culture.

To a large extent, legislation defines social expectations and regulates corporate action in the United States in certain business activities—for example, those relating to the environment, equal employment opportunity, and consumer safety—with the underlying principles of utilitarianism and deontology. Similarly, in other economically developed nations, business behavior is regulated by legislation derived from broad social consensus. However, when the issue involves the international arena, ethical dilemmas arise because no such moral consensus has been reached because of cultural diversity. The problem is compounded when the practices and norms of the MNCs' host and home countries conflict or when there is inadequate regulation and enforcement of desired corporate action by Third World hosts. The "universal minimum," therefore, calls for rejecting the lower standards set by host country laws.

Following these philosophical approaches, some authors have offered further guidance toward incorporating the ethical consideration into decision

making. Extending the ethical principles to the international arena is complicated by cultural differences both within and across countries. Ethical models
that have been adapted to the international sphere have been developed that
consider economic development, cultural values, societal benefit, and individual concerns and integrate them with the major ethical principles discussed
above.[29]

Fritzsche used the decision-tree model of Cavanagh, Moberg, and Velasquez, which based its questions on utilitarian rights, principles of justice, and
exceptional circumstances.[30] He divided the model between macrolevels and
microlevels with three progressive stages. Stage 1 at the macrolevel is concerned with utilitarian benefits to society, while stages 2 and 3 at the micro-
level are concerned with individual freedom and individual justice, respectively. In each case, the effect of corporate decisions are assessed in this
framework; if they pass the tests, the decisions are accepted as being ethical.

Donaldson offered a more detailed model in resolving cultural conflicts in
MNC practices, which is summarized as follows.[31] He developed an algorithm or a conceptual interpretation. Two contexts form the bases: (1) the host
country's level of economic development and (2) purely cultural differences
in dealing with certain situations. Different tests of a practice's permissibility
are used in arriving at ethical decisions in each case. In the case of level of
economic development, the practice with the higher standards may be acceptable to the host country but is subordinated until the country achieves an
economic level that is similar with that of the developed home country. The
formula in this case thus would be that the host nation's practice is permissible if the MNC's home country would regard the practice as permissible if the
same economic conditions prevailed there. An example would be that exceedingly high levels of asbestos pollution would not be acceptable, although
slightly higher than preferred levels would be. The second case of cultural
difference is not that clear. For example, should bribery or nepotism be accepted as a common practice? In such a case, two questions are relevant: (1)
Is it possible to conduct business successfully in the host country without
following the practice? (2) Is the practice a clear violation of human rights? If
the answer to both the questions is negative, then the practice is permissible.
For example, in some South American nations a small and uniform amount of
payment to low-level customs officials is normal practice to clear goods
through customs. Hence, this is an acceptable practice for the MNC, despite
disapproval in the home country. On the contrary, bribery of elected officials
is not permissible according to this formula. Thus, four criteria are relevant:
(1) the level of economic development in the host country, (2) the acceptability of the practice in the home country under similar economic conditions, (3)
the necessity of the practice for conducting business in the host country, and
(4) respect of fundamental rights. In addition to use of the algorithm, Donaldson indicates the need for ethical codes and guidelines that are appropriate to

specific issues, as in the case of the Sullivan Principles, which foster human dignity and equal participation in the workplace.

Other authors have supported the theory of common societal good while emphasizing the duty to respect individual rights, thus recognizing a trade-off between utilitarian and deontological theories.[32] The implication is that the ethical approach is mandated because it is morally appropriate, not because of market pragmatism or governmental regulation that calls for self-regulation and volunteerism by corporations. Nevertheless, research indicates that social considerations have been related to economic performance, thereby adding strength to the legitimacy of corporate social policy.[33]

MANAGEMENT RESPONSE WITH REGARD TO CSR: LEADERSHIP ROLE AND SYSTEMIC CHANGE

Role of the Executive, the Organization, and the Professional

While the corporation has been recognized as a legal entity and hence is expected to perform responsibly, some theorists hold the view that the organization is, in fact, a legal fiction and has no status independent of its members.[34] Accordingly, the locus of ethical responsibility rests with individuals at the strategic and operational levels. Senior executives who represent the corporation set the ethical tone of the entire organization by their attitudes, values, manifest behavior, and messages for performance.[35]

In addition to providing leadership through such role modeling, the executives acculturate and shape the behaviors of members at the operational levels, particularly those of lower-level managers and professionals, by reinforcement through organizational factors. These include performance measures, reviews, rewards and sanctions.[36] The professional and technical group is a broad category that encompasses various functional subgroups. Values of these people as individuals and as members of their professional group will also influence their cognitions and behaviors. Thus, Pruden conceived three reference points for the (marketing) professional in terms of power: (1) organizational authority supported by rewards and sanctions, (2) the power of the individual to offer or withdraw required services, and (3) the power of the individual's professional group to obtain compliance through codes of conduct and sanctions.[37] The influence of the three together forms a dynamic balance that can provide direction to the decision maker in circumstances of conflicting interests.

Bommer, Grato, Gravander, and Tuttle include various individual factors (e.g., life experiences and moral values) and situational factors (e.g., work, professional, legal, and social environments) in the decision-making processes of individuals and their ethical behaviors.[38] Among individual factors, socialization through group membership shapes one's ethical system. Consequently, differences in values are identified according to age, work experience, religious beliefs, sex role, and nationality.[39] Similarly, England concludes that cultural differences in upbringing lead to differences in ethical beliefs of managers.[40] However, recent studies of business students and managers contradict this view.[41] Lee found similarities in ethical beliefs between British and Chinese managers in Hong Kong and attributed this to the acculturation of the British managers.[42] This acculturation process occurs in organizations through the influence of significant others, according to social learning theory.[43] Furthermore, social learning combined with reinforcement can be instrumental in relearning and substituting the newly desired behaviors for the existing inappropriate ones.

Other internal organizational factors were also recognized as influencers of individual behavior, although with negative effects. Specific job demands, (e.g., external contacts) and organizational competition can oftentimes foster ethical dilemmas and must be resolved.[44] A set of empirical studies of marketing practitioners illustrates the influence on this critical professional group.[45] The researchers found that peer pressure and the availability of opportunities for unethical behavior predicted such behavior and that interorganizational influences were not significant. Thus, internal reference groups had greater effects than did external groups such as professional associations and their codes of conduct. This finding on the negative influence is supported by a survey of managers, who ranked the behavior of superiors and peers (that is, the role set of the individuals) as the most important reasons for making unethical decisions.[46] Yet Pruden stresses that the professional ethic is critical in view of changing social demands and technology.[47] When ethical dilemmas arise, the individual perception of inappropriate conduct, if supported by the professional ethic, might lead to a questioning or avoidance of the behavior. For example, Clasen explains the marketing professional's role in protecting consumer interests, and Chamberlain points out the roles of accountant and legal counsel in ensuring ethical decisions.[48] In view of these potentially conflicting and shifting reference points, top management has a leadership imperative to recognize and balance mutual influences and to aid in the convergence and consensus of moral judgments.

Corporate Systemic Change

The MNC's social goals and collaborative role will be supported by its business strategy. The MNC needs to link its internal long-term planning with the host government's national planning objective with regard to environment, technology, or human resources and then translate the strategic plan into operational goals and activities. This implies a systemic change in the culture, structure, and functioning of the organization—that is, a change from a purely economic culture to an ethical culture throughout the entire organizational system. Several models and proposals for ethical transformation have been discussed in the literature, from which the following suggestions have been developed.[49] For example, a study by the Business Roundtable identifies several elements that favorably influence ethical performance in firms considered to be both economically and ethically successful.[50] In the area of strategy formulation, four specific actions are involved: (1) the formulation of a mission statement that specifies the MNC's social purpose and ethical profile, and which forms an ethical core; (2) an environmental scanning of the host society to determine socially desirable needs and issues within the scope of the business as well as an assessment of the effects of the organization and its actions on the host country; (3) integration of the results of such studies with strategic decision making, which is followed by the issuance of a policy statement; and (4) the use of ethical, legal, and efficiency criteria, such as economic and social returns, in the decision process.

To implement social strategy, a kind of systemic change is called for that involves the following dimensions: commitment, communication, and institutionalization.

Commitment. An MNC states its ethical philosophy and translates it into behavior by taking several measures. First, it can create a functional unit headed by high-level position whose holder reports to the chief executive officer (CEO); when filled by an individual with congruent values, this top placement will serve both functional and symbolic purposes. Second, the corporation's board of directors can include or create a subcommittee on CSR that is responsible for defining and reviewing the MNC's social performance. The board thus links the host country's national planning objectives with its own corporate planning, thus ensuring corporate identification with social concerns and values. For this, the board will include either outside members representing different interest groups and the government or outside leaders only, understanding that they would seek the input of interest groups. Third, an MNC can appoint a professional ethics aide to top managers to provide expertise and guidance in implementing social strategy. Fourth, the corporation can require an annual report by the CEO on corporate social performance. Fifth, long-range plans can be required throughout the organization based on its mission and social strategy and supported by budgets, management responsibilities, and organizational systems. And sixth, the MNC can assess existing organizational values to develop a moral inventory of values, dilemmas, strengths, and inadequacies that is suitable for local conditions.

Communication. Top management ensures the transmission of its ethical philosophy and intentions to organizational members. To accomplish this, three actions must be taken. First, a code of conduct should be developed to articulate social values, expectations, and guidelines for their implementation. Usually, this necessitates changing the current codes, whose scope is to avoid adverse effects, to incorporate prosocial concerns and values. Second, the behavior of senior executives must be congruent with the code of conduct; this is imperative, because senior executives set the tone for the entire organization by their values, messages for performance, and manifest behavior. Third, codes and expectations can be communicated throughout the organization by in-house media.

Institutionalization. This step includes internalizing the desired attitudes and behaviors of an organization's members by means of structures and systems. The structures may be departments, committees, and task forces, while the systems include measurements (standards), information and communication, auditing, review and rewards, acculturation, and appeals. The process of institutionalization may include the following steps or procedures. First, a senior-level committee can be appointed to establish standards, develop ethical awareness and orientation, clarify employee ethical dilemmas, and monitor the program. This committee would include managers, staff specialists, and an outside specialist to maintain the integrity of the committee. Other line and staff teams may be formed at lower levels to diffuse the activities throughout the organization. Second, standards of social performance or ethical behavior can be established that are based on corporate codes and policy and which are suited to unit levels and local conditions. Third, information systems can be developed for the purpose of collecting and disseminating information relevant to the firm's prosocial activities. Fourth, social-performance audits can be done with the same rigor as budget reviews. Fifth, managerial responsibilities and criteria for performance review can be defined to include social performance, which would, in turn, be tied to rewards and sanctions. Sixth, disincentives to ethical behavior can be removed, thus strengthening prosocial behavior. Seventh, an acculturation program can be established to clarify the meaning of ethical performance and to handle ethical conflicts and dilemmas. This involves a reorientation of employees through experiential workshops using ethical scenarios and actual incidents, as well as through learning abstract concepts. Following the training, an assessment will be made of the experience in a participatory environment to refine social learning. Eighth, realistic means can be used to resolve problems, report unethical conduct, and prevent crises, thus reinforcing ethical learning and performance. Ninth, ethical screening, selection, and orientation can be used in the recruitment process to increase the likelihood that new employees will enter the firm with some knowledge of and experience in ethical decision making. And tenth the organization's social values can be maintained through the selection of future managers with appropriate attributes and values.

In formulating and implementing social policy in the Third World, the role of an MNC's subsidiary is of special value. The subsidiary in the host country is in a pivotal position. Being in closer contact with the host government, it can act as a liaison between the parent corporation and the host government in resolving situation-specific differences.[51] Furthermore, the subsidiary can receive input from the host government as part of the collaborative strategy between the host and the MNC. Finally, Tavis suggests that the subsidiary's managers become "adoptive stakeholders" to serve in the absence of actual stakeholders, and their concerns, in the host nations.[52] This approach is consistent with the fiduciary responsibility of the MNCs in fulfilling societal needs and values.

NOTES

1. Several authors have documented these factors. For example, W. C. Frederick, K. Davis, and J. E. Post, *Business and Society* (New York: McGraw-Hill, 1988); and J. Naor, "A New Approach to Multinational Social Responsibility," *Journal of Business Ethics, 1* (1982): 219–225.

2. See, for example, J. R. Simpson, "Ethics and Multinational Corporation via-à-vis Developing Nations," *Journal of Business Ethics, 1* (1988): 227–237.

3. D. H. Blake, "The Management of Social Policy by Multinational Corporations: A Research Agenda," in L. E. Preston, ed., *International and Comparative Corporation and Society Research* (Greenwich, Conn.: JAI Press, 1990), pp. 57–78.

4. For example, S. C. Amba-Rao, "Industrial Hazards, Social Responsiveness and the Transformational Imperative of Multinational Corporations: A Conceptual Model," in *The Proceedings, S. W. Decision Sciences Institute Conference* (Houston, Tex.: March 1987); T. Donaldson, "Multinational Decision Making: Reconciling International Norms," *Journal of Business Ethics, 4* (1985), 357–366; and Naor, "New Approach."

5. See, for example, S. C. Amba-Rao, "Whither Bhopal: Technological Hazards and Social Responsiveness in the Third World," *Social Development Issues, 12*(2) (Winter 1989): 11–22; Blake, "Management"; and E. A. Murray, Jr., "Ethics and Corporate Strategy," in R. B. Dickie and L. S. Rouner, eds., *Corporations and the Common Good* (Notre Dame, Ind.: University of Notre Dame Press, 1986), pp. 91–117.

6. On shareholder wealth, see M. Friedman, "A Friedman Doctrine: The Social Responsibility of Business Is to Increase its Profits," *The New York Times Magazine,* September 13, 1970, p. 32; R. Hay and E. Gray, "Social Responsibilities of Business Managers," *Academy of Management Journal, 17* (1974): 135–143; and T. J. Zenisek, "Corporate Social Responsibility: A Conceptualization Based on Organizational Literature," *Academy of Management Review, 4* (1979): 359–368.

7. S. P. Sethi, "Dimensions of Corporate Social Performance: An Analytical Framework," *California Management Review, 12* (1975): 58–64; W. C. Frederick, "Toward CSR3: Why Ethical Analysis Is Indispensable and Unavoidable in Corporate Affairs," *California Management Review, 28* (1986): 126–141; D. Windsor and L. E. Preston, "Corporate Governance, Social Policy, and Social Performance in the Multinational Corporation," in L. E. Preston, ed., *International and Comparative Corporation and Society Research* (Greenwich, Conn.: JAI Press, 1990), pp. 79–92; T. Donaldson, *The Ethics of International Business* (New York: Oxford University Press, 1989); S. P. Sethi and P. Steidlmeier, "A New Paradigm of the Business/Society Relationship in the Third World: The Challenge of Liberation Theology," in W. C. Frederick and L.E. Preston, *Business Ethics: Research Issues and Empirical Studies* (Greenwich, Conn.: JAI Press, 1990), pp. 279–293.

8. Sethi, "Dimensions."

9. Frederick, "Toward CSR3."

10. Hay and Gray, "Social Responsibilities," and Zenisek, "Corporate Social Responsibility."

11. Frederick et al., *Business.*

12. Frederick et al., *Business,* p. 45.

13. Windsor and Preston, "Corporate Governance."

14. Donaldson, *Ethics.*

15. Sethi and Steidlmeier, "New Paradigm."

16. Zenisek, "Corporate Social Responsibility."

17. M. Anshen, ed., *Managing the Socially Responsible Corporation* (New York: Macmillan, 1974); and N. W. Chamberlain, *Social Strategy and Corporate Structure* (New York: Macmillan, 1982).

18. A good review may be found in J. Tsalikis and D. J. Fritzsche, "Business Ethics: A Literature Review With a Focus on Marketing Ethics," *Journal of Business Ethics, 8* (1989): 695–743.

19. K. B. Boal and N. Peery, "The Cognitive Structure of Corporate Social Responsibility," *Journal of Management, 11*(3): 71–82.

20. Frederick et al., *Business.*

21. Donaldson, *Ethics.*

22. D. P. Robin and R. E. Reidenbach, "Social Responsibility, Ethics, and Marketing Strategy: Closing the Gap Between Concept and Application," *Journal of Marketing, 51* (January 1987): 44–57.

23. R. Brandt, *Ethical Theory* (Englewood Cliffs, N.J.: Prentice-Hall, 1959).

24. For example, see Amba-Rao, "Industrial Hazards"; R. Bartels, "A Model for Ethics in Marketing," *Journal of Marketing, 31* (January 1967): 20–26; L. Kohlberg, *The Meaning and Measurement of Moral Development* (Worcester, Mass.: Clark University Press, 1981); H. O. Pruden, "Which Ethics for Marketers," in J. R. Wish and S. H. Gamble, *Marketing and Social Issues* (New York: John Wiley & Sons, 1971), pp. 98–104; and T. J. Von der Embse and R. A. Wagley, "Managerial Ethics: Hard Decisions on Soft Criteria," *SAM Advanced Management Journal* (Winter 1988): 4–8.

25. Kohlberg, *Moral Development.*

26. D. R. Forsyth, "A Taxonomy of Ethical Ideologies," *Journal of Personality and Social Psychology, 39*(1) (1980): 175–184; and J. Fletcher, *Situation Ethics: The New Morality* (Philadelphia: Westminster Press, 1966), p. 95.

27. Donaldson, *Ethics.*

28. Donaldson, *Ethics,* p. 360.

29. See, for example, Tsalikis and Fritzsche, "Business Ethics."

30. D. J. Fritzsche, "Ethical Issues in Multinational Marketing," in G. R. Laczniak and P. E. Murphy, eds., *Marketing Ethics: Guidelines for Managers* (Lexington, Ky.: Lexington Books, 1985), pp. 85–96; G. F. Cavanagh, D. J. Moberg, and M. Velasquez, "The Ethics of Organizational Politics," *Academy of Management Review, 63* (1981): 363–374.

31. Donaldson, *Ethics.*

32. R. B. Blake and D. A. Carroll, "Ethical Reasoning in Business," *Training and Development Journal* (June 1989): 99–104; and S. Hunt and S. Vitell, "A General Theory of Marketing Ethics," *Journal of Macromarketing, 6*(1) (Spring): 5–16.

33. F. D. Sturdivant and J. L. Ginter, "Corporate Social Responsiveness Management Attitudes and Economic Performance," *California Management Review* (Spring 1977): 30–39.

34. M. Velasquez, "Why Corporations Are Not Morally Responsible for Anything They Do," *Business and Professional Ethics Journal* (Spring 1983): 1-18.

35. See, for example, M. C. Mathews, *Strategic Intervention in Organizations,* (Newbury Park, Calif.: Sage Publications, 1988); vol. 169, Sage Library of Social Research; D. L. Worrell, J. G. Stead, and J. B. Spalding, "Unethical Decisions: The Impact of Reinforcement Contingencies and Managerial Philosophies," *Psychological Reports, 57* (1985): 355-365.

36. W. H. Hegarty and H. P. Sims, Jr., "Organizational Philosophy, Policies and Objectives Related to Unethical Decision Behavior: A Laboratory Experiment," *Journal of Applied Psychology, 64*(3) (1979): 331-338; Mathews, *Strategic Intervention*; and Worrell, et al., "Unethical Decision."

37. Pruden, "Which Ethics."

38. M. Bommer, C. Grato, J. Gravander, and M. Tuttle, "A Behavioral Model of Ethical and Unethical Decision Making," *Journal of Business Ethics, 6* (1987): 265-280.

39. Hegarty and Sims, "Organizational Philosophy."

40. G. W. England, *The Manager and His Values: An International Perspective* (Cambridge, Eng.: Ballinger Publishing, 1975).

41. K. H. Lee, "Ethical Beliefs in Marketing Management: A Cross Cultural Study," *European Journal of Marketing, 15*(1) (1981): 58-67; J. Tsalikis and O. Nwachukwu, "Cross-Cultural Business Ethics: Ethical Beliefs' Difference Between Blacks and Whites," *Journal of Business Ethics, 7* (1988): 745-754.

42. Lee, "Ethical Beliefs."

43. A. Bandura, *Social Learning Theory* (Englewood Cliffs, N.J.: Prentice-Hall, 1977).

44. S. Vitell and T. Festervand, "Business Ethics: Conflicts, Practices and Beliefs of Industrial Executives," *Journal of Business Ethics, 6* (1987): 111-122.

45. M. Zey-Ferrell, K. M. Weaver, and O. C. Ferrell, "Predicting Unethical Behavior Among Marketing Practitioners," *Human Relations, 32*(7) (1979): 557-569; M. Zey-Ferrell and O. C. Ferrell, "Role-Set Configuration and Opportunities as Predictors of Unethical Behavior in Organizations," *Human Relations, 35*(7) (1982): 587-604; O. C. Ferrell, M. Zey-Ferrell, and D. Krugman, "A Comparison of Predictors of Ethical and Unethical Behavior Among Corporate and Agency Advertising Managers," *Journal of Macromarketing, 3* (Spring 1983): 1927.

46. B. Z. Posner and W. H. Schmidt, "The Significance of Value Compatibility Between Managers and Their Organizations." Paper presented at 25th annual meeting of Western Academy of Management, Vancouver, Canada, April 1984.

47. Pruden, "Which Ethics."

48. E. A. Clasen, "Marketing Ethics and the Consumer," *Harvard Business Review* (January–February 1967): 79-86; Chamberlain, *Social Strategy.*

49. See, for example, Amba-Rao, "Industrial Hazards"; K. E. Goodpaster, "Ethical Imperatives and Corporate Leadership," in K. R. Andrews, ed., *Ethics in Practice* (Boston: Harvard Business School Press, 1987), pp. 212-228; W. E. Stead, D. L. Worrell, and J. G. Stead, "An Integrative Model for Understanding and Managing Ethical Behavior in Business Organizations," *Journal of Business Ethics, 9* (1990): 233-242; and J. A. Raelin, "The Professional as the Executive's Ethical Aide-de-Camp," *The Academy of Management Executive, 1*(3) (1987): 171-182.

50. Business Roundtable, *Corporate Ethics: A Prime Business Asset* (New York: Business Roundtable, 1988).

51. Amba-Rao, "Whither Bhopal"; and N. A. Ashford and C. Ayers, "Policy Issues for Consideration in Transferring Technology to Developing Countries," *Ecology Law Quarterly, 12*(4) (1985): 871–905.

52. L. A. Tavis, ed., *Multinational Managers and Host Government Interactions* (Notre Dame, Ind.: University of Notre Dame Press, 1988).

Chapter 16

Media Image and Development: Political and Economic Implications of U.S. Media Coverage of Africa

Eronini R. Megwa and Ike S. Ndolo

This chapter examines the economic and political implications of negative portrayals of Africa in the U.S. news media. Using the findings of a content analysis of two leading U.S. weekly news magazines from 1979 to 1989, the authors argue that, in view of recent economic and social changes occurring in some parts of the world system, scanty coverage and negative portrayal of Africa in the U.S. news media could hurt the region economically and politically by serving not only as a disincentive for prospective investors but also by weakening Africa's bargaining power in international negotiations.

INTRODUCTION

Disparaging information about people, groups, organizations, and products has probably been disseminated by word of mouth nearly as long as human communication has existed. However, the ability to transmit negative information quickly to large, disparate, and widely dispersed audiences has increased dramatically with the growth of mass communications.

It has been sufficiently documented that (1) Western news media give scanty and distorted coverage of Africa, and (2) an imbalance exists in the flow of international news between the developed and developing nations of the world, with the former enjoying a disproportionate advantage.[1] Research findings in the area of international news flow further indicate that, even though Western news media's coverage of international news has generally improved in quality and quantity in the last decade, what has remained unchanged is the United States (U.S.) news media coverage of Africa.[2] The U.S. news media give Africa the least attention and the most distorted portrayal of any region of the world.

The U.S. news media have been criticized for scanty coverage of international news. In a 1977 piece, Lent observed that the U.S. news media are not known for their outstanding coverage of international news. European, Latin American, and Caribbean newspapers, he argued, provide proportionately more space for international news than do U.S. newspapers.[3] However, sparse attention has been devoted to the economic and political ramifications of such limited coverage, particularly for Africa.

This chapter examines the political and economic implications of the U.S. media's scanty and distorted coverage of Africa and African issues. Our objective is to address such questions as whether this type of media coverage stunts or facilitates development efforts and the democratization process in Africa.

Do U.S. media reporting and portrayals of Africa provide problem-solving information for their audiences—Western and developing—that will help them interpret and understand the complex process of development as it relates to Africa? Do they allow readers to share ideas that are necessary for the understanding and appreciation of the duality of the African continent and its colonial experience? Does U.S. news media coverage dissuade potential U.S. investors? Finally, does U.S. news media coverage of Africa predispose their audience to contribute to the development not only of themselves but also of their neighbors and, ultimately, their society?

In the "New World Order," there seems to be a greater realization that the world is increasingly becoming interdependent. Under this new dispensation, the media, whether developed or developing, have the entire world as their audience. In most of the developing world, Western media, particularly those of the United States, are widely utilized by elites as a model. Consequently, U.S. media reporting should be responsive and sensitive to these global audiences in raising their aspirations and awareness, in teaching them skills and encouraging their development efforts, and in assisting them in reconstructing their cognitive frameworks to comprehend events in all regions of the world. In our view, these are the responsibilities of the news media in any new world order.

Development has been defined as the improvement in socioeconomic and political conditions of the individual and his or her society. This includes the acquisition of knowledge and skills, expansion of the human mind, the fusion of human confidence, and the growth of new consciousness. In essence, all of this implies freedom, equality, and growth and the opportunity to allow the individual to better realize human values and allow him or her a greater control over the environment and political destiny.[4]

MARKETPLACE ORIENTATION OF U.S. NEWS MEDIA

The U.S. mass media are not isolated social institutions unaffected by their environment. Rather, they exist and function within the ideological framework of U.S. society. Thus, they influence and are influenced by other institutions, groups, and individuals in this social milieu.

In a marketplace news paradigm, news stories are primarily treated as commodities and selected on the basis of their ability to excite and entertain the audience. The assumption is that the more exciting and dramatic the news story, the greater the chance that it will attract a larger audience and, by implication, more advertising revenue. This marketplace approach to news has significantly influenced the contents of international news.

The marketplace mechanism was developed in the latter part of the nineteenth century in the United States and Great Britain. It views news as a commodity that serves particular economic interests and caters to specific cultural tastes. It is characterized by a reporting style that defines news as any recent occurrence with up-to-the-minute, factual information. Furthermore, it demands that news reports be brief, succinct, and clear and able to relate to the audience the *who, what, where, when,* and *why* of an event and *how* it took place.

While it is true that freedom of expression and opinion and freedom of the press are among the most admirable characteristics of Western democracies, the U.S. news media's scanty and distorted coverage of Africa could be seen as a suppression of views and events as they occur in that region of the world. We are aware that not all thoughts, views, or actions in the developed nations are free from all forms of regulation. Part of this control comes from marketplace mechanisms that actively seek to neutralize sentiments and perspectives that are not in the "public interest" or views that do not reflect "what the media audience wants."

The construction of the "ideas market" was one of the most important events of modern Western history, opening the door for individual exposure to expression and diversity of opinions and views. However, such a market destroyed intergroup communication barriers and exposed minority or disenfranchised groups to the ideas of the political and economic majority. In modern society, this exposure is facilitated and nurtured by the mass media. The ideas marketplace undermines the ideological autonomy and cohesion of subordinate groups, forcing them to see the world in nearly the same ways as do the superior groups. It is equally true that the marketplace mechanism exposed the superior class to the views, beliefs, and values of the subordinate class. The ideal touted by the marketplace concept is that truth, regardless of who is its repository, will win in the end.

What this model fails to acknowledge, however, is that, in the business of opinion construction, laissez-faire laws almost always favor the interests of those in superior positions. This is because these groups generally have far more sophisticated mechanisms and far better access to the financial and organizational resources needed for the effective creation and dissemination of ideas than do the subordinate groups.[5] The U.S. news media are established primarily as profit-making institutions, not as human knowledge promoters, that benefit from the production and promotion of opinions and information generated by powerful economic and political groups and institutions. As has been observed, the ultimate importance of the marketplace orientation was to provide an institutional framework within which superior groups and institutions use their superior economic and ideological powers to protect and consolidate their positions. Thus, the superior groups are able to expand and protect their economic and political interests and define and forge the framework within which social reality is perceived at the local, national, and international levels.

The U.S. news media, which are operated by individuals who are themselves products of a socialization process that treats Africa as culturally unimportant and uneventful and economically unattractive, create and perpetuate a grossly inadequate and faulty news-reporting framework. This paradigm of news reporting paints Africa as unproductive, helpless, and hopeless, a region in constant need of direction and assistance from the West. In addition, this inadequate construction forms the viewer through which the perceptions and attitudes of Americans about Africa are framed.

Determinants of International News Coverage

In a piece written in 1973, Hester identified the hierarchy of nations as one of the determinants of international news flow; he also argued that the wider apart new nations are in the hierarchy of international relations, the greater the likelihood of a news imbalance between them.[6] The nation in the lower stratum of this hierarchy suffers a disadvantage.

Structural relationships between senders and receivers of information underscore a superior–subordinate relationship with senders as superiors and receivers as subordinates. Similarly, in the international political arena, the United States and Africa occupy superior–subordinate political positions, respectively. Accordingly, research has shown that the flow of news is enormously tilted in favor of the United States.

Cultural affinity is another criterion used in determining news flow among nations. In several studies of U.S. news media and how they make editorial decisions, it has been found that editorial decisions by U.S. journalists are not value-free. It has also been found that, in covering international news, U.S. journalists give considerations to their own societal values, such as ethnocentricism, altruistic democracy, and responsible capitalism.[7]

Foreign correspondents and foreign news staff select news items that are culturally and socially relevant to their news markets and present them in such a manner as to make sense to their own audiences. To retain this market, the news media consistently provide the U.S. public with news that fits this cultural and social framework. To do otherwise would challenge prevailing but erroneous perceptions about Africa as nonpresent, inefficient, and helpless. In the end, it is Africa that is severely hurt by this news-gathering and news-reporting framework.

International News Flow and Transnational News Agencies

International news agencies and foreign correspondents as we know them today did not exist until the middle and end of the nineteenth century. Systematic international news gathering arose then when newspaper editors began to gather foreign newspapers and reprint foreign news.[8] By 1900, international news assumed a sensational and commercial stature, exhibiting all the attributes of a commodity as defined by Marx: Its development is rooted in the historical context of industrialized, capitalist society; it was utilitarian in value; and it was a product of human labor, produced as a consumer good intended for exchange within a capitalist market system.[9]

The four most dominant transnational news agencies (TNNAs)—United Press International, Associated Press, Reuters, and Agence France Presse—are all U.S.-, British-, or French-owned. And because news selection reflects the personal preferences, journalistic orientations, and social backgrounds of those who edit and report the news, it is reasonable to speculate that news flowing in and out of the developing nations reflects the needs and preferences of those who edit international news for the four TNNAs.

This explains, in part, Righter's 1978 observation that foreign assignments were treated by the transnational news agencies like local assignments.[10] For example, U.S. and British TNNAs filed their foreign reports to suit and to be sensitive to U.S. and British interests, tastes, and values. In addition, the TNNAs administratively divided the world into beats using colonial ties and imperial interests as criteria for these divisions.[11]

These structural arrangements, designed primarily for profit and intended for consumption by Western audiences, unfortunately persist today. They are among the reasons for the imbalance in the international flow of news between developing and developed nations. They discourage the balanced flow of news between the developed and developing nations as well as the horizontal flow of information. Thus, these structural arrangements stifle the genuine exchange of ideas between the industrialized world and developing nations as well as among developing nations.

International News and Uncertainty Reduction

As an uncertainty reduction mechanism, information is crucial in decision making and choice making at both the micro- and macrolevels. Negative media coverage of events in Africa and issues relevant to the African agenda helps to limit further the negotiating ability of African representatives at international markets and international negotiations. In addition, it discourages potential U.S. investors in Africa and further compounds an already complex situation for potential African sympathizers.

Constant negative portrayal of Africa in the U.S. news media transmits distorted images of Africa to the U.S. media audience, which has little or no critical perspective by which it can view short-signed, incomplete, and inadequate information as relayed by their news media. This gross distortion of information often is the basis for erroneous judgments and policy debates about events in Africa and constitutes a significant part of the ammunition used by African critics and detractors to deny Africa much-needed aid.

Cognitive psychologists tell us that people have "schemas" that help them to store and retrieve beliefs, attitudes, values, and preferences. Accordingly, these cognitive structures direct and guide the interpretation of relevant information and assist in its organization and retention. We are aware that the news media sometimes reinforce existing attitudes and preferences rather than help form new ones. Therefore, if the news media reinforce existing attitudes, it is our position that the U.S. media will reinforce existing attitudes and perceptions of their audience about Africa. These perceptions and attitudes have been significantly shaped by distorted and limited U.S. news media coverage of Africa.

The selectivity and inattention hypotheses posit that people will often select information that contradicts and challenges their current views if that information is available. But Americans, Entman tells us in a recent study, have so little knowledge and such weakly anchored beliefs that information provided by the news media can significantly shape their attitudes.[12] In our view, most Americans lack the basis for critical evaluation of international news, particularly news about Africa in the U.S. news media.

Media Image, Power, and Public Perceptions

Some critics of the U.S. news media argue that the media exist to maintain the status quo, citing as their rationale the U.S. news media's inextricable reliance on elite news sources as their main source of raw materials for the production of news. Others claim that the media serve as a change agent in helping to create new attitudes and behavior. In this model, the media could represent a means for maintaining or destroying cultural values—that is, a tool not only for creating awareness but also to destabilize, an effect that could be adverse or destructive to national development efforts.

There is no question that the U.S. public depends, to a large extent, on its mass media to be informed of events around the world. In domestic affairs, the U.S. mass media are a common source of political information and knowledge connecting citizens and officials.

The injection-needle view of the power of the news media sees the media as wielding irresistible influence on their audiences. The agenda-setting concept as enunciated by Cohen and empirically examined by McCombs and Shaw is an offspring of this all-powerful media perspective, espousing the view that the media—through placement and coverage of certain issues in the news flow over time—tell their audiences what is and is not important.[13] Agenda setting in the foreign policy arena is seen as the process by which problems become salient political issues around which policy alternatives can be defined and supported or opposition gathered.[14] Through this strategy, the mass media are able to (1) place issues, regions, or countries on the U.S. foreign policy agenda, and (2) move an issue or country or region to a higher level of policy consideration.[15] However, scanty and negative media coverage of Africa by the U.S. news media makes it difficult for African issues to be added to the foreign policy agenda of the U.S. government.

The theories sketched above will guide our perspectives on the U.S. mass media's coverage of Africa and their ability to exert powerful influence on the U.S. public's knowledge and perceptions of Africa and issues relevant to the African agenda.

Africa in the U.S. News Media

Africa receives the least media attention and the most negative coverage of all the five continents in the U.S. news media. The continent is seen as one of, if not, the least attractive tourist areas to Americans.

In a study of two U.S. news magazines' coverage of Africa from 1979 to 1989, Megwa and Ndolo found that, for the period examined, *Newsweek* and *U.S. News and World Report* carried a total of 550 news items on Africa (247 for the former and 303 for the latter).[16] Political news dominated reports in the two magazines. The researchers also found that 406 of these news items were negative. In addition, Megwa and Ndolo found that southern Africa, particularly South Africa and Zimbabwe, was the most frequently covered of the five regions of Africa with a total of 310 news items, followed by northern Africa with a total of 110 items.[17] These news items emphasized conflict and crisis in these two parts of Africa. The researchers further observed that in the western region of the continent, Nigeria, which enjoyed a relatively peaceful democratic regime during the first half of the study period, received the most coverage in this region—because of the military coups in 1983 and 1985.[18] Apparently, the U.S. news media did not consider Nigeria's 1979 historic peaceful handover of power from the military to civilians newsworthy. Rather, what was newsworthy to the U.S. news media were the disruptive aspects of Nigeria's genuine attempts at American-style democracy.

The resultant effect of scanty and negative U.S. news media attention given to Africa is a negative audience perception of Africa. Furthermore, these audience's have few or no alternative sources of information about Africa that could assist them in challenging the prevailing mode of reporting. As such, the U.S. news media are able to exert tremendous influence on their U.S. audiences on issues relating to Africa.

As a result, Africa does not constitute a salient zone in the U.S. media audience's cognitive threshold. In other words, the U.S. public pays little or no attention to news about Africa. And even if U.S. media reporting of Africa were to be reversed today, this negative perception and nonsaliency of Africa would not disappear immediately. The negative effects of negative information, cognitive psychologists tell us, may persist in the form of affect even after its original cognitive base has been completely invalidated.

What makes this situation worrisome is that the U.S. media, on whose shoulders rests the mantle of reporting Africa to the U.S. public and the world, are themselves not adequately informed about Africa. And it is one of the sources that feed the persistent cycle of distorted coverage of the developing world. Confessions by U.S. media correspondent Ester Schrader when writing about the Lithuanian crisis for the *Washington Post* (July 15, 1990) lent credence to the above observation. It is the proverbial blind leading the blind. Consequently, U.S. news media's distorted coverage of Africa has been nearly catastrophic for Africa because it encourages and perpetuates negative attitudes toward the continent and generates incomplete and limited knowledge of Africa and African issues. This type of reporting, based mainly on a marketplace model of news work that stresses simple, dramatic, and spotty news over complex, human, and soft news, negates the historical background of events and thus discourages a more thorough understanding of the process of development in Africa. In addition, it reinforces and fosters negative stereotypes and myths about the continent.

Why Negative U.S. Media Coverage of Africa?

The structuralist school of thought faults U.S. media coverage by pointing to the content and form of international news: It is essentially neocolonial and imperialistic, intended to maintain and perpetuate the superior–subordinate relationship that exists between industrialized nations and developing nations.[19] Others blame the marketplace orientation of the U.S. news media, which places profit over and above all other considerations. According to the marketplace model, news must be sellable, simple, convenient to gather, and easy to produce.

By implication, therefore, this model is inadequate in dealing with news events in the developing world. For one thing, news in the developing world is not simple. It is neither convenient nor easy to produce. Development news takes into account historical backgrounds and long-range implications of isolated events.[20] Therefore, such news does not fit the frame used by Western news media. The Western news reporting style overlooks the genuine efforts and struggles of Africans to overcome poverty, disease, and malnutrition. In addition, it fails to give attention to those issues and topics that are relevant to the African agenda—for example, agriculture, education, and health.

In response to criticisms of their reporting style, the Western news media argue that development news is "slow," "soft," and unattractive. This may explain, in part, why U.S. news reporting of African events is spotty, incomplete, and disjointed. Consequently, these media do not relate one event in one part of Africa to others in the continent in such a way as to be comprehensible to their audiences.

The methods used by the U.S. news media may be different and more sophisticated from those of the colonialists, but the effects are the same: They place developing nations, particularly those in Africa, in a severely disadvantaged position because they help to curtail and constrain the negotiating ability of African countries and their representatives at international markets. This consistent negative portrayal of Africa conjures up and fosters an image of a dangerous, unstable, and chaotic continent. Ultimately, it engenders a perception among U.S. news media audiences that Africa is undemocratic, helpless, and incapable of self-governance. The cumulative effect of this reporting mechanism is that it sends a powerful negative message to potential U.S. investors and African sympathizers: Investing in Africa is a dangerous economic and political move!

DISCUSSION AND CONCLUSION

Western News Paradigm and Development

The occupational routines of journalists under a marketplace news paradigm, we have argued, ensure the promotion and protection of the interests and needs of elites and mainstream groups in a society and the preclusion of the development of perspectives that challenge the legitimacy of the status quo. We also posited that the U.S. media's overwhelming dependence on high-profile government news sources for the raw materials used in producing news engenders a situation whereby news is highly "bureaucratized" and "routinized." Such news carries with it a significant proportion of elite and mainstream values and interests.[21]

The news media represent a means for maintaining as well as destroying power and authority structures. Not only can they generate awareness but also they are capable of generating and encouraging negative attitudes toward Africa and its issues, thereby creating a destabilizing effect that could be adverse to national development efforts in Africa.

Therefore, consistent distortion of Africa in the U.S. news media fosters and legitimizes the erroneous image of Africa as nonpresent, nonactive, unproductive, and incapable of self-governance—and thus always in dire need of Western salvation. This pattern of reporting is capable of discouraging self-determination and self-initiatives. It creates audience uncertainty about Africa, and diminishes the bargaining power of African representatives in international markets and in international diplomacy.

Today, more than ever before, the U.S. news media have assumed a primordial position as one of the most potent forces that shape the American cultural and political future. The U.S. public, including policy makers and industry leaders, depends on the news media for knowledge of what is happening in both its immediate and international environments. In the area of domestic affairs, the news media are a common source of information connecting the government with citizens. The news media play a similar role in foreign affairs, an arena in which they serve as an almost exclusive information source for the U.S. public. Therefore, the U.S. news media's inextricable reliance on elite sources for public affairs news and international news sends a strong message to the U.S. audience that information from bureaucratic and government institutions is "objective," "correct," and "disinterested." By adopting this structural arrangement, the U.S. media systematically stifle the views of economic and political minorities. Consequently, this type of reporting presents a slanted and incomplete view of the world, one that legitimizes the prevalent political ideology of *laissez faire* and other values that are almost always intolerant of opposing views and preferences.

In the 1960s, political development theorists (notably Pye and Lerner) contended that increased literacy and urbanization constituted the panacea for modernization in the emerging nations of the world.[22] This overly simplistic assumption viewed increased literacy as a stimulant for media use and as a catalyst for a more productive work force. In addition, these theorists claimed that a free press and increased economic output would lead to democratic politics and eventually national development in the developing nations. History has shown that the contrary is true: Uncritical dependence on and use of Western-style news reporting and technology promotes and encourages the increased cultural and economic dependence of developing nations on developed nations.

Nothing in the structure of the present international news flow ensures the promotion and protection of the interests and views of developing nations. Rather, the structure is primarily an economic arrangement designed to protect the interests of the transnational Western news agencies and to guarantee the survival of Western news media institutions. It is, therefore, no surprise that it is economically profitable for the U.S. media to distort images of Africa and its people through consistently inadequate and disjointed coverage, one that makes Africa incoherent, confusing, and problematic for the U.S. public—and, by implication, unimportant and irrelevant both politically and economically. Consequently, sympathizers are discouraged from taking a keen interest in Africa. As such, the resulting attitudes stunt development efforts in the developing nations, disparage African culture and values, and help to support the international status quo by perpetuating dependency. In this scheme of things, the developed nations enjoy a scandalously disproportionate advantage in the hierarchy of nations by monopolizing the international news market to protect their interests.

Domination of international news dissemination by the four TNNAs cited at the beginning of this chapter does not encourage the flow of news between developed and developing nations. It also does not encourage the flow of news among nations of the developing world. The U.S. news media's marketplace orientation to news and their overwhelming reliance on powerful political and economic elite news sources violate liberal values of individual autonomy and are contrary to the concept of pluralistic democracy. The marketplace approach to international news coupled with the Western news agencies' monopoly of this market discourages individual growth. It is capable of stifling not only genuine efforts to promote national unity, but also attempts to build a shared sense of cultural identity. In addition, it helps to displace authentic cultural values. Indeed, marketplace news selection criteria are contrary to the interests of sovereign independence. Finally, it subjugates African interests to those of the Western nations.

There is no question that the world is becoming more and more interdependent. The developing nations are bound to the West, and the West, in turn, is increasingly linked with developing nations. News media—whether Western or developing—are charged with the uneasy burden of reporting events in both developed and developing nations, so they should be more sensitive and responsive to the needs of their increasingly global audience. And where such an audience does not exist, the news media should create one. After all, audience surveys in the United States have consistently indicated, as Stevenson's 1988 study shows, that audiences are highly interested in foreign news.[23]

The U.S. news media can and should provide better coverage of Africa. Whether in the West or in developing nations, news reporting is a highly selective process mediated by personal, professional, and organizational factors. The U.S. news media should assist their audiences in comprehending the complex processes of development and democratization, particularly the nondisruptive and nondramatic aspects of those processes, in the developing nations by making these events more coherent, interesting, and attractive. Their audiences will need such an approach because the world has become increasingly interdependent and their own jobs and future may depend on these events and peoples.

Transnational News Agencies and Cultural Imperialism

The TNNAs are found in every region of the globe, carrying with them complex technologies over which they have exclusive control. Such technologies could create substantial problems for the political economies of Africa.

Critics of the Western news media claim that international news has a decidedly Western bias and that Western news media almost always underreport Africa and present it in a poor light. Negative messages persist and tend to have adverse effects. It is quite possible that this type of reporting could cause or generate negative perceptions on the part of Western news media audiences, ultimately persuading them to see Africa as unimportant and irrelevant.

Both individuals and groups in Africa are exposed to Western media. If such news is only about African crime and violence, then these people are more likely to have negative perceptions about themselves and their African neighbors, become less likely to cooperate and compromise, and make increasing demands on the limited national resources if they are to attain a Western style of living. This type of interregional or intergroup tension increases and reinforces subnational identities, which could, in turn, could severely jeopardize national integration efforts as well as exacerbate ethnic cleavages.

Structuralists argue that the Western monopoly of the international flow of information is a disguised form of cultural imperialism. As such, when developed nations dominate the flow of news or mediate the flow of news from, to, and among the developing nations, there is created a state of dependency, a desire and ability to develop and think more and more like the developed nations.[24]

What could be done? We are not so optimistic about the U.S. news media changing their journalistic perspectives and attitudes toward Africa. This is because a change in their pattern of covering Africa will be considered revolutionary not only because it will place an undue burden upon them, but also because it is incompatible with the market orientation of U.S. society.

What we are sure of, however, is that to change this pattern of reporting will not be to the economic advantage of the U.S. news media and will challenge prevalent myths about Africa held by Americans through constant negative media coverage and recurring distorted images. These images, history has shown us, were created by colonialists and imperialists to further their imperial interests.

It is our position that a deep cultural gulf exists between the U.S. media and Africa that makes it even more difficult for the U.S. news media to understand the problems of African countries and to relate their reporting to the issues relevant to the African agenda. Until this marketplace news-reporting paradigm is repaired, Africa will be underreported and misperceived by U.S. audiences. Consequently, genuine development and democratization efforts in Africa will remain severely hampered.

One of the primary responsibilities of the U.S. news media is to maintain the marketplace of ideas and the self-righting process of truth despite the growing concentration of voices. In an increasingly multicultural and multiethnic marketplace of diverse interests, values, and tastes, it is imperative that the U.S. news media should be acutely aware of and responsive to the needs and interests of this public. These needs and interests include, among other things, being aware of what is happening in other parts of the world—including the developing nations and their efforts to democratize. To be able to accomplish these tasks, the U.S. news media in an interdependent world—one linked by technology—will have to embark on self-regulation and reeducation to sharpen the critical perspectives of their international news staffs regarding the complex and painful processes of development and the genuine efforts at democratization in the developing world. This calls for the U.S. news media to give equal attention to both the disruptive and nondisruptive aspects of development in Africa; provide background information on famine, disease, irrigation projects, and health campaigns; and give fair coverage to corruption, graft, and inefficiency as well as honesty and accountability in government.

NOTES

1. The first position is asserted by E. McAnany, J. F. Larson, and J. D. Storey, "News of Latin America on Network Television, 1972–1982: Too Little, Too Late?" Paper presented at annual meeting of the International Communication Association, Boston, Massachusetts, May 1982. The second position is held by J. Galtung and M. H. Ruge, "The Structure of Foreign News," *Journal of Peace Research, 2* (1965): 64–91; A. Hester, "An Analysis of News Flow from Developed and Developing Nations," *Gazette, 17* (1971): 70–74; and J. A. Lent, "Foreign News in American Media," *Journal of Communication, 27* (1977): 46–51.

2. See, for instance, D. H. Weaver and G. C. Wilhoit, "Foreign News Coverage in Two U.S. Wire Services: An Update," *Journal of Communication* 33(2) (Spring 1983): 132–148.

3. Lent, "Foreign News."

4. For elaboration, see A. Inayatulla as quoted on p. 8 in "The Nature of Development," in Hamadan Bin Adnan et al., *Introduction to Development Communication* (Honolulu: East-West Communication Institute, East-West Center, 1980).

5. B. Ginsburg, *The Captive Public: How Mass Opinion Promotes State Power* (New York: Basic Books, 1986).

6. Hester, "Analysis of News Flow."

7. Herbert Gans, *Deciding What's News: A Study of CBS Evening News, NBC Nightly News, Newsweek and Time* (New York: Vantage Books, 1979).

8. See Robert W. Desmond, *Windows on the World: World News Reporting, 1900–1920* (Iowa City: University of Iowa Press, 1980).

9. William Meyer, *Transnational Media and Third World Development* (Westport, Conn.: Greenwood Press, 1988).

10. See Rosemary Righter, *Whose News? Politics, the Press and the Third World* (New York: Times Books, 1978).

11. Righter, *Whose News?*

12. See R. M. Entman, *Democracy Without Citizens: Media and the Decay of American Politics* (New York: Oxford University Press, 1989).

13. See B. C. Cohen, *The Press and Foreign Policy* (Princeton, N.J.: Princeton University Press, 1963); and M. E. McCombs and D. L. Shaw, "The Agenda-Setting Function of Mass Media," *Public Opinion Quarterly, 36* (1972): 176–184.

14. See Lutz Ebring et al., "Front Page News and Real World Cues: A New Look at Agenda-Setting by the Media," *American Journal of Political Science, 24* (February 1980): 17.

15. See Patrick O'Heffernan, *Mass Media and American Foreign Policy: Insider Perspectives on Global Journalism and the Foreign Policy Process* (Norwood, N.J.: Ablex Publishing, 1991).

16. E. R. Megwa and I. S. Ndola, "Guns, Gavels, and Pens: U.S. Media Coverage of Africa, 1979–1989." Paper presented at annual meeting of African Studies Association, Baltimore, Maryland, November 1990.

17. Megwa and Ndolo, "Guns."

18. Megwa and Ndolo, "Guns."

19. Among the structuralists advancing this view are Johan Galtung, "A Structural Theory of Imperialism," *Journal of Peace Research, 82*(2) (1971): 81–117; and Herbert I. Schiller, *Communication and Cultural Domination* (White Plains, N.Y.: International Arts and Sciences Press, 1976).

20. For elaboration, see Narinda Aggarwala, "New International Information and Communication Order: Setting the Record Straight," *New York Law School Journal of International and Comparative Law, 4*(1) (1982).

21. This observation is borne out by the following studies: Schiller, *Communication*; G. Tuchman, *Making News: A Study in the Construction of Reality* (New York: Macmillan, 1978); D. L. Lasorsa and S. D. Reese, "New Sources Use in the Crash of 1987: A Study of Four National Media," *Journalism Quarterly, 67*(1) (1990): 60–71; Entman, *Democracy*; and E. R. Megwa and J. T. Barber, "Can Minority News Sources Set the Agenda for Mainstream News Media: A Study of the Congressional Black Caucus and the National Media." Paper presented at meeting of International Communication Association, Dublin, Ireland, June 1990.

22. See Lucian Pye, *Aspects of Political Development* (Boston: Little, Brown, 1966); and Daniel Lerner, *The Passing of Traditional Society: Modernizing the Middle East* (New York: Free Press, 1958).

23. R. L. Stevenson, *Communication Development and the World* (New York: Times Books, 1988).

24. Galtung, "Structural Theory."

Part Seven

Conclusion:
Future Prospects and Promises

Chapter 17

Contemporary Issues and Future Challenges for Professionals in Third World Social Change: The 1990s and Beyond

Lewis A. Mennerick and Mehrangiz Najafizadeh

This chapter critically examines the role of professionals in Third World develop-ment and the challenges that they will confront in the 1990s and beyond. We first focus on the traditional sociological concept of "professionals" and then on the emerging redefinition of the role of development professionals. Next, we examine organizational, structural, and ideological constraints confronting and often im-peding such professionals' work. Third, we concentrate on four of the most funda-mental problems facing Third World nations, which professionals are being called upon to help rectify: insufficient educational expansion, rapid population growth, environmental problems, and allocation of scarce economic resources and the proliferation of military technologies. We conclude by emphasizing the changing roles of professionals, the need for greater interorganizational cooperation, and the need to involve laypeople more fully in development activities.

INTRODUCTION

The roles of professionals engaged in Third World development activities have expanded immensely since the end of World War II. No longer is such work restricted to a few select categories such as religious clergy, colonial govern-ment personnel, business entrepreneurs, and philanthropists. Instead, profes-sionals are involved, in one capacity or another, in activities related to Third World development and are found in a diverse array of organizational settings: religious organizations, nonprofit special-interest associations, private-sector consulting firms, commercial business enterprises, multinational corporations,

This is a revised version of a paper presented at the annual meeting of the Association for the Advancement of Policy, Research and Development in the Third World, which was held in Mexico City, Mexico, November 14–17, 1990.

government agencies, and international agencies. Such professionals encompass an equally diverse set of job titles, including social and behavioral scientists, physical scientists and engineers, education specialists, physicians and other health-care workers, environmental specialists, corporate officials, attorneys, religious clergy, and various government personnel.

In examining current and future issues and challenges for professionals in development, we first focus on the traditional sociological concept of "professionals" and on the emerging redefinition of the role of professionals. Next, we examine the organizational, structural, and ideological constraints that professionals confront. Third, we concentrate on four fundamental problems that Third World nations face: problems that professionals are being called upon to help rectify. We conclude by emphasizing the changing roles of professionals and the need to involve laypeople more fully in development activities.

THE ROLE OF PROFESSIONALS IN DEVELOPMENT

Despite the increase in the number and diversity of development professionals, the long-standing tradition of attempting to impose development models from the industrialized Northern nations is still the norm for some professionals. At least implicit in this tradition are ethnocentric attitudes of moral, cultural, educational, and technological superiority. Nonetheless, particularly during the past decade or so, we also have witnessed fundamental changes. Perhaps most significant is the increased realization that particular forms of professionalism and of development planning are now irrelevant, ineffective, or both.

Specifically, professionals traditionally have been characterized as being unique because their positions require relatively high levels of formal education and the mastery of extensive knowledge. Because of their specialized expertise, professionals distinguish themselves from laypeople, and they also emphasize autonomy and control over their work activities. In this conception, professionals are most knowledgeable, and their judgments are not to be disputed.

Two guiding ideas followed from this traditional concept of professionals. First, professionals—*not* laypeople—are most qualified to define the objectives of Third World development, to plan development programs, and ultimately to implement development projects. Whether the professional is from an industrialized Northern nation or is a Third World national who was educated in the North, the dominant notion has been that professionals are unique in status and in their ability to foster development and solve Third World problems. The dominant belief was that advanced formal education, professional certification, and other credentials positioned professionals to lead the development and modernization process.

Second, development should emphasize macrolevel social change. As such, the traditional professional approach to development has emphasized top-down planning and particular development models. For example, to expand access to education, national ministries of education would be established and maintained in Third World countries to plan and implement the building of more schools and the training of more teachers. Professionals, through the centralized ministries, also would determine the appropriate form and content of schooling. Therefore, from this perspective, laypeople (e.g., parents and community members) and other professionals (e.g., classroom teachers) would have little or no input into the school-expansion process. Instead, professionals believed that the products of their professional expertise would trickle down and eventually benefit the citizenry as a whole. Similar examples are common to planning for various other types of development activities such as building and expanding highways, hydroelectric dams, health-care facilities, housing complexes, manufacturing or assembly plants, and so forth.

Through this portrait of traditional development professionals, we do not mean to impugn either the character or the well-intentioned activities of all such professionals. On the contrary, many development professionals have sought and continue to seek viable solutions to Third World problems. Nonetheless, many development professionals increasingly are realizing that formal education and professional certification are not always the only credentials needed in effective development planning. In fact, many professionals have come to recognize that the practical work and life experiences of Third World laypeople can provide especially important insights into alternative avenues for development.

Two additional points are important. First, this emerging redefinition of the role of development professionals now places greater emphasis on understanding the complexities of the social, cultural, organizational, economic, and political contexts in which development projects are to be carried out.[1] Development does not occur in a vacuum. Rather, it occurs within a complex set of structural and ideological forces that, unless they are fully understood and accommodated, will most likely impede even the most theoretically sophisticated development plans.

Second, this emerging redefinition of professional roles calls attention to the fact that development professionals should not restrict their attention solely to the goals of Northern-based development agencies and Third World government officials, the interests of Northern corporate leaders, or those of Third World elites. Traditionally, professionals have failed to give adequate attention to the values, goals, and needs as perceived by the intended lay beneficiaries of development projects.[2] Yet, it is crucial that planners understand development needs from the perspectives of their intended beneficiaries. This includes a potentially diverse range of the Third World citizenry: urban slum dwellers, subsistence farmers, indigenous Indian and other ethnic groups, industrial workers, and so forth. Therefore, in this redefined model, development is not imposed. Rather, development professionals seek increased input and commitment from lay beneficiaries, and both groups ultimately participate to foster social change that more adequately addresses the needs of the citizenry.

CONSTRAINTS ON PROFESSIONALS

Although professionals have traditionally maintained considerable control over their work settings because of their expertise and privileged social positions, they have increasingly confronted a variety of organizational, structural, and ideological constraints. These constraints sometimes become intertwined, and they frequently impede the work of professionals. We will illustrate with a few examples.[3]

Organizational Constraints

Professionals function within complex organizational structures that frequently are characterized by conflicting goals or conflicting methods for achieving particular goals. Such organizations include international agencies, development agencies sponsored by Northern governments, private-sector nonprofit organizations, religious organizations, private-sector corporations, and a wide range of Third World private-sector and governmental organizations that focus on various aspects of development. In some instances, the activities of professionals are constrained by the broader policies and development agendas of international funding agencies. For example, to receive funding, professionals must subscribe to the goals and priorities of the funding agencies. In other instances, professionals are constrained by conflicting or contradictory bureaucratic procedures that impede their work. Further, constraints also sometimes emanate from private-sector commercial enterprises that seek to foster development as well as increase their own financial gains through the establishment of new manufacturing or assembly plants or through the exploitation of natural resources in ways that contradict other development goals such as improved worker safety, the conservation of natural resources, or the reduction or prevention of environmental pollution.

Structural Constraints

The activities of development professionals also are influenced by broader structural issues as in the case of Ethiopia where, during the civil war, opposing factions interfered with attempts by international relief professionals to provide food supplies to famine victims on the grounds that such food might help opposing forces. Even in less dramatic circumstances, constraints arise from inadequate infrastructure to facilitate development projects and from inadequate numbers or uneven distribution of development professionals. Engineers, for example, may have the expertise to design various public-service projects (e.g., highways, electric plants, sanitation systems) but lack adequate finances and support personnel to fully implement the projects. In still other cases, decisions regarding the provision of development assistance by Northern governments is determined not by the recommendations of development professionals but instead by professionals whose major concerns focus on achieving the foreign-policy objectives of Northern donor governments.

Ideological Constraints

Professionals also confront constraints that are linked to broader issues of religion, politics, or professional ideology. In Peru, for example, attempts to encourage family planning to reduce rapid population growth have been met with substantial religious opposition; in certain African countries, similar attempts have been hindered by cultural constraints. Further, in postrevolutionary Iran, government and religious officials, until quite recently, have avoided development cooperation with Northern governments, in part, on the grounds that it would lead to the further secularization of Iran and would conflict with the religious goals of the Islamic revolution. More generally, in some Third World nations, government policies—influenced by such factors as political, ethnic, racial, or religious divisions—have directly or indirectly influenced the distribution of development projects, with particular groups receiving preferential consideration in the allocation of development projects ranging from the provision of electricity, potable water, and sanitation facilities to medical, education, and other social services. In addition, guiding national political ideologies—whether democratic, socialist, authoritarian, or religious—also have affected the work of development professionals. Professionals working within Third World democratic contexts often must be responsive to political leaders and must function within the framework of governmental legislation and regulation, which presumably reflect the will of the citizenry more generally. In socialist or authoritarian contexts, professionals are constrained not by the citizenry per se but by the controlling apparatus of the state (for example, when the state maintains unilateral control of education and health services). In other settings, theocratic decrees may constrain the functioning of professionals. Finally, personal or professional beliefs and values to which professionals adhere also can lead to conflict and constraint as when professional ecologists and professional economists differ on long-term and short-term goals and the consequences of development projects that adversely affect the environment.

THIRD WORLD PROBLEMS AND CHALLENGES

During the 1990s and into the twenty-first century, the Third World will confront a series of major development-related problems for which professionals will be asked to provide solutions. It is important, however, to emphasize that the concept of "development" is not absolute or neutral but, instead, is socially constructed. The meaning of development varies among professionals and among the citizenry more generally depending on the particular beliefs and values to which they subscribe as well as on the varied self-interests of both professionals and citizens. Therefore, the meaning of development depends on one's perception and definition of both current conditions and how or if these conditions should be modified in the future.

More specifically, particular development projects may be favorably viewed by some segments of society as contributing, for example, to overall economic productivity. But they may be viewed quite differently by other segments of the citizenry. To illustrate, the construction of highways through rain forests in the Amazon region is viewed very differently by the engineers and economists who design the highways and project their future contributions to economic development than by the biologists and ecologists who contemplate environmental damage or the social scientists who assess the consequences for both the indigenous population and those citizens who can now more easily migrate to rain forest land. So, too, such projects are viewed quite differently by the indigenous population that wishes to preserve the forests than by the migratory groups that wish to clear forest land and establish their own farms.

In the following, we provide an overview of four of the most fundamental Third World problems that professionals now face and will continue to face in the twenty-first century. Yet, as we have emphasized, not all segments of the world's citizenry view these conditions as problems or as being equally problematic. Further, even where there is consensus that these conditions are problematic, there is no international consensus as to the most appropriate means for solving them.

Insufficient Educational Expansion

We focus first on education because enhanced educational opportunities are fundamental to other aspects of social change that would benefit Third World citizenries. Education alone will not resolve all problems confronting the Third World. Nonetheless, education is a central mechanism for social change that will contribute to increased economic productivity and enhanced understanding and remedying of population, health, and environmental problems as well as providing an intellectual foundation to foster democratization and to promote human rights and civil liberties.

Despite considerable educational expansion since the 1950s, the Third World continues to lack the levels of education found in the industrialized Northern nations. At least 60 million Third World youths still did not have access to primary schooling in the late 1980s, the total number of youths out of school exceeded 290 million, and per-pupil expenditures (as measured in constant dollars) declined in two-thirds of the Third World nations. So, too, financial assistance earmarked for Third World education constituted only 10 percent of the total aid provided by the industrialized Western nations.[4] Overall, during the 1980s, fourteen Third World nations in Africa and three in Asia continued to enroll less than 50 percent of their youths in primary schools. Seventy-four Third World nations, in turn, enrolled less than 50 percent of their youths at the secondary school level.

Added to insufficient access to primary and secondary schooling are questions about inequities in participation in schooling and inequities in the financing of education. Of the 100 million youths who began school in 1990, 40 percent will drop out before completing primary school—and two-thirds of all youths who have never attended school or who drop out are female. In turn, UNICEF estimates that the cost of a university education for one student equals the cost of providing a primary school education for one hundred youths. More specifically, during the 1980s in Africa, the use of international financial assistance heavily favored support for advanced education; only 7 percent was used for primary schools and 16 percent for secondary schooling, compared with 33 percent for vocational or technical and 34 percent for higher education. Similar examples are found in Latin America where, with a tenfold increase in higher-education enrollments from 1960 to the mid-1980s, government subsidies have favored higher education and, in turn, favored the upper classes because Latin American university students are disproportionately drawn from white-collar and urban families. Lower-class children tend to have less access to secondary education and, therefore, also less access to higher education. Indeed, the children of white-collar families are disproportionately represented in higher education throughout the Third World. Gender differences also persist: Male university students tend to concentrate in engineering and technology, whereas female students disproportionately concentrate in education and health-related disciplines.[5] Such social class and gender differences not only demonstrate contemporary inequities in access to and participation in higher education, but also forecast continuing inequities into the twenty-first century as the university students of the 1980s and 1990s assume higher-status leadership and professional roles in their respective countries.

Many Third World nations also face specific problems in determining the educational goals that are most suitable for the needs of their citizens. Should emphasis be placed on basic primary school education to make individuals more self-sufficient or should the goal of primary schooling be to prepare children for secondary school, with secondary schools, in turn, preparing youths for higher education? Further, in some instances, imbalances exist within and between education and the occupational structure. For example, in Zimbabwe, primary school expansion has been so effective that the government has confronted problems of providing adequate buildings, equipment, and trained teachers for secondary schools. In other Third World countries, imbalances exist wherein employment is not available for many of those who graduate from secondary schools or colleges. Indeed, the expansion of higher education in Latin America was accompanied by increases during the 1980s in the total number of unemployed university graduates as well as the number of unemployed graduates relative to unemployment as a whole.[6]

In other cases, questions persist as to the appropriateness of educational models imported from Northern industrialized nations. In Nigeria, for example, debate continues as to whether primary school children should be educated in the English language or in one or more of the three major indigenous languages. In Iran, the 1979 revolution brought the ouster of Western secular education and the implementation of Islamic-based education. And in Tanzania, the long-term emphasis on education for self-reliance has produced disappointing results despite extensive international financial aid. Further, throughout the Third World, professionals confront continuing educational inequities as rural and lower-class youths still tend to receive less education and lower-quality education than do urban and upper-class youths.[7]

Rapid Population Growth

The global community confronts significant population growth, and Third World nations will account for 95 percent of such growth during the next thirty-five years. In 1950, the industrialized North constituted 32 percent of the world population, but by 2025 it will constitute only 16 percent. And by 2025, population in Latin America is projected to increase from 448 million to 760 million; that of East Asia from 1.2 billion to 1.6 billion; that of South Asia from 1.2 billion to 2.174 billion; and that of Africa from 648 million to 1.581 billion. More immediately, the world population, now well in excess of 5 billion, is projected to increase by 1 billion by the end of the 1990s. Such increases vary considerably. South Asia will account for 31 percent of the increase, Africa 23 percent, East Asia 17 percent, and the remainder of the Third World 23 percent, with the industrialized North accounting for only 6 percent. Simultaneously, family planning in the Third World also has expanded greatly: from 9 percent in the early 1960s to an estimated 50 percent in 1990, with East Asia (74 percent) and Latin America (56 percent) manifesting the most marked increases. In addition, average fertility in the Third World has dropped from 6 to 4 children per woman, and, by the late 1980s, 125 governments worldwide directly supported family planning. Nonetheless, the magnitude of population increases continues to impact Third World citizenries. For example, although the Third World overall has experienced a decline in the percentages of citizens living in poverty, the illiterate, and the malnourished, the *total* number in each category continued to increase from 1970 to the mid-1980s.[8] Indeed, future prospects for remedying problems such as educational insufficiency are exacerbated by rapid population growth, as reflected in the fact that in fifty-three of the seventy-four Third World nations that still enroll less than 50 percent of their youths in secondary schools, the population is projected to at least double by 2025.

Environmental Problems

Environmental problems pertain both to damage to the natural environment and also environmental health-related problems that immediately affect the lives of human beings. The Third World confronts an array of problems and, although progress has been made in alleviating some of them, the Third World increasingly is characterized by overall environmental deterioration.

Human health. Life expectancy in the Third World increased from 51 years for men and 53 for women in the 1960s to 59 and 61 years, respectively, in the 1980s. Nonetheless, the magnitude of environmental health problems is enormous. As we approach the end of the twentieth century, more than 1 billion people—roughly 20 percent of all humans—still lack access to safe drinking water, sufficient food, and basic health services. More than 150 million children under the age of five are malnourished, with the total number of malnourished exceeding 500 million. Yet, such numbers alone do not communicate the consequences in the diminution of human potential and of human capital. They communicate neither how these children's physical and cognitive development is impeded by illness or malnutrition nor the consequences for vast numbers of adults who similarly live in environmental settings that are detrimental to physical well-being. At the extreme, more than 35,000 children a day—more than one-quarter of a million each week—die from malnutrition or from diseases that could be prevented or treated at very low financial cost. Such problems exist in the majority of Third World nations but are particularly acute in both Africa and South Asia. In sheer numbers, three nations—Bangladesh, India, and Pakistan—account for 45 percent of all malnourished children and 40 percent of all child deaths.

Yet medical technologies do have significant potential. During the 1980s, roughly two-thirds of all Third World children were immunized against childhood diseases, and one-third of all families now use oral rehydration therapy for diarrheal disease. Even so, current projections indicate that illness and malnutrition will claim the lives of more than 100 million children during the 1990s, two-thirds of them the result of dehydration, pneumonia, tetanus, measles, and whooping cough—all of which could be treated or prevented. Equally important is birth spacing and health services for women. Each year, one-half million women die from childbirth-related causes and another one-half million die from other reproductive problems. Still other health issues focus directly on safe water and sanitation: 25 percent of urban Third World families and 60 percent of rural families continue to lack access to safe water. Indeed, between 1970 and 1988, the number of urban households without safe water *increased* from 138 million to 215 million; the number without adequate sanitation *increased* from 98 million to 340 million.[9]

The natural environment. Potentially irreparable damage to the natural environment also threatens the future well-being of both the global community and the Third World. The industrialized North currently consumes the largest proportion of natural resources and contributes disproportionately to problems such as acid rain, the deterioration of the ozone layer, and the potential for global warming. Some corporations in the industrialized North, in turn, have sought to use the Third World as disposal sites for toxic wastes, while other corporations have moved toxic-producing industries to Third World nations where environmental regulations are lax and the supply of less-expensive labor is abundant. Simultaneously, many Third World nations are experiencing substantial deforestation, which contributes to soil erosion, destroys plants and wildlife, and contributes to the potential for global warming. The current annual destruction of tropical forests entails an acreage equal to Washington state, resulting in the destruction of roughly 100 plant and animal species each day.

In addition, although the industrialized North thus far has been responsible for most emissions of greenhouse gases, current projections suggest that, within the next fifty years, more than one-half of greenhouse gas emissions will originate from Third World nations. Concomitantly, if the greenhouse effect and global warming materialize, such nations as Bangladesh, China, Egypt, India, and Indonesia will likely experience major population displacements because of flooding, and many other Third World nations probably will experience negative effects in agricultural production. Other environmental problems result from inappropriate farming methods and from the search for fuel wood, both of which contribute to desertification and soil erosion and which threaten future food production. In still other instances, the overuse and misuse of chemical fertilizers, pesticides, and herbicides in agriculture have resulted in rural water and soil pollution. And as Third World urbanization and industrialization have increased, so too have air, water, and soil pollution. Finally, added to such continuing environmental damage is the potential for catastrophic environmental destruction, as graphically illustrated in 1991 by the oil spill and the burning of Kuwaiti oil wells in the Persian Gulf War. For "sustainable development" to be realized, major modifications in the use of natural resources, major changes in pollution-creating technologies, major reductions in global population growth, and major new initiatives for international cooperation will be required.[10]

Allocation of Scarce Resources and Proliferation of Military Technologies

Third World military establishments pose two significant problems: (1) They drain scarce economic resources from social programs that could enhance Third World well-being, and (2) they pose the potential for national, regional, and international war and destruction. The growth of Third World military establishments and the proliferation of military technologies reflect several problems: the international community's failure to formulate and maintain effective peace accords, national concerns for maintaining sovereignty, the self-aggrandizement and self-interests of some Third World political and military leaders, and the monetary self-interests of individuals, corporations, and governments who participate in the manufacture and supply of military arms. As do the industrialized Northern nations, Third World countries have the right to ensure their own sovereignty. Most, however, possess finite economic resources, and military expenditures reduce available funding for social programs and infrastructure development, which already are quite inadequate. It is instructive, therefore, to review Third World military expenditures relative to social expenditures.

During the 1980s, Third World nations as a group placed a disproportionate emphasis on military arms imports, with arms expenditures exceeding education expenditures in twelve Third World countries and public-health expenditures in thirty-two countries. In the same period, education expenditures were cut an average of 50 percent and health expenditures an average of 25 percent in the thirty-seven poorest Third World nations. While the Soviet Union and the United States were the major arms suppliers during this period, France and China also played significant roles as Middle Eastern countries purchased roughly two-thirds of all weapons sold to the Third World. At the same time, some arms manufacturers anticipate that concerns about national security resulting from the closure of U.S. military installations in the Philippines will prompt other Southeast Asian nations such as Malaysia, Thailand, Singapore, and Indonesia to dramatically increase arms purchases during the 1990s.[11]

Disproportionate expenditures become even more evident when we consider *total* military expenditures during the past decade. Third World nations spent approximately $150 billion per year in the first half of the 1980s, compared to a little more than $100 billion on education and only $38 billion on public health. Total military expenditures exceeded education and health expenditures in forty-three and eighty-one Third World nations, respectively. *Per capita* military expenditures also exceeded those for education in thirty-eight Third World nations and exceeded public health expenditures in seventy-seven countries. Although overall military expenditures were declining in the late 1980s largely because of budget constraints, the Third World still was spending $145 billion annually on its military.[12]

When we take into account both past military and arms expenditures and the continuing international debt and interest payments that many Third World nations confront, future funding for social programs and infrastructure development faces many questions. Further, because of the decline in social programs in many Third World nations during the 1980s, the decade reflects a lost generation of many Third World youths. This cohort of young people lacked access to adequate health care and schooling, and the negative consequences of this loss of human potential will be manifested within particular Third World nations during the 1990s and into the twenty-first century.

With the recent end to war in the Persian Gulf, Central America, and sections of Africa, it is possible that military expenditures in particular Third World countries will continue to decline. Even so, the global community still confronts the continuing proliferation of military technologies. Ballistic missile capabilities have increased, and at least thirteen Third World nations currently either possess or are developing missiles of varying technological sophistication: Egypt, Iran, Iraq, Libya, Saudi Arabia, and Syria in the Middle East; Pakistan and India in South Asia; Taiwan, North Korea, and South Korea in East Asia; and Argentina and Brazil in South America. In addition to China, both India and Pakistan have nuclear weapons capability, and experts believe that Argentina, Brazil, Libya, and Taiwan also could develop nuclear weapons within ten years. In turn, eight Third World nations—China, Iran, Iraq, Libya, North Korea, South Korea, Syria, and Taiwan—have the technology to produce chemical weapons, the so-called poor person's weapon. And while governments of the industrialized North may attempt to control the transfer of relevant technologies to the Third World, private-sector arms dealers still persist, and some Third World nations also possess or are developing their internal capacity to produce military arms. As such, Third World military establishments and military technologies will continue to pose threats to both regional and international stability.[13]

CONCLUSION

As we have indicated, development professionals confront a variety of constraints that impede their work. These constraints, together with the major problems that Third World nations face, will pose continuing challenges to development professionals in the coming decades. The role of professionals has changed and will continue to change as we enter the twenty-first century. As many Third World nations increasingly focus on the process of democratization, three issues become evident. First, development professionals need to emphasize greater cooperation among various professional groups and greater cooperation among the variety of governmental and private-sector development agencies and organizations. Second, development professionals need to recognize that the concept of development is relative. People perceive and define development in different ways and therefore it is crucial that development professionals understand development from the perspectives of Third World laypeople and that they incorporate them through grass-roots participation and cooperation in the planning and implementation process. In doing so, professionals need to facilitate communication with the lay public and also use laypeople's knowledge and expertise. Third, professionals working in the context of increasing democratization within the Third World need to become more sensitive to issues of social change that go beyond the development programs that disproportionately benefit Third World elites. Professionals need to recognize the cultural uniqueness of particular Third World nations and not merely attempt to transform Third World societies into mirror images of the industrialized North. At the same time, development professionals must continue to address the fundamental problems of educational insufficiency, population growth, environmental deterioration, and the allocation of scarce resources and the proliferation of military technologies. As manifested in these problems, the ultimate challenge for the coming decades is to remedy the persistent inequities that continue to characterize much of the Third World today and thereby enhance the quality of life for all segments of Third World citizenry.

NOTES

1. Also see Dennis A. Rondinelli, John Middleton, and Adriaan M. Verspoor, *Planning Education Reforms in Developing Countries* (Durham, N.C.: Duke University Press, 1990).

2. Also see Lawrence F. Salmen, *Listen to the People: Participant-Observer Evaluation of Development Projects* (New York: Oxford University Press, 1987).

3. Also see Lewis A. Mennerick and Mehrangiz Najafizadeh, "The Role of Professionals in Third World Development: Conflicts and Constraints," *Review of International Affairs, 937* (April 1989): 18–21.

4. UNICEF, *The State of the World's Children 1990* (New York: Oxford University Press, 1990); Nafis Sadik, *The State of World Population 1990* (New York: UNFPA, United Nations Population Fund, 1990).

5. UNICEF, *World's Children 1990*; World Bank, *Education in Sub-Saharan Africa* (Washington, D.C.: World Bank, 1988); World Bank, *World Development Report 1990* (New York: Oxford University Press, 1990); and Donald R. Winkler, *Higher Education in Latin America: Issues of Efficiency and Equity* (Washington, D.C.: World Bank, 1990).

6. O. M. Maravanyika, *Implementing Educational Policies in Zimbabwe* (Washington, D.C.: World Bank, 1990); Winkler, *Higher Education.*

7. Mehrangiz Najafizadeh and Lewis A. Mennerick, "Constraints on Education as a Mechanism for Social Change." Sociology Series Working Paper No. 70 (Lawrence: University of Kansas, 1991); World Bank, *World Development Report 1990.*

8. Sadik, *World Population 1990*; Garvin W. Jones, *Population Dynamics and Educational and Health Planning* (Geneva: International Labor Organization, 1990); World Bank, *World Development Report 1990.*

9. UNICEF, *World's Children 1990*; Sadik, *World Population 1990.*

10. Lewis A. Mennerick and Mehrangiz Najafizadeh, "Third World Environmental Health: Social, Technological and Economic Policy Issues," *Journal of Environmental Health* (Spring 1991): 24–29; Center for Investigative Reporting and Bill Moyers, *Global Dumping Ground: The International Traffic in Hazardous Waste* (Washington, D.C.: Seven Locks Press, 1990); William A. Nitze, "Improving U.S. Interagency Coordination of International Environmental Policy Development," *Environment* (May 1991): 10–13, 31–37; Louis Peck, "The Spoils of War," *The Amicus Journal, 13* (Spring 1991); 6–9; Patti Petesch, *Tropical Forests: Conservation with Development?* (Washington, D.C.: Overseas Development Council, 1990); Cheryl Simon Silver, *One Earth One Future: Our Changing Global Environment* (Washington, D.C.: National Academy of Sciences, 1990); John C. Topping, Jr., *Global Warming: Impact on Developing Countries* (Washington, D.C.: Overseas Development Council, 1990); World Resources Institute, *World Resources 1990–91* (New York: Oxford University Press, 1990).

    11. Najafizadeh and Mennerick, "Constraints."
    12. Najafiszdeh and Mennerick, "Constraints."
    13. Janne E. Nolan and Albert D. Wheelon, "Third World Ballistic Missiles," *Scientific American, 263* (August 1990); 34–40; "The Arms Bazaar Revisited," *South: Emerging World Review, 120* (March 1991); 11–27.

Afterword

From Development to Liberation—The Third World in the "New World Order"

E. San Juan, Jr.

I don't like the [term] "Third World" at all. The term, like "underdeveloped countries," is based on a class concept which refers to a world as "third class" without saying what this word means. . . . But the "Third World" is the most important world in our time. Those countries are the actually developed ones since they alone have reintroduced human dignity. This and this only can we call development in our age and time.

—*Peter Weiss, author of* Marat/Sade *and other works*

Against the background of the recently concluded U.S.-led war against Iraq and the unprecedented change in the former Soviet Union rapidly overtaking academic pontifications, reflections on the twin fates of democracy and development in dependent formations are bound to assume greater urgency and resonance than ever before. The obvious reason for this is that the bulk of the world's population inhabits the periphery but exerts an incalculable force on governments and transnational corporate policy makers in the center (that is, Washington, Tokyo, Bonn). In a world system dominated by the messiahs of the "free market" hard on the tracks of fleeing Kurds, Palestinians, and millions of refugees, the inauguration of a "New World Order" opens up the space for rethinking cherished beliefs and received notions.

In both the Middle East and the late Soviet Union, the erstwhile bastion of "world communism," the talismanic shibboleth of "democracy" broadcast by Western media claimed to promise nothing short of absolute redemption. "Free World" triumphalism preempts all dissent, criticism, and refusal.[1] Meanwhile, in El Salvador, South Africa, the Philippines and other presumed democratic polities, the problems of inter alia poverty, social injustice, military brutality, ecological disasters, and so on continue to confound the technocratic experts of the International Monetary Fund (IMF) and the World Bank. But, as everyone knows, their worry concerns the gigantic debt of countries such as Brazil, Mexico, Argentina, and a dozen others in Africa and Asia; debts whose fore-closure might precipitate a global financial crisis that would be worse—in the minds of the corporate elite—than a nuclear war. In such a scenario, the mean-ings of "democracy" and "development," already highly contested concepts, again become the site of struggle for redefinition and reappropriation.[2]

Mapping the contours of the recent past may help prefigure the shape of what is to come. The impasse of technocratic development in the Third World in the last twenty-five to thirty years—or since the two sessions of the United Nations Conference on Trade and Development (UNCTAD) in 1964 and 1968—returns us to the fundamental and indeed perennial questions: Develop-ment for what? Development for whom?

We know from any historical standpoint that the uneven development of the Third World is the logical consequence of the international division of labor and the accumulation of capital by the colonial powers of the West and North from the sixteenth century to the present.[3] But since then the patterns of imperialist exploitation of the world's labor and resources have undergone a series of mutations. When the prescription of import substitution carried out in the post-war years failed to usher sustained, independent growth, the elite of the depen-dent countries resorted to export-oriented industrialization in the 1950s and 1960s. The result? A rich harvest of massive human rights violations by U.S.-backed authoritarian regimes, systematic corruption of cultures, degradation of work through "warm body exports" (migrant labor), and unrelenting pauper-ization of the masses.[4] In the free trade zones where the global assembly line generates superprofits out of cheap labor, total surveillance and draconian pro-hibitions prevail. Both empirical evidence and substantial testimony demon-strate that the cult of the gross national product (GNP) as institutionalized by the disciples of W. W. Rostow's *The Stages of Economic Growth,* among oth-ers, has brought with it only rampant unemployment, widespread poverty, cy-cles of repression and stagnation, cultures and environments destroyed for peo-ples of color whose underdevelopment is reproduced daily by such development formulas.[5] The plight of Argentina or Chile might well foreshadow the future of the newly industrialized countries (NICs) in Asia.[6]

Long before the crisis of the reformist U.N. "Program of Action on the Establishment of a New International Economic Order," Denis Goulet, in his provocative work *The Cruel Choice,*[7] had already proposed that the philosophy of development involves not only democracy in the political sphere but also "the basic questions about the quality of life in society, the relationship between goods and the good, and human control over change processes. . . . Will 'un-derdeveloped' societies become mere consumers of technological civilization or agents of their own transformation?" To answer this question, we need to con-front the key issue of self-determination in the realm of civil society and the state: Who decides and ultimately determines the goals, means, and process of any development program? This certainly transcends the politics of "who gets what when" or the economics of scarcity and supply and demand.

One of the many virtues of this volume is its attempt to confront headlong the complex dialectics of "development and democratization in the Third World" from a historical and analytic perspective without prejudging the various conflicting approaches to the issues on terms dictated by mainstream banalities and prejudices. Kenneth E. Bauzon's survey of research trends in Chapter 1 provides an excellent mapping of the field, with their emphasis on an integrated vision of democratic practices (together with moral and ethical norms) implicated in and entailed by various processes of economic development. There is a need to stress what he points out as the Social Darwinist genealogy of modernization theory, its founding hypothesis of laissez-faire liberalism, that in various guises still informs the current neoconservative privileging of privatization, entrepreneurial rights, and law and order, all of them subsumed in the untramelled operations of the "free market." While he correctly focuses on a Third World consensus on empowerment of the people—or popular autonomy—as the guiding principle for reversing underdevelopment, Bauzon undercuts somewhat this balance by a postmodernist insistence on the incommensurability of "reality" and any epistemological model or paradigm. In pointing out how method, criteria of evaluation, foci of research, purpose, and conclusion of the inquiry are all determined by "prevailing assumptions of reality" and values held by research practitioners, he questions the status of objectivity, of objective knowledge, and so in a sense jeopardize the validity of his own theoretical claims. But this, I think, is a necessary moment in any project of self-critical understanding.

A symptom of this complicity of underlying value judgments and research methods may be gleaned from accounts of the lack of democracy and equity in Central America that contain no reference whatsoever to the destabilization efforts of the Contras in Nicaragua or the excesses of the U.S.-supported military in El Salvador. In his introductory essay, however, Bauzon highlights the substantive issue of "the establishment of the necessary social and economic conditions that would render the exercise" of formal legal rights prescribed by liberal democracy "both meaningful and effective." These conditions are in fact the subject of controversy rehearsed or implied by several contributors to this volume.

Although it is now (after Kuhn, Foucault, Feyerabend)[8] a prudent gesture to relativize knowledge paradigms and to disavow essentialism as a kind of original sin, I hold that it is still necessary to ground principles in a logic of verifiability or falsification to prevent organized power, or violence as such, from unilaterally imposing the rules.[9] Methodical doubt is, of course, to be discriminated from the rejection of reason for faith. Inquiry into rules and norms invested in pragmatic schemes of development is particularly welcome. Remigio E. Agpalo's questioning of "the iron logic of modernization," the transformation of societies by the scientific and technological revolution, is thus salutary. While he favors pluralism, liberty, and social justice, Agpalo's notion of "civilization" conflated with "civil order" and the "rule of law" betrays a Hobbesian (as well as Eurocentric) bias so dear to the hearts of the New Right and its neoconservative ideologues. The classic problem of political philosophy, the dialectic of order and freedom, cannot be resolved if one fails to question the historical limits of civility in a liberal democracy and to contextualize these ideals.

The enhancement of civilized life as the moral purpose of development is also the theme of Edward Broadbent's essay. Although schematic and universalistic in its claims, its focus on the linkage of economic progress with human rights and dignity realized through grass-roots participation enunciates the axiom for theorizing the organic unity of democratization and the improvement of its material conditions of possibility. This is an inspiring exhortation for all of us. Broadbent invokes the 1986 U.N. Declaration on the Right to Development and calls for Western governments to "integrate economic advancement policies with human rights and democratic practices," a call hitherto left unheeded by scholars long nourished by Cold War dogmatism. Thomas S. Axworthy joins the chorus heeding this call, but his sentiments remain abstract and rhetorical juxtaposed with the facts of unimpeded underdevelopment in the non-Western world (evinced in the cited report by Helmut Schmidt). Western-style "democracy" becomes evacuated of any meaning when the historical contexts of the complicity of Western governments with authoritarian regimes in the Third World (admitted by all empirical-minded liberals) are one-sidedly attributed to indigenous traditions. A civil society that promotes acquisitive or possessive individualism can only foster Social Darwinism disguised as utilitarianism—more development for a few.[10] Or, as in the Philippines, "elite democracy" becomes a model for reinstating "business as usual" (as lucidly demonstrated by Robert Stauffer).[11] Justice and equality are thus ignored for the sake of Eurocentric philanthropy.

In the discourse opened up by liberation theology so eloquently voiced here by Fr. Michael Czerny, distinctions of "left" and "right" become anachronisms. Most North American experts would refuse Fr. Czerny's proposition that "The rights of the poor and the oppressed form the basis for a human community," an insight of paramount significance to which I will return later. But without this vision, all attempts to help the cause of embattled communities in El Salvador and elsewhere who fought for survival, dignity, and independence against "low-intensity warfare" and its accompanying civic actions become mere rhetorical cover for patronage.

Easily the most erudite and radical contribution to this anthology is Enrique Dussel's elaboration of the foundational insight of the person as both an agent of communicative action (in Jürgen Habermas' construal) and as part of "a community of life" (*Lebensgemeinschaft*). This effectively displaces the Hegelian notion of "civil society" rooted in private property, the premise of liberal individualism. I want to underscore here Dussel's historical hermeneutic of "living labor" and communal praxis hidden by the fetishism of the market, capital, investment flows, and so on, a fetishism vitiating all the charitable intentions of the proponents of a free market economy as the guarantee of freedom, democracy, and justice. What I would add to this is the deployment of certain concepts by Baruch Spinoza to distinguish between repressive power (*potestas*) that transforms living labor into exchange value and power (*potentia*), the constitutive and appropriative power of humans in society (collective praxis).[12] Analytical categories such as these are more capable of grasping inequities as historically differentiated modalities, interdependencies, relations of hegemony, and subalternity. Spinoza's *Ethics* can be a heuristic catalyst for recuperating the surplus value of Western knowledge production.[13]

The stark realities of unmitigated poverty and worsening repression in a dependent society such as El Salvador (or South Africa, to cite another case) belie the triumphalist claims of a "New World Order" of peace and prosperity. They make the liberal idiom of Deborah S. DeGraff and Marian A. L. Miller almost irrelevant. While DeGraff's learned study finally ties up "the costs and benefits of population policy" with the "existing political system," her demographic transition theory uses the model of the industrialized societies that marginalizes if not ignores the profound experience of colonization of her target subjects as well as the indigenous cultural processes that elude the secularizing thought machine. Such a framework of judgment is misleading if not reductive.[14] This is also the orientation of Miller's chapter, which tells Third World peoples to demonstrate an initiative and creativity in "addressing resource-management concerns" similar to industrialized powers when they formulate "an environmentally responsible development path." This seems to ignore all the arguments of those who view Third World underdevelopment as the prime motor force and result of First World production and consumption (from Paul Baran, Harry Magdoff, Andre Gunder Frank to Samir Amin, Walter Rodney, and many others).[15] When we think of how, for example, transnational corporations operate their factories in free trade zones in Third World enclaves and how they dump prohibited insecticides, drugs, chemicals, and other commodities in Third World markets, Miller's statement that "developing countries have borne some of the development costs of industrialized countries" seems to be the understatement of the year.

So far the central and controversial role of an institution such as the IMF has not been examined in the preceding essays, and the only one that engages this matter leaves something to be desired. For the IMF is the single global institution that has decided the fates of many nations and peoples since its inception. The IMF's enormous power has literally subverted the "New International Economic Order" dreamed up by the nonaligned nations in the 1970s and made short shrift of the Keynesian recommendations of the much-touted Report of an Independent Commission on International Development Issues chaired by Willy Brandt entitled *North-South—A Program for Survival*.[16] Gerald E. Scott's review of IMF stabilization programs in sub-Saharan Africa is a useful diagnosis. Its tempered criticism of the damage IMF conditionality inflicts on "the quality

of infrastructure, capital stock, and administrative efficiency in the public service" is appropriate in this volume devoted to the task of exploring the interface
of democratic popular participation and bureaucratic, hierarchical development
schemes. Despite the negative evidence of the IMF's record, however, Scott
does not suggest any viable alternative. In this regard, one can appreciate how
Sita C. Amba-Rao's survey of the ethical imperatives confronting multinational
corporate management performs a similar heuristic function, but it begs the
question of the MNCs' "responsibility."

Viewed from a revisionary optic, Scott's suggested modification of IMF
monetary policy pursued at the expense of Third World people's welfare tends
to blame the victim and exonerate the victimizer. Unless the critic of Western
banks and financial institutions (whose welfare the IMF exists to safeguard)
addresses the mode and rationale of capitalist lending as well as its collusion
with antidemocratic tendencies of the elite and other privileged classes, tendencies that are ironically condemned by William L. Ascher as the shortcomings of
what he calls the "interventionist welfare state," the outcome will be a futile
exercise in liberal apologetics. Here is where knowledge finds itself deeply
implicated in concrete actions and effects. That is why, despite or because of its
"good" intentions, traditional development planning geared to promoting "a
strong human resource strategy" (read: cheap labor for multinational corporations) and exports can only underwrite a "democracy" for the propertied few,
as attested to by the intervention of the Alliance for Progress in the 1960s. Not
states, nations or countries, but social classes and sectors (that represent progressive or reactionary agendas) are the actors in the development drama under-
written by the international political economy of growth via foreign investment,
free trade zones, aid, and so forth.[17]

Concerned with the private ownership of land as the key to "efficient resource allocation and enhanced productivity," jargon that captures the scientis-
tic economism of the discipline, Young J. Park's chapter encapsulates the thrust
of orthodox developmentalism in fostering entrepreneurship and marketing. It
presupposes a specific Korean political conjuncture but claims to be universally
applicable. In so doing, it fails to account for the historical context of class and
sectoral conflicts where land reform is occurring, a context in which (as the
Philippine case demonstrates so clearly) ownership of land is only one factor in
the larger equation of oligarchic monopoly of wealth and power maintained by
neocolonial structures and mentalities.[18] It ignores the overriding force of the
international division of labor in the removal of the economic surplus in Third
World countries by foreign capital, a phenomenon that Paul Baran, in his classic
study *The Political Economy of Growth,* has thoroughly analyzed.[19] Baran concludes: "It is the economic strangulation of the colonial and dependent countries by the imperialist powers that stymied the development of indigenous
industrial capitalism, thus preventing the overthrow of the feudal-mercantile
order and assuring the role of the comprador administrations. It is the preservation of these subservient governments, stifling economic and social develop-

ment and suppressing all popular movements for social and national liberation, that makes possible at the present time the continued foreign exploitation of underdeveloped countries and their domination by the imperialist powers."[20] Needless to say, empiricism with its sophisticated algebra cannot envisage what is really at stake in such a life-or-death matter as land reform.

Ultimately, changes for the better in the Third World will come from a convergence of popular initiatives, the catalyzing force of the indigenous intellectuals (in the large sense defined by Antonio Gramsci), and the solidarity of progressive forces in the international arena.[21] Why this is not perceived, or even suspected, by most scholars in the West is partly answered by Eronini R. Megwa and Ike S. Ndolo's excellent description of the institutional apparatus of the U.S. news media and its marketplace ideology. Their cogent analysis of Eurocentric and even racist bias in the mass media confirms Bauzon's argument made earlier that knowledge is always interested; that what passes for truth or commonsensical idea is actually produced, circulated, and consumed according to the code of a contrived disciplinary regime internalized by individuals and supportive of the status quo.

This is perhaps the point to suggest how the absence of a democratizing impulse in mainstream development thought, a characteristic of the ideology of competitive accumulation in the global marketplace, can be traced to two foundations of capitalism as a world system that Immanuel Wallerstein denominates as racism and universalism.[22] While racism functions as a worldwide mechanism to control direct producers by hierarchical and differential distribution of wealth, universalism proclaims truth (in the mind of the ascendant European bourgeoisie) to inhere in technical and instrumental rationality, hence the slogan of progress and modernization justifying the predatory effects of Western cultural imperialism.[23] Opposing universalizing modernization are the diverse nationalisms, ethnic revivals, and traditionalisms of communities sacrificed in the name of productivity and growth. Unfortunately, this volume does not feature any investigation into the contemporary resurgence of ethnically based or religion-oriented nationalisms, particularly the sharp racial antagonisms that are currently renegotiating the boundaries of First and Third World transactions. Nor does it examine sexuality and gender relations as integral to the democratizing project.

This is also the moment for me to register a reservation to David C. Korten's otherwise inspiring vision of "people-centered development." Every social formation exhibits the conjuncture of multiple, historically specific determinations ranging from ethnic and racial conflicts to colonial legacies. While absolutely correct in proposing a "people-centered development" as an alternative to transnational plunder, Korten's globalism—his focus on the global crisis of poverty, environmental destruction, and communal violence—makes short shrift of how inequity, human rights violations, and so on are structural problems involving the overlapping domains of government, business, and communities in their historic relations with foreign governments and corporate interests. To postulate three separate sectors with their distinctive power competences as key to the empowerment of the disenfranchised is to disingenuously consign the "voluntary" sector to marginality. In contrast, the numerous cause-oriented groups in the Philippines (such as the Congress for People's Agrarian Reform, Freedom from Debt Coalition, Nuclear Free Philippines Coalition, the federation Green Forum) are mobilizing people in business, government, farms, factories, private associations, churches, and elsewhere.[24] Moreover, no one would disagree with Korten's three principles of authentic development—justice, sustainability, inclusiveness—that Goulet, Brandt, and even conservative developmentalists would applaud. But when he concludes that "people-centered development agenda is a human agenda that unites the interests of all people irrespective of class, race, religion, or nationality," then one begins to suspect that a metaphysical functionalism committed to pacification and equilibrium begins to take over. The critique of specific powers and the adjudication of responsibilities in each national milieu then becomes subordinate to a homogenizing call for unity in the name of "global change." Meanwhile, the Gulf War and the recent dissolution of the Soviet Union serve as stark reminders of the contemporary resurgence of ethnic, racial, and nationality forces that any vision of "people-centered development" needs to take into account. For who indeed are the specific peoples, nations, and classes concerned? What is the concrete character of their historical relations? Who suffers and who benefits in particular processes of social change? Any agenda of global transformation needs to begin with historical givens, their causes and effects, and the power of national traditions and class interests that up to now continue to shape the course of international affairs.

To return to Megwa and Ndolo's essay: In elucidating the liaisons between transnational news agencies and "cultural imperialism," our two authors belie the neutrality of MNCs and their alleged "fiduciary responsibility." Considering how 600 transnational corporations today produce 25 percent of everything made in the world and account for 80 percent to 90 percent of the exports of the United States, Japan, Britain, and Canada, no substantive appraisal of programs for democratic development can be conducted without interrogating the role and impact of such corporations in the social and political transformation of the Third World. This is precisely what Armand Mattelart has done in his perspicacious commentary *Transnationals and the Third World*, where the transnational apparatus for the production of cultural commodities is dismantled to reveal how the ideology and ethos of Western business practice, legitimized by such notions as security, freedom, efficiency, and so forth, are normalized in Third World societies through the virtually unconstrained operations of the monopolistic information and knowledge industry.[25]

Finally, the two contributions of Mehrangiz Najafizadeh and Lewis A. Mennerick are exceedingly important in that they enable us to gain insights into the critical but problematic role of professionals (the mediating stratum of the intelligentsia) in the mobilization and dynamic polarization of underdeveloped for-

mations. It is understandable how our authors tend to inflate the role of professionals in rectifying such problems as "insufficient educational expansion,
rapid population growth, environmental problems, the allocation of scarce resources, and the proliferation of military technologies." But their underscoring
of the "cultural uniqueness" of Third World nations in their insistence that they
not be reduced to "mirror images of the industrialized North" and their attempt
to synthesize professional knowledge and grass-roots participation to infuse
difference into the otherwise homogenizing, Eurocentric perspective of development paradigms are positive indices in the deconstruction of canonical truths
in the social sciences and humanities.[26] We are just beginning to witness here
the emergence of Third World peoples as historic agents in the shaping of their
own ethnic, racial, and national histories vis-à-vis the industrialized center that
seek to maintain their supremacy over a world system where exchange value
and the commodification of everything still continue to govern our sensibilities
and fantasies, the performance of our everyday lives.

From the perspective of liberation theology, this radically democratic aspira-
tion of peoples of color (a more exact designation for underdeveloped communities in both the metropolis and the periphery), as Dussel and others have
shown, is in essence a struggle for liberation, a process of self-empowerment.
This process of transition involves difficult choices, zigzags and detours, vex-
ing ambiguities and paradoxes.[27] Refusing to be seduced by "ethnocentric
thinking of the white North," the struggle of peoples of color will have to
choose, as Goulet puts it, between two principles of social organization: one
that values efficiency and social control, the other social justice and "the creation of a new man." While the rhetoric is oppositional and even utopian, the
two principles need not be interpreted strictly as being exclusive. Fetishisms of
both technology and untamed nature rule out the attainment of social justice and
the shaping of new alternative forms of life that Raymond Williams foresees as
the challenge of the twenty-first century.[28] The spirit of people's liberation encompasses both order and freedom, discipline and social justice.

What is at stake in this initiative of reconceptualizing development? Precisely the answer to the questions introduced earlier: For whom? For what?

In redefining by renegotiating the praxis of development, *The People's Development Agenda*,[29] an instructive document drawn up by the Council for People's Development in the Philippines, sums up the lessons of half a century of
mass struggles for popular democracy and national liberation: development
"refers to the struggle to advance the socioeconomic rights of the poor majority, to strengthen their capacity to gain control of production resources, to
improve their capability to meet basic needs, and to create the means towards
their sustained development. It is an integral part of the process of transferring
political and socioeconomic power from the elite to the majority who are poor."
This Filipino desideratum of "democratic participation of the people in development processes" echoes the sentiment of Third World self-determination expressed, for example, in "The Pastoral Letter from the Third World" issued by

fifteen Latin American bishops headed by Dom Helder Camara in 1968. It informs also the Cocoyoc (Mexico) Declaration formulated in 1974 by the participants of the Symposium on Models of Resources Utilization: A Strategy for the Environment and Development organized by UNCTAD and UNPE (United Nations Programs for the Environment). This declaration affirms the primacy of self-reliance even as it valorizes the solidarity of peoples: "reliance on the capacity of people themselves to invent and generate new resources and techniques, . . . to take a measure of command over the economy, and to generate their own way of life." It upholds production for equitable use, not for profit or power, to satisfy basic human needs (which includes self-fulfillment, participation, togetherness, conviviality). It also calls for affirming the first principle of human dignity, "namely that human beings as well as their culture need to be treated by others with due respect, for their own sakes and on their own terms." Surpassing the demand for formal democratic rights, this principle of cultural diversity and integrity repudiates outright the instrumentalizing strategy of technocratic development in favor of preserving and enriching culture as "an integral whole of accumulated resources, both material and non-material, which they [Third World subalterns] utilize, transform and transmit in order to satisfy their needs, assert their identity and give meaning to their lives."[30]

In 1973, the Trilateral Commission sponsored by David Rockefeller of the Chase Manhattan Bank sought to firm up the ideological perspective of transnational corporations. It endeavored to reconcile the tensions among the major powers. It tried to demarcate the uneven geopolitics of the periphery: the oil-producing countries (organized in OPEC), the NICs, and the underdeveloped countries now baptized the "Fourth World." It did not, of course, seek to alter the system's imbalance in which a quarter of the world's population enjoys four-fifths of the world's income, nor did it seek to realign business ethics with the welfare of consumers. It was essentially a maneuver to retool the global division of labor, bringing us nearer to what can now be conceived of as the refeudalized or recompradorized terrain of the underdeveloped world.

A decade after this hegemonic response to the threat of a New International Economic Order, Samir Amin posed the major contradiction at that historical stage: "between the pressures of globalization (or "transnationalization") imposed by the predominance of capital, and the aspirations of working classes, peoples and nations for some autonomous space."[31] To remedy the disarticulating effects of the new "electronic revolution" based on the microprocessor, the postmodernist compression of time and space that fuses opposed tendencies of capital to reify and dissolve forms, the Third World has come up with an array of ingenious forms of collective resistance and mobilization.[32] To cite only the most well-known instances, witness the 1986 "people power" insurrection in the Philippines, the student rebellions in South Korea, the revival of revolutionary opposition in Brazil after decades of military rule, and the inexhaustible resourcefulness of Nelson Mandela's African National Congress when faced with the vicious terrorism of the apartheid state. Sparks of hope in the wasteland of the global megamall? Perhaps. This intervention of new historical subjects—peoples of color dispersed throughout the planet—carving out a self-emancipatory space across the East–West ideological divide that is now becoming rapidly obsolescent, is a protean movement that may bridge the gulf between North and South, between rich and poor nations, between the past and the future.

Of late, some activists in the United States believe that the Brundtland U.N. Report of 1987 on Environment and Development focusing on the theme of "sustainable development" can serve as a basis for a political and ethical alliance between North and South.[33] Resource depletion, environmental injury, burgeoning human populations, oppression—these are surely urgent concerns with broad appeal. But can the project of participatory democracy and self-reliance survive the new world order born from an unfinished war? There are, in fact, several wars raging today. With the demise of Soviet and East European socialism as a counterbalance to the domination of the commodity, the cash nexus, and the market, increased rivalry among the European states, the United States, and Japan is bound to complicate the relations between the three centers, notwithstanding the establishment of free-trade linkages and respective spheres of influence. Some observers predict that the compradorization of Eastern Europe and the former Soviet Union as a result of the weakening and fragmentation of state structures will open up new markets of cheap labor and capital in the wake of revitalized racisms and ethnocentrisms, along with the recrudescence of sexist, chauvinist, and traditionalist intolerance of all sorts.[34] What is the alternative?

In a recent lecture delivered at Tribhuvan University in Kathmandu, Nepal, Sam J. Noumoff, Director of the Center for Developing Area Studies at McGill University, described the dismal prospects of development in the Third World unless countermeasures are taken: greater penetration of these societies by transnational market's control of the production process (knowledge-intensive industries), loss of leverage with the decline of the need for raw materials, decrease of agricultural earnings because of Western protectionism, the traps of the "green revolution" and debt (this last administered by the IMF and the World Bank prevents indigenous capital formation), export-led growth ensuring permanent dependency through import of capital-intensive technology, the rule of comparative advantage freezing the Third World in a dual economy, and so on.[35] As countermeasures, Noumoff suggested regional cooperation in research to break the technological monopoly of the North, integrated training in joint ventures to break the MNCs' marketing monopoly, and internal diffusion of technology throughout society, among others.

In retrospect, Noumoff's proposal evokes the vision of self-reliance expressed by the 1974 Cocoyoc Declaration, the theme of empowerment in the Filipino "people's agenda," and the prophetic passion of the Latin American theology of liberation: "One must institute a program which uses as a measure of development the most deprived in the society. The measure of a developed society is not how the best live; the measure of a society is what is the state of the poorest person, and one must start there. . . . It is through internal strength and empowerment at the local level that self-sustained development will occur which will be the basis of the prosperity of this country [Nepal]." Only in that way, I think, will the antinomy of democracy and development as inscribed in Western rationality be transmuted by those whom Frantz Fanon designated as "the wretched of the earth" into the protracted process of liberation, the conquest of autonomy through self-reliance, the empowerment of the people, that will also guarantee the preservation of the earth's biosphere.[36] Against the Leviathan of a universal commodification marching on the ruins of Baghdad and the Kremlin, one can oppose the solidarity of peoples of color, their history of creativity and resourcefulness, their heterogeneous cultures of resistance, their commitment to the dignity and freedom of specific communities as the best hope of humankind's survival and regeneration at the turn of this explosive century.

NOTES

1. A recent article in *Newsweek* (September 9, 1991), "How the West Can Win the New World Order" (p. 23), registers this Establishment triumphalism in a mass media style.

2. See Keith Buchanan, "Reflections of a 'Dirty Word.'" *Dissent, 31* (Summer 1974): 25–31; reprinted in Richard Peet, ed., *Radical Geography* (Chicago: Maaroufa Press, 1977).

3. For elaboration, see Arthur MacEwan, "Capitalist Expansion, Ideology, and Intervention," and Thomas Weisskopf, "Capitalism and Underdevelopment in the Modern World." Both in Richard Edwards, Michael Reich, and Thomas Weisskopf, eds., *The Capitalist System* (Englewood Cliffs, N.J.: Prentice-Hall, 1972); and Eric Wolf, *Europe and the People Without History* (Berkeley: University of California Press, 1982).

4. Eqbal Ahmad, *Political Culture and Foreign Policy* (Washington, D.C.: Institute for Policy Studies, 1980).

5. Walt W. Rostow, *The Stages of Economic Growth: A Non-Communist Manifesto* (Cambridge: Cambridge University Press, 1960).

6. This point is discussed further by Hamza Alavi and Teodor Shanin, eds., *Introduction to the Sociology of "Developing Societies"* (New York: Monthly Review Press, 1982); Samir Amin, *Imperialism and Unequal Development* (New York: Monthly Review Press, 1977); and Jack Woddis, *Introduction to Neo-Colonialism* (New York: International Publishers, 1972).

7. New York: Atheneum, 1973.

8s. Paul Feyerabend, *Against Method* (London: Verso, 1975); Michael Foucault, *Power/Knowledge* (ed. by Colin Gordon) (New York: Pantheon, 1980); and Thomas S. Kuhn, *The Structure of Scientific Revolutions* (Chicago: University of Chicago Press, 1970).

9. Peter Dews, *Logics of Disintegration* (London: Verso, 1987).

10. Samuel Bowles and Herbert Gintis, *Democracy and Capitalism* (New York: Basic Books, 1986).

11. See his "Philippine Democracy: Contradictions of Third World Redemocratization," *Kasarinlan; Philippine Quarterly of Third World Studies, 6* (1–2) (Third and Fourth Quarters 1990): 7–22.

12. As discussed in Antonio Negri, *The Savage Anomaly* (Minneapolis: University of Minnesota Press, 1991).

13. See Gilles Deleuze, *Spinoza: Practical Philosophy* (San Francisco: City Lights Books, 1988).

14. See further discussion on this score by Lars Bondestam, "The Political Ideology of Population Control," in Hamza Alavi and Teodor Shanin, eds., *Introduction to the Sociology of "Developing Societies"* (New York: Monthly Review Press, 1982).

15. See the following works: Amin, *Imperialism*; Paul A. Baran, *The Political Economy of Growth* (New York: Monthly Review Press, 1957); Andre Gunder Frank, *Capitalism and Underdevelopment in Latin America* (New York: Monthly Review Press, 1969); Harry Magdoff, *Imperialism: From the Colonial Age to the Present* (New York: Monthly Review Press, 1978); and Walter Rodney, *How Europe Underdeveloped Africa* (London: Bogle L'Ouverture, 1972).

16. Willy Brandt et al., *North–South—A Programme for Survival* (London: Pan, 1980).

17. Michael Barratt Brown, "Developing Societies as Part of an International Political Economy," in Hamza Alavi and Teodor Shanin, eds., *Introduction to the Sociology of "Developing Societies"* (New York: Monthly Review Press, 1982).

18. A succinct background to the problems of land reform and social inequality, and to the prospect of popular democracy, in the Philippines may be found in Mamerto Canlas, Mariano Miranda, and James Putzel, *Land, Poverty and Politics in the Philippines* (London: Catholic Institute for International Relations, 1988).

19. Baran, *Political Economy.*

20. Paul A. Baran, "A Morphology of Backwardness," in Hamza Alavi and Teodor Shanin, eds., *Introduction to the Sociology of "Developing Societies"* (New York: Monthly Review Press, 1982), pp. 203–204.

21 See Gramsci, *Selections from the Prison Notebooks, 1929–35* (New York: International Publishers, 1971).

22. See Wallerstein, *Historical Capitalism* (London: Verso, 1983).

23. See also A. Sivanandan, *A Different Hunger* (London: Pluto Press, 1982).

24. For instance, Thomas M. M. O'Brien, *Crisis and Instability; The Philippines Enters the Nineties* (Davao City: Philippine International Forum, 1990).

25. *Transnationals and the Third World* (Westport, Conn.: Bergin & Garvey, 1983).

26. For a brilliant specimen of deconstructive analysis dealing with asymmetrical North–South encounters and which also epitomizes the dialectic of an exploitative modernity and popular resistance, see Susan Buck-Morss, "Semiotic Boundaries and the Politics of Meaning: Modernity on Tour—A Village in Transition," in Marcus Raskin and Herbert Bernstein, *New Ways of Knowing* (New Jersey: Rowman and Littlefield, 1987).

27. Richard R. Fagen, "The Politics of Transition," in Richard Fagen, Carmen Diana Deere, and Jose Luis Coraggio, eds., *Transition and Development* (New York: Monthly Review Press, 1986).

28. Raymond Williams, *The Year 2000* (New York: Pantheon Books, 1983), pp. 175–217.

29. See Council for People's Development, *People's Development Agenda* (Manila: Council for People's Development, 1990).

30. Mattelart, *Transnationals,* p. 25.

31. Samir Amin, "The Crisis, the Third World, and North-South, East-West Relations," in Stephen Resnick and Richard Wolff, eds., *Rethinking Marxism* (New York: Autonomedia, 1985), p. 2.

32. For elaboration, see David Harvey, *The Condition of Postmodernity* (Oxford: Basil Blackwell, 1989).

33. For such activisms, see Oliver Loud, "Socialism in the 1990s: Where Do We Go From Here?" *Monthly Review, 43* (June 1991): 45–53. For the North–South alliance, see World Commission on Environment and Development (popularly known as the Brundtland Commission in deference to its chair, Gro Harlem Brundtland, former Prime Minister of Norway), *Our Common Future* (New York: Oxford University Press, 1987).

34. See, for instance, James Petras, "World Transformations: The Challenges for the Left," *Against the Current,* no. 34 (September-October 1991): 17–22.

35. See Noumoff, "The New International Order as an Impediment to Third World Development." Lecture presented at the Center for Nepal and Asian Studies, Tribhuvan University, Kathmandu, Nepal, June 11, 1991.

36. See Fanon, *The Wretched of the Earth* (New York: Grove Press, 1963).

Bibliography

I. BOOKS AND MONOGRAPHS

Adnan, Hamadan bin, et al. "The Nature of Development." In *Introduction to Development Communication*. Honolulu: East-West Communication Institute, East-West Center, 1980.

Adorno, T. W., and Associates. *The Authoritarian Personality*. New York: Harper & Row, 1950.

Agpalo, Remigio E. *The Filipino Polity: Historical Perspective and New Goals in the 1980s*. Quezon City: University of the Philippines, 1976.

———. *Models of Political Systems and the Philippines*. Quezon City: University of the Philippines Press, 1978.

———. *The Organic-Hierarchical Paradigm and Politics in the Philippines*. Quezon City: University of the Philippines Press, 1973.

———. "The Philippine Executive." In Froilan M. Bacungan, ed., *The Powers of the Philippine President*. Quezon City: University of the Philippines Law Center, 1983.

———. *The Political Elite and the People: A Study of Politics in Occidental Mindoro*. Manila: College of Public Administration, University of the Philippines, 1972.

Ahmad, Eqbal. *Political Culture and Foreign Policy*. Washington, D.C.: Institute for Policy Studies, 1980.

Alavi, Hamza, and Teodor Shanin, eds. *Introduction to the Sociology of "Developing Societies."* New York: Monthly Review Press, 1982.

Almond, Gabriel, and Sidney Verba. *The Civic Culture*. Boston: Little, Brown, 1963.

Amin, Samir. "The Crisis, the Third World, and North-South, East-West Relations." In Stephen Resnick, ed., *Rethinking Marxism: Struggles in Marxist Theory*. New York: Autonomedia, 1985. Pp. 1–8.

———. *Imperialism and Unequal Development*. New York: Monthly Review Press, 1977.

Amba-Rao, S. C. "Industrial Hazards, Social Responsiveness and the Transformational Imperative of Multinational Corporations: A Conceptual Model." In Timothy P. Cronan, ed., Decision Sciences: Theory and Application (The Proceedings of the S.W. Decision Sciences Institute Conference). Houston, Tex.: Decision Science Institute, March 1987. P. 121.

Amnesty International USA. *Amnesty International Report 1990*. New York: Amnesty International Publications, 1990.

Anderson, C. Arnold, and Mary Jean Bowman. *Education and Economic Development.* Chicago: Aldine, 1965.

Andrews, K. R., ed. *Ethics in Practice.* Boston: Harvard Business School Press, 1987.

Anshen, M., ed. *Managing the Socially Responsible Corporation.* New York: Macmillan, 1974.

Apel, Karl-Otto. *Transformation Der Philosophie.* Frankfurt, Germany: Suhrkamp, 1973. Vols. I–II.

Arendt, Hannah. *The Origins of Totalitarianism.* New York: Harcourt, Brace & World, 1951.

Arens, Edmund. *Habermas und die Theologie.* Dusseldorf, Germany: Patmos, 1987.

Ascher, William. "Risk, Politics and Tax Reform: Lessons from Some Latin American Experience." In Malcolm Gillis, ed., *Tax Reform in Developing Countries.* Durham, N.C.: Duke University Press, 1988. Pp. 417–472.

Ascher, William, and Ann Hubbard, eds. *Central American Recovery and Development; Task Force Report to the International Commission for Central American Recovery and Development.* Durham, N.C.: Duke University Press, 1989.

Ash, Timothy Garton. *The Magic Lantern.* New York: Random House, 1990.

———. *The Uses of Adversity: Essays on the Fate of Central Europe.* New York: Vintage Books, 1989.

Assmann, Hugo. *Teología desde la praxis de la liberación* (Theology from the praxis of liberation). Salamanca, Spain: Sigeume, 1973.

Assman, Hugo, and Franz Hinckelammert. *Teología y economía.* Petropolis, Brazil: Vozes, 1989.

Austin, John Langshaw. *How to Do Things With Words.* Oxford: Oxford University Press, 1962.

Austruy, Jacques. *Le Scandale du Development.* Paris: Marcel Riviere, 1965.

Bacungan, Froilan M., ed. *The Powers of the Philippine President.* Quezon City: University of the Philippines Law Center, 1983.

Bandura, A. *Social Learning Theory.* Englewood Cliffs, N.J.: Prentice-Hall, 1977.

Banister, Judith. *China's Changing Population.* Stanford, Calif.: Stanford University Press, 1987.

Baran, Paul A., "A Morphology of Backwardness." In Hamza Alavi and Teodor Shanin, eds., *Introduction to the Sociology of "Developing Societies."* New York: Monthly Review Press, 1982. Pp. 195–204.

———. *The Political Economy of Growth.* New York: Monthly Review Press, 1957.

Bauzon, Kenneth E. *Liberalism and the Quest for Islamic Identity in the Philippines.* Durham, N.C.: Acorn Press in association with Duke University, Islamic and Arabian Development Studies, 1991.

Bauzon, Kenneth E., and Charles Frederick Abel. "Dependency: History, Theory and a Reappraisal." In Mary Ann Tetreault and Charles Frederick Abel, eds., *Dependency Theory and the Return of High Politics.* Westport, Conn.: Greenwood Press, 1986. Pp. 43–69.

Bauer, Peter T., and Basil S. Yamey. *The Economics of Under-developed Countries.* Chicago: University of Chicago Press, 1926.

Bello, Walden. *Brave New Third World? Strategies for Survival in the Global Economy.* Food First Development Report No. 5. San Francisco: Institute for Food and Development Policy, February 1989.

Bhaskar, Roy. *Scientific Realism and Human Emancipation.* London: Verso, 1986.

Black, Cyril E., Marlus B. Jansen, Herbert S. Levine, Marion J. Levy, Jr., Henry Rosovsky, Gilbert Rozman, Henry D. Smith, and S. Frederick Starr. *The Modernization of Japan and Russia.* New York: Free Press, 1975.

Blake, D. H. "The Management of Social Policy by Multinational Corporations: A Research Agenda." In L. E. Preston, ed., *International and Comparative Corporation and Society Research.* Greenwich, Conn.: JAI Press, 1990.

Bondestam, Lars. "The Political Ideology of Population Control." In Hamza Alavi and Teodor Shanin, eds., *Introduction to the Sociology of "Developing Societies."* New York: Monthly Review Press, 1982. Pp. 252–259.

Boserup, Ester. *Economic and Demographic Relationships in Development.* Baltimore, Md.: Johns Hopkins University Press, 1990.

Boulding, Kenneth E. "The Economics of the Coming Spaceship Earth." In Henry Jarrett, ed., *Environmental Quality in a Growing Economy.* Baltimore, Md.: Johns Hopkins University Press, 1968. Pp. 3–14.

———. *Three Faces of Power.* Newbury Park, Calif.: Sage Publications, 1989.

Bowles, Samuel, and Herbert Gintis. *Democracy and Capitalism.* New York: Basic Books, 1986.

Bradford, Colin I., Jr. "East Asian 'Models': Myths and Lessons." In John P. Lewis and Valeriana Kallab, eds., *Development Strategies Reconsidered.* Washington, D.C.: Overseas Development Council, 1986.

Brandt, R. *Ethical Theory.* Englewood Cliffs, N.J.: Prentice-Hall, 1959.

Brandt, Willy, et al. *North-South—A Programme for Survival.* London: Pan, 1980.

Brockman, S. J., James R., *The Word Remains: A Life of Oscar Romero.* Maryknoll, N.Y.: Orbis Books, 1990.

Brown, Lester R. "Redefining National Security." In Steven L. Spiegel, ed., *At Issue: Politics in the World Arena.* New York: St. Martin's Press, 1988. Pp. 517–530.

———. *State of the World 1984.* New York: W.W. North & Co., 1984.

Brown, Lester R. et al. *State of the World 1991.* New York: W.W. Norton, 1991.

Brown, Michael Barratt. "Developing Societies as Part of an International Political Economy." In Hamza Alavi and Teodor Shanin, eds., *Introduction to the Sociology of "Developing Societies."* New York: Monthly Review Press, 1982. Pp. 153–171.

Brzezinski, Zbigniew. *The Grand Failure.* New York: Scribner's, 1989.

Buchbinder, Reinhard. *Bibelzitate, Bibelanspielungen, Bibelparodien, Theologische Vergleiche und Analigien bei Marx und Engels.* Berlin: Erich Schmidt Verlag, 1976.

Buck-Morss, Susan. "Semiotic Boundaries and the Politics of Meaning: Modernity on Tour—A Village in Transition." In Marcus Raskin and Herbert Bernstein, eds., *New Ways of Knowing.* Totowa, New Jersey: Rowman and Littlefield, 1987. Pp. 200–236.

Business Roundtable. *Corporate Ethics: A Prime Business Asset.* 1988.

Cacnio, Alberto, and Guillermo Pablo, Jr. *Roberto Concepcion: Chief Justice of the Philippines.* Manila: Cacnio and Pablo Publications, 1974.

Canlas, Mamerto, Mariano Miranda, and James Putzel. *Land, Poverty and Politics in the Philippines.* London: Catholic Institute for International Relations, 1988.

Cardoso, Fernando Henrique. *Empresario industrial e desenvolvimento economico no Brasil.* São Paulo: Difusao Europeia do Livro, 1964.

Center for Investigative Reporting and Bill Moyers. *Global Dumping Ground: The International Traffic in Hazardous Waste.* Washington, D.C.: Seven Locks Press, 1990.

Chamberlain, N. W. *Social Strategy and Corporate Structure.* New York: Macmillan, 1982.

Chaudhury, Rafiqul H. "Population Pressure and its Effects on Changes in Agrarian Structure and Productivity in Rural Bangladesh." In G. Rodgers, ed., *Population Growth and Poverty in Rural South Asia*. New Delhi: Sage Publications, 1989. Pp. 151–182.

Cheung, Paul P. L. "Recent Changes in Population Policies." In IUSSP, *IUSSP International Population Conference*. New Delhi: IUSSP, 1989. Vol. I, pp. 133–142.

Cheung, Stephen N. C. *The Theory of Share Tenancy.* Chicago: University of Chicago Press, 1969.

Chilcote, Ronald, ed. *Dependency and Marxism.* Boulder, Colo.: Westview Press, 1981.

Chirot, D. *Social Change in the Twentieth Century.* San Diego: Harcourt Brace Jovanovich, 1977.

Choucri, Nazli. *Multidisciplinary Perspectives on Population and Conflicts.* Syracuse, N.Y.: Syracuse University Press, 1984.

Coale, Ansley J., and Edgar M. Hoover. *Population Growth and Economic Development in Low-Income Countries*. Princeton, N.J.: Princeton University Press, 1958.

Cohen, B. C. *The Press and Foreign Policy.* Princeton, N.J.: Princeton University Press, 1963.

Concepcion, Roberto. "The Rule of Law: A Collective Responsibility of All Citizens." In Alberto Cacnio and Guillermo Pablo, Jr., *Roberto Concepcion: Chief Justice of the Philippines*. Manila: Cacnio and Pablo Publications, 1974. Pp. 31–46.

Council for People's Development. *People's Development Agenda.* Manila: Council for People's Development, 1990.

Dahrendorf, Ralf. *The Modern Social Conflict.* Berkeley: University of California Press, 1988.

———. *Reflections on the Revolution in Europe.* New York: Random House, 1990.

Daly, Herman E., and John B. Cobb, Jr. *For the Common Good: Redirecting the Economy Toward Community, the Environment and a Sustainable Future*. Boston: Beacon Press, 1989.

Dasgupta, Partha. "The Ethical Foundations of Population Policy." In D. G. Johnson and R. D. Lee, eds., *Population Growth and Economic Development; Issues and Evidence*. Madison: University of Wisconsin Press, 1987. pp. 631–659.

Dell, Sidney. "Stabilization: The Political Economy of Overkill." In John Williamson, ed., *IMF Conditionality*. Washington, D.C.: Institute for International Economics, 1983.

Deleuze, Gilles. *Spinoza: Practical Philosophy.* San Francisco: City Lights Books, 1988.

D'Encause, Helene Carrere. *Stalin: Order Through Terror.* New York: Longman, 1981.

Desmond, Robert W. *Windows on the World: World News Reporting 1900–1920.* Iowa City: University of Iowa Press, 1980.

Deutsch, Karl W. *Nationalism and Social Communication: An Inquiry into the Foundations of Nationality*. Cambridge, Mass.: MIT Press, 1966.

Dews, Peter. *Logic of Disintegration.* London: Verso, 1987.

Diamond, Larry, Juan Linz, and Seymour Martin Lipset, eds. *Democracy in Developing Countries*. Boulder, Colo.: Lynee Rienner, 1987–199 . 4 vols.

Diamond, Larry, Juan J. Linz, and Seymour Martin Lipset. "Democracy in Developing Countries: Facilitating and Obstructing Factors." In Raymond D. Gastil, ed., *Freedom in the World: Political Rights and Civil Liberties, 1987–88*. New York: Freedom House, 1988. Pp. 229–258.

Dickie, R. B., and L. S. Rouner, eds. *Corporations and the Common Good.* Notre Dame, Ind.: Notre Dame Press, 1986.

Donaldson, T. *The Ethics of International Business.* New York: Oxford University Press, 1989.

Dos Santos, Theotonio. *El nuevo caracter de la dependencia.* Santiago: Cuadernos de Estudios Socio-Economicos, Centro de Estudios Economicos, Universidad de Chile, 1968.

Drucker, Peter F. *The New Realities.* New York: Harper & Row, 1989.

Durning, Alan. "How Much is Enough?" In Lester R. Brown, Alan Durning, Christopher Flavin, Hilary French, Jodi Jacobson, Nicholas Lenssen, Marcia Lowe, Sandra Postel, *State of the World 1991.* New York: W.W. Norton, 1991. Pp. 153–169.

Dussel, Enrique. *Ética comunitaria* (Community ethics). Dusseldorf, Germany: Patmos, 1988. [English edition, *Ethics and Community* (Maryknoll, N.Y.: Orbis, 1988).]

———. *Filosofía de la liberacion* (Philosophy of liberation). Maryknoll, N.Y.: Orbis Books, 1985.

———. *Hacia un Marx desconocido (1861–1863). Comentario a la segunda redacción de "El Capital"* [Toward an unknown Marx (1861–1863): Commentary on the second printing of *Das Kapital*]. Mexico City: Siglo XXI, 1988.

———. *Herrschaft und Befreiung.* Freiburg, Switzerland: Exodus, 1985.

———. *Historia general de la Iglesia en América Latina* (General history of the Church in Latin America). Salamanca, Spain: Sígueme, 1983.

———. *A History of the Church in Latin America: Colonialism to Liberation, 1492–1979.* Grand Rapids, Mich.: William B. Eerdmans, 1981.

———. *La ideología alemana* (German ideology). Barcelona: Grijalbo, 1970.

———. *El Marx definitivo (1863–1882). Un comentario sobre la tercera y cuarta redacción de "El Capital"* [The definitive Marx (1863–1882): A commentary on the third and fourth editions of *Das Kapital*]. Mexico City: Siglo XXI, 1990.

———. *Para uma etica da Libertacao Latino-americana* (Toward an ethic of Latin American liberation). São Paulo, Brazil: Loyola, 1984.

———. *La pedagógica latinoamericana* (Latin American pedogogy). Bogotá, Colombia: Nueva America, 1980.

———. *La producción teorética de Marx* (The theoretical production of Marx). Mexico City: Siglo XXI, 1985.

———. *Religión.* Mexico City: Edicol, 1977.

Edwards, Richard, Michael Reich, and Thomas Weisskopf, eds. *The Capitalist System.* Englewood Cliffs, N.J.: Prentice-Hall, 1972.

Eisenstadt, S. N. *Modernization: Protest and Change.* Englewood Cliffs, N.J.: Prentice-Hall, 1966.

Ellacuria, Ignacio S. J. "Entorno al concepto y a la idea da liberación." In Ignacio Ellacuria et al., eds., *Implicaciones sociales y politicas de la teología de la liberación.* Madrid: Escuela de Estudios Hispanoamericanos, Instituto de Filosofía, 1985.

England, G. W. *The Manager and His Values: An International Perspective.* Cambridge, Eng.: Ballinger Publishing, 1975.

Entman, R. M. *Democracy Without Citizens: Media and the Decay of American Politics.* New York: Oxford University Press, 1989.

Evans, Peter B., and John D. Stephens. "Development and the World Economy." In Neil J. Smelser, ed., *Handbook of Sociology.* Newbury Park, Calif.: Sage Publications, 1988. Pp. 739–773.

Fagen, Richard R. "The Politics of Transition." In Richard Fagen, Carmen Diana Deere, and Jose Luis Coraggio, eds., *Transition and Development.* New York: Monthly Review Press, 1986. Pp. 249–263.

Fanon, Frantz. *The Wretched of the Earth.* New York: Grove Press, 1963.

Farooq, Ghazi M., and Deborah S. DeGraff. *Fertility and Development: An Introduction to Theory, Empirical Research and Policy Issues.* Geneva: International Labor Office, 1988.

Feinberg, Richard E., and Valeriana Kallab, eds. *The Adjustment Crisis in the Third World.* Washington, D.C.: Overseas Development Council, 1984.

Fernando, Enrique M. *The Constitution of the Philippines.* Quezon City: Central Law Book Publishing, 1974.

Feyerabend, Paul. *Against Method.* London: Verso, 1975.

Fiorenza, Francis Schlüssler, "Die Kirche als Interpretations-gemeinschaft." In Edmund Arens, *Habermas und die Theologie.* Düsseldorf, Germany: Patmos, 1987. Pp. 115–144.

Fletcher, J. *Situation Ethics: The New Morality.* Philadelphia: Westminster Press, 1966.

Foucault, Michel. *Power/Knowledge.* Ed. by Colin Gordon. New York: Pantheon, 1980.

Foxley, Alejandro. *Latin American Experiments in Neo-Conservative Economics.* Berkeley: University of California Press, 1983.

Frank, Andrè Gunder. *Capitalism and Underdevelopment in Latin America.* New York: Monthly Review Press, 1969.

———. *Dependent Accumulation and Underdevelopment.* New York: Monthly Review Press, 1969.

———. *Latin America: Underdevelopment or Revolution.* New York: Monthly Review Press, 1969.

Frederick, W. C., K. Davis, and J. E. Post. *Business and Society.* New York: McGraw-Hill, 1988.

Frederick, W. C., and L. E. Preston. *Business Ethics: Research Issues and Empirical Studies.* Greenwich, Conn.: JAI Press, 1990.

Freedman, R., ed. *Population: The Vital Revolution.* Garden City, N.Y.: Anchor Books, 1964.

Freire, Paulo. *Cultural Action for Freedom.* Monograph No. 1, Harvard Educational Review and Center for the Study of Development and Social Change. Cambridge, Mass.: 1970.

———. *Pedagogy of the Oppressed.* Hammondsworth: Penguin Books, 1972.

Friedman, Milton. *Capitalism and Freedom.* Chicago: University of Chicago Press, 1982.

Friedman, Milton, and Rose Friedman. *Free to Choose: A Personal Statement.* New York: Avon Books, 1979.

Friedrich, Carl, and Zbigniew K. Brzezinski. *Totalitarian Dictatorship and Autocracy.* New York: Praeger, 1965.

Fritsche, D. J. "Ethical Issues in Multinational Marketing." In G. R. Laczniak and P. E. Murphy, eds., *Marketing Ethics: Guidelines for Managers.* Lexington, Ky.: Lexington Books, 1985. Pp. 85–96.

Fukuyama, Francis. *The End of History and the Last Man.* New York: The Free Press, 1991.

Galbraith, John Kenneth. *The Nature of Mass Poverty.* Cambridge, Mass.: Harvard University Press, 1979.

Gans, Herbert. *Deciding What's News: A Study of CBS Evening News, NBC Nightly News, Newsweek and Time.* New York: Vantage Books, 1979.

Gastil, Raymond D., ed. *Freedom in the World: Political Rights and Civil Liberties, 1987–88.* New York: Freedom House, 1988.

Gillis, Malcolm, ed. *Tax Reform in Developing Countries.* Durham, N.C.: Duke University Press, 1988.

Ginsberg, B. *The Captive Public: How Mass Opinion Promotes State Power.* New York: Basic Books, 1986.

Goodpaster, K. E. "Ethical Imperatives and Corporate Leadership." In K. R. Andrews, ed., *Ethics in Practice.* Boston: Harvard Business School Press, 1987. Pp. 212–228.

Goulet, Denis. *The Cruel Choice: A New Concept in the Theory of Development.* New York: Atheneum, 1973.

Gramsci, Antonio. *Selections from Prison Notebooks 1929–35.* New York: International Publishers, 1971.

Greenpeace International. *The International Trade in Toxic Wastes.* Washington, D.C.: Greenpeace International, 1988–89.

Greenstein, Fred I., and Nelson W. Polsby, eds. *Handbook of Political Science.* Reading, Mass.: Addison-Wesley, 1975.

Grossholtz, Jean. *Politics in the Philippines.* Boston: Little, Brown, 1964.

Guitan, Manuel. "Economic Management and International Monetary Fund Conditionality." In Tony Killick, ed., *Adjustment and Financing in the Developing World.* London: International Monetary Fund, 1982.

Habermas, Jürgen. *Economía y sociedad* (Economy and society). Mexico City: FACE, 1984.

——. *Erkenntnis Und Interesse.* Frankfurt, Germany: Suhrkamp, 1968.

——. *Moral Bewusstsein und Communikatives Handeln.* Frankfurt, Germany: Suhrkamp, 1983.

——. *Theorie Des Kommunikasten Handelns.* Frankfurt, Germany: Suhrkamp, 1981. Vols. I–II.

——. *Theorie Des Kommunikativen Handelns.* (Spanish ed.) Madrid: Taurus, 1987.

Harberger, Arnold. "Investment in Men Versus Investment in Machines: The Case of India." In C. Arnold Anderson and Mary Jean Bowman, *Education and Economic Development.* Chicago: Aldine, 1965. Pp. 11–50.

Harvey, David. *The Condition of Postmodernity.* Oxford: Basil Blackwell, 1989.

Havnevik, Kjell, ed. *The IMF and the World Bank in Africa: Conditionality, Impact and Alternatives.* Uppsala, Sweden: Scandinavian Institute of African Studies, 1987.

Hayek, Friedrich. *The Road to Serfdom.* Chicago: University of Chicago Press, 1976.

Hegel, Georg W. *Lectures on the Philosophy of Religion.* Ed. by Peter Hodgson. Berkeley: University of California Press, 1984, 1985, and 1987. Vols. I–III.

Hegel, Georg W. *Religionsphilosophie.* Frankfurt, Germany: Suhrkamp.

Helleiner, G. K., ed. *Africa and the IMF.* Washington, D.C.: International Monetary Fund, 1986.

Henfrey, Colin. "Dependency Modes of Production, and the Class Analysis of Latin America." In Ronald Chilcote, ed., *Dependency and Marxism.* Boulder, Colo.: Westview Press, 1981. Pp. 17–54.

Hinckelammert, Franz. *Las armas ideológicas de la muerte* (The ideological weapons of death). San José, Costa Rica: DEI, 1977.

Hirschman, Albert. *Essays in Trespassing: Economics to Politics and Beyond.* New York: Cambridge University Press, 1981.

Hishimoto, Choji. *Study of Chōsen [Korea] Rice Production.* Tokyo: Chiguru Shobō, 1938.

Hobbes, Thomas. *Leviathan.* New York: E.P. Dutton, 1950.

Honore, A. M. "Social Justice." In Robert B. Summers, ed., *Essays in Legal Philosophy.* Berkeley: University of California Press, 1968. Pp. 61–94.

Hsueh, S. S., ed. *Political Science in South and Southeast Asia.* Asia Political Science Association, 1966.

Huntington, Samuel. *Political Order in Changing Societies.* New Haven, Conn.: Yale University Press, 1968.

Huntington, Samuel P., and Clement Moore. *Authoritarian Politics in Modern Society: The Dynamics of Established One Party Systems.* New York: Basic Books, 1970.

Institute for Food and Development Policy. *Food First Resource Guide.* San Francisco: IFDP, 1979.

International Monetary Fund. *IMF Survey.* Washington, D.C.: IMF, 1980.

International Monetary Fund. *World Economic Outlook.* Washington, D.C.: International Monetary Fund, 1989.

The International Trade in Toxic Wastes. Washington, D.C.: Greenpeace International, 1988–89 ed.

IUSSP. *IUSSP International Population Conference.* New Delhi: IUSSP, 1989.

Jay, Martin. *Marxism and Totality.* Berkeley: University of California Press, 1982.

Jarrett, Henry, ed. *Environmental Quality in a Growing Economy.* Baltimore, Md.: Johns Hopkins University Press, 1968.

Jessop, B. *The Capitalist State.* Oxford, England: Martin Robertson, 1982.

Jevons, William. *The Theory of Political Economy.* 5th ed. New York: Kelly and Millman, 1957.

Johnson, D. G., and R. D. Lee, eds. *Population Growth and Economic Development: Issues and Evidence.* Madison: University of Wisconsin Press, 1987.

Jones, Garvin W. *Population Dynamics and Educational and Health Planning.* Geneva: International Labor Organization, 1990.

Kant, Immanuel. *Perpetual Peace and Other Essays.* Trans. by Ted Humphrey. Indianapolis, Ind.: Hackett Publishing, 1983.

Keohane, Robert, and Joseph S. Nye, eds. *Transnational Relations and World Politics.* Cambridge, Mass.: Harvard University Press, 1972.

Kidd, Benjamin. *The Control of the Tropics.* New York: Macmillan, 1898.

Killick, Tony, ed., *Adjustment and Financing in the Developing World.* London: International Monetary Fund, 1982.

———. *The Quest for Economic Stabilization: The IMF and the Third World.* London: Heinemann Educational Books, 1984.

Killick, Tony, Graham Bird, Jennifer Sharpley, and Mary Sutton, "The IMF: Case for Change in Emphasis." In Richard E. Feinberg and Valeriana Kallab, eds. *The Adjustment Crisis in the Third World.* Washington, D.C.: Overseas Development Council, 1984. Pp. 59–89.

Kohlberg, L. *The Meaning and Measurement of Moral Development.* Worcester, Mass.: Clark University Press, 1981.

Koo, A. Y. C. *The Role of Land Reform in Economic Development: A Case Study of Taiwan.* New York: Praeger, 1968.

International Commission for Central American Recovery and Development, *The Report of the International Commission for Latin American Recovery and Development; Poverty, Conflict, and Hope, A Turning Point in Central America.* Durham, N.C.: Duke University Press, 1989.

Korean Ministry of Agriculture. *Yearbook of Agriculture and Forestry Statistics.* Seoul: KMA, 1970.

Kornhauser, William. *The Politics of Mass Society.* New York: Free Press, 1959.

Korten, David C. *Getting to the 21st Century: Voluntary Action and the Global Agenda.* West Hartford, Conn.: Kumarian Press, 1990.

Kuhn, Thomas S. *The Structure of Scientific Revolutions.* Chicago: University of Chicago Press, 1970.

Laclau, Ernesto. *Politics and Ideology in Marxist Theory.* London: New Left Books, 1979.

Laclau, Ernesto, and Chantal Mouffe. *Hegemony and Socialist Strategy: Towards a Radical Democratic Politics.* London: Verso, 1985.

Laczniak, G. R., and P. E. Murphy, eds. *Marketing Ethics: Guidelines for Managers.* Lexington, Ky.: Lexington Books, 1985.

Lamb, Matthew. "Kommunikative Praxis und Theologie." In Edmund Arens, *Habermas und die Theologie.* Düsseldorf, Germany: Patmos, 1989. Pp. 241-270.

Larson, James F. *Television's Window of the World: International Affairs Coverage on the U.S. Networks.* Norwood, N.J.: Ablex, 1984.

Lebret, Louis. *Manifeste pour une Civilisation Solidaire. Economie et Humanisme.* 1959.

Lee, Hoon K. *Land Utilization and Rural Economy in Korea.* Chicago: University of Chicago Press, 1936.

Lerner, Daniel. *The Passing of Traditional Society: Modernizing the Middle East.* New York: Free Press, 1958.

Lewis, John P., and Valeriana Kallab, eds. *Development Strategies Reconsidered.* Washington, D.C.: Overseas Development Council, 1986.

Linz, Juan J. "Totalitarian and Authoritarian Regimes." In Fred I. Greenstein and Nelson W. Polsby, eds., *Handbook of Political Science.* Reading, Mass.: Addison-Wesley, 1975. Vol. 3, *Macropolitical Theory,* pp. 187-192.

――――. *The Breakdown of Democratic Regimes: Crisis, Breakdown and Reequilibrium.* Baltimore, Md.: Johns Hopkins University Press, 1978.

Lipset, S. M. *Political Man: The Social Basis of Politics.* New York: Anchor Books, 1963.

Little, Ian. *Economic Development: Theory, Policy, and International Relations.* New York: Basic Books, 1982.

Loxley, John. "Alternative Approaches to Stabilization in Africa." In G. K. Helleiner, ed., *Africa and the IMF* (Washington, D.C.: International Monetary Fund, 1986). Pp. 117-147.

――――. "The IMF, World Bank and Sub-Saharan Africa: Policies and Politics." In Kjell Havnevik, ed., *The IMF and the World Bank in Africa: Conditionality, Impact and Alternatives.* Uppsala, Sweden: Scandinavian Institute of African Studies, 1987. Pp. 47-63.

McCarthy, George. *Marx's Critique of Science and Positivism*. Boston: Kluwer Academic Publishing, 1987.

MacEwan, Arthur. "Capitalist Expansion, Ideology, and Intervention." In Richard Edwards, Michael Reich, and Thomas Weisskopf, eds., *The Capitalist System*. Englewood Cliffs, N.J.: Prentice-Hall, 1972.

McKeown, Thomas. *The Modern Rise of Population*. New York: Academic Press, 1976.

McNeeley, Jeffrey A., et al. *Conserving the World's Biological Diversity*. Washington, D.C.: International Union for Conservation of Nature and Natural Resources, et al., 1990.

Magdoff, Harry. *Imperialism: From the Colonial Age to the Present*. New York: Monthly Review Press, 1978.

Maravanyika, O. M. *Implementing Educational Policies in Zimbabwe*. Washington, D.C.: World Bank, 1990.

Marcos, Ferdinand E. *Notes on the New Society of the Philippines*. Manila: Marcos Foundation, 1973.

———. *Presidential Speeches*. Manila: Marcos Foundation, 1979.

Marini, Mauro. *Dialéctica de la dependencia* (Dialectic of dependency). Mexico City: Era, 1973.

Martin, Linda G. "Emerging Issues in Cross-National Survey Research in Ageing in Asia." In IUSSP, *IUSSP International Population Conference*. New Delhi: IUSSP, 1989. Vol. III, pp. 69–80.

Marx, Karl. *Capital*. Mexico City: Siglo XXI, 1979.

———. *Grundrisse*. Berlin: Dietz, 1974.

———. *Theories of Surplus Value*. Spanish ed. Mexico City: FACE, 1980. 3 vols.

Mattelart, Armand. *Transnationals and the Third World*. Westport, Conn.: Bergin & Garvey, 1983.

Matthews, M. C. *Strategic Intervention in Organizations*. Vol. 169, Sage Library of Social Research. Newbury Park, Calif.: Sage Publications, 1988.

Meyer, William. *Transnational Media and Third World Development*. Westport, Conn.: Greenwood Press, 1988.

Mikesell, Raymond. "Appraising Fund Conditionality: Too Loose, Too Tight, or Just Right." In John Williamson, ed., *IMF Conditionality*. Washington, D.C.: Institute for International Economics, 1983. Pp. 47–62.

Moore, Barrington. *Social Origins of Dictatorship and Democracy*. Boston: Beacon Press, 1966.

Munck, Ronaldo. *Politics and Dependency in the Third World: The Case of Latin America*. London: Zed Books, 1985.

Murray, E. A., Jr. "Ethics and Corporate Strategy." In R. B. Dickie and L. S. Rouner, eds., *Corporations and the Common Good*. Notre Dame, Ind.: Notre Dame Press, 1986. Pp. 91–117.

Myint, Hla. *The Economics of Developing Countries*. New York: Praeger, 1966.

National Academy of Sciences. *Rapid Population Growth: Consequences and Policy Implications*. Baltimore, Md.: Johns Hopkins University Press, 1971. 2 vols.

National Agricultural Cooperative Federation. *Agricultural Yearbook 1957*. Seoul: NACF, 1957.

———. *Agricultural Yearbook 1970*. Seoul: NACF, 1970.

———. *Analysis of Korean Agriculture*. Seoul: NACF, 1963.

———. *Korean Agricultural Problems.* Seoul: NACF, 1969.

———. *Twenty Years of Korean Agricultural Policy.* Seoul: NACF, 1965.

National Research Council. *Population Growth and Economic Development: Policy Questions.* Washington, D.C.: National Academy Press, 1986.

Negri, Antonio. *The Savage Anomaly.* Minneapolis: University of Minnesota Press, 1991.

Nwuneli, O., ed. *Mass Communication in Nigeria: A Book of Reading.* Enugu, Nigeria: Fourth Dimension Publishers, 1985.

Novak, Michael. *The Spirit of Democratic Capitalism.* New York: American Enterprise Institute, 1982.

O'Brien, Thomas M. M. *Crisis and Instability: The Philippines Enters the Nineties.* Davao City: Philippine International Forum, 1990.

O'Donnell, Guillermo. *Modernization and Bureaucratic Authoritarianism: Studies in Latin American Politics.* Berkeley: University of California Press, 1973.

O'Donnell, Guillermo, Philippe Schmitter, and Lawrence Whitehead, eds. *Transitions from Authoritarian Rule: Prospects for Democracy.* Baltimore, Md.: Johns Hopkins University Press, 1986. 4 vols.

O'Heffernan, Patrick. *Mass Media and American Foreign Policy: Insider Perspectives on Global Journalism and the Foreign Policy Process.* Norwood, N.J.: Ablex Publishing, 1991.

Outarra, Alhasane. "Design, Implementation and Adequacy of Fund Programs in Africa." In G. K. Helleiner, ed., *Africa and the IMF.* Washington, D.C.: International Monetary Fund, 1986. Pp. 68–92.

Payer, Cheryl. *The Debt Trap: The IMF and the Third World.* New York: Monthly Review Press, 1974.

Peet, Richard, ed. *Radical Geography.* Chicago: Maaroufa Press, 1977.

Perroux, Francois. *L'economie du XXieme Siecle.* Paris: Presses Universitaires de France, 1964.

Petesch, Patti. *Tropical Forests: Conservation with Development?* Washington, D.C.: Overseas Development Council, 1990.

Peuckert, H. "Kommunikatives Handelin, Systeme der Machsgteigerung." In Edmund Arens, *Habermas und die Theologie.* Düsseldorf, Germany: Patmos, 1989. Pp. 39–64.

Peuckert, Helmut. *Wissenschaftstheorie, Handlungstheorie, Fundamentales Theologie.* Frankfurt, Germany: Patmos, 1976.

Poulantzas, Nicos. *Political Power and Social Classes.* London: Verso, 1978.

Preston, L. E., ed. *International and Comparative Corporation and Society Research.* Greenwich, Conn.: JAI press, 1990.

Pruden, H. O. "Which Ethics for Marketers." In J. R. Wish and S. H. Gamble, eds., *Marketing and Social Issues.* New York: John Wiley & Sons, 1971. Pp. 98–104.

Pye, Lucian W. *Aspects of Political Development.* Boston: Little, Brown, 1966.

Raskin, Marcus, and Herbert Bernstein, eds. *New Ways of Knowing.* New Jersey: Rowman and Littlefield, 1987.

Rawls, John. *Theory of Justice.* Cambridge, Mass.: Harvard University Press, 1971.

Resnick, Stephen, and Richard Wolff. *Rethinking Marxism.* New York: Autonomedia, 1985.

Ricoeur, Paul. *Du texte à l'action. Essai d'hermeneutique.* Paris: Seuil, 1986.

Ridker, Ronald G. *Population and Development: The Search for Selective Interventions.* Baltimore, Md.: Johns Hopkins University Press, 1976.

Righter, Rosemary. *Whose News? Politics, the Press and the Third World.* New York: Times Books, 1978.

Roberts, Brad, ed. *The New Democracies: Global Change and U.S. Policy.* Cambridge, Mass.: MIT Press, 1990.

Rodgers, G., ed. *Population Growth and Poverty in Rural South Asia.* New Delhi: Sage Publications, 1989.

Rodney, Walter. *How Europe Underdeveloped Africa.* London: Bogle L'Ouverture, 1972.

Rondinelli, Dennis A., John Middleton, and Adriaan M. Verspoor. *Planning Education Reforms in Developing Countries.* Durham, N.C.: Duke University Press, 1990.

Rossiter, Clinton. *Constitutional Dictatorship: Crisis Government in Modern Democracies.* New York: Harcourt, Brace and World, 1963.

Rostow, W. W. *Eisenhower, Kennedy and Foreign Aid.* Austin: University of Texas Press, 1985.

———. *The Stages of Economic Growth: A Non-Communist Manifesto.* Cambridge: Cambridge University Press, 1960.

Rousseau, Jean-Jacques. *The Social Contract and Discourses.* New York: Dutton, 1973.

Rouyer, Alwyn R. "The State and Fertility Decline in Low-Income Countries." In IUSSP, *IUSSP International Population Conference.* New Delhi: IUSSP, 1989. Vol. I, pp. 201–214.

Rustow, Dankwart A. *A World of Nations: Problems of Political Modernization.* Washington, D.C.: The Brookings Institution, 1967.

Sadik, Nafis. *The State of World Population 1990.* New York: UNFPA, United Nations Population Fund, 1990.

Salmen, Lawrence F. *Listen to the People: Participant-Observer Evaluation of Development Projects.* New York: Oxford University Press, 1987.

San Juan, E. *From People to Nation: Essays in Cultural Politics.* Manila: Asian Social Institute, 1990.

San Juan, E., Jr. *Ruptures, Schisms, Interventions; Cultural Revolution in the Third World.* Manila: De La Salle University Press, 1988.

Schiller, Herbert I. *Communication and Cultural Domination.* White Plains, N.Y.: International Arts and Sciences Press, 1976.

Schelling, Friedrich Wilhelm Joseph von, *Philosophie der Offenbarung.* Paris: Presses Universitaires de France, 1989.

Schmitt, David E. *Dynamics of the Third World: Political and Social Change.* Cambridge, Mass.: Winthrop Publishers, 1974.

Schultz, T. Paul. *Economics and Population.* Reading, Mass.: Addison-Wesley Publishing, 1981.

Sethi, S. P., and P. Steidlmeier. "A New Paradigm of the Business/Society Relationship in the Third World: The Challenge of Liberation Theology." In W. C. Frederick and L. E. Preston, *Business Ethics: Research Issues and Empirical Studies.* Greenwich, Conn.: JAI Press, 1990. Pp. 279–293.

Siebert, R. J. *The Critical Theory of Religion.* Hawthorne, N.Y.: Mouton de Gruyter, 1985.

Silver, Cheryl Simon. *One Earth One Future: Our Changing Global Environment.* Washington, D.C.: National Academy of Sciences, 1990.

Simon, Julian L. *The Ultimate Resource.* Princeton, N.J.: Princeton University Press, 1981.

Simon, Julian L., and Herman Kahn. *The Resourceful Earth: A Response to Global 2000.* New York: Basil Blackwell, 1984.

Sivanandan, A. *A Different Hunger.* London: Pluto Press, 1982.

Sivard, Ruth L. *World Military and Social Expenditures 1989.* Washington, D.C.: World Priorities, 1989.

Smelser, Neil J., ed. *Handbook of Sociology.* Newbury Park, Calif.: Sage Publications, 1988.

Smith, Adam. *The Wealth of Nations.* New York: Penguin, 1985.

Smith, Anthony. *The Geopolitics of Information: How Western Culture Dominates the World.* New York: Oxford University Press, 1980.

So, Alvin Y. *Social Change and Development: Modernization, Dependency, and World Systems Theories.* Newbury Park, Calif.: Sage Publications, 1990.

Sobrino, Jon. "The Divine Element in the Struggle for Human Rights." In Jon Sobrino, ed., *Spirituality of Liberation: Toward Political Holiness.* Trans. by Robert R. Barr. Maryknoll, N.Y.: Orbis Books, 1988. Pp. 103–116.

Spiegel, Steven L., ed. *At Issue: Politics in the World Arena.* New York: St. Martin's Press, 1988.

Spinoza, Baruch Benedict de. *Ethics: Works of Spinoza.* Trans. by R. H. M. Elwes. London: George Bell and Sons, 1883. Reprinted in 1955 by Dover Publications, New York.

Sraffa, Piero. *Production of Commodities by Means of Commodities: Prelude to a Critique of Economic Theory.* Cambridge: Cambridge University Press, 1960.

Steedman, Ian. *Marx After Sraffa.* London: Verso, 1981.

Steedman, Ian, Paul Sweezy, Anwar Shaikh, Erik Olin Wright, Geoff Hodgson, Pradeep Bandyopadhyay, Makoto Itoh, Michael De Vroey, G. A. Cohen, Susan Himmelwelt, Simon Mohun, *The Value Controversy.* London: Verso, 1981.

Stewart, Frances. "Should Conditionality Change?" In Kjell Havnevik, ed., *The IMF and the World Bank in Africa: Conditionality, Impact, and Alternatives.* Uppsala, Sweden: Scandinavian Institute of African Studies, 1987. Pp. 29–45.

Stevenson, R. L. *Communication Development and the World.* New York: Times Books, 1988.

Stolnitz, George J. "The Demographic Transition: From High to Low Birth Rates and Death Rates." In R. Freedman, ed., *Population: The Vital Revolution.* Garden City, N.Y.: Anchor Books, 1964. Pp. 30–46.

Streeten, Paul. *Development Perspectives.* London: Macmillan, 1981.

Summers, Robert B., ed. *Essays in Legal Philosophy.* Berkeley: University of California Press, 1968.

Szymanski, A. *The Logic of Imperialism.* New York: Praeger, 1981.

Talmon, J. L. *The Origins of Totalitarian Democracy.* New York: Beacon Press, 1952.

Tavis, L. A., ed. *Multinational Managers and Host Government Interactions.* Notre Dame, Ind.: University of Notre Dame Press, 1988.

Tetreault, Mary Ann, and Charles Frederick Abel, eds. *Dependency Theory and the Return of High Politics.* Westport, Conn.: Greenwood Press, 1986.

Thomas, C. Y. *The Rise of the Authoritarian State in Peripheral Societies.* New York: Monthly Review Press, 1984.

Timmer, C. Peter, Walter P. Falcon, and Scott R. Pearson. *Food Policy Analysis.* Baltimore, Md.: Johns Hopkins University Press for the World Bank, 1983.

Topping, John C., Jr. *Global Warming: Impact on Developing Countries.* Washington, D.C.: Overseas Development Council, 1990.

Tuchman, G. *Making News: A Study in the Construction of Reality.* New York: Macmillan, 1978.

UNESCO. *Statistical Yearbook 1989.* Paris: UNESCO, 1989.

UNICEF. *The State of the World's Children 1990.* New York: Oxford University Press, 1990.

United Nations. *Progress in Land Reform, Third Report.* New York: United Nations, 1962.

United Nations Development Program. *Antalya Statement on Change: Threat or Opportunity for Human Progress.* New York: United Nations Development Program, 1991.

———. *Human Development Report 1990.* New York: Oxford University Press, 1990.

———. *Human Development Report 1991.* New York: Oxford University Press, 1991.

United Nations Economic Commission for Africa. *Alternative Framework to Structural Adjustment Programmes for Socio-Economic Recovery and Transformation.* Addis Ababa: UNECA, 1989.

United Nations Economic Commission for Latin America. *The Economic Development of Latin America and Its Principal Problems.* New York: United Nations. E/CN.12/89/Rev.1.

Vanhanen, Tatu. *The Process of Democratization: A Comparative Study of 147 States 1980–88.* Washington, D.C.: Crane Russak, 1990.

Vega, Claudio Gonzales, and Jeffrey Payo. "Central American Financial Development." In William Ascher and Ann Hubbard, eds., *Poverty, Conflict, and Hope: Central American Recovery and Development: Task Force Report to the International Commission for Central American Recovery and Development.* Durham, N.C.: Duke University Press, 1989. Pp. 181–211.

Wallerstein, Immanuel. *Historical Capitalism.* London: Verso, 1983.

———. *The Modern World System.* New York: Academic Press, 1974.

Wangwe, Samuel M. "Impact of IMF/World Bank Philosophy, The Case of Tanzania." In Kjell Havnevik, ed., *The IMF and the World Bank in Africa: Conditionality, Impact, and Alternatives.* Uppsala, Sweden: Scandinavian Institute of African Studies, 1987.

Weisskopf, Thomas. "Capitalism and Underdevelopment in the Modern World." In Richard Edwards, Michael Reich, and Thomas Weisskopf, eds., *The Capitalist System.* Englewood Cliffs, N.J.: Prentice-Hall, 1972. Pp. 442–458.

Williams, Raymond. *The Year 2000.* New York: Pantheon Books, 1983.

Williamson, John, ed. *IMF Conditionality.* Washington, D.C.: Institute for International Economics, 1983.

Windsor, D., and L. E. Preston. "Corporate Governance, Social Policy, and Social Performance in the Multinational Corporation." In L. E. Preston, ed., *International and Comparative Corporation and Society Research.* Greenwich, Conn.: JAI Press, 1990. Pp. 79–92.

Winkler, Donald R. *Higher Education in Latin America: Issues of Efficiency and Equity.* Washington, D.C.: World Bank, 1990.

Wish, J. R., and S. H. Gamble, eds., *Marketing and Social Issues.* New York: John Wiley & Sons, 1971.

Woddis, Jack. *Introduction to Neo-Colonialism.* New York: International Publishers, 1972.

Wolf, Eric. *Europe and the People Without History.* Berkeley: University of California Press, 1982.

World Bank. *Education in Sub-Saharan Africa.* Washington, D.C.: World Bank, 1988.

———. *External Debt of Developing Countries.* Washington, D.C.: World Bank, 1989.

———. *World Development Report 1984.* New York: Oxford University Press, 1984.

———. *World Development Report 1989.* New York: Oxford University Press, 1989.

———. *World Development Report 1990.* New York: Oxford University Press, 1990.

World Commission on Environment and Development. *Our Common Future: Report of the World Commission on Environment and Development.* Oslo, Norway: WCED, 1987.

World Resources Institute. *World Resources 1988–89.* New York: Basic Books, 1988.

———. *World Resources 1990–91.* New York: Oxford University Press, 1990.

Worldwatch Institute. *State of the World 1986: A Worldwatch Institute Report on Progress Toward a Sustainable Society.* New York: W.W. Norton & Co., 1986.

Yang, Martin C. *Socio-economic Results of Land Reform in Taiwan.* Honolulu: East-West Press, 1970.

Yi, Zeng. "Ageing of the Chinese Population and Policy Issues: Lessons from a Rural-Urban Dynamic Projection Model." In IUSSP, *IUSSP International Population Conference.* New Delhi: IUSSP, 1989. Vol. III, pp. 81–102.

II. PROFESSIONAL JOURNALS AND OCCASIONAL PAPERS

Aggarwala, Narinda. "New International Information and Communication Order: Setting the Record Straight," *New York Law School Journal of International and Comparative Law, 4* (1) (1982). Pp. 66–68.

Agpalo, Remigio E. "The Iron Logic of Modernization." Inaugural lecture for the Aurelio Calderon Professorial Chair in Philippine–American Relations, delivered at De La Salle University, June 10, 1985. Published in *Praxis, III* (December 1988): 37–38.

———. "*Pangulo* Regime and Civilization," *Solidarity,* no. 12 (1985): 18–27.

Amba-Rao, S. C. "Whither Bhopal: Technological Hazards and Social Responsiveness in the Third World," *Social Development Issues, 12* (2) (Winter 1989): 11–22.

"The Arms Bazaar Revisited," *South: Emerging World Review, 120* (March 1991): 11–27.

Arthur, Brian W., and Geoffrey McNicoll. "An Analytical Survey of Population and Development in Bangladesh," *Population and Development Review, 4* (1) (1978): 23–80.

Ascher, William. "On the Convergence of Efficiency and Equity via Neoclassical Prescriptions," *Journal of Interamerican Studies and World Affairs, 31* (1–2) (Spring-Summer 1989): 49–62.

Ashford, N. A., and C. Ayers. "Policy Issues for Consideration in Transferring Technology to Developing Countries," *Ecology Law Quarterly, 12* (4) (1985): 871–905.

Bauzon, Kenneth E. "Breakdown of a Military Regime: The Case of Pakistan, 1969–1971," *Asia Quarterly,* no. 2 (1977): 121–142.

———. "Development Administration and Asian Political Processes in Retrospect" (a review essay), *Philippine Journal of Public Administration, 19* (3) (July 1975): 237–246.

———. "The Multilateral Assistance Initiative and Democratization in the Philippines," *Contemporary Southeast Asia, 12* (2) (September 1990): 120–133.

———. "Neo-Marxism: End of a Career or Start of a New One?" *Kasarinlan: Philippine Quarterly of Third World Studies,* 6(4) & 7(1): 113–126 (Second and Third Quarters, 1991).

———. "Social Knowledge and the Legitimation of the State: The Philippine Experience in Historical Perspective," *Political Communication; An International Journal,* 9 (3) (July–September 1992). In press.

Bartels, R. "A Model for Ethics in Marketing," *Journal of Marketing, 31* (January 1967): 20–26.

Berelson, Bernard, and J. Lieberson. "Government Efforts to Influence Fertility: The Ethical Issues," *Population and Development Review, 5* (4) (1979): 581–613.

Blake, R. B., and D. A. Carroll. "Ethical Reasoning in Business," *Training and Development Journal* 43(6) (June 1989): 99–204.

Boak, K. B., and N. Peery. "The Cognitive Structure of Corporate Social Responsibility," *Journal of Management, 11* (3): 71–82.

Bommer, M., C. Grato, J. Gravander, and M. Tuttle. "A Behavioral Model of Ethical and Unethical Decision Making," *Journal of Business Ethics, 6* (1987): 265–280.

Bongaarts, John, and Susan Greenhalgh. "An Alternative to the One-Child Policy in China," *Population and Development Review, 11* (4) (1985): 585–617.

Bond, M. E., "Agricultural Responses to Prices in Sub-Saharan African Countries." IMF Staff Papers 30, no. 4, Washington, D.C. (December 1983). Pp. 703–726.

Broad, Robin, and John Cavanagh. "No More NICs," *Foreign Policy* 72 (Fall 1988): 81–103.

Brown, David L., and David C. Korten. "Understanding Voluntary Organizations: Guidelines for Donors." Working Paper No. WPS 258. Country Economics Department, World Bank, Washington, D.C. (September 1990).

Buchanan, Keith. "Reflections of a 'Dirty Word,'" *Dissent, 31* (Summer 1974): 25–31.

Bulatao, Rodolfo A. "Fertility Targets and Policy Options in Asia," *Asian and Pacific Census Forum, 11* (2) (1984): 1–4; 8.

Caiden, G. E. and N. J. Caiden, "Administrative Corruption," *Public Administration Review,* 37 (3) (May-June 1977): 301–309.

Cain, Mead T., and Samuel S. Lieberman. "Development Policy and the Prospects for Fertility Decline in Bangladesh," *Bangladesh Development Studies, 11* (3) (1983): 1–38.

Caldwell, John C. "Toward a Restatement of Demographic Transition Theory," *Population and Development Review, 2* (3–4) (1976): 321–366.

Cavanagh, G. F., D. J. Moberg, and M. Velasquez. "The Ethics of Organizational Politics," *Academy of Management Review, 63* (1981): 363–374.

Clasen, E. A. "Marketing Ethics and the Consumer," *Harvard Business Review* 45(1) (January-February 1967): 79–86.

Cooper, R. N. "Currency Devaluation in Developing Countries," *Essays in International Finance No. 86,* International Finance Section, Princeton University (1971).

Dell, Sidney, "Stabilization: The Political Economy of Overkill," *World Development,* 10 (8) (1982): 597–612.

Diaz-Alejandro, C. F. "A Note on the Impact of Devaluation and the Redistributive Affect," *Journal of Political Economy, 71* (1963): 577–580.

Donaldson, T. "Multinational Decision Making: Reconciling International Norms," *Journal of Business Ethics, 4* (1985): 357–366.

Dussell, Enrique. "La base en la teología de la liberación: Perspectiva latinoamericana" ("The base in the theology of liberation: A Latin American perspective"), *Concilium, 104* (1975): 76–89.

———. "Christian Art of the Repressed in Latin America," *Concilium, 15* (2) (1980): 215–231.

———. "Comentario a la 'Introducción' de la *Transformación de la Filosofía* [de K. O. Apel]" ("Commentary on the 'Introduction' of the *Transformation of Philosophy* [of K. O. Apel]"), *Argument* (Hamburg), (1990).

———. "Le pain de la célébration: signe communinautaire de justice," *Concilium, 17* (2) (1982): 89–101.

East-West Population Institute. "Policies for Fertility Reduction: Focus on Asia," *Asia-Pacific Population and Policy,* no. 9 (1989).

Ebring, Lutz, et al. "Front Page News and Real World Cues: A New Look at Agenda-Setting by the Media," *American Journal of Political Science, 24* (February 1980): 16–49.

Ellacuria, Ignacio. "Funcion liberadora de la filosofía," *Estudios Centroamericanos, 40* (435–436) (Enero-Febrero 1985): 45–64.

———. "Historizacion de los derechos humanos desde los pueblos oprimidos y las mayorias populares," *Estudios Centroamericanos, 45* (502) (Agosto 1990): 589–596.

Evans, Peter. "Beyond Center and Periphery: A Comment on the Contribution of the World System Approach to the Study of Development," *Sociological Inquiry, 49* (4) (1979): 15–20.

Ferrell, O. C., M. Zey-Ferrell, and D. Krugman. "A Comparison of Predictors of Ethical and Unethical Behavior Among Corporate and Agency Advertising Managers," *Journal of Macromarketing, 3* (Spring 1983): 19–27.

Forsyth, D. R. "A Taxonomy of Ethical Ideologies," *Journal of Personality and Social Psychology, 39* (1) (1980): 175–184.

Foster-Carter, Aidan. "Marxist Approaches to Development and Underdevelopment," *Journal of Contemporary Asia, 3* (1) (1973): 7–33.

Frederick, W. C. "Toward CSR3: Why Ethical Analysis Is Indispensable and Unavoidable in Corporate Affairs," *California Management Review, 28* (1986): 126–141.

Galtung, Johan. "A Structural Theory of Imperialism" *Journal of Peace Research, 82* (2) (1971): 81–117.

Galtung, Johan, and M. H. Ruge. "The Structure of Foreign News," *Journal of Peace Research, 2* (1965): 64–91.

Gasiorowski, Mark J. "Economic Dependence and Political Democracy: A Cross-National Study," *Comparative Political Studies, 20* (4) (January 1988): 489–515.

Gold, Joseph. "Conditionality." IMF Pamphlet Series No. 31, Washington, D.C. (1979).

———. "Financial Assistance by the IMF—Law and Practice." IMF Pamphlet Series No. 27, Washington, D.C. (1979).

Greenhalgh, Susan. "Shifts in China's Population Policy, 1984–86: Views from the Central, Provincial, and Local Levels," *Population and Development Review, 12* (3) (1986): 491–515.

Guitan, Manuel. "Fund Conditionality: Evolution of Principles and Practices." IMF Pamphlet Series No. 38, Washington, D.C. (1979).

Haggard, Stephan. "The Newly Industrializing Countries in the International System" (a review essay), *World Politics, 38* (2) (January 1986): 343–370.

Hardee-Cleaveland, Karen, and Judith Banister. "Fertility Policy and Implementation in China, 1986–88." *Population and Development Review, 14* (2) (1988): 245–286.

Hay, R., and E. Gray. "Social Responsibilities of Business Managers," *Academy of Management Journal, 17* (1974): 135–143.

Heady, Earl O. "Economics of Farm Leasing Systems," *Journal of Farm Economics, 29* (3) (August 1947): 599–678.

Hegarty, W. H., and H. P. Sims, Jr. "Organizational Philosophy, Policies and Objectives Related to Unethical Decision Behavior: A Laboratory Experiment," *Journal of Applied Psychology, 64* (3) (1979): 331–338.

Hester, A. "An Analysis of News Flow from Developed and Developing Nations," *Gazette, 17* (1971): 70–74.

Hunt, S., and S. Vitell. "A General Theory of Marketing Ethics," *Journal of Macromarketing, 6* (1) (Spring 1986): 30–39.

Huntington, Samuel P. "Will More Countries Become Democratic?" *Political Science Quarterly, 9* (1984): 193–218.

Issawi, Charles. "Farm Output Under Fixed Rents and Share Tenancy," *Land Economics, 33* (1) (February 1957): 74–77.

Johnson, D. Gale. "Resource Allocation Under Share Contracts," *Journal of Political Economy, 58* (2) (April 1950): 111–114.

Katseli, Louka T. "Devaluation: A Critical Appraisal of IMF's Policy Prescriptions," *American Economic Review* 73(2) (May 1983): 359–363.

Khan, M. R. "Economic Development and Population Policy in Bangladesh," *Bangladesh Development Studies, 12* (3) (1984): 1–18.

Khan, Moshin, and Malcolm D. Knight. "Fund Supported Adjustment Programs and Growth." IMF Occasional Paper No. 41 (1985).

Klitgaard, Robert. "Incentive Myopia," *World Development, 17* (4) (1989): 447–459.

Kohli, Atul. "The Political Economy of Development Strategies: Comparative Perspectives on the Role of the State" (a review essay), *Comparative Politics, 19* (2) (January 1987): 233–246.

Korten, David C. "International Assistance: A Problem Posing as a Solution," *Development, 3*(4) (1990): 87–94.

Krueger, Anne O. "The Political Economy of the Rent-Seeking Society," *American Economic Review, 64* (3) (1974): 291–303.

Krugman, P., and L. Taylor. "Contractionary Effects of Devaluation," *Journal of International Economics, 8* (1978): 445–456.

Kydd, Jonathan. "Policy Reform and Adjustment in an Economy Under Siege: Malawi 1980–87," *Institute of Development Studies Bulletin, 19* (1) (1988).

Lasorsa, D. L., and S. D. Reese. "News Sources Use in the Crash of 1987: A Study of Four National Media," *Journalism Quarterly, 67* (1) (1990): 60–71.

Lee, K. H. "Ethical Beliefs in Marketing Management: A Cross Cultural Study," *European Journal of Marketing, 15* (1) (1981): 58–67.

Lent, J. A. "Foreign News in American Media," *Journal of Communication, 27* (1) (1977): 46–51.

Leonard, H. Jeffrey. "Multinational Corporations and Politics in Developing Countries," *World Politics, 32* (3) (April 1980)454–483.

Lipset, Seymour M. "Some Social Prerequisites of Democracy: Economic Development and Political Legitimacy," *American Political Science Review, 53* (1) (March 1959): 69–105.

Loud, Oliver. "Socialism in the 1990s: Where Do We Go From Here?" *Monthly Review, 43* (June 1991): 45–53.

McCombs, M. E., and D. L. Shaw. "The Agenda-Setting Function of Mass Media," *Public Opinion Quarterly, 36* (1972): 176–184.

McNicoll, Geoffrey. "Consequences of Rapid Population Growth: Overview and Assessment," *Population and Development Review, 10* (2) (1984): 177–240.

Masmoudi, M. "The New World Information Order," *Journal of Communication, 29* (1979): 172–179.

Mennerick, Lewis A., and Mehrangiz Najafizadeh. "The Role of Professionals in Third World Develoment: Conflicts and Constraints," *Review of International Affairs, 937* (April 1989): 18–21.

———. "Third World Environmental Health: Social, Technological and Economic Policy Issues," *Journal of Environmental Health* (Spring 1991): 24–29.

Montgomery, John D. "How Facts Replace Fads," *Comparative Politics, 22*(2) (January 1990): 237–248.

Mouzelis, Nicos. "Marxism or Post Marxism?" *New Left Review,* no. 167 (January-February 1988): 107–123.

Najafizadeh, Mehrangiz, and Lewis A. Mennerick. "Constraints on Education as a Mechanism for Social Change." Sociology Series Working Paper No. 70. Lawrence: University of Kansas, 1991.

———. "Worldwide Educational Expansion from 1950 to 1980: The Failure of the Expansion of Schooling in Developing Countries," *The Journal of Developing Areas, 22* (April 1988): 333–358.

Naor, J. "A New Approach to Multinational Social Responsibility," *Journal of Business Ethics, 1* (1982): 219–225.

Nitze, William A. "Improving U.S. Interagency Coordination of International Environmental Policy Development," *Environment 33* (4) (May 1991): 10–13, 31–37.

Nolan, Janne E., and Albert D. Whellon. "Third World Ballistic Missiles," *Scientific American, 263* (August 1990): 34–40.

Otsuka, Keijiro, and Yujiro Hayami. "Theories of Share Tenancy: A Critical Survey," *Economic Development and Cultural Change, 37* (1) (October 1988): 31–68.

Park, Jin Whan. "The Comparison of Farm Income and Land Productivity by the Landownership Pattern," *Agricultural Economy* (Ministry of Agriculture and Forestry) (December 1965): 114.

Park, Young J. "The Effects of Land Reform on Labor Input Use: Theory and a Case Study of Korean Agriculture," *The Korean Economic Journal, 15* (2) (June 1976): 214–235.

Peck, Louis. "The Spoils of War," *The Amicus Journal, 13* (Spring 1991): 6–9.

Petras, James. "State Capitalism and the Third World," *Development and Change, 8* (1977): 1–17.

———. "World Transformations: The Challenges for the Left," *Against the Current,* no. 34 (September-October 1991): 17–22.

Portes, Alejandro. "On the Sociology of National Development: Theories and Issues," *American Journal of Sociology, 82* (July 1976): 55–85.

Prebisch, Raul, "The Economic Development of Latin America and Its Principal Problems," *Economic Bulletin for Latin America, 7*(1) (1962): 1–22.

Raelin, J. A. "The Professional as the Executive's Ethical Aide-de-Camp," *The Academy of Management Executive, 1* (3) (1987): 171–182.

Ramaswamy, V. "A New Human Rights Consciousness," *IFDA Dossier, 80* (January-March 1991): 3–16.

Reichman, Thomas. "The Fund's Conditional Assistance and Problems of Adjustment, 1973–75," *Finance and Development, 15* (4) (1978): 38–41.

Reichman, Thomas, and Richard Stillson. "How Successful are Programs Supported by 'Stand-by' Arrangements?" *Finance and Development, 14* (1) (1977): 22–24.

Robin, D. P., and R. E. Reidenbach. "Social Responsibility, Ethics, and Marketing Strategy: Closing the Gap Between Concept and Application," *Journal of Marketing, 51* (January 1987): 44–57.

Rojas, Paul. "Das Unvollendete Projekt. Zur Entstehungsgeschichte von Marx 'Kapital,'" *Argument* (Hamburg) (1989).

Rustow, Dankwart. "Transitions to Democracy: Towards a Dynamic Model," *Comparative Politics, 2* (1970).

Sandbrook, Richard. "The State and Economic Stagnation in Tropical Africa," *World Development, 14* (3) (1986): 319–332.

Schickele, Rainer. "Effects of Tenure Systems on Agricultural Efficiency," *Journal of Farm Economics, 23* (1) (February 1941): 185–207.

Schmidt, Helmut. "Facing One World." Report by an Independent Group on Financial Flows to Developing Countries, Hamburg, Germany (1989).

Schydlowsky, Daniel M. "Alternative Approaches to Short Term Economic Management." Discussion Paper No. 50, Center for American Development Studies. Boston: Boston University, 1981.

Sethi, S. P. "Dimensions of Corporate Social Performance: An Analytical Framework," *California Management Review, 12* (1975): 58–64.

Shils, Edward. "Observations on Some Tribulations of Civility," *Government and Opposition, 15* (3/4) (Summer-Autumn 1980): 528–545.

Simpson, J. R. "Ethics and Multinational Corporation vis-à-vis Developing Nations," *Journal of Business Ethics, 1* (1982): 227–237.

Solidum, Estrella D., Roman Dubsky, and Teresita Saldivar-Sali. "Security in a New Perspective," *Asian Perspective, 5* (2) (Fall-Winter 1981).

Stauffer, Robert B. "Philippine Democracy: Contradictions of Third World Redemocratization," *Kasarinlan; Philippine Quarterly of Third World Studies, 6* (1–2) (Third and Fourth Quarters 1990): 7–22.

Stead, W. E., D. L. Worrell, and J. G. Stead. "An Integrative Model for Understanding and Managing Ethical Behavior in Business Organizations," *Journal of Business Ethics, 9* (1990): 233–242.

Sturdivant, F. D., and J. L. Ginter. "Corporate Social Responsiveness: Management Attitudes and Economic Performance," *California Management Review 19* (3) (Spring 1977): 30–39.

Sunkel, Osvaldo. "Politica nacional de desarollo y dependencia externa," *Estudio Internacionales, 1* (April 1967).

Supreme Court of the Philippines. "Resolution" (With Regard to Marcial A. Edillon),

Journal of the Integrated Bar of the Philippines, 6 (3) (Third Quarter, 1978): 229–234.

Tsalikis, J., and O. Nwachukwu. "Cross-Cultural Business Ethics: Ethical Beliefs' Difference Between Blacks and Whites," *Journal of Business Ethics, 7* (1988): 745–754.

Tsalikis, J., and D. J. Fritzche. "Business Ethics: A Literature Review With a Focus on Marketing Ethics," *Journal of Business Ethics, 8* (1989): 695–743.

Velasquez, M. "Why Corporations Are Not Morally Responsible for Anything They Do," *Business and Professional Ethics Journal 2* (3) (Spring 1983): 1–18.

Vitell, S., and T. Festervand. "Business Ethics: Conflicts, Practices and Beliefs of Industrial Executives," *Journal of Business Ethics, 6* (1987): 111–122.

Von der Embse, T. J., and R. A. Wagley. "Managerial Ethics: Hard Decisions on Soft Criteria," *SAM Advanced Management Journal* (Winter 1988): 4–8.

Weaver, D. H., and G. C. Wilhoit. "Foreign News Coverage in Two U.S. Wire Services: An Update," *Journal of Communication 33* (2) (Spring 1983): 132–148.

Wellhofer, E. Spencer. "Models of Core and Periphery Dynamics," *Comparative Political Studies, 21* (2) (July 1988): 281–307.

Winjberger, Sweder van. "Exchange Rate Management and Stabilization Policies in Developing Countries," *Journal of Development Economics, 23* (1986): 227–247.

Williamson, John. "On Seeking to Improve IMF Conditionality," *American Economic Review 73* (2) (May 1983): 354–358.

World Bank. "Environmentally Sustainable Economic Development: Building on Brundtland." Robert Goodland, Herman Daly, and Salah El Serafy, eds. Working Paper, Environmental Department. Washington, D.C.: World Bank, 1991.

Worrell, D. L., J. G. Stead, and J. B. Spalding. "Unethical Decisions: The Impact of Reinforcement Contingencies and Managerial Philosophies," *Psychological Reports, 57* (1985): 355–365.

Wynne, Bryan. "The Toxic Waste Trade: International Regulatory Issues and Options," *Third World Quarterly 11* (3) (July 1989): 120–146.

Zenisek, T. J. "Corporate Social Responsibility: A Conceptualization Based on Organizational Literature," *Academy of Management Review, 4* (1979): 359–368.

Zey-Ferrell, M., K. M. Weaver, and O. C. Ferrell. "Predicting Unethical Behavior Among Marketing Practitioners," *Human Relations, 32* (7) (1979): 557–569.

Zey-Ferrell, M., and O. C. Ferell. "Role-Set Configuration and Opportunities as Predictors of Unethical Behavior in Organizations," *Human Relations, 35* (7) (1982): 587–604.

Zulu, Justin, and Saleh M. Nsouli. "Adjustment Programs in Africa, The Recent Experience." IMF Occasional Paper No. 34. International Monetary Fund, Washington, D.C. April (1985).

III. NEWSPAPERS, NEWSMAGAZINES, AND NEWSLETTERS

Bauzon, Kenneth E. "The Fallacy of the New World Order," *Manila Chronicle,* May 4–10, 1991, p. 9.

Branigin, William. "Mexico Adopts Campaign to Save the Environment," *Washington Post,* June 6, 1990, p. A18.

———. "North America's Largest Rain Forest Faces Destruction," *Washington Post,* July 17, 1989, p. A17.

Brooke, James. "African Nations Barring Foreign Toxic Waste, *The New York Times,* September 25, 1988, p. 18.

Browne, Malcolm W. "93 Nations Move to Ban Chemicals that Harm Ozone," *The New York Times,* June 30, 1990, p. 1.

Bulletin Today, December 28, 1981, p. 32.

"Coral Reefs off 20 Countries Face Assaults from Man and Nature," *The New York Times,* March 27, 1990, p. C4.

Friedman, M. "A Friedman Doctrine: The Social Responsibility of Business Is to Increase Its Profits," *The New York Times Magazine,* September 13, 1970. P. 32.

Greenhouse, Steven. "U.N. Conference Supports Curbs on Exporting of Hazardous Waste," *The New York Times,* March 23, 1989, p. 1.

Hardin, Blaine. "Africans Turn to Hostages in Battle Against Foreign Waste," *Washington Post,* July 16, 1988, p. A18.

―――. "Outcry Grows in Africa over West's Waste-Dumping," *Washington Post,* June 22, 1988, p. A15.

House, Richard. "Brazil Declines Invitation to Conference on Ecology," *Washington Post,* March 4, 1989, p. A20.

"How the West Can Win the New World Order," *Newsweek,* September 9, 1991, p. 23.

Mookerjee, Subimal. "New Guidelines for Use of Fund's Resources Follow Review of Practice of Conditionality," *IMF Survey, 8* (March 29, 1979).

"News in Brief," *Jamaican Weekly Gleaner,* November 5, 1990, p. 22.

Orme, William J. Jr. "Treaty to Protect Caribbean Advances at Mexico Conference," *Washington Post,* April 27, 1985, p. A10.

"Ship Heads for West Africa with Cargo of Unwanted Ash," *Washington Post,* June 12, 1988, p. A10.

Toporowski, Jan. "Togo: A Structural Adjustment that Destabilizes Economic Growth," *Institute of Development Studies Bulletin, 29* (1) (January 1988).

"UN Index on Freedom Enrages Third World," *The New York Times,* June 23, 1991, p. 11.

IV. OFFICIAL DOCUMENTS AND PUBLICATIONS

Bureau of Census and Statistics. *Journal of Philippine Statistics, XXI* (2) (Second Quarter 1970): ix.

Calalang v. *Williams,* 48 O.G. 9th Supp. 239 (1940). [Philippines]

Constitution of the Republic of the Philippines (1973)

The Philippine Civil Service: A Personal Profile. Quezon City: Civil Service Commission [Republic of the Philippines], 1974.

Philippine Yearbook 1971. Manila: Bureau of Census and Statistics, 1973.

Philippine Yearbook 1977. Manila: National Census and Statistics Office, 1977.

Population Reference Bureau. *World Population Data Sheet.* Washington, D.C.: National Academy Press, 1986.

―――. *World Population Data Sheet.* Washington, D.C.: National Academy Press, 1990.

Statistical Handbook of the Philippines. Manila: National Census and Statistics Office, 1984.

V. UNPUBLISHED MANUSCRIPTS

Bauzon, Kenneth E., "The Current State of Dependency Research" (1991).
————. "Knowledge and Ideology in Philippine Society" (1990).
Diamond, Larry. "Beyond Authoritarianism: Strategies for Democratization." Paper presented at the Conference on "Pluralism, Participation and Democracy: Prospects and Prescriptions into the 21st Century," sponsored by the Center for Strategic and International Studies, Washington, D.C., and held in Lisbon, Portugal, June 19–21, 1988.
Hinckelammert, Franz. *La coherencia lógica de la construcción de una merchancía patrón* (*The logical coherence of the construction of a merchandise pattern*). San José, Costa Rica: 1988.
Linz, Juan J. "The Transition from Authoritarian Regimes to Democratic Political Systems and the Problems of Consolidation of Political Democracy." Paper presented at the International Political Science Association, Tokyo Roundtable, held March 29 to April 1, 1982.
McAnany, E., J. F. Larson, and J. D. Storey. "News of Latin America on Network Television, 1972–1982: Too Little Too Late?" Paper presented at Annual Conference of International Communication Association, Boston, Massachusetts, May 1982.
Megwa, E. R., and I. S. Ndolo. "Guns, Gavels, and Pens: U.S. Media Coverage of Africa, 1979–1989." Paper presented at annual meeting of African Studies Association, Baltimore, Maryland, November 1990.
Megwa, E. R., and J. T. Barber. "Can Minority News Sources Set the Agenda for Mainstream News Media? A Study of the Congressional Black Caucus and the National Media." Paper presented at meeting of International Communication Association, Dublin, Ireland, June 1990.
Noumoff, Sam J. "The New International Order as an Impediment to Third World Development." Lecture presented at the Center for Nepal and Asian Studies, Tribhuvan University, Kathmandu, Nepal, June 11, 1991.
Posner, B. Z., and W. H. Schmidt. "The Significance of Value Compatibility Between Managers and Their Organizations." Paper presented at 25th Annual Meeting of Western Academy of Management, Vancouver, Canada, April 1984.
Scott, Gerald, and Richard Cebula. "The Impact of Government Policies on Economic Growth in Africa." (1991).

Index

About the Editor

Kenneth E. Bauzon, currently Adjunct Assistant Professor of Political Science at Yeshiva University in New York City, has also taught at Lafayette College in Easton, Pennsylvania, and at Lynchburg College in Lynchburg, Virginia. He received his B.A. degree in political science from Silliman University in the Philippines, and his graduate degrees (master's degrees in history and in political science and a doctorate in political science) from Duke University in Durham, North Carolina. His fields of specialization are development studies and social change in the Third World, international political economy, and foreign and strategic policy in East Asia and the Pacific. He was a recipient of the Faculty Development Fellowship from the University of the Philippines as well as the Lockheed Leadership Fund Fellowship through the Islamic and Arabian Development Studies of Duke University. He has authored *Martial Law in the Philippines: Paradigms of Explanation* (Université Libre de Bruxelles, 1978) as well as the more recent *Liberalism and the Quest for Islamic Identity in the Philippines* (Acorn Press, 1991; co-published by the Ateneo de Manila University Press, 1991). He has contributed to the volumes *Asian Panorama: Essays in Asian History, Past and Present* (Vikas Publishing, 1990), *Dependency Theory and the Return of High Politics* (Greenwood Press, 1986), and *Protest Movements in South and Southeast Asia: Traditional and Modern Idioms of Expression* (University of Hong Kong, 1987). He has also contributed to the journals *Asia Quarterly; Asian Thought and Society: An International Review; Contemporary Southeast Asia;* and *Kasarinlan: Philippine Quarterly of Third World Studies.* He is book review editor for *Pilipinas, A Journal of Philippine Studies,* and serves on the editorial board of *Political Communication: An International Journal.*

About the Contributors

Remigio E. Agpalo, Professor Emeritus of Political Science at the University of the Philippines, Quezon City, was the first recipient of the National Social Science Award in Political Science by the Philippine Social Science Council. Certainly one of the leading political scientists in the Philippines, he has contributed to a definition of the research agenda for social scientists, particularly political scientists, in the Philippines.

Sita C. Amba-Rao, Associate Professor of Management at the Division of Business and Economics at Indiana University at Kokomo, earned her graduate degrees from Purdue University and has served, in addition to teaching, as senior personnel officer and chief personnel manager at V.S. Space Center (Indian Space Research Organization) and at Bharat Dynamics Ltd., respectively.

William L. Ascher is Project Director of the International Commission for Central American Recovery and Development, and Co-director of the International Development Policy Center of Duke University in Durham, North Carolina. With a doctorate degree in political science from Yale University, he has received numerous awards. Currently, he edits the journal *Policy Sciences* and serves on the editorial boards of the journals *Technological Forecasting and Social Change* and *International Journal of Forecasting.*

Thomas S. Axworthy, with a doctorate in political science from Queen's University in Kingston, Ontario, Canada, currently serves as Adjunct Lecturer at the John F. Kennedy School of Government at Harvard University in Boston, Massachusetts, and concurrently as Executive Director of the CRB Foundation in Montreal, Canada. He has also served in various capacities including as assistant principal secretary and senior policy advisor to the office of the Prime Minister of Canada.

Edward Broadbent, a former member of the Canadian Parliament, became the first and current President of the International Centre for Human Rights and Democratic Development based in Montreal. He earned his doctorate in political science from the University of Toronto. He served as professor at York University immediately prior to entering politics.

Michael F. Czerny, S.J., is Professor of Philosophy and Theology and Vice Rector for Social Outreach at the Central American University in San Salvador, El Salvador. He concurrently serves as the Director of the university's Institute for Human Rights (IDHUCA). He did his graduate work at the University of Chicago where he earned his doctorate in 1978. In 1979, he co-founded the Jesuit Centre for Social Faith and Justice and served as its director until 1989. In 1982, he co-founded the Canada Central America Caribbean Policy Alternatives (CAPA), a group of social activists working toward a re-orientation of policy toward the Caribbean and Central America.

Deborah S. DeGraff, until recently a research fellow at the Carolina Population Center of the University of North Carolina at Chapel Hill, is currently Assistant Professor of Economics at Bowdoin College in Brunswick, Maine. She earned her doctorate in Economics from the University of Michigan in 1989, specializing in economic demography and economic development.

Enrique Dussel, Professor of Theology at the National University of Mexico in Mexico City, also serves as President of the Commission on Studies for Church History in Latin America (CEHILA). Born in La Paz, Argentina, he became active when he was eight years old in the Catholic Action movement. He received his licentiate in philosophy from the Universidad Nacional del Cuyo in Mendoza in 1957. While at that university, he was president of the Young Christian Student Movement (JEC). He then went to Europe where he earned his doctorate in philosophy at Universidad Central de Madrid. In 1981, an honorary doctorate degree in theology was conferred on him in Freiburg, Switzerland. Upon returning to Latin America in 1967, he taught at various times at the Pastoral Institute of Latin America in Quito, Ecuador, the Universidad Nacional de Resistencia in Chaco, Argentina, and the Universidad Nacional del Cuyo also in Argentina. A political refugee from his country since 1976, he has been living and teaching in Mexico. A prolific writer, he wrote the *History of the Church in Latin America: Colonialism to Liberation (1492–1979),* first published in Spanish in 1967 and in English in 1981. One can say with confidence that Dr. Dussel has been the single most important intellectual force in setting the agenda of liberation theology in Latin America and beyond.

David C. Korten is Founder and President of the People-Centered Development Forum, a global network of intellectual activists engaged in the creation and advancement of a global people's movement for social transformation, and Visiting Professor at the Asian Institute of Management in Makati, Metro Manila, Philippines. He holds M.B.A. and Ph.D. degrees from the Graduate School of Business at Stanford University. Many of his views on development are derived from nearly thirty years of experience in Asia, Latin America, and Africa, including eight years as a resident advisor to the U.S. Agency for International Development and numerous consultancies with other international assistance agencies.

George Lister is currently Senior Policy Advisor at the Bureau of Human Rights and Humanitarian Affairs of the United States Department of State in Washington, D.C. He is a retired foreign service officer with many years of diplomatic experience. He has specialized in Eastern European and Latin American affairs, and his foreign assignments have included Moscow, Warsaw, Rome, and Bogota. He was educated in New York City and graduated from the College of the City of New York. He was one of the founders of the U.S. human rights policy and he holds the distinction of being the first human rights officer appointed to the Bureau of Inter-American Affairs, in 1974. Since 1981, he has been with the Bureau of Human Rights and Humanitarian Affairs, working on human rights problems worldwide.

Eronini R. Megwa, until recently an assistant professor of mass communications in the School of Communications at Howard University in Washington, D.C., is now a Professor of Communication Studies at the University of Swaziland in southern Africa. He earned his master's degree in mass communication from Iowa State University and his doctorate in journalism from the University of Missouri. His current research is in political and development communications as well as in the strategic use of the media for economic and political development.

Lewis A. Mennerick, Associate Professor of Sociology and Associate Departmental Chair at the University of Kansas in Lawrence, Kansas, received his B.A. from Knox College in Galesburg, Illinois, and his M.A. and Ph.D. from Northwestern University. His research interests focus on Third World educational development and on the social history of the expansion of schooling as well as on environmental problems and public well-being as they relate to Third World development.

Marian A. L. Miller, currently Assistant Professor of Political Science at the University of Akron in Ohio, earned her M.A. and Ph.D. degrees from the University of Southern California, where she specialized in international relations. Her research focuses on development as well as on resource and environmental policy concerns. She has presented papers on resource management in the Third World and on developing countries' options and interests in merchant shipping.

Mehrangiz Najafizadeh, Associate Professor of Sociology at Mount Saint Mary's College in Emmitsburg, Maryland, has studied both in Iran and in the United States. She received her B.A. from Tehran University, her M.A. from Ohio University, and her Ph.D. in sociology from the University of Kansas. In addition to research on education and on environmental problems in Third World countries, her major interests include the sociology of comparative cultures, the sociology of the family, and sociological theory.

Ike S. Ndolo, Assistant Professor of Mass Communication at the School of Communications at Howard University in Washington, D.C., where he earned his doctorate in 1987. Between 1979 and 1983 he was producer and director of international programs for KTSU-FM radio station in Houston, Texas. His research interests are communication patterns and behavior of peoples of African descent, and mass media and national development.

Young J. Park, Professor of Business and Economics at California University of Pennsylvania in California, Pennsylvania, received his undergraduate degree in public administration from Korea University and his graduate degree in economics from Temple University in Philadelphia. He has also taught at Central State University in Ohio and at Wright State University, also in Ohio.

E. San Juan, Jr., Professor of English and Comparative Literature at the University of Connecticut in Storrs, received his undergraduate degree from the University of the Philippines and his graduate degrees from Harvard University. He has taught at the University of California, the Brooklyn College of the City University of New York, and the Inter-University Center of Postgraduate Studies, Yugoslavia. In 1987–89, he was a Fulbright lecturer in American literature and critical theory at the University of the Philippines and the Ateneo de Manila University. His writings have been translated in Italian, and Japanese.

Gerald E. Scott, Assistant Professor of Economics at Florida Atlantic University in Boca Raton, Florida, earned his undergraduate degree from the University of Sierra Leone in Sierra Leone, his M.A. degree from Yale University, and his Ph.D. degree in economics from the University of Maryland, College Park. His fields of specialization include economic development, international economics, and microeconomics.

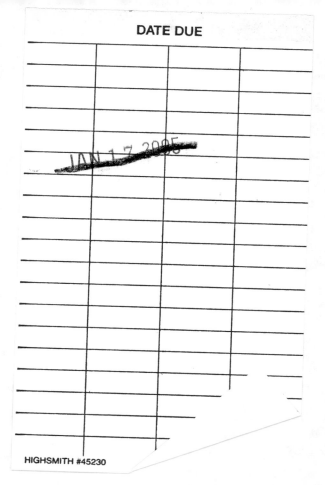

DATE DUE

JAN 1 7 2005

HIGHSMITH #45230